MATERIALS AND MEAN
IN ARCHITECTURE

MATERIALS AND MEANING IN ARCHITECTURE

ESSAYS ON THE BODILY EXPERIENCE
OF BUILDINGS

Nathaniel Coleman

BLOOMSBURY VISUAL ARTS
LONDON • NEW YORK • OXFORD • NEW DELHI • SYDNEY

BLOOMSBURY VISUAL ARTS
Bloomsbury Publishing Plc
50 Bedford Square, London, WC1B 3DP, UK
1385 Broadway, New York, NY 10018, USA

BLOOMSBURY, BLOOMSBURY VISUAL ARTS and the Diana logo are trademarks of
Bloomsbury Publishing Plc

First published in Great Britain 2020

Cover design: Eleanor Rose
Cover image © R.Tsubin / Getty Images

A catalogue record for this book is available from the British Library.

Library of Congress Cataloging-in-Publication Data
Names: Coleman, Nathaniel, 1961- author.
Title: Materials and meaning in architecture: Essays on the bodily
experience of buildings / Nathaniel Coleman.
Description: New York: Bloomsbury Visual Arts, Bloomsbury Publishing Plc,
[2020] | Includes bibliographical references and index.
Identifiers: LCCN 2019021039| ISBN 9781474287746 (hb) | ISBN 9781474287753 (pb)
Subjects: LCSH: Architecture–Human factors. | Building materials.
Classification: LCC NA2542.4 .C645 2020 | DDC 720.1/03–dc23 LC record available at
https://lccn.loc.gov/2019021039

ISBN HB: 978-1-4742-8774-6
PB: 978-1-4742-8775-3
ePDF: 978-1-4742-8772-2
ePUB: 978-1-4742-8773-9

Typeset by Deanta Global Publishing Services, Chennai, India
Printed and bound in India

To find out more about our authors and books visit www.bloomsbury.com and
sign up for our newsletters.

Dedicated to P, Z & E

CONTENTS

ILLUSTRATIONS

Figures

Illustrations

Plates

1   Kärntner Bar (American Bar or Loosbar), (1908), Vienna, Austria. Adolf
    Loos, Architect. Materials: marble (coffered ceiling, pillars and floor), onyx
    (clerestory above entrance), mahogany (bar and other furnishings) and
    brass (accents). [Photo: Nathaniel Coleman, 2017]
2   Museo di Castelvecchio (1957–64; 1968–69; 1973–75), Verona, Italy. Carlo
    Scarpa, Architect. [Photo: Nathaniel Coleman, 2007]
3   Stone and Concrete (?) Render, above Vals, Graubünden, Switzerland.
    [Photo: Nathaniel Coleman, 2007]
4   Quarzite Roofs Slates, Vals, Graubünden, Switzerland. [Photo: Nathaniel
    Coleman, 2007]
5   Water and Stone, Vals, Graubünden, Switzerland. [Photo: Nathaniel
    Coleman, 2007]
6   American Folk Art Museum, NYC (1998–2001, Demolished 2014).
    Tombasil Façade, 53rd Street. Tod Williams and Billie Tsien, Architects.
    [Photo: Nathaniel Coleman, 2008]
7   American Folk Art Museum, NYC (1998–2001, Demolished 2014).
    Tod Williams and Billie Tsien, Architects. *Carceri* Qualities of Folk Art
    Museum. [Photo: Nathaniel Coleman, 2008]
8   Scottish Parliament, Edinburgh, Scotland (1999–2004). EMBT (Enric
    Miralles and Benedetta Tagliabue, Architects). Member of Scottish
    Parliament (MSP) Block ('Skating Minister'). [Photo: Nathaniel
    Coleman, 2012]
9   Scottish Parliament, Edinburgh, Scotland (1999–2004). EMBT (Enric
    Miralles and Benedetta Tagliabue, Architects). Debating Chamber. [Photo:
    Nathaniel Coleman, 2012]
10 Querini Stampalia Bridge (1961–63), Venice, Italy. Carlo Scarpa, Architect.
    Steel arch and structure, Istrian stone step/abutments, metal uprights,
    wood handrails with brass accents, wood. [Photo: Nathaniel Coleman, 2007]
11 Barbican Estate Housing (1969–76), City of London, United Kingdom.
    Chamberlin, Powell and Bon, Architects. Timber window frames make
    the flats more homelike, internally and externally. [Photo: Nathaniel
    Coleman, 2017]
12 Dulwich Picture Gallery (1811–17), Dulwich, London, UK. Sir John
    Soane, Architect. Altered, added to, damaged by Second World War
    bombing, rebuilt (as original) after the War, and altered later. A direct,
    almost ancient use of brick. [Photo: Nathaniel Coleman, 1999]
13 Town Hall, Hilversum, The Netherlands (1928–31). Willem Marinus
    Dudok, Architect. Early Modernist Civic Building. Yellow buff glazed
    brick; taut unbrick-like skin. Emphasis on forms, scale of individual
    material is revealed close-up. [Photo: Nathaniel Coleman, 2015]

ACKNOWLEDGEMENTS

Inevitably, a project of this sort incurs too many debts to fully acknowledge here. Suffice it to say, I am particularly grateful to the many individuals who generously welcomed me to visit and photograph the buildings I've written about in what follows (and more that could not be included), without whom this project would have been impossible, particularly those able guides who enthusiastically shared *their* buildings with me.

A special debt of gratitude goes to Tod Williams and Billie Tsien who I interviewed in their Manhattan studio a number of years ago. Their openness and generosity – of time and spirit – have been recollected often as a spark to keep this project alive. I am also grateful to Annalisa Zumthor for permitting me unrestricted access to the Therme Vals, and for making my visit so pleasurable.

The project would also have been impossible without the generous support of funders during the development of its many aspects across the unanticipated extended timeframe of primary research undergirding this book, including the British Academy, the Leverhulme Trust and departmental, school and faculty-based research funding from Newcastle University, in a variety of forms, on numerous occasions, over many years. I am also indebted to the ever-growing group of architecture students I have worked with, particularly at Newcastle University, who good-naturedly engage with the *lab* experiments they encounter in the design studios and seminars I lead, which are invaluable opportunities for testing ideas, including those developed in what follows. I am also deeply grateful to friends and colleagues. Though too numerous to acknowledge all by name, a few require special mention: Ufuk Ersoy, Tom Moylan, Carlos Calderon, Andrew Ballantyne, James Craig, David Boyd and Elliot Payne.

James Thompson, Bloomsbury architecture commissioning editor, and Sophie Tann, former assistant editor, and Alexander Highfield, now in that role, deserve special appreciation for their faith in this project and forbearance. James in particular for his enthusiasm for the book from when it was an idea we discussed, through his close readings of the proposal and invaluable insights throughout.

My greatest debt is to my children for tolerating the demands producing this book has made on my time, and to my wife, Elizabeth, for her support and prodding. The family cats' welcome company and interruptions also require acknowledgement.

INTRODUCTION
READING MATERIAL

CHAPTER 1
MATERIAL AS REALITY PRESERVE: HISTORY, THEORY, DESIGN

The method elaborated on throughout this book is both descriptive and productive: architectural themes are outlined through detailed analyses of particular buildings, which, although worth studying for themselves, are equally valuable for the insights they offer on how future architecture might be imagined *otherwise*. In each instance, a first step entails recuperating what German philosopher Theodor W. Adorno (1903–69) described as the 'double sense' of art's representation of 'truth': maintaining 'the image of its aim, which has been obscured by rationality', while convicting 'the status quo of its irrationality and absurdity'.[1] As Adorno asserts, art's rationality – architecture here – takes shape in works that outmanoeuvre our 'overadministered world', by revealing the 'absurdity' of the 'faulty irrationality of the rational world', which 'Capitalist society hides and disavows'.[2] As a 'refuge for mimetic comportment', art allows 'the subject' to expose 'itself, at various levels of autonomy, to its other, separated from it and yet not altogether separated', a theme Adorno took up in an explicitly architectural context in his 'Functionalism Today' address.[3]

In the balance between case studies of buildings and readings of theories, the material reality of architecture as produced and as manifesting disruptive ideas – the predicament of art as simultaneously separated from the world and inevitably bound to it – is central. By giving similar weight to theories (texts/ideas) and practices (modes of producing built form), theory is presented as kind of practice, while practice is conceptualized as incomplete without theory. Key to this argument is conceptualization of architecture as a constructed material thing experienced by the whole body, rather than primarily an aesthetic object, the making of space or the production of signs. Architecture and architectural theory are emphasized as enmeshed, accentuating construction – physicality rather than visuality. Ultimately, interweaving theories and practices facilitates augmented understandings of the world, beyond what the imagined autonomy of either can offer. By countering the alienation of practice both from theory and from everyday life, the overarching theme developed is that *material can make architecture a reality preserve*. Importantly, rather than attempting to produce a comprehensive history, the thematic approach entails an interplay between ideas and buildings, with specific built works reinforcing general concrete and theoretical reflections on architecture.

Matter provides a framework for introducing the ideas of a range of thinkers from within architecture and beyond it, in support of multidimensional explorations of material use and meaning in building. When tied to, and interpretive of, local features and conditions, material imagination can contribute to establishing place identity. Locality counteracts intensifying elimination of material and place specificity, and difference. Specificity resists colonization of the world by non-places: the omnipresent global spaces of exchange. As used here, 'place identity' should not be confused with *genius loci*, which in contemporary discourse suggests essential or fixed meanings of a place that need only be excavated to achieve something 'authentic'. Rather, place identity is always made, or constructed; never a given certainty: it must be cultivated. Arguing for architecture as primarily experienced by the whole body, rather than chiefly with the eyes, asserts concreteness (the potentially real) over abstractness (the impossibly visionary).

Material imagination

Conceptualization of 'material imagination' (as opposed to 'formal imagination') owes much to French philosopher Gaston Bachelard's (1864–1962) coinage of the term and suggests that the substance of specific materials is as much a matter of matter as of individual and cultural memory. Accordingly, inventive engagements with material emerge out of a circular process in which specific individual and group associations with them are shaped by experience, memory and cultural imaginaries through time and use. The inherent qualities of particular materials are also relevant. However, 'qualities' is understood here in both a poetic sense and in relation to the specific properties of a given material. As Bachelard observes: 'To the various material elements correspond phantoms that keep their strength as long as they are faithful to their matter or, what amounts to almost the same thing, as long as they are faithful to original dreams.'[4]

As employed here, 'material imagination' is also indebted to Italian novelist and literary critic Umberto Eco's (1932–2016) conceptualization of the 'connotative' and 'denotative' in relation to architectural elements.[5] The everyday bits out of which buildings are assembled – stairs, doors and columns, for example – function in two senses: intimating the activities they support and facilitate, while simultaneously embodying poetic associations. Material imagination also recollects German architect and theorist Gottfried Semper's (1803–79) consideration of the 'Four Elements of Architecture'.[6] For each, architecture's 'thingness' is enriched by imaginaries of technical and emotional function.

Globalized practices and modes of architectural production, dominated by spectacle, virtualization and exchange overwhelm the total body, material imagination and place identity.[7] Design imagination, disciplined by modes of architectural representation, and building assembly that exaggerate generalization dissolve the specificity of experience. Conceptualizations of architecture and its consumption dominated by abstraction and the visual displaces the use value of backdrops and settings for everyday life by emphasizing exchange value, thereby commodifying architecture into aesthetic objects.[8]

Concentrating on architecture as an assemblage of materials and forms experienced bodily (individually and socially) counters prevailing conceptions of it as primarily image making, the production of space, or as responses to complex technical problems.

Thinking of architectural significance in terms of bodily experience foregrounds use, in its broadest sense, including reflection on appropriations of built environments as responses to emotional and practical needs. Embodied experience counters the alienation of form from content and matter; mind from body; and everyday use from formal (or theoretical) virtuosity. The prospect that making space and the production of signs could be re-joined by bodily experience through use is an admittedly utopian hope provoked by its high risk of failure.

Practising theory

The commonalities and differences of the architects and theorists considered in this book contribute to developing a multidimensional exploration of materiality (material use, presence and meaning) in architecture, and help to establish connections with architectural practice in one direction, and thinkers on architecture (philosophers, theorists and architects) in the other (construed as practitioners of thought in action); while building design and construction are engaged with as a practical theoretic. Prior to building, architectural ideas are introduced by verbal, textual and two- and three-dimensional visual representations, only fully fleshed out as they take on a material presence through construction, and use.

Non-places and beyond

French sociologist and philosopher Henri Lefebvre's (1901–91) conception of the 'possible-impossible' is borrowed to develop on his conviction that possible alternatives are immanent within the apparently totalized spaces of planned modernity.[9] Although present practices appear to exclude alternatives by making possible other spaces seem impossible, they are latent nonetheless. Lefebvre's assertion that the more absolute the pose of totality, the more fragile its construct is echoed in French anthropologist Marc Augé's (b. 1935) proposition that 'place and non-place are rather like opposed polarities: the first is never completely erased, the second never totally completed', suggesting the latency of alternatives.[10]

Augé asserts that *place* is distinguished from non-place by being 'anthropological': 'relational, historical and concerned with identity', and held in common, whereas *non-place* lacks locational specificity, characterized by anonymity and solitude.[11] Anonymity is an aesthetic designation for the non-descript (or rather, uninflected, continuous) landscape that characterizes the built environment since the Second World War, whereas solitude is a psychological or critical observation, or in Augé's terms, an anthropological one, inasmuch as it takes account of the social conditions of such places: the alienation they foster as much the alienated practices from which they emerge. Constructed out of alienation as a manifestation of it, the contemporary built environment makes alternatives seem inconceivable. Alternatives that do emerge are evidence of extravagant will, operating against the tide of history and society alike. Achievement of something other than transparent reflections of *what is*, is so unexpected that Italian architectural historian and theorist Manfredo Tafuri (1935–94) described its appearance as 'golden'.[12]

If the inevitably alienating apparent totality of the built environment is apprehended as a 'production'(organized for reproducing its own conditions), its status as a sort of natural phenomenon crumbles, making previously impossible alternatives construable. When apparent totality is revealed as a perishable ideological armature for conserving itself at any cost, the balance of risk shifts slightly from nearly assured failure to anticipatory illumination of conceivable alternatives. Following Lefebvre, Augé's belief that place (or its possibility) 'is never completely erased' suggests a recuperation of the sort French Jesuit scholar Michel de Certeau (1925–86) (echoing Lefebvre) imagined. According to him, the ordinary practice of walking the city could re-inscribe controlling environments of bureaucratic modernity with subversive specificity.[13]

The unlikely persistence of anthropological place and the daily resistance enacted by walking the city confound plans for complete management. Accordingly, in everyday life, Lefebvre could identify the prospect of 'concrete' space, as a real possibility in opposition to 'abstract' space.[14] When not simply compliant, persistence of the everyday traces the concrete specificity of anthropological place within the abstract spaces of the present. Relational materialized places, imbued with communal and individual identity, will have 'real historical precedent'.[15] Lefebvre's preoccupation with thinking the possible-impossible (as the necessary mindset for exceeding the impasses of present conditions) reveals the radical dimension of tradition as simultaneously transgressive and self-renewing.[16]

Conceptualizing tradition as self-renewing reveals it as fertile ground for radical inventions, exceeding adherence to pre-existing habits, static conditions or some mythical past. Reintroducing tradition to its etymological origins discloses it as also a 'handing over', a surrender of the past to the present, and of both to the future, rather than solely faithfully 'handing down' what came before, in perpetuity. Tradition and the persistence of anthropological places resist the solvent of modernity (particularly the creative destruction endemic to global capitalism), which makes them reservoirs of everyday practices and places not yet erased (or overwhelmed by abstraction). Accordingly, pre-modern conditions materialize as radical counterpoints to the present, rather than solely nostalgic, or atavistic. If dissolution of tradition is the cultural logic of late capitalism, the appeal of the past resides in the future action it models as a robust critique of modernity.[17]

Mindful engagement with the tangibility of materials in architecture guarantees nothing but is nonetheless a first step to overcoming the abstract with the concrete. Like material, the everyday can act as a mode of resistance to the abstract blueprint utopianism of planners, technocrats and architects of the modern city. The undisciplined nature of the everyday harbours capacities for confounding attempts to rationalize it, so long as pliant conformity gives way to embodied subversion. Liberating tradition and everyday life from preconceptions of enervating nostalgia or repetition depends on conceiving of the former beyond fixity and the latter as more than code for the primitive. Unhinged from commonplaces, tradition and everyday life can be generative, carrying within them capacities for renewal, prompting material imaginaries exceeding convention, codes or industry standards. Reinvention requires surrendering, or betraying, inheritances, rather than obedience to them.

Material as reality preserve

In building, 'concrete' most obviously suggests a particular material, identified with the architecture of the twentieth century to the present. But 'concrete' also signifies 'specificity', as opposed to 'abstractness' (perhaps of much contemporary architectural theory, dislocated from materials, construction and use). Likewise, 'concrete' suggests the antithesis of abstract uses of materials in construction as well as conceptualizations of material as captured image. Concreteness structures building blocks for social settings perpetually renewed by disobedient experiencing subjects, who defy limited narratives of occupation and use.

The proposition of a specific, concrete, architecture developed here has much in common with the ethos introduced in British architectural historian Kenneth Frampton's (b. 1930) *Studies in Tectonic Culture* but is intentionally less systematic in its aims.[18] Central to the approach here is the paradox of specificity born of non-essentialist, constructionist conceptions of material. The assertion is that this oscillation anticipates how the dominance of encroaching non-places carpeting the world might be countered. It is in this sense primarily that material is asserted as potentially a 'reality preserve' in contemporary architecture.

'Reality Preserve' in relation to architecture emphasizes its thingness, its concrete reality and material presence, as modes of resistance to the abstractness that dominates the built environment in relation to use, and in obscured, or hidden, construction. While this has less to do with 'truth' or 'honesty', it argues that human beings are most at home in settings analogous to bodily physicality, perishability, endurance and sensuality. The reality preserved is that of physical experience and emotional resonance, manifest in architectural works that persist as usable for elaborating individual and community life, contrary to commoditization of buildings as products of exchange (as art object, city brand icon or lever for real estate investment and development).[19]

The conviction that material, and material imagination, constitutes the core of architecture's capacity to persist as a *reality preserve* depends on productions that evade the panoptic sweep of capitalist realism or neoliberalism. Manifesting countercurrents to the seemingly unstoppable dissolution of places of social appearance, such work resists transformation into products for exchange and consumption, not least in its obdurate material specificity. As defined here, 'reality' might signify the 'unreality' of a non-existent utopian counter-condition, a Not Yet, potentially achievable nonetheless. The consideration of material advanced here does not propose absolutes. In and of itself, material represents no fixed positive value: all brick may be hand-scaled, but not all brick is made or used in the same way. Consequently, no totalizing statement (one way or another) can be made about brick; any statement about it (or any other material) is inevitably situational. Brick can recollect its humanizing capacities associated with its original modes of production, including weathered mellowness but it can just as easily be a shallow veneer, as paper thin in conception as in deployment, constituting little more than simulacrum of its assumed inherent value, perhaps not even that. Brick has darker associations as well.

If materials actually embodied fixed positive values, then even their most banal use would be enough to distinguish a building as a 'work', rather than a 'product' (in Lefebvre's terms). For him, 'a work has something irreplaceable and unique about it', whereas 'a product can be reproduced exactly, and is in fact the result of repetitive acts and gestures'.[20] As Lefebvre conceptualizes it, 'a work' relates to 'spontaneity and naturalness', not 'art's intentionality' (which is a first step to it becoming 'a specialized activity', and therefrom transforming into 'products destined to be exchanged, traded and reproduced *ad infinitum*)'.[21] In most instances, according to Lefebvre, superficial differences between like products are simply matters of (re)packaging: 'The predominance of visualization … serves to conceal repetitiveness. People look, and take sight, take seeing, for life itself.' The generally 'increasingly pronounced visual character' of buildings confirms only that

> They are made with the visible in mind: the visibility of people and things, of spaces and of whatever is contained by them. We build on the basis of papers and plans. We buy on the basis of images. Sight and seeing, which in the Western tradition once epitomized intelligibility, have turned into a trap: the means whereby, in social space, diversity may be simulated and a travesty of enlightenment and intelligibility ensconced under the sign of transparency.[22]

While the topic of transparency is returned to in a later chapter on glass, for the moment, Lefebvre's observations support the conclusion that apparent difference achieved by emphasizing the visual presence of material – mostly as a simulacrum of itself – does little more than attempt 'to conceal repetitiveness'. Using material as an image, or sign, of some supposed significance is no substitute for the quality of the imaginary transposed into the work, and of labour's impress upon it. In Lefebvre's estimation, when 'repetition' defeats 'uniqueness', and 'the artificial and contrived' drive out 'spontaneity and naturalness', 'products' will 'have vanquished works'.[23] Accordingly, current preoccupations with materials as a topic of architectural theory and practice are, in many ways, the antithesis of the argument advanced here: throughout, material as a reality preserve in contemporary architecture is considered as avowedly non-essentialist. No special status is given to matter beyond tangible presence.

Despite the exaggeration of value commodities trading encourages – precious metals or stones for example – the argument here is twofold: material has no necessary intrinsic value. Because of this, values accrue to material relative to the context of its use; according to *how* it is used, and to *what* end. Because labour adds symbolic value to material, what matters is what is done with it. Vapid, or exhibitionist, use of precious (expensive because rare) materials in much corporate (or even institutional) architecture bears this out.

In Thomas More's *Utopia* (1516), the Utopians' 'eat from pottery dishes and drink from glass cups, all well made but inexpensive, their chamber pots and stools – all their humblest vessels, for use in the common halls and private homes – are made of gold and silver'.[24] The double significance of this turns first on the most obvious point: More's satire would have been incomprehensible if gold and silver were not generally considered inherently valuable. Accordingly, More identifies obsession with the preciousness of gold and silver as a kind of enslavement – of individual, community and desire alike. Only by reconceptualizing precious materials as *base* could their hold upon us be loosened. Thus, liberation (including of the imagination) entails overcoming material fetishes. More drives his point home as follows:

> The chains and heavy shackles of slaves are also made of these materials. Criminals … are forced to wear golden rings in their ears and on their fingers, golden chains around their necks, and even golden headbands. Thus they [the Utopians] hold up gold and silver to scorn in every conceivable way.[25]

As social critique rather than rulebook, the Utopians' disdain for gold and silver voices More's criticism of his own society: fetishizing material is inseparable from acquisitiveness and thus corruption (spiritual and otherwise). Although written more than half a millennium ago, More's consideration of silver and gold still cautions against getting carried away with the relative richness of any material, especially in terms of its imagined accrued worth, even on account of scarcity.

Material and meaning

The reality that is preserved by material in architecture is the intensified reality that art and experiencing it can give access to. Even in an age when art is consumed as leisure time entertainment, a distraction from the disappointments of everyday life and as an investment opportunity, it can still offer the prospect of a more intense reality. But this is no plea for an architecture that impresses itself on experiencing subjects by overwhelming either use or the capacity to inhabit it in distraction. Concentration on material presence and use is what joins the apparently unrelated work considered in this book. Adolf Loos, Carlo Scarpa, Peter Zumthor, Tod Williams and Billie Tsien, and Enric Miralles and Benedetta Tagliabue might appear to share little, but only if preoccupation with coincidences of certain superficial formal characteristics (*style*) is exaggerated. Rather, what links their works is mindfulness of architecture's potential for exceeding the limitations of technique and standardization, imposed by a building industry organized according to the logic of mechanized production, consumption and the profit motive. The works discussed are radical and resistant, which makes them utopian as well, inasmuch as each articulates alternatives to what *is*; to the limitations of the generally *given*, and do so as offerings for appropriation in ways suggestive of new (social and spatial) conditions.

Most discussions of material turn on a consideration of an apparent 'form/matter' split, which represents one or the other as dominant. Either the overall form of a work of architecture – its perception as a unitary object of consideration – is privileged, or the stuff out of which it is made is.[26] In a number of ways, this opposition parallels another; the *form/content* split, which represents the meaning of a work of art, or architecture, as somehow separate from its substance. As Ceylonese Tamil philosopher Ananda K. Coomaraswamy (1877–1947) observed: 'For the most part, our "aesthetic" approach stands between us and the content of the work of art, of which only the surface concerns us.'[27] For him, 'outward appearance' is the same as 'shape', 'form' and 'style'. In each instance: 'As shape is the outward expression of theme, so form is the outward manifestation of content; subject is made known by shape, actual value by form.'[28] According to Coomaraswamy, 'content' is obscured by the tendency to think of form as the substance of a work; content is read into form by being attached to it as an afterthought, rather than as intrinsic. The dominance of vision and exchange overemphasizes image, while exaggerating dependency on description, which inevitably undervalues bodily – or visceral (emotional) – experience of architecture, and other aspects of the world.

French-American artist Marcel Duchamp's (1887–1968) *Fountain* (1917) provides an object lesson in the form/content split: he transformed a ready-made urinal simply by signing it as an artist, and rechristening it a 'Fountain', and placing it in an art exhibition, which made it a work of art representing a fountain, thereby attaching a meaning to it only vaguely related to its actual use. Fountains and urinals may both pass water but whereas urinals use running water to flush captured urine into the sewer, fountains issue water in exuberant celebrations of its capacities. The association of both with water and certain shared technical and mechanical characteristics might make their correlation less counterintuitive but mostly intensifies the ironic effect. Arguably, the man imagined using the urinal is more the fountain, which highlights the readiness to separate form from content in the modern world, which could lead to the conclusion that alienation, as a central condition of contemporary existence, problematizes embodied use. Perhaps that was precisely Duchamp's point.

Mindful of *Fountain*, recuperating the inextricable association of form to content, and thereby the bond between form and matter, is urgent. Even if these bonds tend to elude contemporary appreciations of art, understandings of architecture and even day-to-day experience of the world, the mode of encountering buildings developed here places form and matter, and form and content, on equal footings; not as pairs of reconciled oppositions but rather as means for recollecting experiencing bodies as the source of meaning and understanding of the world.

Material matters, depending

Although spectacle can make material seem a value in itself, as an antidote to ocular dominance, the triumph of image threatens to vanquish bodily experience as central to comprehending architecture as felt meaning.[29] Perhaps reflecting general cultural devolution, imagining buildings in computers and digital representations of them parallels a general flattening of the world. The ebbing of shadow and craft in building detail mirrors expanding use of computers, which is likely more symptom than cause.[30]

Even if construction always involves manipulating materials, attitudes towards them differ widely. Some architects view material as simple necessity, required to construct buildings or to achieve a particular image or finish. For others, material has a nearly mystical value, as though worth was inbuilt. Often absent is reflection on the value added to material by thoughtful labour: what is done with it, how it is conceptualized and the way construction re-imagines it. Apart from mind, making and use, material is meaningless. The enduring expressive possibilities of material deriving from effort expended are initially discussed in the chapters on Ruskin and Loos. The pervasiveness of spectacle notwithstanding, noteworthy architecture recollects touch as the sense with which the world is experienced and learned from our earliest days. Such architecture engages material as the first point of physical contact between individuals and buildings.

Dematerialization of the built realm diminishes its adequacy as a stage for unfolding human interaction and events. Resisting depersonalizing abstraction in a weakening material realm is crucial. Although not without risk, material expression has the capacity for responding to a real human need to locate shared places in the built environment, able to house bodies, desires and senses. A generally common bodily form establishes relations of human beings to one another by linking past and future through a shared inheritance of birth, with touch, the earliest navigation system for mastering the environment, by crawling over, under and through things.

The drama of material expression engages experiencing subjects and makers in a middle realm that links nature with culture and art with science. The world is alive with material possibilities, from trees to sand, stone, earth and water (amongst others). The ability to do something with the material possibilities of the world and at the same time leave some part of their origin intact inscribes building with the ethical drama of balancing desires to master the world for human inhabitation with a capacity to leave it alone. Inevitably, culture makes a stand against nature, and is often defeated by it. Art can reveal something about this perpetual drama, while science and technology transform the natural world into a set of availabilities artists and architects could manipulate in re-enactments and retellings of it.

Structure

Organized into a three-part structure, the book comprises the following sections: 'Introduction: Reading Material', including this Preface and two essays, the first considers English art and social critic John Ruskin (1819–1900), the second, Austrian-Czech architect, theorist and satirist Adolf Loos (1870–1933); section two, 'Part One: Stones, Buildings, Land and Interiors', comprises four separate discussions of work by individual architects or studios in relation to the key themes introduced previously and in the introductory chapters. Section three, 'Part Two: The Long View of Materials in Play', includes five reflective essays on specific materials, considering how meaning accrues to wood, brick, concrete, steel and glass across time, through use, in relation to the human body. A final chapter recapitulates and concludes the discussion. The three-part structure is intended to clarify the aims developed throughout, while making it easier for readers to focus on individual sections, chapters and/or themes according to specific interests.

Notes

1. Theodor W. Adorno, *Aesthetic Theory* (1970), Robert Hullot-Kentor (trans.), London and New York: Continuum, 1997, p. 54.

2. Ibid., p. 53.

3. Ibid., p. 53. See also, Adorno, 'Functionalism Today', Jane Newman and John Smith (trans.), *Oppositions*, 17 (Summer 1979): 31–41. Originally presented to the German Werkbund, 1965.

4. Gaston Bachelard, *Water and Dreams: An Essay on the Imagination of Matter* (1942), Edith R. Farrell (trans.), Dallas, TX: The Pegasus Foundation, 1983, p. 17.

5. Umberto Eco, 'Function and Sign: The Semiotics of Architecture' (1973), reprinted in *Rethinking Architecture: A Reader in Cultural Theory*, Neil Leach (ed.), London and New York: Routledge, 1997, pp. 173–93.

6. Gottfried Semper, 'The Four Elements of Architecture: A Contribution to the Comparative Study of Architecture' (1851), in *The Four Elements of Architecture and Other Writings*, Harry Francis Mallgrave and Wolfgang Herrmann (trans.), Cambridge: Cambridge University Press, 1989, pp. 74–129.

7. Henri Lefebvre, *The Production of Space* (1974), Donald Nicholson-Smith (trans.), Oxford: Blackwell, 1991.

8. Ibid., See also, Nathaniel Coleman, *Utopias and Architecture*, London and New York: Routledge, 2005; Coleman, *Lefebvre for Architects*, London and New York: Routledge, 2015.

9. Lefebvre, 'Time and History' (1970), from *La Fin de l'histoire*, Paris: Éditions de Minuit, and 2 e édn. (2001), Paris: Anthropos, reprinted in Henri Lefebvre, *Key Writings*, S. Elden, E. Lebas and E. Kofman (eds), (trans. unspecified), New York: Continuum, 2003, pp. 177–87; Coleman, *Lefebvre for Architects*.

10. Marc Augé, *Non-Places: Introduction to an Anthropology of Supermodernity* (1992), John How (trans.), London and New York: Verso, 1995, p. 79.

11. Ibid., pp. 77, 120.

12. Manfredo Tafuri, *History of Italian Architecture, 1944–1985*, Cambridge, MA: MIT Press, 1989, p. 111.

13. Michel de Certeau, 'Walking in the City', in *The Practice of Everyday Life*, Steven Rendall (trans.), Berkeley, CA: University of California Press, 1984, pp. 91–110.

14. Lefebvre, *The Production of Space*.

15. Augé, *Non-Places*, pp. 117–18.

16. Ibid., p. 118; Henri Lefebvre, *Critique of Everyday Life Volume II, Foundations for a Sociology of the Everyday* (1961), John Moore (trans.), London: Verso, 2008; Lefebvre, *Key Writings*;

Lefebvre, *Writings on Cities*, E. Kofman and E. Lebas (trans.), Oxford: Wiley-Blackwell, 1996.

17. Michael Löwy and Robert Sayre, *Romanticism Against the Tide of Modernity*, Catherine Porter (trans.), Durham, NC: Duke University Press, 2001.

18. Kenneth Frampton, *Studies in Tectonic Culture: The Poetics of Construction in Nineteenth and Twentieth Century Architecture*, John Cava (ed.), Cambridge, MA: MIT Press, 2001.

19. The conception of 'reality preserve' outlined owes its origins – albeit obliquely – to Ignasi de Sol à Morales, 'Weak Architecture', in *Differences: Topographies of Contemporary Architecture*, Sarah Whiting (ed.), Graham Thompson (trans.), Cambridge, MA: MIT Press, 1996, pp. 57–71.

20. Lefebvre, *The Production of Space*, p. 70.

21. Ibid., pp. 74–5.

22. Ibid., pp. 75–6.

23. Ibid., p. 75.

24. Thomas More, *Utopia* (1516), Norton Critical Edition, Second Edition, Robert M. Adams (trans. and ed.), New York: W. W. Norton, 1992, p. 47.

25. Thomas More, *Utopia* (1516), Cambridge Texts in the History of Political Thought, Third Edition, Robert M. Adams (trans.), George M. Logan (ed.), Cambridge: Cambridge University Press, 2016, p. 64.

26. Katie Lloyd Thomas, *Material Matters: Architecture and Material Practice*, Katie Lloyd Thomas (ed.), New York and London: Routledge, 2007, pp. 2–12; Esra Sahin, 'Exchange of Forces: Environmental Definition of Materials in the Works of Vitruvius, Alberti, Le Corbusier, and Peter Zumthor' (2009). Dissertations available from ProQuest. AAI3405397. https://repository.upenn.edu/dissertations/AAI3405397

27. Ananda K. Commaraswamy, 'Saṁvega, "Aesthetic Shock,"' *Harvard Journal of Aesthetic Studies*, 7, no. 3 (1943): 174, n. 2.

28. Ananda K. Commaraswamy, 'Indian Art', *Studies in Comparative Religion*, 15, no. 3 & 4 (Summer–Autumn, 1983). Available online at: http://www.studiesincomparativereligion.com/Public/articles/Indian%20Art-by_Ananda_K_Coomaraswamy.aspx (Accessed 21 May 2018).

29. Lefebvre, *The Production of Space*; Guy Debord, *The Society of the Spectacle* (1967), Donald Nicholson-Smith (trans.), New York: Zone Books, 1994. See also: Steen Eiler Rasmussen, *Experiencing Architecture, Second Edition*, Cambridge, MA: MIT Press, 1964; Juhani Pallasmaa, *The Eyes of the Skin: Architecture and the Senses*, Chichester, West Sussex: Wiley & Sons, 2005; Juhani Pallasmaa, *The Thinking Hand: Existential and Embodied Wisdom in Architecture*, Chichester: Wiley & Sons, 2009.

30. Richard Sennett, *The Craftsman*, London: Allen Lane, 2008.

CHAPTER 2
JOHN RUSKIN (1819–1900): STONES OF ARCHITECTURE

The nineteenth-century English social theorist and art and architecture critic John Ruskin's (1819–1900) best-known and clearest statement of the virtues of architecture and architectural values, *The Seven Lamps of Architecture* (1849, Second Edition, 1880) (hereafter *The Seven Lamps*; *Seven Lamps*; *The Lamps*; or *Lamps*), is transmuted in this chapter to reveal its surviving relevance. In the main, Ruskin concentrates on works as expression but does so from an imaginatively critical historical perspective that culturally situates the architecture he considers. Importantly, Ruskin considered 'all art' to be 'abstract in its beginnings', inasmuch as 'it expresses only a small number of the qualities of the thing represented.' Equally, 'how much' of a work can 'be supposed good, depends … more on place and circumstance than on general laws'. And, while 'sculpture is the representation of an idea, … architecture is itself a real thing.'[1] In many ways, these three points render *The Lamps* timely.

Despite its age, Ruskin's *Seven Lamps* is supple enough to portray architecture's dynamism. Rendering the *Lamps* current entails reading twentieth- and twenty-first-century architecture through it, particularly works by US architect Frank Lloyd Wright (1867–1959), Swiss-French architect Le Corbusier (1887–1965), US architect Louis I. Kahn (1901–74), Italian architect Carlo Scarpa (1906–78), Dutch architect Aldo van Eyck (1918–99), Swiss architect Peter Zumthor (b. 1943) and US architects Williams (b. 1943) and Tsien (b. 1949).

The apparent mismatch between the architecture of a specific time and place Ruskin analyses in *Lamps* and claims for its continuing relevance is precisely the point – to problematize style and aesthetics as the primary modes of architectural sorting by shifting focus towards material presence and bodily experience as more stable sources of imagining future work.

Ruskin's importance for Le Corbusier is well documented, less considered is his transmission of this influence to younger architects. The radical dimension of the *Lamps* is Ruskin's proposition of architectural significance as work culture silted up in physical artefacts, which outsmarts style-bound conceptions of value by bridging the pre-modern past with the nineteenth century and the origins of twentieth-century modernist architecture, extensible to the present and future.

Architecture as building

Buildings are inflected by social, political, economic, technical, aesthetic and ethical forces (amongst others). Although material and meaning in architecture is the focus of this book, material is construed as a tool for developing more comprehensive readings of architecture that begin with use and experience rather than exchange.

In the development of twentieth-century modernist architecture, sorting reached its apotheosis with the 1932 International Style exhibit at the Museum of Modern Art (MoMA), in New York City. Organized at the behest of then MoMA director, Alfred Barr (1902–81), by Philip Johnson (1906–2005) and Henry-Russell Hitchcock (1903–87), the exhibit ethos was codified in their simultaneous book, *The International Style* (1932).[2]

Despite the association of modernist architecture with form following function, the International Style exhibit emphasized formal unity as the defining feature of the movement. Industrial elements and industrial production were represented – or depicted – by the works displayed. Although the hoped-for stylistic unity no longer obtains, formalism and industrial (and technological) myths continue to dominate *auteur* architecture. Faithful to the MoMA exhibit, images of buildings (or buildings as images) dominate over considerations of use, bodily experience or production, despite the dominance of the building industry.

Examining buildings in-situ, as Ruskin did, experiencing them bodily, rather than primarily visually, recorded by drawing and painting, is how architects and aesthetes once cultivated architectural knowledge. Resisting digital methods of virtual representation and production is all but impossible but recuperating dynamic, multidimensional modes of conceptualizing and representing architecture is prerequisite for recuperating a built environment worthy of bodily experience.

The body of architecture

Architectural value appraises qualities buildings possess thought of as desirable, or necessary, for them to be considered worthy. Comprehensive rather than reductive, the range of topics addressed in thinking and practising architecture is now more limited. In general, worthiness is reduced to just three qualities: image, economy and efficiency. A fuller sense of use, the urban realm and bodily experience is largely neglected. Positively or negatively, positioning buildings along a spectrum of worth, including concern for inhabitants and civic adornment, is most immediately determined by prevailing attitudes towards materials, and evident in how they are used. Recollecting those qualities Ruskin believed fundamental to the invention, purpose and value of architecture could enrich appraisals of it, and the work we might produce ourselves.

In affinity with Italian Renaissance architect and theorist Leon Battista Alberti (1404–72), Ruskin believed that buildings are analogous to bodies (animals for Alberti). Bodies and buildings are both made up of mostly hidden internal organs and obscured structure, protected by external layers of skin forming a visible weather-resisting membrane.[3] For

Ruskin, architecture is also analogous to human behaviour, especially of acting in the world: good, bad or exemplary. A building or person can be either noble or debased. As a topic, decorum might seem particularly anachronistic, since it is now mostly overwhelmed by exhibitionist self-disclosure and regimes of display. But by conflating building demeanour with human comportment, Ruskin delineates the virtuous qualities of both: 'we require from buildings, as from men, two kinds of goodness: first, the doing their practical duty well: then that they be graceful and pleasing in doing it; which last is itself another form of duty.'[4]

Ruskin's use of 'practical duty' is more nuanced than modernist 'function' (or 'functionalism'), which suggests 'fulfilling' technical conceptions of use: mechanistic readings of activities emphasizing efficiencies of time and motion in their performance. 'Function' also has some relation to 'type', which is equally reductive, relating to the fidelity of the most recent iteration of a thing to an idealized first example of its 'kind', akin to Platonic conceptions of an 'ideal', or *essence*. In practice, 'type' concerns suitability of building character to intended occupation, gauged in relation to a supposedly 'essential' first of its kind, as the foundation of typicality.

'Function', 'type' and 'practical purpose' are associable with the second component of first century BC Roman architect and theorist Vitruvius's triad: *utilitas*; utility, usefulness or functionality. However, neither his conception nor Ruskin's 'practical duty' is solely technical, in the way 'functionalism' has come to be understood. For Vitruvius, *utilitas* (usefulness) was inseparable from the other two components of his triad: *firmitas* (strength), or *venustas* (beauty). Ruskin's assertion that buildings and people be 'graceful and pleasing' in doing their 'practical duty well' renders his estimation of architectural virtue proximate with Vitruvius's triad:

> practical duty divides itself into two branches, acting and talking: acting, as to defend us from weather or violence; talking, as the duty of monuments or tombs, to record facts and express feelings; or of churches, temples, public edifices, treated as books of history, to tell such history clearly and forcibly.[5]

Ruskin's 'acting' recollects Vitruvius's *firmitas* and 'firmness' (unyielding, secure and forceful) and 'commodity' (material, useful or valuable). The second branch of a building's 'practical duty' is 'talking': it must 'record facts and express feelings' (memorial buildings), and communicate embodied history by recording and transmitting it, 'clearly and forcibly' (religious and public buildings). For buildings to do either well, they must be more robust in conception than in execution. Nonetheless, material choice, in relation to execution (construction and detailing), is central to construing architectural significance. Ruskin's 'three great branches of architectural virtue' match Vitruvius's triad in number and spirit, with each indicating what 'we require of any building':

1. That it act well, and do the things it was intended to do in the best way.

2. That it speak well, and say the things it was intended to say in the best words.

3. That it look well, and please us by its presence, whatever it has to do or say.[6]

Akin to Vitruvius's firmness, commodity and delight; or strength, functionality and beauty, Ruskin's branches of 'architectural virtue' define architecture's vocation. His second and third virtues – speaking well and looking well – map onto Vitruvius's *venustas*, or beauty. More so than Ruskin, Vitruvius's and Alberti's ideas of beauty derive from Socrates's definition in Plato's *Symposium*. Vitruvius calls it *eurythmia*, whereas Alberti calls it *concinnitas*. Both are the underlying causes of beauty, related to balance in bodies, analogous to natural (or divine) order. Paraphrasing Socrates, Alberti defines beauty as:

> that reasoned harmony of all the parts within a body, so that nothing may be added, taken away, or altered, but for the worse. It is a great and holy matter; all our resources of skill and ingenuity will be taxed in achieving it; and rarely is it granted, even to Nature herself, to produce anything that is entirely complete and perfect in every respect.[7]

Although Alberti's definition presumes wholeness as an ideal, Ruskin's appropriation does not require bilateral symmetry, or static balance, but rather extols striving for completeness, which, because unachievable, permits roughness and wildness. Despite being unattainable, the perfection and wholeness of beauty ought to be aimed for. According to Ruskin, because perfection exceeds human achievement, only limited aims and meagre aspirations are completely reachable but only as chimera, which explains his conviction that fallibility is the nature of human work.

Despite his influence on the development of modernist architecture, Ruskin has been largely rejected, perhaps for describing architecture's desirable qualities in terms of 'virtues'. Italian-French author of the 'Futurist Manifesto' (1909), Filippo Tommaso Marinetti (1876–1944), encouraged jettisoning Ruskin for being burdensome and moralizing. Granted, Ruskin 'suffers from a tendency to dogmatic exaggeration and petulance which makes even his best writing repugnant to some readers'.[8] But that is also a source of his charm. More so, Ruskin's consideration of architecture's intrinsic worth provides enduring points of reference.

Aims and objectives

Ruskin's division of 'practical duty' into 'acting' and 'talking' is also suggestive of Italian semiotician Umberto Eco's (1932–2016) identification of the 'connotative' and 'denotative' function of architectural elements.[9] Ruskin's *acting* is akin to Eco's *denotative* function. Fundamentally, technical or literal, function requires building elements to accommodate the bodily activities they are intended to facilitate. Ruskin's *talking* is akin to Eco's *connotative* function, which refers to the emotional, or associative, functions buildings must also fulfil. According to Ruskin, for a building to discharge this duty well, it must embody the reality of its time and making and communicate this effectively. The double sense of *doing well* – persuasively in the most appropriate way – joins technical function to emotional function, without valuing one over the other. A building that effectively fulfils its rhetorical functions and practical ones in more or less equal measure is worthy of praise.

Careful consideration of the elements out of which it is assembled, as much as the material presence of its construction and cladding, inside and out, is required for a building to do well (formally, technically, functionally). Materials must 'act' well, and 'speak' well, by being simultaneously durable and meaningful (denotatively and connotatively). In this regard, notions of 'appropriateness', or 'propriety', collapse divides between technical and emotional functions, as well as between 'form' and 'content'. Because material meaning is associative, it is largely culturally determined, even if suggested by physical qualities: smooth, rough, hard, malleable, dark, light, absorptive, reflective, opaque, translucent, transparent and so on.

Growing up in a culture, as architectural historian and theorist David Letherbarrow has observed, equips each of us with comprehensive social understandings of the world. Bodily memories of a given spatial and temporal context (or analogous ones) make it possible to decode the built environment through reference to socially grounded direct experiences, so that content can be read through form.[10] Ruskin's approach is bidirectional: identifying the qualities or characteristics that architecture ought to embody in one direction, and revealing what architects ought to strive for in the other.

The criteria are proposed as transcendent, in the sense of being relevant to evaluating *any* work of architecture, regardless of age or location. Although Ruskin's judgements constitute *moral* principles, which could invite their rejection as anachronistic, his stalwart belief in the endurance of morals paradoxically renews the relevance of his ideas. In their intimate relation to human will to survive, and stewardship of the planetary habitat, morals, like Ruskin's Lamps, are adaptively related to evolving perceptions of the biosphere.

In the 'Preface to the First Edition' of *The Seven Lamps*, Ruskin asserts that the architectural examples selected to illustrate his laws are representative rather than authoritative. Whatever his reasons for choosing them, his chief aim was to make a 'statement of principles'.[11] Encapsulating multiple senses of the term 'principles', Ruskin's use includes conceptions of 'truth' and 'morals', and a 'doctrine', out of which he constructs an architectural ethics, in parts philosophical and ideological.

As the argument goes here, Ruskin's laws of architecture are supple enough to be reusable across time and space. He surely hoped so: 'I could as fully … have illustrated the principles' with 'the architecture of Egypt, India, or Spain, as from that which the reader will find his attention chiefly directed, the Italian Romanesque and Gothic'.[12] Even so, it is doubtful Ruskin would have esteemed architecture now, which is produced by the repetitive actions of industrialized mass production, performed by semi-skilled labourers, or technicians. His geographical and temporal openness, though, suggests a future orientation.[13] He set for himself 'the task of determining some law of right, which we may apply to the architecture of all the world and of all time', in order to make possible 'judgement … [of] whether a building is good or noble'.[14]

Although speaking from another time, alongside Loos (subject of the next chapter), the spirit of Ruskin's laws – if not the letter – undergirds the present study. Both made statements of architectural principles complex and comprehensive enough to support fuller accounts of more recent divergent architecture. Together, Ruskin's *Lamps* constitutes a method dynamic enough to sustain it beyond its original spatiotemporal context; individually, each offers a powerful interpretive tool on its own. As foremost a social theorist and reformer, Ruskin's *Lamps* should be read as commentaries on the architecture of his time, which hint at horizons of future possibility.

Sacrifice

For Ruskin, there are five classes of structures: Devotional, Memorial, Civil, Military and Domestic, with only the first two benefitting from his first Lamp, 'Sacrifice', which concerns distinctions between *building* and *architecture*. For him, pure necessity produces *building*, whereas *architecture* is a matter of the unnecessary (encompassing building but exceeding it), a division still generally accepted.[15] Although the grandeur characterizing devotional and memorial architecture is discretionary, sacrifice is not a matter of cost alone. What is most valued is dearest to us emotionally. Hence, what is sacrificed must be treasured enough to be felt. Value may accrue through scarcity and perishability but Ruskin had more than money in mind.

Sacrifice divides superlative architecture from banal according to material selection and meaning, determined coequally by preciousness (cost), the investment of thought (conception and execution: labour) and cultural associations (memory and history). According to Ruskin, architecture is enhanced by offering 'precious things simply because they are precious; not as necessary to the building, but as an offering, surrendering, and sacrifice of what is to ourselves desirable'.[16] Despite his belief that devotional and memorial buildings alone required sacrifice, new social conditions suggest widening this to include all civic and institutional structures: hospitals, terminals, schools, museums, governmental buildings and civil engineering works, amongst others.[17] Ruskin promoted the 'opposite of the prevalent feeling of modern times … to produce the largest results at the least cost' supports such expansion.[18]

The assembly of buildings predominantly from premade, or mass-produced, elements has made craft redundant. Despite persisting attachments to craft and ornament, material selection and assembly have largely replaced both. The connections, details and joints that mediate materials and assemblies of parts in construction have become the primary sources of architectural signification. However, until enriched by material, details and finish, assemblages of forms are little more than constructed diagrams. Accordingly, when mindful, construction transmits architectural ideas and underlying ethical and aesthetical convictions.[19]

Buildings enhanced by sacrifice exceed problems of simple necessity, which generous forms and spaces, quality of construction and attention to detailing further augments. Enrichment results as much from material selection, as from munificence. In Ruskin's terms, such buildings express 'the desire to honor or please someone else by the costliness of the sacrifice'. Sacrifice must be public, intended to honour the commonweal. Extravagant displays of private wealth – ostentatious corporate headquarters or outrageous private homes, for example – would not constitute sacrifice.[20] Although expenditure is central, the richness of conception and labour invested are more important. As Ruskin asserts: 'I do not want marble churches for their own sake, but for the sake of the spirit that would build them.'[21] He continues, for the 'Spirit of Sacrifice' to be in evidence, 'we should in every thing do our best; and secondly, that we should consider increase in apparent labour as an increase of beauty in the building.'[22]

In contrast to the values of the building industry – economy, efficiency and return on investment – practising Ruskin's virtues constitutes radical resistance: going slower, caring more, increasing the quality and quantity of labour. Equally, mass production entails misconstruing *completeness* as *perfection*, and *technique* as *imagination*. Throughout *The Seven Lamps*, as elsewhere in his writing, Ruskin reminds readers that completeness does not ensure perfection. Apparent perfection can only seem to have been achieved when ambition is set sufficiently low. For Ruskin: 'better our work unfinished than all bad.' In relation to material selection, he argues:

> if you cannot afford marble use Caen stone, but from the best bed; and if not stone, brick, but the best brick; preferring always what is good of a lower order of work or material, to what is bad of a higher; for this is not only the way to improve every kind of work, and to put every kind of material to better use; but it is more honest and unpretending[23]

The preceding anticipates the enduring problem of how to dignify industrialized construction (assembled onsite with ready-made parts mass-produced offsite), without the benefit of humanizing imagination brought to bear on raw materials.

Truth

Although contested by competing subjectivities, 'truth', Ruskin's second Lamp, is conceptually robust enough to withstand disbelief. What work of architecture would not be improved by avoiding 'direct falsity of assertion respecting the nature of material, or the quantity of labour'? Early modernist architects sought to achieve just such honesty by rejecting stylistic eclecticism and material deception, in the belief that *truth to materials* and *honesty of construction* would produce a more *authentic* built environment.[24]

Directly communicating the materials and methods of construction discloses relations to gravity and nature that contribute to physically, socially and emotionally orientating individuals and communities. According to Ruskin, upholding the 'Lamp of Truth' entails avoiding three primary 'Architectural Deceits':

> 1st. The suggestion of a mode of structure or support other than the true one … 2nd. The painting of surfaces to represent some other material than that which they actually consist … [And] 3rd. the use of cast or machine-made ornaments of any kind. Now, it may be broadly stated, that architecture will be noble exactly in the degree in which all these false expedients are avoided.[25]

As an alternative to deceitful construction, Ruskin proposes noble architecture as a 'building' that reveals 'the great secrets of its structure'.[26] Considering his modernist tone, it is easier to gauge his influence on twentieth-century modernist architecture and after. Because deception asserts an unreality as true, the question of comprehensible construction is above all else an ethical one, which, although identifiable with Greek temples and Gothic churches, is a decidedly proto-modernist conception:

> the moment that conditions of weight are comprehended, both truth and feeling require that the conditions of support be also comprehended. Nothing can be worse … than affectedly inadequate supports – suspensions in air, and other such tricks and vanities.[27]

Equally troubling would be, 'deceptive assumptions of [structure] – the introduction of members which should have, or profess to have, a duty, and have none'.[28] Being 'true' also applies to materials for building walls: 'to cover brick with cement, and to divide this cement with joints that it may look like stone, is to tell a falsehood'.[29] Although concealing actual qualities of material and structure should be avoided, Ruskin's laws are not absolute: 'certain degrees of' false expedients are 'admissible' on account of 'frequent usage', so long as one thing is not confused for another. For example, 'gilding, which … in architecture' is not mistaken 'for gold' is not deceitful. However, 'in jewellery it is a deceit, because' it is taken for solid gold. Accordingly, despite his 'strict rules of right', Ruskin tolerates 'exceptions and niceties of conscience'. Ultimately, judgement outstrips law.[30]

The actual physical properties and qualities of materials ground understandings of structures, and orientate the body by touching emotion at the moment of experience. Taking stone as an example, Ruskin argues that if 'the whole fragility, elasticity, and weight of the material are to the eye, if not in terms, denied', this would constitute a 'deliberate treachery'. Accordingly, apparent virtuosity in denying, or attempting to defeat, material attributes, structure or gravity produces bad faith work, in relation to bodily and emotional expectations.[31]

For Ruskin, 'the false representation of material', painting wood or cement to appear as marble, for example, is unpardonable. The more convincing the deception, the worse it is. Because 'whatever is pretended is wrong … all such imitations are utterly base and inadmissible.'[32] Anticipating problems of 'truth' associated with modernist layered construction, Ruskin deemed cladding permissible, so long as perceptible as 'dressing', by not feigning solidity. Avoiding confusion is key: if 'marble facing does not pretend or imply a [solid] marble wall, there is no harm in it'.[33] Starker modernist assertions of 'truth to materials' are difficult to imagine. However, if Ruskin shares moralizing with modernism, it was out of fealty to divine truths, not modernists' idealization of industrial production.

Paradoxically, Ruskin's complete prohibition of the 'substitution of cast or machine work for that of the' hand anticipates the ascendance of unadorned assembled architecture (and the disappearance of craft and ornament) from the nineteenth century onwards. Once industrialized production made craft redundant, design methods and production processes appropriate to the new condition would be more 'truthful' than mimicking handwork with machines (as Loos argued). Disregarding this inescapable condition of modern construction has perpetually frustrated endeavours to produce modern ornament, including stylistic postmodernists' ill-fated adornments of reductionist modernist architecture.

Ruskin's unconditional rejection of 'all cast and machine work', because it 'is bad as work', and 'dishonest' – despite its inevitability – articulates a persisting bind: if cast and machine work can never reproduce 'the sense of human labour and care spent upon' ornament (or other aspects of architecture), as the assured outcome of handwork, industrial production *must* make architecture strange to human beings. Not least because no longer a 'record of [the] thoughts, and intents, and trials, and heart-breakings – of recoveries and joyfulness of success' of the workers who crafted it.[34] If the marks of human labour — as records of toil and thought — make works worthy, then exiling human impress makes them worthless, whether machine-made, or handmade in a machine-like manner.[35]

Although anachronistic, Ruskin's definition of a work's integrity as dependent on its honesty, unity and soundness is proto-modernist in character, inasmuch as the unadorned is preferable to the deceitful: 'Leave your walls as bare as a plane board, or build them of baked mud and chopped straw if need be; but do not rough-cast them with falsehood.'[36] He hoped that 'the dishonesty of machine work would cease, as soon as it became universally practised.'[37]

Above all else Ruskin venerated thoughtful labour. Accordingly: 'The definition of the art of architecture … is independent of its materials.' Concept precedes construction and dominates it, so any reasonable material can be used in building. Whilst he rejected metal architecture, he acknowledged that no ultimate rule prohibited it. But using new, unknown or non-traditional, materials require development of 'a new system of architectural laws' of proportion and structure for working with them. He reasoned that because theories and practices of architecture are interdependent, materials and methods of construction determine the structure and proportion of buildings. Until the beginning of the nineteenth century, 'clay, stone, or wood' were the dominant building materials. Their use in construction formed the basis for 'the sense of proportion and the laws of structure' developed for using them. Accordingly, new materials would initially 'be generally felt as a departure from the first principles of the art'.[38] Novel materials and advanced engineering may expand limits but risk making the built environment alien.

Following Ruskin, emergent theories and practices of modernist architecture demanded new principles; a revised sense of proportion, and modified laws of structure adapted to new materials and methods of construction. The disruption new modes of production cause could perpetually renew architecture but only if conception outstrips execution. Years of developing theory and practice have made modernist architecture into a tradition in its own right. For example, Le Corbusier's *modulor* updates traditional proportional systems for industrial construction, whereas Kahn's 'adoration of the joint' as 'the beginning of ornament' compensates for the loss of traditional ornament. And van Eyck's theorization of the *problem of vast number* accommodated great scale and modularized construction without a loss of signification.[39] While the modernist 'truth to materials' would be inconceivable without Ruskin's 'Lamp of Truth', the proposition that taking greater care with materials and methods of assembly could make buildings less alienating is more permanent, because a matter of imagination rather than technique.

Power

According to Ruskin, the most memorable architecture falls into two categories: one 'characterised by an exceeding preciousness', recollected 'with a sense of affectionate admiration', is *beautiful*. The other, 'by a severe, and, in many cases mysterious majesty', is recollected 'with an undiminished awe, like that felt at the presence and operation of some great Spiritual Power', is sublime.[40] Although 'intermediate examples' exist between the two, buildings are 'always distinctively marked by features of beauty or of power'.[41] Architecture that stirs memory and emotion is thus either sublime or beautiful.[42]

As noted earlier, Ruskin most highly values the human mind's impress on material, reiterated in his conviction that – fair or beautiful – architecture imitates 'natural forms', but receives its 'dignity' from [the] human mind', as 'the expression of the power of that mind'.[43] *Beautiful* architecture (in the Classical sense of approximating wholeness or completeness) derives its authority from imitating nature, as 'a just and humble veneration for the works of God upon the earth'.[44] In contradistinction, *sublime* architecture expresses human mental power, consisting 'in an understanding of the dominion over those works [of nature/architecture] which has been vested in man'.[45]

The power and majesty Ruskin attributes to sublime architecture is foremost a product of its large size, contrasted to more diminutive surroundings; big enough to 'make a living figure look less than life beside it', which conjures up post-Second World War cubic concrete architecture.[46] Art historian Arnold Hauser (1892–1978) observed something similar: 'The purposefulness and solidity of modern architecture and industrial art are very largely the result of Ruskin's endeavours and doctrines,' deriving mostly from writing on twelfth- to fourteenth-century Italian Romanesque and Gothic architecture.[47] Anticipating later developments, Ruskin believed, if resources or skill are lacking, size is always preferable to failed attempts at ornamentation. Despite the banality of much big architecture, whether commercial, or so-called iconic, Ruskin's assertion remains germane: in the absence of ornament, the significance of material, form, size and assembly (particularly how joints are detailed) increase in importance. As examples, the unrelieved masses of Le Corbusier's La Tourette and the mature work of Kahn echo Ruskin.[48] In laying out the virtues of size, Ruskin anticipates the problem of monumentality arising during the late 1940s but also how it might have been resolved:

Let, therefore, the architect who has not large resources, choose his point of attack first, and if he choose size, let him abandon decoration; for unless they are concentrated, and numerous enough to make their concentration conspicuous, all his ornaments together will not be worth one huge stone.[49]

The preceding could describe much architecture from the 1950s through the 1970s, including the Barbican Estate in the City of London (1960s–80s). But does 'every increase in magnitude' really promise to 'bestow upon [even a mean design] a certain degree of nobleness'?[50] Surely, size alone is not enough. For Ruskin, shape is also important: a building whose form approaches that of a cube will have 'a nobler character than that of mere size' could lend it; evident in buildings by Kahn, Le Corbusier and Zumthor, amongst others.[51]

Ruskin believed a building approximating a 'mighty square', with 'bold and unbroken' surfaces would be perceived as having 'the light of heaven upon it, and the weight of earth in it'.[52] For him, the 'square and cylindrical column' are 'the elements of utmost power in all architectural arrangements', to which the 'cube and the sphere' may be added, recalling ancient Greek temples, platonic solids and modernist architecture.[53]

A building's power also depends on a 'certain respect for material', and mindfulness of how 'time and storm' weather them.[54] Boldness of material expression, revelation of its weight and awe-inspiring size demonstrate architectural authority, but so does shadow: 'after size and weight, the Power of architecture may be said to depend on the quantity (whether measured in space or intenseness) of shadow'.[55] Kahn's Salk Institute, La Jolla, California (1959–65), is an example of architectural power but especially of shadow, rendered as significant *material*. According to Ruskin, darkness of shadow enhances architecture's scope for receiving the fullness and depth of human tragedy: 'the reality of its works, and the use and influence they have in the daily life of men … require of it that it should express a kind of human sympathy, by a measure of darkness as great as there is human life'.[56]

The gloominess of shadow, its pools of blackness, reveals architecture as capable of emotional communication the equal of any expressive art. In this, building can shelter the plight of being human, affecting us in much the way great poems and fiction do, with 'the majesty of their masses of shade', which Ruskin argues has a greater capacity for taking 'hold upon us' than 'lyric sprightliness' does. Serious work, which is often melancholy, reveals architecture as a 'magnificently human art', capable of expressing the 'truth of this wild world of ours': 'the trouble and wrath of life', made out of 'its sorrow and its mystery', which it can 'only give by depth or diffusion of gloom, by the frown upon its front and the shadow of its recess'.[57]

Ruskin asserted: 'truly great' buildings will have 'mighty masses, vigorous and deep, of shadow mingled with its surface'. Light, form, structure and material speak directly to the body and emotion, so even buildings devoid of traditional ornament or carving, like the Salk, can embody qualities Ruskin believed make 'great' architecture.[58]

The 'size and boldness . . . and solidity' of the Salk, with its many 'points or masses of energetic shadow' and penetrations 'which, seen from within, are forms of light, and from without, are forms of shade', harmonizes with Ruskin's descriptions.[59] Deep shadows may protect the Salk's lab interiors from the intense Southern California sunlight but the resulting 'simplicity and force of the dark masses' heightens the powerful effect.[60] More so, the 'masses of light and darkness' at the Salk result from the 'composition of the whole' as a kind of 'proportioning and shaping of the darks' to produce 'grand masses of shadow', augmented by a 'strange play of light and shade'.

Figure 2.1 Salk Institute for Biological Studies (1959–65), La Jolla, CA, USA. Louis I. Kahn, Architect. Mass and Shadow; Exposed Poured-in-Place Concrete. [Photo: Nathaniel Coleman, 1999].

Without the extremes of light and dark produced by the sun's play on the building's 'broad, dark and simple' masses, the emotional effect of the Salk would be greatly diminished.[61] Shadow, more than concrete, gives the Salk its mighty physical presence; anticipated by Ruskin's conviction that in works embodying power;

> the relative majesty of building depends more on the weight and vigour of their masses, than on any other attribute of their design: mass of everything, of bulk, of light, of darkness, of colour, not mere sum of any of these, but breadth of them; not broken light, nor scattered darkness, nor divided weight, but solid stone, broad sunshine, starless shade.[62]

The Salk verifies the pragmatic bent of Ruskin's seemingly romantic impressions: 'It matters not how clumsy, how common, the means are, that get weight and shadow ...; get but gloom and simplicity, and all good things will follow in their place and time.'[63] The sculptural power of Le Corbusier's and Kahn's architecture transposes many of the qualities Ruskin affirms in 'The Lamp of Power', shaped by embracing the limitations of modern spatial practices and modes of production as sources of poetry taken to their expressive limits.

By the time *The Seven Lamps of Architecture* was first published, architectural production was already transforming, reflecting profound sociological and technological changes. Large-scale engineering projects materialized these new conditions first but architects during the nineteenth century already felt the urgency of developing new forms of symbolic expression; responsive to new materials and industrialized modes of production, in tandem with the rise of mass society, which rendered traditional modes of making obsolete.

Beauty

Ruskin's fourth Lamp, 'Beauty', is perhaps the most problematic of the seven, for being philosophically grounded in seemingly defunct Western Classical ideals of beauty as wholeness or completeness; aligned with his attachment to craft production and independent skilled labour. Because beauty is now generally understood as pure visuality bound to surface appearance, conceiving of it as an underlying, invisible, idea made visible by (now absent) ornament is meaningless. Idealized conceptions of the (male) body, balance, symmetry and proportion are outmoded, on account of their association with power. Most significantly, semi-skilled mechanized production and technocratic functionalist myths largely place the built environment outside almost any possible conception of beauty; even if 'there is no other way to control the machine than to accept it and conquer it spiritually.'[64]

Nevertheless, Ruskin argued if power in architecture is a product of human intellect and will, beauty 'bears the image of natural creation'.[65] Beautiful works are 'adaptations of those [beautiful lines or natural objects] which are commonest in the external creation' of nature, whereas 'forms which are not taken from natural objects must be ugly'.[66] While 'forms are not beautiful *because* they are copied from Nature', doing so is prerequisite for its achievement, since beauty is inconceivable without nature.[67] As evidence of God's genius for perfection, nature, according to Ruskin, is the necessary source of beauty but not its guarantee. While he believed nature results from Divine design, human creations are 'at the best, a faded image of God's daily work'.[68] Although recollecting non-human forces, secularized nature represents only itself, whereas beauty now images only its own appearance.

Despite 'universal and instinctive' conceptions beauty being out of the question, Ruskin's conviction that beauty is a product of the naturalness of forms, combined with their frequency, is suggestive. If it is possible to 'reason from Frequency to Beauty, [so] that knowing a thing to be [visibly] frequent [in nature], we may assume it to be beautiful', as Ruskin asserts, then it follows that typicality in nature confers beauty to an object, despite present associations of beauty with novelty.[69] Yet, there is some logic to basing the repetitive manufactured elements out of which buildings are assembled on sources in nature which imitate 'that limited and isolated frequency which is characteristic of all perfection'.[70] However, Ruskin's emphasis on 'limited and isolated frequency' is not interchangeable with 'multitude'.[71] The apparent pervasiveness of materials, forms and elements is qualified by the 'limited and isolated' instances when they approach beauty, in nature, as in architecture.

Ruskin goes on to identify crystalline forms, akin to right angles in nature, as a source of architectural beauty.[72] By associating cubic forms in architecture with their source in nature, Ruskin makes a case for continuing to study nature. That is where Le Corbusier began, following Ruskin. For example, ancient stone inspired his use of concrete as a recollection of traditional masonry architecture, including at La Tourette. Accordingly, profound engagement with material possibilities, rooted in their earthly origins, and reinforced by sensitive interpretation, contributes to building quality, especially when mediated by the realities of production and use.

Life

Ruskin's fifth Lamp, 'Life', refers to the enduring evidence of labour as love gathered into things by the effort (intellectual and manual) exerted in making them. For him, a thing done without love can bring neither pleasure nor substantial satisfaction, so would best be left undone. Although *The Seven Lamps* affirm that only crafted things can be loved, because mass-produced or machine-made things must be bereft, Ruskin was aware that his was a quixotic stand against the tide of modernity. Agonistic perhaps but not morbidly nostalgic.[73] His abhorrence of 'machine ornament and cast-iron work' was a critical response to developing facts, despite the futility of resistance.[74] Raising the alarm, rather than promoting illusions of return, 'The Lamp of Life' identifies carving ornament with love in labour, 'done with enjoyment' by craftsmen made happy by doing it. His apparent sentimentalism is radically future orientated: humanizing machine-made, metal, cast and assembled architecture demands inventing new ways to introduce 'tender touch' and 'warm stroke' to buildings, by returning joy in labour to workers (including architects), that inhabitants experience.[75]

Since the dawn of the twentieth century, the facts of machine production have become confused with the aims of architectural expression, leading to alienating reproductions of mechanistic logic in buildings. As they become more machine-like, evidence of the hand in making – as marks of life – disappears from buildings. Against waves of homogenized modes of production, including the alienation this inscribes within the built environment, the problematic of how to reintroduce *warmth, tenderness, touch* and *human scale* and *human making* to architecture persists, right at the centre of modern industrialized architecture. Williams and Tsien's work negotiates this by traversing a knife-edge between reminiscences of craft and amenability to industrialized production.

Although diminished, architecture retains a figurative capacity for touching emotion, but only if joy in labour is transposed to the logic of assembly. For Ruskin, the mind and hand alone are capable of leaving the imprint of life on architecture. He asserted, 'noble' work is proportionate 'to the fullness of life which' it enjoys (shelters), as evidence of the liveliness of those who made it. The more objects 'bear [the] impress … of the' human mind, and 'the energy of that mind', the nobler the work. Ultimately, architecture is incapable of any 'other life than this'; the 'dignity and pleasurableness' of which is dependent 'upon the vivid expression of the intellectual life which has been concerned with [its] production'.[76]

Lifeless because made from otherwise meaningless inert matter, with the structural aim of remaining motionless, whatever liveliness architecture has, comes from the impress of the builder's, more so labourer's, mind upon the static material out of which it is made, and from bodily experience of it. While this explains the predominantly enervated character of the modernist built environment, recuperating alternative modes of production – thus liveliness – would only be possible if the division of labour that has reduced craftsmen to semi-skilled workers, building to an industry and architects to technicians was overcome. Throughout *The Seven Lamps*, Ruskin's concern is with craftsmen, not architects. Yet, if 'the expression of intellectual life' is most important in relation to 'production', then architects caught in the webs of the building industry must construe ways to introduce liveliness to their work, despite the diminished role they share with labourers.

Ruskin's conviction that 'Frankness and its Audacity' produce liveliness is an enduring rejoinder to the machine-like slickness of bureaucratic modernist architecture. In frankness, 'there is never any effort to conceal the degree of the sources of its borrowing', therefore, the independence of the work must be proven by a 'mind of power capable of transforming and renewing whatever it adopts', as in Scarpa's work.[77] No stylistic revival, adoption of historical forms or ornaments, extreme formal novelty or structural virtuosity is sufficient to breathe life into the banalities of reductive, unornamented, assembled architecture, because in each, flaccid imitation and optimized technique overwhelm audacity. 'Audacity', according to Ruskin, results from frank transformative borrowing, entailing 'the unhesitating and sweeping sacrifice of precedent where precedent becomes inconvenient', again recollecting Scarpa.[78]

More than anything, according to Ruskin, the liveliness of a building correlates with the 'visible subordination of execution to conception', which inverts the conventional dominance of execution over conception. Only a conceiving mind powerful enough to exceed the capacity of production to replicate its aims exactly ensures subordination of execution. To achieve the liveliness of approximate and rough results, wildness of conception *must* outstrip desires for 'perfect finish', which Ruskin believes 'belongs to the perfected art'. But 'perfected art' is completed, or dead, in contradistinction to living art, which is yet to be perfected. In short, 'progressive finish belongs to progressive art.'[79] Vital architecture shows signs of a 'struggle toward something unattained', because unattainable.[80] The production limitations of early modernist buildings made them livelier than later slicker orthodox modernist architecture, despite efforts to subordinate conception to execution. The closer modernist architecture comes to achieving machine-like perfection, the more dead it becomes.

Memory

As the embodiment of culture, place, time and labour, for Ruskin, art and more so architecture, is memory made concrete. Accordingly, his sixth Lamp, 'of Memory', is not only a lens on life but also its framework. Buildings open windows onto the day-to-day life of people, present and past, suggesting also the contours of the future.

Architecture, the built environment more generally, including industrial arts, are indisputably central to individual and community life, which would scarcely be possible without them. The fundamental status of architecture, though, is paradoxical: despite its prosthetic nature as extension and augmentation of bodily capacities, it is now largely determined by forgetting. Its steady transformation into exchangeable commodity, subordinated to land value, weakens architecture's relation to memory, life and the body, mirrored in dissipation of its material presence and truncated duration.

The catastrophe of progress is forgetting. Markers of the past are perpetually in danger; as much from destruction, as from renovation. Wiping the world clean of silted-up records of life and thought is often misconstrued as progressive but only in eradicating memory and physical associations with the world. Because it banishes life and age, freezing heritage in time through preservation is no better. Alienation of new buildings from their spatiotemporal milieu and old ones from their age disavows memory. Material only becomes memory by recording the impress of time and touch through weathering or use.

Ruskin's sensitivity to architecture as a necessary armature of life and memory that orientates individuals and communities, emotionally and physically, makes 'Memory' the most powerfully presented of the *Seven Lamps*:

> We may live without her [architecture], and worship without her, but we cannot remember without her. How cold is all history, how lifeless all imagery, compared to that which the living nation writes, and the uncorrupted marble bears! – how many pages of doubtful record might we often spare, for a few stones left one upon another![81]

The assertion that architecture constitutes memory is more than merely romantic overstatement. At its core, Ruskin's message is as ethical as aesthetical. He advocated for the reform of modern life in its entirety, arguing for humane alternatives to the emphasis of conventional political economic thinking on the already possible, including the production of buildings. He stood on the side of what *ought* to be rather than surrendering to what *is*. His conviction that old, even dead, art and architecture continues to speak articulates a critical stance against the alignment of modernist forgetting with dominant modes of production:

> There are but two strong conquerors of the forgetfulness of men, Poetry and Architecture; and the latter in some sort includes the former, and is mightier in its reality: it is well to have, not only what men have thought and felt, but what their hands have handled, and their strength wrought, and their eyes beheld, all the days of their life.[82]

Obviously, Ruskin's avowal does not extend to all architecture. The body *knows* when emotion has been touched by architecture. Experience is the only sure guide to its profundity, in much the way poetry's impact is *felt*, despite being read. Enduring art is future orientated, it is made in one epoch and gains in significance through time for future ones. Past work thereby constitutes inexhaustible reservoirs for present invention, and future contexts. A work's endurance is as dependent on material and execution, as it is on conception. Importantly, Ruskin's idea of building as memory encompassed the grandest structures as well as the humblest, including 'domestic architecture'.[83] If permitted to, historical buildings persist through time if loved enough by communities to be maintained, which protects their significance for successive generations. For Ruskin, it is better to preserve the architecture 'of past ages ... as the most precious of inheritances' than to conserve it as heritage, in the current sense.[84] By 'preservation', he means lavishing a structure with continuous care, out of affection for it. Accordingly, preserving buildings has little to do with 'renovation', which involves rescuing redundant structures from certain ruin but does violence to them by erasing signs of age and use (memory): a loved building *never* requires restoration.[85]

Building survival begins with care from the outset, comprising the most durable materials, as solidly constructed as possible, subordinate to conceptions that make it as emotionally engaging as imaginable. However, when building is primarily an investment opportunity, a novelty or the land it is constructed upon exceeds its exchange value from the start, quality – of material, construction and conception – becomes an uneconomical conceit. According to Ruskin, present limitations – intellectually, politically or economically – are no justification for bequeathing a meaner world to future generations. What is produced in the present – 'planting forests'; 'raising cities' – is as much for 'our descendants' as for 'future nations', because 'our part' is not 'fitly sustained upon the earth, unless the range of our intended and deliberate usefulness include, not only' our contemporaries 'but [our] successors' as well.[86]

Because a work's worth is measured by memory, in proportion to how well it makes good on its standing debt to an unknowable future, short-term adornment of the *now* betrays the as-yet unborn, who ought to be the intended beneficiaries of the present. As Ruskin put it: we are 'lent ... the earth for our life' but 'it belongs as much to those who are to come after us.' Accordingly, 'we have no right, by anything we do or neglect, to involve them in unnecessary penalties, or deprive them of benefits it was in our power to bequeath.' Thus, we ought to 'place our aim[s]' far off into the future, with little 'desire to be ourselves the witness of what we have laboured for', which promises that 'the measure of our success' will be wider and richer.[87]

Expedience guarantees failure, with impulse and economy the enemies of durability, poetry and care. Intensity of conception, material selection and quality of construction prefigure memory, making enduring architecture a reality preserve against disorientating waves of creative destruction. For Ruskin, the greatest glory of any building is its age, not as a rejection of a deficient present, but because lasting structures bridge past and future in the present. Witnesses to events, repositories of life's dramas in all their depth, memory silts up in buildings through time, recollected in marks left by labour, weathering and use.[88]

The glory of age for a building lies far in the future; contemporary constructions accrue value by transacting in memory, analogously to ancient structures, constructed in a *now* long past but durable enough to survive beyond any immediate present. How would architecture today be different if it were built as if for forever, not 'for present delight, nor for present use alone'. What if the aim was to produce work 'our descendants will thank us for', in the belief that our buildings 'will be held sacred because' we 'touched them'; with 'the labour and wrought substance of them' looked upon affectionately as something past generations bequeathed to future ones.[89]

Impermeable buildings able to resist imprints of life upon them, and replacement cycles shorter than lifetimes, banish the glory of age (time and memory) from buildings. Marketplace limitations on procurement, and the production and consumption of buildings dominated by technique, entraps structures within *now time*. Diminishing opportunities for individuals and groups to leave their impress upon the world through use betrays architecture's vocation for establishing receptacles and levers of cultural memory.

Obedience

Ruskin's final lamp, 'of Obedience', is at first glance more problematic than even 'The Lamp of Beauty'. The prospect of submitting to a higher order is antithetical to rugged individualism and radical subjectivity. Myths of artistic autonomy make restrictions (such as use) disagreeable. Maybe but everything takes place within systems of organization and domination more total (closed) than discontinuous (open), even if cracks of possibility can always be found. For architects, economics and engineering are the most obvious limitations, so are legal frameworks, site restrictions and deadlines, as well as education and professional culture. Obligations to the body and to life, however, place the most significant demands for obedience upon architecture.

German Jewish cultural critic Walter Benjamin (1892–1940) outlines a conception of architecture close to Ruskin, declaring that because 'the human need for shelter is lasting', architecture 'is more ancient than any other art', making 'buildings … man's companions since primeval times'.[90] Fetishized high-profile structures notwithstanding, buildings are artefacts experienced 'by a collectivity in a state of distraction'.[91] Overemphasis on exchange transforms architecture into a product, which obscures its configuring role in venerating the everyday through use. When this occurs, the 'twofold manner' of building appropriation Benjamin observes is halved; splitting 'use' from 'perception', thereby estranging 'touch' from 'sight'. He continues, when use/touch and perception/sight are conjoined, the 'appropriation' of structures 'cannot be understood in terms of the attentive concentration of a tourist before a famous building'.[92] Misconstruing buildings as primarily objects of visual perception neglects their *world-making* role, which Benjamin alludes to:

> On the tactile side there is no counterpart to contemplation on the optical side. Tactile appropriation is accomplished not so much by attention as by habit. As regards architecture, habit determines to a large extent even optical reception. The latter, too, occurs much less through rapt attention than by noticing the object in incidental fashion.[93]

In addition to rendering the gist of Ruskin's 'Lamp of Obedience' comprehensible to modern ears, Benjamin clarifies the centrality of material and use for making meaning in architecture. Appropriation of buildings by use/touch and perception/sight highlights the role of 'habit' in construing architectural meaning, with touch as the first point of physical contact with any building, which has little to do with style or destination architecture.

To satisfy the complex range of purposes Ruskin demands of architecture, strict enough rules are required to limit 'individual caprice' from subverting 'use' and 'touch' as the primary concerns of building.[94] For him, striving to be 'original', or attempting 'to invent a new style', should be resisted at all costs.[95] The problem of 'what style' to adopt is 'immaterial', so long as its development can admit ample 'room for originality', even when adhered to judiciously, or generally. Although calling modernist architecture an 'international style' overstates consistency, beyond the limitations of the building industry, existing spatial practices and modes of production, already taking shape in Ruskin's time, do constitute a universal of sorts that can either be adhered to slavishly or engaged with imaginatively through processes of negation and reaffirmation.[96]

When associated with modernist architecture, Ruskin's 'Lamp of Obedience' becomes less restrictive: a matter of spatial practices and modes of production, more than of 'style'. Despite seeming to restrict free expression by requiring adherence to a national style, Ruskin's rules exceed pedantic adherence by allowing for some licence, accommodated by an interpretative spirit open to the influence of multiple dialects. Architectural invention is less dependent on choosing between styles than on perfecting the one selected.

Recuperating Ruskin

Ruskin's evangelical tone in *The Seven Lamps of Architecture* tends to obscure the fullness of his influence on the founders of the Bauhaus (1919–33), Wright and Le Corbusier, in the quest to articulate principles for an unornamented, yet dignified, machine-made and assembled, modern architecture. English architectural critic Reyner Banham (1922–88) sums up modernist intolerance of Ruskin: 'there is a test that divides the men from the boys in say 1912, it is their attitude to Ruskin. Men whose view of the aims of art and the function of design were as diverse as could be, nevertheless united in their hatred of *ce deplorable Ruskin*.'[97] The last three words quoted from Banham come from Futurism founder Marinetti, who at a 1910 London lecture challenged his English audience to renounce Ruskin:[98]

> When, when will you disembarrass yourselves of the lymphatic ideology of that deplorable Ruskin [*ce deplorable Ruskin*], which I would like to cover with so much ridicule that you would never forget it?

> With his morbid dream of primitive and rustic life, ... with his hatred for the machine, steam power, and electricity, that maniac of antique simplicity is like a man who ... still wants to ... recover his thoughtless infancy.[99]

For Marinetti, only the storm and tumult of modernity, machine noise and creative destruction in the service of overwriting history would do, the influence of which has been overstated as 'the charter for aesthetic modernism as a whole'.[100] Uncritical embrace of progress and machines as decisive-markers of being modern deprives successive accomplishment (including progressive failure) of its depth. Although modernism is often defined as rejecting all that came before, Ruskin's Romanticism is radical: offering clues to reform and productive ways forward that are generative negations of what *is*.

Writing just before the dawn of modernist architecture, Ruskin's lament for fading craft traditions, overwhelmed by industrialization and burgeoning mass production, is foreknowledge of the myriad problems of signification still confronting unornamented, assembled and reductive architecture. Proposing Ruskin's relevance for a discussion of material and meaning in architecture, more than a century after his death, depends on open readings of him. Rendering the *Seven Lamps* relevant for the present requires thinking of his promotion of four specific styles as the levers of his argument. No doubt, the Romanesque and Gothic architecture Ruskin preferred have significant virtues but their greater usefulness was to aid his elaboration of practical advice for inventing significant architecture post-craft.

Notes

1. John Ruskin, *The Seven Lamps of Architecture* (1849), *Second Edition* (1880), New York: Dover, 1989, pp. 131, 132, 137.

2. For a brief introduction to the legacy of the International Style exhibit and book, see, Coleman, *Utopias and Architecture*, pp. 68–71, 95–6.

3. Ruskin, *Seven Lamps*, pp. 35, 44–5.

4. John Ruskin, *The Stones of Venice* (1851–53), J. G. Links (ed.), Volume I (*The Foundations*), Chapter II ('The Virtues of Architecture'), New York: Da Capo Press, 2003 (1960), p. 29.

5. Ibid.

6. Ibid.

7. Leon Battista Alberti, *On the Art of Building in Ten Books*, Joseph Rykwert, Neil Leach and Robert Tavernor (trans.), Cambridge, MA: MIT Press, 1998, Book 6, Chap. 2, p. 156.

8. John Unrau, *Looking at Architecture With John Ruskin*, London: Thames and Hudson, 1978, p. 7.

9. Eco, 'Function and Sign: The Semiotics of Architecture' (1973), pp. 182–202.

10. David Leatherbarrow, 'Architecture Its Own Discipline', *The Discipline of Architecture*, Andrzej Piotrowski and Julia Williams Robinson (eds), Minneapolis: University of Minnesota Press, 2001, pp. 83–102.

11. Ruskin, *Seven Lamps*, p. xi.

12. Ibid.

13. See: Nikolaus Pevsner, *Pioneers of Modern Architecture from William Morris to Walter Gropius* (1949), London: Penguin Books, 1968. For Ruskin's influence on Le Corbusier see, Coleman, *Utopias and Architecture*.

14. Ruskin, *The Stones of Venice*, 'The Virtues of Architecture', p. 29.

15. Pevsner declared: 'A bicycle shed is a building. Lincoln Cathedral is a piece of architecture.' Nikolaus Pevsner, *An Outline of European Architecture* (1943), London: Penguin Books, 1990, p. 16.

16. Ruskin, *Seven Lamps*, p. 10.

17. Ibid.

18. Ibid., p. 11.

19. See: Kenneth Frampton, *Studies in Tectonic Cultures: The Poetics of Construction in Nineteenth and Twentieth Century Architecture*, John Cava (ed.), Cambridge, MA: MIT Press, 1995; Alberto Pérez-Gómez, *Architecture and the Crisis of Modem Science*, Cambridge, MA: MIT Press, 1984; Alberti, *On the Art of Building in Ten Books*; Edward R. Ford, *The Architectural Detail*, New York: Princeton Architectural Press, 2011; Klaus Herdeg, *The Decorated Diagram: Harvard Architecture and the Failure of the Bauhaus Legacy*, Cambridge, MA: MIT Press, 1983.

20. Ruskin, *Seven Lamps*, p. 17.

21. Ibid., p. 18.

22. Ibid., pp. 20–1.

23. Ibid., p. 22.

24. Ibid., p. 34.

25. Ibid., p. 35.

26. Ibid.

27. Ibid., p. 37.

28. Ibid.

29. Ibid., p. 46.

30. Ibid., p. 35.

31. Ibid., p. 63.

32. Ibid., pp. 50, 48.

33. Ibid., pp. 50–1.

34. Ibid., pp. 53–4.

35. Ibid., pp. 55–6.

36. Ibid., p. 55.

37. Ibid., Note 19, bottom of page 55.

38. Ibid., p. 39.

39. On Le Corbusier's modulor system, see: Rudolf Wittkower, 'Le Corbusier's Modulor' (1961), in *In the Footsteps of Le Corbusier*, Carlo Palazzola and Ricardo Vio (eds), New York: Rizzoli, 1991, pp. 11–19. Source of Kahn quote: Louis I. Kahn, *Light is the Theme*, Fort Worth: Kimbell Art Museum, 1975, p. 43. For van Eyck's consideration of the problem of number, see Aldo van Eyck, 'Steps Toward A Configurative Discipline', *Forum 3*, August 1962, reprinted in, Aldo van Eyck, *Collected Articles and Other Writings: 1947–1998*, Vincent Ligtelijn and Francis Struaven (eds), Amsterdam: Sun, 2008, pp. 327–43; For consideration of Le Corbusier (La Tourette), Louis Kahn (Salk Institute), and Aldo van Eyck (Amsterdam Orphanage), within a broader historical and theoretical context (including discussion of Ruskin), see Coleman, *Utopias and Architecture*.

40. Ruskin, *Seven Lamps*, p. 70.

41. Ibid., p. 71.

42. Ruskin's conception of the sublime and beautiful (and reference to it in this chapter) is largely informed by, Edmund Burke (1729–1797), *A Philosophical Enquiry into the Origin of our Ideas of the Sublime and Beautiful* (1779), James T. Boulton (ed.), Notre Dame: University of Notre Dame Press, 1958.

43. Ruskin, *Seven Lamps*, p. 70.

44. Ibid., p. 72.

45. Ibid.

46. Ibid., p. 74.

47. Hauser writes: Ruskin 'was indubitably the first to interpret the decline of art and taste as the sign of a general cultural crisis, and to express the … principle that the conditions under which men live must first be changed, if their sense of beauty and their comprehension of art are to be awakened … His influence was extraordinary, almost beyond description' (Arnold Hauser, *Naturalism, Impressionism, The Film Age: The Social History of Art, Volume 4*, Stanley Goodman (trans.) London and New York: Routledge, 1999 [1958], pp. 66, 67).

48. Coleman, *Utopias and Architecture*.

49. Ruskin, *Seven Lamps*, p. 74.

50. Ibid.

51. Ibid., p. 77.

52. Ibid., pp. 73, 74, 78.

53. Ibid., p. 79.

54. Ibid., pp. 78, 82.

55. Ibid., p. 84.

56. Ibid.

57. Ibid., pp. 84–5.

58. Ibid., p. 101.

59. Ibid., pp. 92, 101.

60. Ibid., p. 92.

61. Ibid., pp. 93, 94, 95, 98, 100.

62. Ibid., pp. 99–100.

63. Ibid., p. 100.

64. Hauser, *Social History of Art, Volume 4* (1958), p. 116.

65. Ruskin, *Seven Lamps*, p. 103.

66. Ibid., pp. 104, 105.

67. Ibid., p. 105.

68. Ibid., p. 147.

69. Ibid., pp. 103, 106.

70. Ibid., p. 107.

71. Ibid.

72. Ibid., p. 109.

73. For this topic, see Löwy and Sayre, *Romanticism against the Tide of Modernity*, esp. pp. 127–46.

74. Ruskin, *Seven Lamps*, p. 174.

75. Ibid., p. 173.

76. Ibid., pp. 148–9.

77. Ibid., pp. 152–3.

78. Ibid., p. 153.

79. Ibid., p. 154.

80. Ibid., p. 155.

81. Ibid., p. 178.

82. Ibid.

83. Ibid., p. 181.

84. Ibid., p. 178.

85. Ibid., pp. 194–8.

86. Ibid., p. 185.

87. Ibid., pp. 185–6.

88. Ibid., pp. 186–7. See also, Moshen Mostafavi and David Leatherbarrow, *On Weathering: The Life of Buildings Through Time*, Cambridge, MA: MIT Press, 1993.

89. Ibid., p. 186.

90. Walter Benjamin, 'The Work of Art in the Age of Mechanical Reproduction' (1936), *Illuminations*, Hanna Arendt (ed.), New York: Schocken, 1969, pp. 239, 240.

91. Ibid., p. 239.

92. Ibid., p. 240.

93. Ibid.

94. Ruskin, *Seven Lamps*, p. 202.

95. Ibid, pp. 202, 203.

96. Ibid., p. 202.

97. Reyner Banham, *Theory and Design in the First Machine Age, Second Edition*, New York: Praeger Publishers, 1967, p. 12.

98. Filippo Tommaso Marinetti, 'The Futurist Speech to the English' ('*Un Discours Futuriste aux Anglais*'), Lyceum Club, London (December 1910), in *Futurism: An Anthology*, L. Rainey, C. Poggi and L. Wittman (eds), New Haven and London: Yale University Press, 2009, pp. 70–4.

99. Ibid., pp. 70–4. The editors of the *Anthology* indicate that the quoted portion of the address 'is present only from the 1915 edition onward' (p. 74).

100. Lionel Trilling, *Sincerity and Authenticity*, Cambridge, MA: Harvard University Press, 1973, p. 128.

CHAPTER 3
LOOS (1870–1933): NOT THE MATERIAL BUT WHAT IS DONE WITH IT

Viennese architect Adolf Loos's (1870–1933) complex relationship with modernity and industrial modes of production undergirds much of the argument developed throughout this book. Although known for seeking to eliminate ornament from design, he was simultaneously attached to traditional and ancient architecture and suspicious of industrialization. Loos's meditations on architecture as art, and on ornament, are as subtle as they are satirical. For example, although he believed contemporary design and architecture should be free of newly invented ornament (art nouveau), his own interiors were lavished with rich materials and echoes of classical ornamentation. The paradoxes mount up when one considers Loos's conviction that architects are dissociated from the living traditions of vital cultures, of the sort he believed farmers, vernacular builders and engineers inhabited. For him, engineers were especially intimate with the cultural currents of their time. Like farmers, the source of their ingenuity was proximity to culture's fertile ground. Accordingly, they understood modern materials, assemblies and forms in a way no architect (inevitably) estranged from the wellspring of civilization could.

Because the new materials and methods of industrial production demanded unadornment, Loos prohibited embellishing manufactured goods and architecture. Reproducing historic ornament with new materials was also outlawed. Above all else, inventing new ornament is maladaptive. Although Loos recalls Ruskin, their imaginaries of the future differ. Whereas Ruskin recollected medieval craft traditions as models of reform, Loos looked to antiquity, ancient Rome in particular, as prefiguring modern society. His conviction was that architecture must be more modern, not less so, but in the spirit of ancient Rome, with its bold civic forms and volumes. More a child of Vitruvius than Ruskin, Loos sought to redefine architecture for modernity. An appropriate attitude to ornament would thus be determined by conditions of modern life and consciousness, alongside modern means of production. Nineteenth-century eclecticism was rejected, as was reform based on decorating modern industrial production with newly invented ahistorical ornament. According to Loos, 'Modern ornament' – without ancient Greek or Roman origins – 'has no parents and no offspring, no past and no future'.[1] But as his own work confirms, continuing use of traditional, ancient and exotic ornament is permissible.

Mixing progressive thought and conservative ideals, Loos envisioned recuperating architectural *essences* as a corrective to nineteenth-century cultural decline identified with eclecticism. The near Old Testament tone of many of his pronouncements derives from this but his ironic aims should not be underestimated. For example: 'Behold, the time is at hand, fulfillment awaits us. Soon the streets of the cities will shine like white walls! Like Zion, the Holy City, Heaven's capital. Then fulfillment will be ours.'[2] Fulfilment begins with accepting the impossibility of inventing new ornament. Although previous historical styles of architecture are characterized by distinct programmes of ornament, nineteenth-century architecture collapsed under their accumulated weight. Excavating a modern architecture from this eclectic debris requires the progressive removal of ornament, to achieve smoothness reflecting modern materials and production methods. But pragmatism must be joined by poetic imagery: 'the greatness of our age resides in our inability to create new ornament.'[3] Because the individuality of modern persons is so evolved (culturally, psychologically) he or she no longer needs to cover human-made things – especially mass-produced everyday objects – with decoration. Inventing new ornament anyway is doomed: out of step with modern consciousness and modes of industrialized production, which makes it wasteful of time, energy, resources and labour.

Workmen-craftsmen

Loos identified the crucial difference between him and Ruskin as their respective positions on the matter of production. Whereas Ruskin extolled an independence of spirit verging on wildness in the infinitely inventive artistic expressions of 'craftsmen', Loos admired 'workmen' who were skilled at exploiting the limitations of specific modes of production, while maintaining material consistency in high-quality workmanship, including when directed by architects. For Ruskin, the craftsmen's wilful invention of ornament – as an expression of joy in labour – made Gothic architecture great. For Loos, what matters most 'are the materials and perfect workmanship', which at first was difficult for him to embrace: 'Because people felt it was shameful to say that was what was right. It is Ruskin, by the way, who is to blame for all this. I am his sworn enemy.'[4] According to British architectural historian Kenneth Frampton:

> Loos' ultimate argument against ornament was not only that it was a waste of labor and material, but that it invariably entailed a punitive form of craft slavery that could only be justified for those to whom the highest achievements of bourgeois culture were inaccessible – for those craftsmen who could only find their aesthetic fulfillment in the spontaneous creation of ornament.[5]

Ruskin believed almost exactly the opposite. If there was waste, it was of intellect, or inventiveness, when craftsmen are deprived of the expressive opportunities provided by inventing ornament. By Loos's time, such individuality in production was either impossibly expensive (in all senses), or relegated to the mists of time by industrial manufacture:

> the harm done by ornament to the ranks of the producers is even greater. Since ornament is no longer a natural product of our culture, but a symptom of backwardness or degeneracy, the craftsman producing ornament is not fairly rewarded for his labor … Ornament means wasted labor and therefore wasted health.[6]

Nevertheless, British architectural historian Sir John Summerson (1904–92) believed that the topic of 'waste' brought Loos closer to Ruskin than he admitted: 'what Loos intended in his assault on ornament was not the elimination of ornament as such but the elimination of *waste* – the waste of human labor and human skill (in this he showed himself a disciple of Ruskin).'[7] 'Waste' by itself is not enough to resolve their differences, especially since Loos's position is defined by negation, including of Ruskin (despite points of contact).

Sublimating ornament

As a self-professed modern, Loos's paradoxical relation to tradition was radical. His architectural theory is a story of cultural evolution charted in everyday objects, ornament and conduct (including manners and dress). Successive liberation of useful objects from ornament manifests an evolutionary classical orientation: encrustation is a sign of decline. The intellectual and cultural development he projected reflects the realities of industrial production, inflected by an unadorned Classical (Greco-Roman) sensibility. Accordingly, Loos declared: 'The evolution of culture is synonymous with the removal of ornament from objects of daily use.'[8]

Loos's attitude towards ornament is analogous to Freudian psychoanalytic conceptions of 'repression' and 'sublimation'. Repression connotes unsophisticated – primitive even – rigid, often violent, reactions to uncomfortable content, whereas sublimation re-channels energy, even if previously discharged self-destructively, towards more productive cultural ends.[9] For Sigmund Freud (1856–1939), who fathered Psychoanalysis in Vienna, civilization demands renunciation of instinct, anticipating rerouting the excess energy released towards positive activities.[10] Inevitably, civilization requires some repression to thrive but sublimation is a signal achievement of evolutionary development. Loos's best-known essay, 'Ornament and Crime', most explicitly corresponds with Freud's schema of human development and progress, charting human evolution from *primitive* to *civilized*.[11] However, temporal coexistence prevails, infusing the present with the past, making ancient and exotic ornament valued cultural inheritances. Intersections between Loos and Freud were inevitable. Indeed, Freud's architect son, Ernst (1892–1970), was a student in Loos's private school of building.[12]

Although creating new ornament is maladaptive, buildings (and objects) dedicated to extraordinary uses could still be ornamented, following Loos's distinction between 'art' (memorial function) and 'building' (mundane utility); the first acceptably ornamented, the second necessarily unadorned: 'Only a tiny part of architecture comes under art: monuments. Everything else, that serves some practical purpose, should be ejected from the realm of art.'[13] If the fullness of the definitional terms of 'monument' is considered, primarily domestic architecture is excluded, which runs against the decorative and applied arts vogue of his time to ornament *everything*. However, by describing as 'art' only architecture that does not 'serve some practical purpose', Loos's definition is arguably too restrictive, especially measured against his own work. Nevertheless, he offers a powerful description of architecture that is difficult to fault: 'If we were to come across a mound in the woods, six foot long by three foot wide, with the soil piled up in a pyramid, a somber mood would come over us and a voice inside us would say, "There is someone buried here." That is architecture.'[14] The distinction is less between *use* and *uselessness*, than it is a matter of emotion and community.

In 'Ornament and Crime', Loos identifies certain forms of conduct with criminality, or as degenerate precursors of criminality, which challenged supposedly civilized moderns to channel expressions of excess erotic energy and instinctual drives – manifested as aggression and violence, and their symbolizations as ornamentation (including of the self) – towards less wasteful endeavours. Sublimation achieves this by redirecting excess energy away from antisocial activities and waste (of labour, material and intellect), towards more abstract and cerebral endeavours, thereby advancing civilization while ensuring species survival. As suggested by Loos, prudence, which presupposes sublimation, promises achievement of authentically modern cultural ends, encompassing human evolution and industrialized modes of production, informed by ancient Roman virtues.[15]

Loos's notion of virtue as combining propriety with prudence explains his conception of domestic architecture as a retreat walled off from public exposure. While important civic buildings (public and private institutions, and even commercial enterprises) could still benefit from ornamentation, residential exteriors (whether individual houses or apartment blocks) should be completely unadorned, safeguarding private life within. Invisibility from the outside mediates the public realm of the street with the private realm of domestic interiors. The external sparseness of Loos's villas is less modernist impulse than a classical or traditional one, antithetical to modernist fantasies of social existence without masks, or with over-embellished ones. Separating private individuals inside from the public life outside is not pathological but a social necessity that makes civic life possible. While many modernists saw exposure as confirming self-expressive liberation from the stifling confines of bourgeoisie life, manifest in its dark encrusted nineteenth-century interiors, Loos's rooms embody the complex ideal of *gemütliche*. Although a modernist, he was not one in an orthodox Bauhaus/International Style vein. His complex relationship to ornament and tradition prophesizes modernism, while voicing early doubts. Despite Loos's guidance, modernist architects are persistently more adept at repressing ornament than sublimating it, attested to by its periodic return as ever more enfeebled or outlandish solutions to problems of signification. Hence, post-1960s attempts to enlist him as a proto-theorist of stylistic postmodernism neglect the subtlety of his conceptions.[16]

Ornament and illusion

Loos's 1898 essay 'Potemkin City' lampoons the monumental effects of Vienna *Ringstrasse* (the Ring) architecture as projecting fraudulent claims to be more than it is by using 'imitation stones and other sham materials', in its construction and by appending ornaments. Both aim to fool citizens into believing 'they have been transported to a city inhabited by no one but the nobility.'[17] In the main, Renaissance Italian palazzi provided the borrowed style for duping residents of individual flats into imagining they were masters of an entire palace, rather than just one box amongst many. Spatial, decorative and material deception are bad enough, worse still, according to Loos, is the illusion of status produced by theatrical facades deployed to convince inhabitants that they are more privileged than they actually are.

Loos argues, 'Poverty is no disgrace,' so using anachronistic ornaments to obscure one's socio-economic position is dysfunctional. A central condition of modernity is mass society and the rise of a neither abjectly poor nor extravagantly wealthy middle class. As Loos observes, 'Not everyone can be born in a baronial hall. But to try and make others think so is ridiculous and immoral. We should stop feeling ashamed of living in the same building as many other people of the same social status.'[18] The material mirror of acceptance is adapting to new straitened conditions of production: 'We should stop feeling ashamed of the fact that there are building materials we cannot afford.'[19] With the social and architectural grandeur of earlier times out of reach, and inventing new ornament inconceivable, accepting given conditions is the necessary framework of vital cultural expression, an assertion more radical than resigned.

At the city scale, the deluding confections of the 'New Vienna' produced a tantalizing urban false self. Loos observes, 'Every city gets the architects it deserves … The one who can best meet the wishes of the inhabitants will be the one who designs the most buildings,' which is indicative of market savvy alone, rather than of any higher ability.[20] As Loos tells it, the excrescences of latter nineteenth-century Viennese urban and architectural developments were driven by consumer demand met by compliant architects. If economic considerations prevailed, 'the property speculator would far prefer to have the façade covered in smooth plaster from top to bottom'.[21] Although reductive smoothness now dominates, Loos believed it followed 'an instinct that is right, true, artistic'.[22] In joining economics to art, rather than opposing them, Loos's paradoxical equation reflects his conviction that architects of his time – spanning from nineteenth-century eclecticism to early twentieth-century art nouveau, or *Jugendstil* – were culturally lacking; because estranged from tradition as the source of *authentically* modern expression, including reduction as the *true* shared characteristic of both.

Loos was appalled that scenographic facades mimicking Renaissance and Baroque palaces, encrusted with ornaments 'not even constructed of the materials they appear to be', were pinned to otherwise modern underlying structure. He observed, 'Some pretend to be built of stone, like Roman and Tuscan palaces, some of plaster, like Viennese Baroque buildings. They are of neither. Their ornamental features … are cast in cement and pinned on'.[23] While his criticism presages *truth to materials* orthodoxies of twentieth-century modernism, this was not Loos's primary concern. He was more relaxed about technique, or structural expression, than with propriety of effect (including for construction). For him, particular materials are associated with mood, atmosphere or the status of a particular use, rather than with some essential material *truth*. Accordingly, he asserts that the 'technique [of casting elements in cement]', developed during the nineteenth century, 'has its own validity'. 'But it is not right to use it for forms, the development of which is closely connected with the qualities of a particular material, simply because there are no technical difficulties to stop one using it.' The issue is association and habit rather than truth; thus, 'the artist's task should be to find a new language for the new material', because 'anything else is imitation'.[24]

Despite his association with modernist prohibition of ornament, Loos was preoccupied with tradition; as a looking forward to more *authentically* modern architecture *and* backward to ancient roots, as the inexhaustible reservoir of signification. For him, the 'modern age' will only ever 'have its very own architectural style' when it is one that could be handed 'down to posterity with a clear conscience, a style people will still look on with pride, even in the distant future'.[25] Successive spent styles, from the end of the Baroque to the present day, demonstrates the fragility of tradition, and the difficulty of meeting Loos's challenge.

Unlike most modernist architects' uncritical identification with mechanization, Loos had suspicions about the machine; industrial means of architectural production; architectural photography; and seductively slick architectural drawings. In his view, inherited forms should be copied exactly, whereas new objects and uses require distinctly new forms. Imitating inherited forms in new materials, or dressing new forms in an old way are deceptions. Equally, contemporary materials and modes of invention make reuse and reinvention of Classical orders and ornaments problematic, more so as cultural development shifts intellectual energies to other forms of invention. Since inheritances from classical antiquity still function (persisting as the *lingua franca* of Western civilization), attempting to invent alternatives is largely irrelevant and wasteful; of manual and intellectual resources. Inevitably, modern ornament is alienated from the form and structure of culture: mostly made with materials inconsistent with its ancient expressive origins, it is confectionery and is simply tacked on to buildings.

Ornament classical

The many references to the elements and ornaments of the ancients in Loos's architecture manifest his conviction that 'A level of culture such as humanity reached during the time of classical antiquity simply cannot be erased from our memory. Classical antiquity was and is the mother of all subsequent cultural epochs.'[26] According to him, 'the superiority of classical antiquity' rests permanently within our 'hearts and minds', making it an inescapable content of Western consciousness, and a perpetual source of cultural imaginaries, whether acknowledged or disavowed.[27] As a modern, Loos asserted: 'Lack of ornamentation is a sign of intellectual strength' but as an ancient, he allowed: 'Modern man uses the ornaments of earlier or foreign cultures as he likes and sees fit.' Foreign ornament is permissible because it can 'influence a stylistic renewal'.[28] Moderns, however, concentrate their 'inventive power on other things', which makes inventing new ornament impossible.[29]

Loos's architecture verifies his theory, for example, the Doric temple front of his Villa Karma (1904–06), Montreux, Switzerland, leads into an opulent entry hall, with marble revetment, accented by gold mosaic tiles, amongst many other allusions to earlier models, from antiquity through the Renaissance. While the building takes a largely classic villa form, with elements conjuring up fragments of the Acropolis, and ancient Roman farmhouses, Loos never slavishly reproduces past architecture. The coffered ceiling of his American Bar (also known as the Loosbar, and Kärntner bar) (1908), Vienna, recollects the ceiling of the Pantheon but at a much-reduced scale and in marble, with a social function in tune with its time (Plate 1). The monolithic columns of his Michaelerplatz building (also known as the Looshaus) (1909–11), Vienna – originally occupied by the Goldman & Salastch men's clothing shop on the lower levels, with apartments above – more directly recollects the character and scale of the Pantheon (amongst other classical references), reasserting the sacrality of dressing for Loos; the smoothness and directly expressed materials of the Michaelerplatz building, including its monolithic columns, are, on the other hand, negations of *Ringstrasse* architecture.

Loos's submission to the Chicago Tribune competition (1922) is especially perplexing: seemingly deadly serious and satirical at the same time. Taking the form of a gargantuan Doric column, he explained his entry in 1923 as follows: '*This huge Greek Doric Column will be built. If not in Chicago, then in another city. If not for the Chicago Tribune, then for someone else. If not by me, then by another architect.*'[30] Though the internal and external elements of his buildings often had Classical origins, unlike later twentieth-century stylistic postmodern architecture, Loos was deeply serious about their use, which preserves the generative tension between authenticity and irony in his writing and architecture.

In Loos's mind, architecture could only be *timeless* if it recollected great works from antiquity to the Renaissance. As a modern, this presented a conundrum: how could a present-day building constructed using up-to-date materials and methods of production – free of redundant traditional craft, irrelevant new ornament and falsity – establish direct links to classical antiquity in line with the consciousness of the times? Not

Figure 3.1 Michaelerplatz 3 (Looshaus) (1909–11), Vienna, Austria. Adolf Loos, Architect. 'Let us be clear about it: a pillar is not an ornament but a load-bearing architectural element. Whether the building would still stand if the pillars were absent is my affair' (Adolf Loos, 'My Building on the Michaelerplatz' 1911, *On Architecture*, 2002, pp. 97–98. Materials: steel-concrete construction, marble revetment and pillars, smooth plaster render. Constructed for Loos's tailors, Goldman & Salatsch. Foreground, arrangement of Roman ruins; Hans Hollein, Architect (1991). [Photo: Nathaniel Coleman, 2017].

only does this predicament still obtain, it animates the material imaginaries of enduring works, which develop out of critical historical perspectives, while accommodating bodily memories.

Meaning and material

In Loos's work, surface is signification but not sign, which re-establishes links to premodern, especially Classical, architecture. If inventing new ornament is futile, and reduction – of means, as much as of expression (though not conception) – is progressive, acting faithfully to the ancient world in the present requires methods for achieving works durable enough to outlive rootless modern ornament, sham materials and wasteful methods. Richness of material, in all senses of 'rich', and a classical approach to finish, could accomplish this and is something architects can still explore. Classically influenced materials and finishes invest cladding with long-lasting signification, resisting accelerated fashion and production cycles alike, and with them, transformation into transient signs. By working with material as multi-determined complex physical presences, Loos's architecture communicates directly to the body, while engaging cultural muscle memories through touch and reverie.

Even though a distinct characteristic of Loos's use of materials was to subject them to very little manipulation – mostly deployed as cladding – he did not believe any to be innately meaningful. Direct application of material, with little additional treatment beyond finishing, does not presence significance. Rather, Loos selected materials for their culturally produced associations with classical antiquity; their ready availability in a specific place; or with reference to material meaning silted up over long durations of use, associable with a certain mood, effect or building's status. Akin to Vitruvius, he believed in the cultural, as well economical, value of using indigenous materials, and adhering to local building traditions wherever possible. According to Loos, 'the true artist, the great architect' begins 'with the effect he wants to produce', and only then determines its frame, or support'.[31] For him, cladding is guided by a precise rule: 'there should be no possibility of confusing the cladding with the material it covers.'[32] Even so, this method allowed for playing with the hierarchies of qualities he indexed, by using materials in unexpected ways, as at the Loos American Bar. Above all else, he attributed more significance to material surface than to underlying structure, or frames, supporting it.

Pronouncing building purpose and status by correlating building use, architectural form and material, contributes to intelligibility, beginning with the architect imagining the effect he or she 'wants to arouse in the observer – for example fear and terror in a dungeon, divine awe in a church, respect for the power of the state in a government building, reverence in a funeral monument, homeliness in a house, cheerfulness in a tavern – comes from materials used and form'.[33] For Loos, 'effect' is foremost determined by materials and form, rather than structure or details, with tombs and monuments the structures most meriting the designation 'art'. All other structures may be so by degree, or not at all. He argues that because 'Architecture arouses moods in people,' the architect's task 'is to give these moods concrete expression. A room must look cozy, a house comfortable to live in. To secret vice the law courts must seem to make a threatening gesture. A bank must say, "Here your money is in the hands of honest people."'[34]

Enduring associations of materials are far more important in determining their selection for Loos than cost, which differs from Ruskin's belief that the most expensive material possible should be chosen, because costliness is analogous to desirable sacrifice, imbuing work with higher spiritual value and overall significance. Loos, however, largely rejected notions of sui generis material value or significance. For him, what is done with material inscribes it with meaning; the material itself is negligible. However, 'If, for the artist, all materials are equally valuable, that does not mean they are equally suitable for all purposes.'[35] Use and meaning derive from cultural associations built up over time, and inform material selection.

Loos's conception of materials was close to German architect and theorist, Gottfried Semper's (1803–79) ideas on cladding (as a skin), outlined in his *The Four Elements of Architecture* (1851).[36] Semper conceptualized wall hangings and rugs as the principle space-defining elements in structures. For Loos, revetment took on this role. He also shared with Semper the conviction that cultural value accrues to artefacts through the process of making; as the hand transforms the material out of which objects are produced. Ultimately, materials are 'intrinsically worthless'. Accordingly, the value of a work 'is independent of the value of the raw material' used to make it. Object value is determined 'not only' by 'the quantity but also the quality of labor involved' in producing it. In short, Loos asserted that when 'people say material, they mean labor'.[37]

Architects and farmers

Loos's observation that architects are culturally alienated, whereas farmers are rooted, contributes to reflections on material meaning. If working the land implants farmers within culture, architects' preoccupation with aesthetics and exchange, instead of use, isolates them. Cultivating the soil, or the self, culture emerges at the intersection between desire and subsistence and between destruction and construction. Neglecting either, according to Loos, skews the axis of invention and production:

> May I take you to the shores of a mountain lake? The sky is blue, the water is green and everywhere is profound tranquillity. The clouds and mountains are mirrored in the lake, the houses, farms and chapels as well. They do not look as if they were fashioned by man, it is as if they come straight from God's workshop, like the mountains and trees, the clouds and the blue sky. And everything exudes an air of beauty and peace.[38]

In the preceding, Loos describes an immemorial cultural context, juxtaposed to self-conscious 'artistic', or aesthetic, production. The bucolic scene he sketches contrasts with his denunciation of architects' unspontaneous creations – villas – for introducing discord, akin to an 'unnecessary screech', amidst 'local's houses' built 'by God'. Less important than relative ability, architects' spoliation of prior 'tranquillity, peace and beauty', leaves Loos wondering: 'why is it that any architect, good or bad desecrates the lake?'[39] In self-consciously attempting to *actually* realize the *new* – dislocated from cultural wellsprings – architects inevitably ruin the environment, rather than sustaining it.

In contradistinction, because guided by 'instinct', farmers' houses do not violate the environment, nor do engineers when they build railways:

> The farmer marks out the site for his new house in a green meadow and digs out the trenches for the foundations … Is the house beautiful? Yes, just as beautiful as a rose or a thistle, as a horse or a cow … Like almost all city dwellers, the architect lacks culture. He lacks the sure touch of the farmer, who does possess culture … What I call culture is that balance between our physical, mental, and spiritual being which alone can guarantee sensible thought and action.[40]

Despite Loos's idealized claims, the rhetorical value remains: rootless architects are split off from instinct (habit/tradition) and obsessed with their imagined status as artists, which translates into an absence of culture. Their own disconnectedness dooms architects to reproducing alienation with their buildings. Nevertheless, Loos argues that constructing work with readily available and widely used local materials could assist architect's to produce disalienated buildings, as he proposed to do for a 'porter's lodge' he 'was entrusted' to erect 'on the beautiful banks of Lake Geneva':

> There were many stones lying around on the lakeside and the people who lived beside the lake had all built houses of them, I decided to do the same. In the first place it would be cheap, which would be reflected in my fee – I would be paid less – and in the second place transport would be easier.[41]

In the preceding quote, Loos outlines multiple levels of propriety: material availability and its situational appropriateness; thrift also, in terms of architect's fees as well as in reduced material and transport costs, including minimizing wasted labour. In articulating this ethos, Loos reveals a way forward, beyond 'the coldness' German philosopher Theodor W. Adorno identifies as 'the basic principle of bourgeois subjectivity', bound up negatively with 'individual profit' and 'indifference'.[42] Alternatively, Loos's approach is obligated to 'tradition', conceived of as social habits and bodily events associated with use, rather than idealizations of old ways, or their representation. Adorno suggests how Loos's relevance might be maintained for thinking architecture in ways so far barely entered upon post-Second World War; by enacting its contradictions rather than attempting to resolve them:

> Architecture contradicts the needs of the here and now as soon as it proceeds to serve those needs — without simultaneously representing any absolute or lasting ideology … Because architecture is in fact both autonomous [a form of art] and purpose-oriented [functional], it cannot simply negate men as they are. And yet it must do precisely that if it is to remain autonomous.[43]

Architecture's double bind, produced by the necessity of affirmation and negation simultaneously, is the source of its invention and possible resistance to total capture by capitalist modes of production and consumption (or any other totalizing conception). Only honouring its obligation to 'use', by fulfilling needs, prevents architecture from becoming oppressively abstract:

> Living men, even the most backward and conventionally naive, have the right to the fulfillment of their needs, even though those needs may be false ones. Once thought supersedes without consideration the subjective desires for the sake of truly objective needs, it is transformed into brutal oppression ... Even in the false needs of a human being there lives a bit of freedom. It is expressed in what economic theory once called the 'use value' as opposed to the 'exchange value'.[44]

Paradoxically, Adorno's problematization of Loos's apparent binary opposition between architecture and art – between function (use) and uselessness – outlines possibilities even more faithful to Loos than he was at times to himself: 'Aesthetic thought today must surpass art by thinking art. It would thereby surpass the current opposition of purposeful and purpose-free, under which the producer must suffer as much as the observer'.[45]

The double condition Adorno outlines, operative in the tension between 'purpose' and 'purpose free', is remarkably promising, albeit perplexing. Of the three principal sorts of architecture today – *continuity as kitsch*; the *New as achieved*; or *invisibility* – all shy away from Adorno's contradiction by attempting to be either autonomous or not; obedient to dominant spatial practices and systems of production or not; or functional or not. Though Loos's theory could give the impression of binaries, in practice, his work is delectably contradictory.

Authentic culture?

Loos's conviction that moderns are incapable of inventing new ornament but could use inherited ornamentation sets him apart from, for example, orthodox adherents of the so-called *International Style* who sought to sever present from past, primarily by suppressing *all* ornament in architecture. His complex relationship to time and history, encompassing the coexistence of past and future, thereby making modernity part of an eternally renewable living tradition, is unique for modernist architecture by suggesting how future oriented meaningful work could be imagined in the present:

> I am for the traditional manner of construction ... Each new day creates man and the new man is incapable of making the same thing as the old man created. He believes he is making the same thing and it turns into something new. Something imperceptibly new, but after a hundred years the difference can be perceived ... My pupils know that a change from the traditional way of doing things is only permissible if the change means an improvement ...

The best form is always there already and no one should be afraid of using it, even if the basic idea for it comes from someone else. Enough of our geniuses and their originality. Let us keep on repeating ourselves! Let one building be like another.[46]

According to Loos's thinking, past achievement inevitably grounds present effort, which in turn provides the foundations of the future. His bidirectional orientation reveals the past, ancient Rome in particular, as a corrective of present cultural deficiencies. Similarly, the future is assimilable – across the present – by way of critical historical encounters with it. Future promise – the evolutionary flow of civilization – is only fulfillable as springing from tradition (radiating from the golden model of classical antiquity). Futures choked off from the wellspring of the past are inevitably ill-conceived, prefiguring a new barbarism. Possible change, however, only comes about by unselfconsciously working in the present, so long as it improves use. On its own, formal originality is meaningless.

Creation imbedded within inherited tradition makes the old new simply by working in one's own place in time. Reversing the naïve modernist belief that invented *forms determine use*, Loos reveals how asserting *use determines form* could be a powerful corrective of contemporary shortcomings. For him, because conventional forms are perpetually renewed by situated workmen (artists and architects), who honour them in their work, any form continuing to function for its original purpose requires no change. Echoing Adorno, *desire for the new*, rather than the new itself, renews work. The *new* is always already there – waiting to be revealed – rather than requiring *ex novo* invention. Loos's doubts about the cultural production of his time constituted a quest for what is missing. For him, only architecture's ancient origins harbour the secrets of its renewal, to make it powerful enough to counteract the unfolding rootlessness of contemporary culture.

Because closer to direct experience, unselfconscious making could rejuvenate architecture. Simultaneously, Loos envisioned a civilized city people free of inauthentic desires to invent ornament; even as classical or exotic ornament binds present architecture with the past, while enhancing legibility. Modern urbans, he believed, are evolved enough to work like ancients, free of urges to ornament. Rome in particular embodied for him 'the all-transcending greatness of classical antiquity', making it the foundation of 'our culture', while providing the outlines of a renewed architecture, free of nineteenth-century eclecticism and anachronistic late nineteenth- and early twentieth-century ornamentation:

Our manner of thinking and feeling we have adopted from the Romans who taught us to think socially and discipline our emotions. The masters of architecture believed they built like the Roman architects. They were mistaken. Period, place, climate frustrated their plans. But whenever lesser architects tried to ignore tradition, whenever ornament became rampant, a master would appear to remind us of the Roman origins of our architecture and pick up the thread again.[47]

Ancient Rome represented freshness for Loos, evident in its relatively austere architecture enhanced by ornaments inherited from ancient Greece, rather than wasting effort on inventing new ornament. He equated expressive restraint – of the self, of objects for daily use and architecture – with advancing culture because of its association with the classical. His epoch, he imagined, 'had more of a classical cast of mind' than any other 'since the fall of the Roman Empire'.[48] Accordingly, Loos believed this made it possible to pursue superlatives: 'we should not be trying to create a new chair for our age [or any other object of daily use], but the best chair.'[49] Optimistically, he asserted that 'the Romans were incapable of inventing a new order of columns, a new ornament … [Instead,] the Romans invented social organization and governed the whole world … The Romans were more advanced than the Greeks, we are more advanced than the Romans.' Moderns' inability to invent new ornament confirms a more general move away from excessive embellishment.[50]

Into the void

An outsider by birth as much as by temperament; despite being a citizen of the multi-ethnic Austro-Hungarian Empire – born in Brno (currently in the Czech Republic), just 100 kilometres from Vienna – Loos would have been seen as an immigrant. As one author observes: 'though culturally "German" (by language) and Catholic, he was a Moravian-born cosmopolite with many Jewish friends at a time when Czechs and Jews were the largest categories of "others" in Vienna.'[51] Vienna remained anxiously multicultural even after the Austro-Hungarian Empire collapsed in 1918, following its defeat in the First World War, until the *Anschluss* – Nazi annexation of Austria – in 1938 (less than five years after Loos's death).

Loos's choice of title for his short-lived journal, 'Das Andere', 'The Other' (2 issues, 1903), subtitled, 'A Journal for the Introduction of Western Culture into Austria', and *Ins Leere gesprochen, 1897–1900* (1920), translated as *Spoken Into the Void: Collected Essays 1897–1900* (1982), pronounced his outsider status. His alienation from official *Fin de Siècle* Viennese culture set him apart, while establishing his association with other vanguard modernist artists. As he saw it, his project consisted of nothing less than attempting to introduce authentic modernity to a Vienna of masks, repression and self-deception, manifested in the excesses, and excrescences, of later-nineteenth-century and early-twentieth-century Viennese architecture, fine and applied arts.

Although modernism identifies decisive breaks from the past with supposedly achieving the *New*, the subtleties of Loos's thought align with Adorno's insight, that 'The new is the longing for the new, not the new itself: That is what everything new suffers from. What takes itself to be utopia remains the negation of what exists and is obedient to it.'[52] In this, Adorno gets to the heart of Loos's unique negotiation with modernity/modernism. By asserting that architecture is conservative, Loos avoids the false duality that opposes *past* to *future*. Rather, he conceptualizes them as coequal, without obliterating contradictions between them. Adorno further clarifies this point by reflecting on modern art's profoundest contradiction: 'At the center of contemporary antinomies is that art must be and wants to be utopia, and the more utopia is blocked by the real functional order, the more this is true; yet at the same time art may not be utopia in order not to betray it by providing semblance and consolation.'[53] In short, the conundrum of modernist artistic production persists in the contradiction between claiming that a work is the *New* achieved, thereby suggesting utopia has also been realized, and the inevitability that this betrays the eternal desires of both by transforming artworks into consolatory semblances decorating the existing order.

Although utopia was not foremost amongst Loos's explicit considerations, his paradoxical preoccupations with authenticity are illuminated by Adorno's distinction between *desire for utopia*, and believing it has been *fulfilled*. According to Adorno, longing for the new of utopia, in whatever form hope takes, may motivate efforts to exceed the limits of the imaginable but believing it has been fulfilled erases desire's generative capacities.[54] Loos sought to remake architecture and culture in the image of unachievable new conditions, grounded in the past. Holding firm to this is what his work holds in reserve. Had Loos ever fulfilled his desire, his work would have been at an end, exhausting its unspent surplus of meaning. This aporia resides at the heart of his double position as a pioneer of modernist architecture *and* a committed classicist.

Adorno assists in resolving Loosian disjunction, asserting that 'a structure of invariants' of the sort Loos posited (antiquity as inviolate) is a necessary 'reaction to an idea drafted by conservative culture critics in the nineteenth century and popularized since: that the world has become formless'.[55] The perplexity of Loos being best known for prohibiting all ornament – classical, exotic and modern – rather than only the invention of new ornament supports Adorno's reading. By misconstruing Loos as rejecting architectural signification in its entirety (all ornament) – the whole of historical inheritance – rather than specifically the excesses and falsehood of the succession of nineteenth-century architectural styles, and continuance of the same general spirit into the twentieth century, he could be evaluated as contributing to the ensuing formlessness of the world. Adorno continues:

> The idea [that the world has become formless] fed on art-historical theses like the one of an extinguished style-building force; originating in aesthetics, it spread as a view of the whole. The basic assumption of the art historians – that this loss is in fact a loss, and not indeed a powerful step toward unshackling the productive forces – is by no means established.[56]

The strong reaction against Loos's ideas and work in his day, by representatives of bourgeois culture, and his relative invisibility in the foundation stories of modernist architecture, from its origins until later in the twentieth century, including his absence from the famous 1932 Museum of Modern Art International Style exhibition in New York City, and its companion book, *The International Style*, becomes comprehensible: Loos did not see the apparent loss of a 'style-building force' as a loss but rather as an 'unshackling' of 'productive forces', requiring 'a structure of invariants', such as classical antiquity furnishes. In this regard, Adorno observes: 'Esthetically revolutionary theoreticians such as Adolf Loos still dared to say so at the beginning of the century [that the apparent formlessness of the world was actually an unshackling of productive forces]; it has been forgotten only by the frightened culture critics, oathbound since to the existing culture.'[57] The speed with which the official *New* architecture (Bauhaus; CIAM; International Style) transformed from apparent negation, and supposedly concrete evidence of utopia realized, to the banalities of mainstream style, reveals its obedience to the existing culture from the start.

The redemptive power Adorno attributes to 'unshackling', of the sort Loos theorized and practised, is not the equivalent of novelty, or illusions of escape. As Adorno observes, attempting to escape the constraints of orthodox modernist architecture by jettisoning invariants is illusory: 'If out of disgust with functional forms and their inherent conformism it [architecture] wanted to give free reign to fantasy, it would fall immediately into kitsch.'[58] Here, 'kitsch' is interchangeable with the inauthentic Loos rejects. Both are evidence of false feeling, of disconnectedness, in search of conciliatory objects, or content, akin to the 'invention' of new ornament (even at building scale). Moreover, total rejection of function, as if ensuring nonconformity, and thus utopia, is also false; at best compensatory, at worst delusional. In Adorno's view, 'Art is no more able than theory to concretize utopia, not even negatively. A cryptogram of the new is the image of collapse; only by virtue of the absolute negativity of collapse does art enunciate the unspeakable: utopia.'[59]

As introduced earlier in this chapter, if the supposedly *new* is misconstrued as somehow utopia actually realized, its only achievement is recapitulation of failure. Accepting the *New* as unachievable and utopia as unrealizable, but going after both anyway, animates art's vocation for opening up prospects onto both, no matter how fugitive. According to Adorno: 'In this image of collapse all the stigmata of the repulsive and loathsome in modern art gather [which is a good thing]. Through the irreconcilable renunciation of the semblance of reconciliation, art holds fast to the promise of reconciliation in the midst of the unreconciled.'[60]

In the negation of reconciliation, reconciliation reasserts its promise, even if it must remain only ever that. The value of this enigma for developing deeper understandings of Loos's thinking and architecture, in particular his use of material, is in clarifying how what might otherwise appear formless, or even unserious, is actually a sophisticated encounter with modernity in the midst of its collapse. Gathering tremors, preceding and following the First World War not only signalled the looming catastrophe of the Second World War but also unshackled productive forces previously concentrated on traditional modes of craft (and artistic) production, which made it possible for Loos to be at once the most modern and classical architect; committed to the solidity of marble while using it as a space-defining textile (almost like a hanging rug, or even as wallpaper) inside, and as cladding (akin to clothing, or skin) outside, in tandem with a search in his writing for *authenticity*, in the guise of an acerbic ironist. Loos shows how embracing the negation of negation, by stubbornly refusing to believe that either the *New* or utopia has been realized, conserves desire for the New as its own aim. The message Loos perpetually sends to the present is that the incompleteness of the broken world can never be made whole, even if maintaining desire for this is compulsory.

Creative destruction

In asserting that existing forms refined through use and time are best, Loos further confounds his status as a pioneer of modernism. Existing forms inflected by transformed materials, modes of production and spatial practices are in turn reshaped by the dominant system of social, political and economic organization at any given moment. Change thus derives from more pliable *ways of doing*, whereas bodily events, habits and established uses – sitting for example – are relatively fixed.

Loos asserted that for an object 'to be considered "beautiful"', it must 'not contravene the rules of practicality'. However, 'being functional alone does not make it beautiful.' Paraphrasing Alberti, he observes, 'An object is beautiful if it is so perfect you could not add anything or take anything away without spoiling it.' Suggestive of Ruskin as well, he continues: 'Nothing in nature is superfluous, and it is the degree of functional value, when combined with the harmony of the other parts, that we call pure beauty.' Accordingly, 'the beauty of a practical object can be determined only in relation to its function.'[61]

Although the body changes little across millennia, dress and mores do; even if the primitive lives on as an inheritance of psyche and physique. In acknowledging this continuum, and present debt to it, Loos did not presume subservience: 'Isn't it remarkable that the most audacious innovators, that is, the most capable people are also those who profess the deepest respect for the work of their predecessors? Actually not. For competence can only be valued again by competence.'[62] In a nod to Vitruvius and his stonemason and sculptor father, Loos writes:

> Our education is based on classical culture. An architect is a bricklayer who has learned Latin. The starting point for drawing instruction should be classical ornamentation. Classical education has created, despite differences of languages and frontiers, a common Western culture, to abandon it would be to destroy this last common ground.[63]

In the preceding, Loos outlines (and attempts to resolve) what he sees as the central conflict of the architect against craftsman, of the classical against modern and of architecture against art. Learning Latin would bind architects to Rome, while being a bricklayer (or 'stonemason', in some translations) is a reminder that architects deal in material, are bound by its limits; obligated to building traditions and to the specifics of use. Learning Latin places architects into the orbit of Vitruvius. Loos's friend, Czech-Austrian writer and journalist Karl Kraus' (1874–1936), supports this reading:

> Adolf Loos and I – he literally {*wörtlich*} and I linguistically {*sprachlich*} – have done nothing more than show that there is a distinction between an urn and a chamber pot and that it is this distinction above all that provides culture with running-room {*Spielraum*}. The others, the positive ones [who fail to make this distinction], are divided into those who use the urn as a chamber pot and those who use the chamber pot as an urn.[64]

Kraus's distinction between urn and chamber pot turns on notions of propriety, manifested in different uses but also in the specifics of material and decoration. As utilitarian, the chamber pot (its form and material) is determined by its use (robust, unobtrusive, easy to clean). On the other hand, as decorative, or memorial, urns allow for freer play with material, form and ornament. The unrestricted movement of culture paradoxically depends on a degree of invariants – with traces back to at least classical antiquity – rather than on either the absence of boundaries, or absolute transparency. Knowing the difference between a chamber pot and an urn ensures against mistakenly using one for the other, and depends on knowing something about comportment within a culture.

Loosening the relation between tradition as self-renewing and historical ideas of the past as fixed clears mental space for gathering past achievements into present efforts, thereby enriching making by furnishing contents for imaginaries of the future. For Loos, this is the only method for producing enduring work in a complex relationship to its age. Unselfconsciously working in the present is enough to simultaneously dignify tradition while renewing it; by producing architecture bound by the realities of its age while transposing these; though it problematizes mythologies of *originality*. Addressing this, Loos ventured:

> A copy of an old picture is also a work of art … But what is unworthy of the name of true art is the conscious effort to clothe new ideas in the style of an old master … Nothing should be altered in an object being copied … We always have some criticism to make of old artifacts … We always delude ourselves into thinking we can improve them in some way … The old model, or an exact copy, still [shines] forth in its authenticity [while] we [cannot] stand the imitation and its 'embellishments'.[65]

Summarizing the paradoxical idea that the *truly* modern is only conceivable within a continuum of tradition, Loos writes: 'Fashion progresses slowly, more slowly than one usually thinks. Objects that are really modern stay so for a long time. If one hears of an article of clothing which is out of date by the very next season, then one can be sure it was never truly modern, but merely feigned modernity.'[66] Despite the soundness of Loos's insights, his notions of authenticity and architects' obligations to tradition, production and use are difficult to reconcile with reality this side of twentieth-century catastrophes. As little more than technicians in a building industry, or mediating decorators of capital, architects' neoliberal compensations make Loos more of an outsider today than he was even in his lifetime. But the outrageousness of his propositions in one direction and their extreme conservativeness in the other are equally radical, which safeguards him from oblivion and misappropriation.

Unlike the many fundamentalist modernists who followed him, Loos's sensitivity to the most disruptive aspects of modernity and industrialization is distinctive: uprootedness; diminishing quality of workmanship; a fading grasp on tradition; and the rise of consumerism. However, his critique of contemporary society was no reactionary call for return to the past. Rather, he sought to act within tradition, while taking ownership of new and alien conditions by determining the most appropriate materials and forms to extend use. Although opposed to planned obsolescence, he accepted machine production. And while bound to tradition, he found the idea of an aestheticized vernacular absurd. Likewise, he rejected the transformation of objects of practical use – furniture, utensils, houses – into art objects, as contrary to their everyday function.

In his essay 'Karl Kraus', German Jewish cultural critic, Walter Benjamin (1892–1940) suggests that Kraus, along with his *comrade-in-arms* Loos, stood paradoxically between past and future, attempting to reconcile the two as they sought authenticity and purity. To get at the truth, a destructive act would be necessary, to pull away all the stuff that obscures and confuses; Kraus with language, Loos with architecture:

> Loos found his providential adversaries in the arts-and-crafts mongers, who, in the ambit of the 'Vienna Workshops' were striving to give birth to a new art industry. He sent out his rallying cry in numerous essays … 'what may be touched cannot be a work of art, and that a work of art must be out of reach.' It was therefore Loos' first concern to separate the work of art from the article of use, as it was that of Kraus to keep apart information and the work of art. The hack journalist is in his heart at one with the ornamentalist … The empty phrase of the kind so relentlessly pursued by Kraus is the label that makes a thought marketable, the way that flowery language, as ornament, gives its value for the connoisseur.[67]

Benjamin observes that 'Kraus deftly tied the knot binding technology to the empty phrase', which he describes as an 'an abortion of technology', not least because divisions between intellectual work and manual labour, and between production and consumption, entail alienating separations; separations that splinter signified and signifier, obliterating the possibility of something akin to *authentic* value, and with it the private capacity for judgement.[68] According to Loos, divisions of labour disrupt the balance between destructive and constructive work: 'the division of labor' is 'nerve-destroying' because it 'allocates the constructive and destructive process to different people'. If the constructive process is not complemented by the destructive, workers 'will waste away, both spiritually and physically'.[69] He goes further:

> He who, during the day, was compelled by the division of labor to do constructive work alone felt a need for destructive labor. Every human activity consists of

destroying and constructing … People can live if their only activity is destruction, for that is the primal instinct … But people who because of the division of labor are compelled to perform constructive tasks alone, become stunted. They lose their humanity. Work becomes a terrible drudgery.[70]

As primal, destruction is a real human act, close to the baseline of existence: devouring, savage and aggressive. Even though hard-won attributes of sublimation, creativity and civilization must be balanced by some outlet for destruction (not managed by repression), which promises ostensibly less alienated results.

As Benjamin understood it, the destructiveness Loos extols when he says that 'If human work consists only of destruction, it is truly human, natural, noble work' is a revelation promising liberation from the distorting encumbrances produced by 'the dilettante luxuriating in creation' (of an 'innocent and pure sort'); engaged in 'consuming and purifying masterliness', which is as alienating as alienated.[71] According to Benjamin, destructiveness dismantles what obscures and confuses, to reveal 'a more real humanism', defined by an assimilation of life to technology.[72] An assimilation only achievable by *taking away* through destruction, rather than by *giving to* through construction. But not until the 'fetish of creative existence' that clogs the way is relinquished.[73] Benjamin's powerful conceptualization is reflected in Loos's assertion that allotment gardening, provided as part of social housing developments, are 'the product of a [bloodless] revolution of the workers against the barracks-like constraint of the factory system'.[74] The end result would echo Benjamin: 'uniting … life with technology', by responding to 'a deep psychological need' to balance *constructive* labour with the *destructive* activity of working the land.[75]

While Loos never sought to abolish ornament, and did not even think it a crime, prohibiting its invention or imitation in sham materials, or application to objects of daily use, was a taking of the sort described in the preceding paragraph, intended to destroy the 'fetish of creative existence', as a means to clearing spaces for the invention of architecture unifying life with technology, without subjugation to the machine, or factory labour. The machine and its methods of production so debased craft traditions that this reality had to be absorbed for modern architecture to evolve, including sublimation of ornament. But the destructive potential of the machine has proven so great – industrialized slaughter of the First World War, perfected by its combination with bureaucratic rationality in the Second World War – that it is incapable of providing a definitive model for architecture (our home on earth). Technical functionalism, explicit structural expression and the dominance of prosaic considerations over poetic ones, blunts correspondences between form, structure and material.

By severing bodily memories from ancient sources, architecture produces alienating settings ill-equipped for sheltering emotional depth. The stand-off between architecture and engineering only hardens disunity between life and technology. Modern myths of pure rationality and perfection, suggested by the elegance of machines, and machine production, are only sustainable apart from the frailty of the human body and fallibility of the human mind.[76] Meditating on use, the way the body determines it, and the best forms to facilitate it are more promising than imagining the *New* achieved. According to Loos, good work is developed out of inventive play with tradition, inflected by contemporary realities – especially production – reconciled materially.

The analogy Loos makes between public comportment and buildings retains its significance. The high value he places on individual restraint, as a counterweight to exhibitionism, such that a person of culture does not stand out at its centre, is analogized by the stern facades of his domestic buildings, counterbalanced by materially opulent, comfortably intimate, rooms within. Although Loos's words and work still hold reserves of relevance, he lived and died before Hitler's 1938 annexation of Austria *ended* modernism in Vienna, foreshadowing subsequent catastrophes that severed ties with the lost world he inhabited. Consequently, Loos's optimistic belief in modernist individualism and the traditions of Western civilization as a viable continuity are irrecuperable, though desire persists.

Notes

1. Adolf Loos, 'Ornament and Crime' (1929 [1908]), in *Ornament and Crime: Selected Essays*, Michael Mitchell (trans.), Riverside, CA: Ariadne Press, 1998, p. 171.

2. Ibid., p. 168. See also, Joseph Rykwert, *On Adam's House in Paradise: The Idea of the Primitive Hut in Architectural History*, Cambridge, MA: MIT Press, 1981 (1972), pp. 27–9, for Loos and the renewal of architecture.

3. Ibid., Loos, 'Ornament and Crime' (1929 [1908]), p. 168.

4. Adolf Loos, 'On Thrift' (1924), in *On Architecture*, Michael Mitchell (trans.), Riverside, CA: Ariadne Press, 2002, p. 183.

5. Kenneth Frampton, *Modern Architecture: A Critical History*, Third Edition, New York: Thames and Hudson, 1992, p. 91.

6. Loos, 'Ornament and Crime' (1929 [1908]), pp. 170–1.

7. Sir John Summerson, 'Foreword', in *The Architecture of Adolf Loos*, Yehuda Safran and Wilfried Wang (eds), London: Arts Council of Great Britain, 1985, p. 6.

8. Loos, 'Ornament and Crime' (1929 [1908]), p. 167.

9. For concise psychoanalytic definitions of 'Repression', 'Sublimation', and the 'Return of the Repressed', see Charles Rycroft, *A Critical Dictionary of Psychoanalysis*, London: Penguin, 1995, pp. 157, 176–7.

10. See esp. Sigmund Freud (1929), *Civilization and Its Discontents*, New York: W.W. Norton, 1961, pp. 22–52.

11. Though traditionally dated 1908, 'Ornament and Crime' was first presented in 1910, published in French in 1913, and finally in German in 1929 (Janet Stewart, *Fashioning Vienna: Adolf Loos's Cultural Criticism*, London and New York: Routledge, 2000, p. 173, n. 5).

12. Volker M. Welter, *Ernst L. Freud, Architect: The Case of the Modern Bourgeois Home*, New York and Oxford: Berghahn, 2011, pp. 41–6.

13. Adolf Loos, 'Architecture' (1910), in *On Architecture*, Michael Mitchell (trans.), Riverside, CA: Ariadne Press, 2002, p. 83.

14. Ibid., p. 84.

15. Loos, 'Ornament and Crime' (1929 [1908]), pp. 167–76.

16. Aldo Rossi, 'Introduction', Adolf Loos, *Spoken Into the Void: Collected Essays 1897–1900*, S. Sartarelli (trans.), Cambridge, MA: MIT Press / Opposition Books, 1982, p. xiii.

17. Loos, 'The Potemkin City' (1898), in *On Architecture*, Michael Mitchell (trans.), Riverside, CA: Ariadne Press, 2002, p. 26.

18. Ibid., p. 28.

19. Ibid.

20. Ibid., p. 27.

21. Ibid., p. 26.

22. Ibid.

23. Ibid.

24. Ibid., p. 27.

25. Ibid., p. 28.

26. Loos, 'A Review of Applied Arts I' (1898), in *Ornament and Crime: Selected Essays*, Michael Mitchell (trans.), Riverside, CA: Ariadne Press, 1998, p. 136.

27. Loos, 'The Old and the New Style' (1898), in *On Architecture*, Michael Mitchell (trans.), Riverside, CA: Ariadne Press, 2002, p. 33.

28. Ibid.

29. Loos, 'Ornament and Crime' (1929 [1908]), p. 175.

30. Emphasis in original. Loos, 'The Chicago Tribune Column' (1923), in *On Architecture*, Michael Mitchell (trans.), Riverside, CA: Ariadne Press, 2002, p. 171.

31. Loos, 'The Principle of Cladding' (1898), in *On Architecture*, Michael Mitchell (trans.), Riverside, CA: Ariadne Press, 2002, p. 42.

32. Ibid., p. 44.

33. Ibid., p. 42.

34. Loos, 'Architecture' (1910), p. 84.

35. Ibid., p. 42.

36. Semper, 'The Four Elements of Architecture' (1851), pp. 101–26.

37. Loos, 'Building Materials' (1898), in *On Architecture*, Michael Mitchell (trans.), Riverside, CA: Ariadne Press, 2002, p. 37.

38. Loos, 'Architecture' (1910), p. 73.

39. Ibid.

40. Ibid., pp. 73–4.

41. Loos, 'My First Building' (1910), in *On Architecture*, Michael Mitchell (trans.), Riverside, CA: Ariadne Press, 2002, p. 70.

42. Theodor W. Adorno, *Negative Dialectics*, E. B. Ashton (trans.), London: Routledge, 1973 [1966], pp. 362–3.

43. Adorno, 'Functionalism Today', p. 38. Originally presented to the German Werkbund, 1965.

44. Ibid., p. 38.

45. Ibid., p. 41.

46. Loos, '*Heimatkunst*' (1912), in *On Architecture*, Michael Mitchell (trans.), Riverside, CA: Ariadne Press, 2002, pp. 112–13, 117.

47. Loos, 'Architecture' (1910), pp. 84–5.

48. Loos, 'A Review of Applied Arts I' (1898), p. 134.

49. Ibid., p. 135.

50. Loos, 'Architecture' (1910), p. 84.

51. Joseph Masheck, *Adolf Loos: The Art of Architecture*, London: I.B. Taurus, 2013, p. 109.

52. Theodor W. Adorno, 'Situation', in *Aesthetic Theory* (1970), p. 32.

53. Ibid.

54. Ibid.

55. Adorno, *Negative Dialectics*, p. 94.

56. Ibid.

57. Ibid.

58. Adorno, 'Situation', p. 32.

59. Ibid.

60. Ibid., pp. 32–3.

61. Loos, 'Chairs' (1898), in *Ornament and Crime: Selected Essays*, Michael Mitchell (trans.), Riverside, CA: Ariadne Press, 1998, p. 63.

62. Loos, 'Tours of the Austrian Museum' (1898), in *Spoken Into the Void: Collected Essays 1897–1900*, Jane O. Newman and John H. Smith (trans.), Cambridge, MA: Oppositions Books/MIT Press, 1982, p. 112.

63. Loos, 'Ornament and Education' (1924), in *Ornament and Crime: Selected Essays*, Michael Mitchell (trans.), Riverside, CA: Ariadne Press, 1998, p. 187.

64. Karl Kraus, *Werke*, Vol. 3, Munich, 1965, p. 341, quoted in, Hal Foster, *Prosthetic Gods,* Cambridge, MA: MIT Press, 2004, p. 91.

65. Loos, 'The New Style and the Bronze Industry' (1898), in *Ornament and Crime: Selected Essays*, Michael Mitchell (trans.), Riverside, CA: Ariadne Press, 1998, pp. 47–8.

66. Loos, 'Gentlemen's Hats' (1898), in *Ornament and Crime: Selected Essays*, pp. 92–3.

67. Walter Benjamin, 'Karl Kraus' (1931), in *Reflections: Essays, Aphorisms, Autobiographical Writings*, Peter Demetz (ed.), Edmond Jephcott (trans.), New York: Shocken Books, 1978, pp. 240, 241, 242.

68. Ibid., pp. 240–1.

69. Loos, 'Rules for Social Housing Development' (1920), in *On Architecture*, Michael Mitchell (trans.), Riverside, CA: Ariadne Press, 2002, p. 142.

70. Loos, 'Social Housing Development Day' (1921), in *On Architecture*, Michael Mitchell (trans.), Riverside, CA: Ariadne Press, 2002, p. 160.

71. Loos quoted by Benjamin, source: Adolf Loos, *Trotzdem, 1900–1930*, Vienna: Prachner, 1981 (1931), p. 184. Benjamin, 'Karl Kraus' (1931), p. 272.

72. Benjamin, 'Karl Kraus' (1931), p. 272.

73. Ibid.

74. Loos, 'Social Housing Development Day' (1921), p. 161.

75. Benjamin, 'Karl Kraus' (1931), p. 272. Loos, 'Social Housing Development Day' (1921), p. 161.

76. Benjamin, 'Karl Kraus' (1931), p. 272.

PART ONE
STONES, ARCHITECTURE, LAND AND INTERIORS

CHAPTER 4
TIME SILTED UP: SCARPA AT THE GIPSOTECA CANOVIANO (1955–57) AND MUSEO DI CASTELVECCHIO (1957–75)

Italian architect Carlo Scarpa's (1906–78) method could be summarized as situated, autobiographical and poetic. Best known for constructing an evocative poetics of building out of intense details, and the inventive use of materials, his work gathers past into present with a Janus glance backward towards fading traditions and forward towards unspecified futures.[1] The conditions and qualities of Scarpa's architecture are concisely rendered as 'a history of materials and the work of the hand', in which

> the materials, and even more the use he makes of them in every phase of his development are a telling of the truth. The figure of the ruin, the decay of bodies, all bodies, which Carlo learned in the readings of his Venetian days – Venice being the great text of decomposition – reappears in the way he exposes materials to weather and history without any pretense of compassion.[2]

In Scarpa's work, past coalesces into figurations of an *eternal present*, which deepens and gentles the mystery of death (including at the Brion Cemetery). Although the Brion Family Tomb complex, San Vito d'Altivole, Italy (1969–78), is perhaps Scarpa's best-known work, his gallery and exhibit designs, including display cases, pedestals and hardware, reveal the full extent of his craft sensitivities, elaborated on in presenting diverse artworks from a range of periods.

Scarpa's galleries, including the Museo di Castelvecchio (1957–64; 1968–69; 1973–75), Verona, Italy, and the Museo Canoviano Gipsoteca (1955–57), Posagno, Italy, recuperate relationships between architecture and the fine arts broken by the rationalization of design, reduction of building to an industrial process and the atomization of art. In his work, architecture, painting and sculpture are reunited by details, colour, material, building elements and display apparatus, mediated by the body. By piercing veils separating spectators from artworks, architects from art and the public from the processes of the artist, his galleries heighten emotional experiences and bodily perceptions of art.

Figure 4.1 Museo Canoviano Gipsoteca (1955–57), Posagno, Italy. Carlo Scarpa, Architect. [Photo: Nathaniel Coleman, 2007].

Figure 4.2 Museo di Castelvecchio (1957–64; 1968–69; 1973–75), Verona, Italy. Carlo Scarpa, Architect. [Photo: Nathaniel Coleman, 2007].

Scarpa and locality

Scarpa's localness is unmatched by almost any noteworthy post-Second World War architect: he built only in Italy, mostly in the provinces of Veneto, especially Venice. Working regionally deepened his practices, even as the dissipating tendencies of

Figure 4.3 Brion Family Tomb complex (1969–78), San Vito d'Altivole, Italy. Carlo Scarpa, Architect. [Photo: Nathaniel Coleman, 2007].

globalization came to dominate contemporary imaginaries. Although cosmopolitanism fosters broader perspectives possibly prerequisite for species and planetary survival, it diffuses cultural specificity, producing a conundrum: emplaced practices can give rise to more profound results but localness risks becoming enervating provincialism, analogous to insipid globalism.[3]

Staying local guarantees nothing but might sustain those qualities that first distinguished an architect, as it did for Scarpa, even as tensions between local and global, as between tradition and modernity, enriched his work. Rooted in a place and modes of production, while participating in the metropolitan currents of modern art, Scarpa interpreted traditions with a rare degree of cultural depth and fluency. The tense play of these contradictions were a source of his work's vitality.

Though an Italian architect, Scarpa's self-identification as a 'man of Byzantium who came to Venice by way of Greece' disclosed his hunger for the world.[4] Originating in 'Byzantium' is a place time reference, conjuring up the ancient Greek colony that in late Roman, and Eastern Roman, or Byzantine, periods (330–1453) became the city of Constantinople (the Second Rome, now Istanbul, Turkey). Then as now, a bridge between Europe and Asia, linking East and West. Identifying 'Greece' as his transit way from Byzantium to Venice is as much a temporal as a geographical reference to ancient Greece. Venetian birth (dying in Sendai, Japan, seventy-two years later) infused his imaginaries with the Eastern Roman Empire (Byzantium). A Republic between the fifth and eighteenth centuries, Venice's strong trading ties with the Byzantine Empire marked the city with distinct Eastern influences.

His East/West (Occidental/Oriental) sensibility, originating in the Venetian archipelago, is a localized biographical detail suggestive of play with tradition as a method for resisting the economic imperatives of off-the-shelf ready-made components, and projects determined by performance specifications. Even architects concerned with details mostly construct distantly cool atmospheres cognate with industrialized mass production but Scarpa's adoration of the joint and love of material mediated ancient sources to fabricate architectural *machines* for engendering detailed immediacy. Assembled from elements bridging past and future, and part and whole, the physicality of his architecture is manifest resistance to dominant modes of production, still modelling alternative practices for architects.[5]

US architect Louis I. Kahn's meditation on Scarpa concentrates on his method as a poetics of joints. In Scarpa's work, 'Beauty', 'Art' and 'Wonder' are indivisible in manifestations of 'the inner realization of "Form"', as a sense of 'wholeness' construed from 'inseparable elements': materials as much as 'shapes'. It is the joint, however, that renders the 'whole' of 'inseparable elements' comprehensible as such: 'In the elements the joint inspires ornament, its celebration. The detail is the adoration of Nature.'[6]

Venetian clues

The key elements of Scarpa's architecture – metal, wood, stone, glass and water – originate in Venice as demonstrations of ancient denotation, persistently open to modern connotation.[7] Decay, stucco falling off brick, headless and/or weather-beaten statues, wind-swept stone, crumbling marble strapped together with bits of iron, bridges of stone, of stone and metal, of metal, of wood and metal and the defining play of light and water everywhere are his lexicon of material presence, cultivated in the fertile soil of associations that nourished his detail imaginaries. Material fragments embedded in ancient walls throughout Venice bridge time, structuring encounters with various *pasts* that a multitude of *presents* negotiate, suggestive of open futures. He cultivated the ground of his work in two senses: turning the earth to urge growth, and through increasing sophistication. A living past was his ground of radical invention, laden with constellations of perpetually renewable significance, translated by transgressive modes of interpretation. Details in particular – redolent with Venetian decay – were his method for recuperating something of architecture's classical fine arts tradition.

Suggestive of the tragic Venetian mood infusing Scarpa's work, Ruskin believed the long decline of Venice, following the 1797 fall of its Republic, so enhances its fatal beauty as to make it a successor to the Garden of Eden:

> like her in perfection of beauty, though less in endurance of dominion, is still left
> for our beholding in the final period of her decline: a ghost upon the sands of the
> sea, so weak – so quiet, so bereft of all her loveliness, that we might doubt, as we

watched her faint reflection in the mirage of the lagoon, which was the City, and which the shadow.[8]

Transformed through time, including to accommodate visitors like Ruskin, Venice maintains an overwhelming atmosphere of perpetual mourning and corporeal pleasure; as eternal commemorations of human ingenuity. Despite the touristic throng, Scarpa's details are spectres of the city's enduring seductiveness. As the living record of its own demise, Venice is a great city of death, heralding inescapable individual finality as life affirming. Tracing this, dramatic tensions between tragedy and comedy play out continuously in Scarpa's work.

Echoing Venice, Scarpa's work mediates life and death by embracing mortality as a source of deepened existence and vitality, built upon fragility and certain decay: a simultaneously elegiac and exultant character the Brion Family Tomb powerfully embodies. Determined, disciplined and rigorous, but mostly supple; jokes of displacement appear throughout his work, locating it within an ambit of surrealism.[9] Dislocation of near-sacred antique objects, as at the Querini-Stampalia Foundation Garden (1961–1963), liberates cultural inheritances by reintroducing them to everyday life.

Joining seemingly irreconcilable materials – perishable wood and durable metal, for example – heightens senses of things by displacing them. Estrangement disrupts expected perception, thereby returning something of the original *shock* of initial contact, while sustaining refreshing defamiliarization through subsequent encounters.[10]

Figure 4.4 Querini-Stampalia Foundation Garden (1961–63), Venice, Italy. Carlo Scarpa, Architect. [Photo: Nathaniel Coleman, 2007].

As practical applications of his method, Scarpa's museum and gallery interventions demonstrate how his dichotomous modernism refreshes encounters with historic artworks by disobediently playing with the past. Tradition is never simply received but is tilled to form tangible records of its material presence in new work. Accordingly, newness is built upon ground originally cultivated in the past, to form the foundation of future work. Scarpa's material meditations are future-orientated transformations of physical presence that structure reflections on possibilities beyond the given.

Accounting for otherness

Despite his pessimism about post-Second World War architecture, Italian architectural historian and theorist Manfredo Tafuri (1935–94) praised Scarpa for his incomparable escape from capitalism's foreclosure on architectural possibility, which makes him deserving of careful study. But, according to Tafuri, his singular achievement is non-transferable, making his relative autonomy an anomaly, in comparison with most architects, who are tormented by false 'hopes in design' and are little more than technicians in a building industry:[11]

> The detachment of the 'outmoded' threw light on collective and subjective situations and allowed (or stimulated?) 'the courage to speak of roses.' Historiographical treatment must be suspended in the case of such golden, isolated individuals, and give way to 'classical' monographs.[12]

As another kind of architect, Scarpa operates beyond historical materialism, resisting both historiography and dominant modes of production, necessitating independent treatment of his work, as the production of a 'golden' (auspicious), and 'isolated' (autonomous) 'individual'. According to Tafuri, Scarpa's relative autonomy derived from his 'isolation and uniqueness' in relation to mainstream architectural production.

His remoteness from conformist professional culture, and the constraints of industrial production, allowed Scarpa to resist capitalism's corrosive influence, as he 'proudly' defended 'the magic circle enclosing the architect and his private *codes*.'[13] Acting against the tide of modernity set his architecture apart from the main currents of contemporary theories and practices, situating it in and out of its time simultaneously. Scarpa's unorthodox encounters with tradition – conceptualized as unfolding and self-renewing – suffused his spatial, formal and material imaginaries.

Although he saw himself as an ancient, who bridged East and West, past and future, with his own body, Scarpa 'always believed in the modern movement [in architecture]'.[14] Recollecting coming across Le Corbusier's *Vers un architecture* (*Toward An Architecture*, 1923) shortly after art school, he declared: 'It opened my soul: since then my spiritual state was radically changed.'[15] He also felt close to Viennese modernism, including Loos, one imagines.[16] Above all else, Scarpa's work articulates an ardent (though promiscuous) relationship to the past, evident in a 1931 letter supporting Italian Rationalist architecture, which, though it aligns with Fascist modernizing myths, surpasses factionalist argumentation:

> We need a new sense of architecture. This modern architecture we invoke will be rational, precisely because that which preceded it for more than a century was not rational, nor was it architecture.
>
> We are not saying that the word 'rational' should be understood as an aesthetic term. We know that all great architecture in the past was rational. It was so because it used the materials available and employed them for civil, social, religious, and therefore rational purposes. Great art was created only when [the] spiritual and imaginative element appeared in it – the irrational, which constitutes its inspired, creative function.[17]

Scarpa here outlines the core ideas that continuously informed his work: the desire to be rational, because 'all great architecture in the past was' but modern too, by using the 'new building materials', especially 'reinforced concrete', which he did with great sophistication. He did not support a modernist break with tradition, certainly not with the 'great architecture' of 'the past' but with the style confusion of nineteenth-century eclectic revivalism. For him, 'rational' is a consciousness, not a style, so does not preclude the 'spiritual and imaginative', which he names the 'irrational'. As such, historical depth, the spiritual, imaginative or irrational, is not banished, further distinguishing Scarpa from most twentieth-century orthodox modernist architecture (Bauhaus or International Style), while revealing affinities with the theories and practices of Loos and Wright.

Scarpa's disobedient encounters with the past are neither quite modern nor antiquarian, which perplexed him. He hoped for a 'critic to discover in' his 'works certain intentions' he 'always had', which he characterizes as 'an immense desire to belong inside tradition, but without having capitals and columns, because you just can't do them any more'.[18] He was also 'always concerned' with 'the problem of historical materials, which' cannot be ignored but cannot be imitated 'directly either'. For him, 'The stupid imitations imposed now, …in Venice, lead in the wrong direction. They don't solve anything.'[19] In Scarpa's view, only living traditions survive but because modes of production are spatially and temporally situational, direct imitation is unimaginative, and not rational.

His drawings, collaboration with craftsmen, use of material and encounters with the past in new work, particularly interventions in historical buildings, constitute evidence of the singularity of his processes and results. Because his work resisted the conceptual and material trivialization of architecture identified with modernity, Tafuri considered 'Scarpa's designs … among the most significant in the history of contemporary Italian architecture'.[20] As an exception that proves the rule of decline – paralleling capitalism's development into a nearly 'total system' – Scarpa confirms depressing inevitabilities with signs of resistance.[21]

Revolutionary act of new space

Scarpa's drawings and buildings are desiring *machines* that renew hope by exceeding professional banalities enforced by dominant modes of production. Italian architecture theorist, and student of Scarpa, Marco Frascari (1945–2013), defines architects' utopian vocation as making 'tangible what is intangible', by producing 'the physical and perhaps metaphysical frameworks of any interart relationship', since, 'no art can interrelate to another art without architecture.'[22] No architecture, no museum; no hospital, no operating theatre; no auditorium, no performance; and so on. Architecture, Frascari argues, is happiest when fulfilling its role as 'the theater of the constructed world.'[23] According to him, Scarpa produced 'nontrivial buildings', which exemplify and suggest, rather than determine or impose; achieved by making 'technology' into an 'expression of pleasure … rather than an objective procedure to which the client and architect must be subjected.'[24] Frascari's assertions about building suggestiveness and pleasurable technology illuminate key countercurrent aspects of Scarpa's modes of production: drawing, modernist extensions of craft and encounters with material.

Frascari enlarges architecture's vocation to include material concern for 'sensible human nature', manifest in the organization of 'time, space, and artifacts in a place', which is the theoretical basis of nontrivial 'architecture' that lives 'among the arts'; knowing 'how to judge and arrange them in a proper environment.'[25] Supporting many of the propositions already introduced, Frascari construes Scarpa's work as 'corporeal time machine[s] where the past, the present, and the future [are] architecturally related through memory.'[26] From inception through inhabitation, the central importance of experiencing bodies to Scarpa's work is mediated by memory and expressed in pronounced materiality; as manifestations of the 'corporeal dimension of memory.'[27]

For Frascari, as practitioners of the trivial, professional businessmen-architects assume 'that design is a service, a transitive activity supporting another more important endeavor – the functioning of a building, from image to HVAC [heating, ventilation, and air-conditioning]'. They subjugate architecture to 'tasks', thought to be 'more important' than 'making tangible what is intangible.'[28] Frampton observes that the 'tectonic authenticity' of Scarpa's intensively detailed, materially sophisticated, architecture constitutes a poetics of construction and 'a critique' of dominant modernist myths of an organic architecture disappearing into the land, and the techno-utopianism 'of modern functionalism'. While Scarpa's 'responsiveness' meant that he 'always addressed the specific terms of the brief and the boundaries of the site; … he never allowed his imagination to be stifled by precedent.'[29]

Scarpa's rebel practices challenged the 'political and economic' context of institutionalized orthodox modernist architecture, including calling himself an 'architect', though not officially *qualified*, which flouted legal restrictions on use of the title. However, his *non-professional* status made it easier to disregard the default positions of conventional design offices, including technocratic modes of representation and building industry organized construction labour. Undisciplined by clockwork time, Scarpa expanded the temporal frame of projects as needed, which contravened professional norms. Ultimately, working on the edges and in the cracks of architectural practice nourished Scarpa's capacity for exceeding productivist limits by identifying otherwise hidden poetic possibilities of post-Second World War building.[30]

Scarpa's canny achievement

Embeddedness within tradition; irregular professional status and working methods; unique collaborative relationships with craftsmen; deep knowledge of materials; and intense details could be construed as the identikit either of an elitist set against his time or of obsolescence. But these countercurrents actually make the strongest case for the continuing relevance of Scarpa's methods. Another former student, Giuseppe Zambonini (1942–90), saw it differently, for him, 'Scarpa's era is over and cannot be prolonged', because increasing societal inequity demands restraint. He argues: 'The art of our time must have the intention of producing buildings of meaning with the utmost economy of means.'[31] In short, because Scarpa's *aristocratic* architecture intensifies all forms of inequality, it is just too out of step.[32] Tafuri offers a surprisingly hopeful rejoinder: 'Surely the characteristic of Scarpa's art is that it indicates the outlines of the happiness that is possible even in a "time of crisis."'[33]

Although only bodily experience can disclose Scarpa's architecture, studying its irrecuperable process and unique forms from afar still has value. Zambonini shows how by analysing its key themes, which he asserts are expressions 'of a design and building process, rather than' of 'fully realized' forms. Accordingly, the final result is unknowable because subjected to continuous open processes. Or, in Ruskin's terms, *conception* outruns *execution* to produce living work. Supporting this reading, Zambonini describes Scarpa's architecture as 'incomplete' rather than 'fragmented'. For him, the first suggests 'an infinite joinery system, the finality of which is quite unknown – or at least unpredictable', whereas the second presupposes 'unity and relationships of parts within the whole'. He continues, 'because of its inherent resistance to precise definition', Scarpa's work has been criticized 'from the standpoint of [absent] unity'. However, in its incompleteness, 'the work possesses the basis for a renewed understanding of the future – if distant – completion it portends.'[34]

Scarpa's resistance to plastic unity sets his work apart from conventional preoccupations with form and imageability.[35] As such, for all the allure of its materials and details, the refusal to deliver a readily apprehended coherent form translates into structures that are not instantly photogenic, reminiscent of Loos's delight in the un-photographability of his interiors. Assembled out of 'discontinuous' elements whole in themselves, Scarpa's architecture constitutes a 'dialectic between celebration of form and the scattering of its parts'.[36] Tafuri augments Zambonini's analysis with an overview of Scarpa's recurrent themes:

There runs all through Scarpa's *oeuvre* a series of variations on the underlying themes of erosion and interval … What seemed no more than an array of fragments turns out to be a landscape from which references emerge to the complex interplay of recognition and recomposition, a network of possible routes. But the threads that guide the way are tenuous and allow for an infinite range of different groupings. So it would really be more correct to speak not of poetic fragments but of a poetic composed of 'figures'. *Figures*, not images or nostalgic scraps of a whole, are the 'hermetic icons' that we have identified in Scarpa's architecture … Scarpa's 'figures' [are] iconic signals from a broken-up labyrinth, alluding to 'new modes of completion'.[37]

The discontinuous (or scattered) coherent elements Tafuri identifies in Scarpa's architecture undermines totalizing unities. Joints (or details) pronounce the intentionality of this by suturing materials, elements or parts of the building together thematically. Although the detail – as a join – is the most identifiable aspect of Scarpa's work, emphasis on the part as the microcosm of a discontinuous, incomplete or potential whole could encourage faulty interpretations of it as fragmented. But there is no missing whole. The figures contribute to a developing narrative that only takes hold by resisting totalization. This reversal of expectation *subordinates the whole to the joint*, as 'the fertile detail', or the physical moment 'where both the construction and construing of architecture take place', emphatically expressed by material assemblies.[38]

For Frascari, the joint is the 'minimal unit in the process of signification (that is the manipulation of meaning)' in architecture, apprehended preconsciously through bodily experience.[39] For Frampton, Scarpa's details are simultaneously critical and compensatory: 'excessively articulated joints may be read as a critical commentary on the economic expediency of our utilitarian age, or alternatively, as a heroic attempt to compensate for our inability to equal the poetic authority of classical form'.[40] While Scarpa's joints critique utilitarian efficiencies, by compensating for poetic deficiencies; slowing time so bodily rhythms can overwrite clockwork time is his work's most radical gesture: 'The slowing down of the time of reading, the expansion of the instant imposed by his work on forms and materials implies an arrest of the nihilistic succession of "measurable" time and space, just as his *figures* imply going beyond the totalizing claims of the "design"'.[41]

Tafuri's observation that discontinuousness in Scarpa's work slows time; Frascari's assertion that architectural signification originates with the joint; and Frampton's proposition that Scarpa's details critique economic expedience, while recollecting classical ornament, suggest that his immoderate assemblies are also partly satiric (in a Loosian mode). The collection of historical events (materials, making and setting) in series (pronounced by intensively detailed joints), formed into a narrative (a succession of episodes: rooms, joints, links between independent forms or parts of buildings), with a plot (structured by corporeal experience), produce discontinuities that Scarpa's architectural assemblages render differently coherent, while intensifying concrete experience. And by slowing time, Scarpa's drawings and buildings resist the status quo.

Supra real

Generally supportive of the reading provided here, Frascari observes: 'At the base, surrealist technology is an adoration of the nature of reality, where the real is made surreal through the powerful tool of fantasy.'[42] Accordingly, the critical edge of Scarpa's work is produced by surrealist sensibilities, as taunts to the meagre efforts of routine practice. Playfully provocative, his 'architecture eschews mundane reality for the unknown world of surreality – not the unreal, but the heart of the real.'[43] But is 'surreality' revolution enough?[44] Arguably yes. As Tafuri asserts: *'icons of the possible ... can be found in* Scarpa's allusive space', which is 'a universe of coexisting possibilities ... left open and ... expressed in multivalent forms, inviting one, especially in his last work, to embark upon interpretative voyages that question the "one way streets" of the "bad modern"', of disenchanting myths of optimizing techno-scientific progress.[45] Tafuri continues, speculating that German philosopher 'Ernst Bloch [1885-1977] might have read, in Scarpa's details, positive responses to his attempt to recover the time of *experience*.'[46]

As characterized by Tafuri, Scarpa's 'forms' and 'details' reveal the work's utopian dimension as searches for *something missing*. Although forever out of reach, the absent is continuously approached through transactions with pre-modern – pre-capitalist – realities, as substructures of alternative futures. Albeit spatially and temporally unique, Zambonini identifies in Scarpa's work lasting models of nontrivial practice:

> Scarpa ... produce[d] nearly universal meanings in his work, although he is more commonly known for his use of rare materials: cast bronze spouts, glass tiles, ebony, ivory and gold. Demanding a craftsmanship based on centuries of experience, Scarpa's work – and his poetic architectonic language capable of touching so many distant cultures – establishes a unique reference for any use of materials.[47]

Of particular relevance is Zambonini's identification of the 'nearly universal meanings' produced by Scarpa's work and its 'unique reference for any use of materials'. While the 'meanings' persist because deeply enrooted, as almost *natural symbols*, the 'use of materials' is far less certain. The artistic limitations of an architecture subjugated to bureaucratic rationality and capitalist production makes construing the meanings Scarpa could, by conceiving and constructing the way he did, less a matter of knowing better, or of desire, than of a particular consciousness.[48]

Drawing, detailing, resisting

Discontinuousness (or incompleteness) in Scarpa's architecture conserves material traces of the design process as reservoirs of methods and significance and of the vitality invested in it by drawing. Drawings are tools for thinking architecture as rhythmically unfolding, prefiguring disclosures of meaning to experiencing bodies. Simultaneously invention and representation, Scarpa's drawings are not the approximate picturing of something absent believed to already fully exist elsewhere (in the imagination, or as a future construction). Accordingly, sketches are not preliminary to contract or construction documents; they really are 'working drawings', mechanisms for inventing projects and solving problems as they arise. Projects are *drawn out* in both senses: by the revelatory processes of design, with the results guiding building construction. Durational rather than fragmentary, Scarpa's architecture analogizes its invention, with construction a kind of *drawing* on the earth that material embodiments of the four elements of *earth*, *water*, *air* and *fire* fix upon it.

Neither copies of nature nor instrumental contractual blueprints, Scarpa's drawings recollect the intellectual and physical activity of inventing and constructing architecture, which makes them unsuitable as gallery art. Exhibition as the aim of representation alienates drawings from making buildings by transforming them into ocularcentric objects of exchange. Similarly, digital representations collapse the generative tripartite translatory process of architecture – imaginaries; representations; construction, preceding inhabitation – into a deceptively singular process of imaging simulations, with construction approximating extrusion. Increasingly optimized processes of depicting and production isolates architecture from the imaginative process of design as demonstration. Ultimately, standardized industrialized modes of production and digital representations, simulated by built form, are distant from every aspect and phase of Scarpa's work.[49]

Through drawing, Scarpa translated his intense engagement with artworks into narrativized museum and gallery settings facilitating encounters with things displayed, by recollecting the artistic processes that brought them into existence. Inflected craft sensibilities, and attendant organization of labour – an artisan's workshop populated with collaborators – made it possible for Scarpa to orchestrate *interart* encounters that were unique in their time but nearly unimaginable now. Combined with exacting assemblages of material, mediated by lavishly articulated joints, Scarpa's work remains countercultural.

The joint

While Scarpa's drawings prefigure joy in making, demonstrable delight is most emphatically pronounced by details. The materials they join and how they are made make Scarpa's joints the signal *events* of revivified craft. Overall perceivable form or image is subordinated to multiple lines of sight and directions of travel. Planes; solids; and thresholds; changes of level; variations of finish and colour; and modulated light (controlled effects of natural light and manipulation of shadows) are all mediated by joints. Visible marks of manufacture throughout – of the old, the new and points of intersection between them – introduce temporal lines that contribute to the prefigurative incompleteness of his architecture, which only movement makes sensible.

The unique artworks and other objects housed in Scarpa's museums and galleries are material components of his spatiotemporal narratives that return a purpose to them, thereby augmenting their significance rather than diminishing it. As space-defining elements, artworks and display apparatus accentuate the three-dimensionality, and experiential richness, of the galleries. Materials and elements of existing buildings are integral to interventions in them, as generative of Scarpa's new work. Similarly for internal and external found conditions, as for garden and building, and materials and elements, including earth, sky and water. Each is integrated as generative material in ways that do not overwrite them.

While Kahn and Scarpa conceptualized the joint as the origin of ornament, they manifested it differently. In Kahn's work, ornament persists in joints, as the resolution of constructed connections between parts and materials. He emphasizes the generative originary power of details as ornament fantasies of degree-zero moments in architecture. Kahn's joints are minimalist expressions of material and construction, as are Scarpa's though more elaborately articulated. By making details explicitly ornamental, Scarpa recollects Renaissance architect Alberti's conception of beauty as an underlying – invisible – idea made perceptible by the auxiliary light of ornament. Baroque where Kahn is elemental, Scarpa's joints are equally details emerging out of adoration for construction, rather than compensating for its limits. Despite the coldness of industrial production, Scarpa and Kahn conserved joy in making with detailed connections between two or more elements, or materials.

With Classical ornament inoperative, details are substitutes for carving.[50] Inevitably, Scarpa's extravagant details analogize buildings of the past adorned with figures. By recollecting the carving, reliefs and statuary, of Classical architecture as post-figurative abstractions, Scarpa's architecture is viscerally comprehensible, which aligns him with modernist architecture only up to a point. Both may achieve signification through structural expression, attentiveness to detailing and material richness but Scarpa's joints (between materials, spaces and elements) are more intensely configured than coolly technical. Although when expression in Scarpa's work verges towards the literal it begins to suggest kitsch but this achieves figurative resonances.

The surplus energy of Scarpa's details bridges oppositions beyond materials that modernism deemed irreconcilable: past and future; tradition and innovation; craft and industrial production. Manifestly physical, and emphatically made, the circular rhythms of Scarpa's joints confound the clockwork time and linearity of modernity, to reveal materials, components and artworks as figuratively functional. Mediating time and place is the central story, intensified by the surreality of Scarpa's encounters with existing historic buildings and artworks in his exhibit designs.

Tactility of vision

Desire for proximity to artworks in museums tends to be frustrated by imperatives of conservation and security: *do not touch*; *do not cross the line*. Such acts 'of authority' fill visitors with a 'sense of constraint'.[51] Captivating works of art draw one closer, intensifying longing for physical contact. Unresolved tensions between wanting to touch and its prohibition defeat most museum displays, alienating visitors and exacerbating museum fatigue. Frustrated desire for proximity is a primary cause of the psychophysical condition of museum fatigue; physical exertions associated with trying to get closer are a secondary cause.[52]

In his meditation on the 'Problem of Museums', French poet, essayist and philosopher Paul Valéry (1871–1945) indexes their conventional deficiencies. According to him: 'Only an irrational civilization, and one devoid of a taste for pleasure could have devised such a domain of incoherence … Modern man, worn out as he is by the immensity of technical resources is also impoverished by the sheer excess of his riches.'[53] In tandem with overabundance; poor lighting (natural or artificial); stale internal air; and frustrating displays contribute to museum fatigue:

> Dreariness, boredom, the fine weather I left outside, my pricks of conscience, and a dreadful sense of how many great artists there are, all walk along with me. … I stagger out of this temple with a splitting head – and extreme fatigue, accompanied sometimes by an almost painful activity of mind[54]

Though drawn to museums out of desire or obligation, the experience disappoints Valéry: 'delight has little to do with the principles of classification, conservation and public utility.'[55] In contradistinction, Scarpa's pleasurable galleries court delight. A deeper understanding of this achievement is facilitated by Adorno's reflections on the contradictory conditions of museums. According to Adorno, the very existence of museums makes them collections of, 'objects to which the observer no longer has a vital relationship and which are in the process of dying. They owe their preservation more to historical respect than to the needs of the present.'[56] Although museums are valued as secular temples (dedicated to the revelatory mysteries of art), Valéry introduces doubts: 'Presently I lose all sense of why I have intruded into this wax-floored solitude, savouring of temple and drawing room, of cemetery and school. . . . Did I come for instruction, for my own beguilement, or simply as a duty and out of convention?'[57]

Short of permitting forbidden access, museum design is challenged to make vision a surrogate for touch, which Scarpa achieves by responding to each of Valéry's complaints, including alleviating the cognitive overload affiliated with crowding *stuff* together. Experientially, the distinctive qualities of Scarpa's museum and exhibit designs are sensual rejoinders to Valéry's lamentations, which take account of the paradoxes Adorno outlines: 'Museums are like family sepulchres of works of art. They testify to the neutralization of culture. Art treasures are hoarded in them, and their market value leaves no room for the pleasures of looking at them. Nevertheless, that pleasure is dependent on museums.'[58] Adorno raises a paradox: *museums are unpleasurable tombs but pleasure in art depends on them.* Since Valéry's time, and Adorno's commentary, museum design has improved. Nevertheless, the general condition persists; though Scarpa's Canoviano and Castelvecchio are exceptions that make intimate interactions with art possible (even without touching).

Scarpa's museums

By recuperating architecture's traditional role as the *mother of the arts* (their first home), Scarpa's museums and galleries address one of Valéry's harshest criticisms:

> Painting and sculpture, says my Demon of Analysis are both foundlings. Their mother, Architecture is dead. So long as she lived, she gave them their place, their function and discipline. They had no freedom to stray. They had their exact allotted space and given light, their subjects and their relationship. . . . While architecture was alive, they knew their function. . . .[59]

As living architecture sheltering art, Scarpa's museums respond comprehensively to Valéry's assertions. By revealing touch – even virtual – as a precondition of making, they adroitly facilitate close (revelatory) experiences of two- and three-dimensional artworks. As distinctly modern places for art, they are built out of the sort of dialectical predicaments Adorno introduces, including:

> When discontent with museums is strong enough to provoke the attempt to exhibit paintings in their original surroundings or in ones similar ... the result is even more distressing than when the works are wrenched from their original surroundings and then brought together ... [into the] the hodge-podge of collections.[60]

In the absence of one's own art collection, it is only possible to 'become familiar with painting and sculpture ... in museums'.[61] If replicating the original surroundings of specific works of art, or the secondary settings of private collections, is worse than dislocation, Scarpa's galleries are alternatives that neither fatigue nor cajole. For example, his Castelvecchio galleries overcome problems of rehousing displaced site-specific artworks without producing simulacra of the original settings, even in restructured existing buildings.

Scarpa's galleries respond to the ruptured ontological conditions that make continuity fantasies untenable on this side of twentieth-century catastrophes. The pragmatic approach to the predicament of severed tradition Adorno outlines is suggestive of Scarpa's valuing of cultural inheritances, even as he confronted the irresolvable conundrum of what to do with them now:

> Anyone who thinks that art can be reproduced in its original form through an act of the will is trapped in hopeless romanticism. Modernizing the past does it much violence and little good. But to renounce radically the possibility of experiencing the traditional would be to capitulate to barbarism out of devotion to culture. That the world is out of joint is shown everywhere in the fact that however a problem is solved, the solution is false.[62]

Architecturally transposing Adorno's philosophical assertions, Scarpa deftly avoids futile reappropriation of the past, without renouncing tradition. For Scarpa, the joint is the mediating element of revitalized interart relationships but also responds to an unhinged world by articulating momentary respite. The carefully orchestrated supports for painting and other works in Scarpa's galleries deconstruct virtual barriers between visitors and artworks, prefiguring convergences that are surrealist in spirit. For example, distancing pedestals become inviting imaginary steps towards sculpture, while painting displays recollect easels.

Gipsoteca Canoviano

Scarpa's Gipsoteca Canoviano is a purpose-built addition to the Museo Canoviano, comprising Neoclassical sculptor Antonio Canova's (1757–1822) studio, birth house, plaster studies for marble statues, plaster copies of completed works, original works in marble and other artefacts. Although an extension of the original barrel-vaulted Neoclassical Gipsoteca gallery, Scarpa's intervention is reasonably autonomous, perceived as independent from the rest of the complex (internally and externally) while also intensifying the uncanny qualities of Neoclassical art and architecture (the stark white casts housed in the likewise original gallery). Mediating between the pre-existing gallery structure, seventeenth-century house, grounds and surroundings,

Figure 4.5 Museo Canoviano. Gipsoteca, Carlo Scarpa, Architect. [Photo: Nathaniel Coleman, 2007].

Scarpa's intervention opens up readings of Neoclassicism otherwise concealed by its preternatural starkness.

By being *almost perfect – thereby complete – in nearly every way, such that nothing could be added to it nor taken away but for the worse*, the gallery discloses itself as a heuristic of architectural poetics; amplified by its relatively small size and exceedingly clear purpose (adding display area to the Gipsoteca). The structure is a masterful demonstration of display and analogy, affirming Scarpa's preoccupation with internal sources of architectural significance: material, finish, form, structure; lighting, colour, sequence, level changes, site negotiation; details and mechanisms of display. In short, architectural meaning derives from building elements and use, rather than from represented contents external to it, or random meanings dumped into it, as though it were empty.

The structure is neither an isotropic white box nor is it burdened by the stifling qualities of the existing gallery, and of museums in general. As in all of his display work, visitors are invited to partake of the processes of artist and architect alike. Lighting and spatial clarity contribute to the airiness of the building, echoing but not mimicking certain Neoclassical qualities; making the setting a suitable homage to Canova and appropriate to the works housed. Materials, colours and natural illumination augment the lightness produced by the spatial planning. Light colours, offset by darker metal and wood displays, windows and a door contribute to the gallery's luminosity, which, combined with the white sculptures on view, gesture towards the conceptually hermetically sealed older Neoclassical gallery it extends. Although adjacent to it, Scarpa's agile topographical negotiations of the confined site establishes his structure's – volumetrically enhanced – independence from the original gallery. His Canoviano addition is lateral; a sort of architecture of landscape, which its interstitial character amplifies. Though woven into the site, it is not self-abnegating but rather unmonumental. Anticipated movement – use – determines the arrangement more so than either form or image.

Seemingly illuminated from all directions, the space is flooded with natural light but glare is expertly controlled. In particular, four varying sized metal and glass cubic roof lights, above each corner of the tallest gallery space, conduct the sky's varying colours and streams of light inward. In contrast to the tomblike earlier gallery, its airiness, loose planning and abundance of light make the Canoviano reminiscent of an artist's studio.

Neoclassical in spirit only, the Canoviano echoes the blank walls, emphatically defined columns, precise geometric forms, light and whiteness, of the style, including its references to idealized ancient classical models (especially Greek) and degree-zero primitive huts. These qualities inevitably also suggest twentieth-century modernist architecture, because Neoclassical clarity – in response to Rococo excrescence – was a crucial source for modernist reforms of nineteenth-century eclecticism.

As with all of his gallery work, Scarpa's Cannoviano would be meaningless without the art displayed, which is content as much as material. The interaction between displayed objects and building prepares it to receive visitors, who are also integral. In almost every detail, the nuanced appropriateness of Scarpa's galleries overcomes clinical, or scientific, display (of typical modernist exhibit spaces) with visceral sensuality. By dissolving

Figure 4.6 Canoviano Interior Roof Lights. Carlo Scarpa, Architect. [Photo: Nathaniel Coleman, 2007].

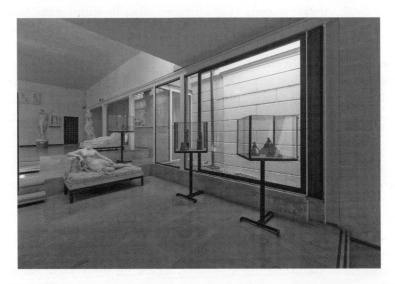

Figure 4.7 Canoviano Interior. Carlo Scarpa, Architect. [Photo: Nathaniel Coleman, 2007].

emotional distance, the settings are less archive, or machines for cultural consumption, than spaces of encounter.

Italian architecture historian Luciana Miotto (1936–2008) puts Scarpa's Canoviano gallery into perspective: 'The only museum Scarpa built *ex novo* is in Possagno: with that small building he produced in embryonic form (*in nuce*) the most significant evolution of museums in our time, one need only consider Libeskind's [Jewish] museum in Berlin.'[63] (Translation by author.)

Castelvecchio Museum

Scarpa's discontinuous restructuring of the Museo di Castelvechhio between 1957 and 1975 plots an emotional, temporal and spatial collapse between visitors and artworks. As in his work generally, the Castelvecchio Museum returns architecture to the fine arts but this reworking is the most concentrated demonstration of his display method. In existence since 1925, the Museum is housed in a building of several parts within a fortified complex constructed and altered over a long duration, from medieval origins to Napoleon era expansion. Scarpa's reimagining of the municipal museum comprises a unique reinstallation of its large collection of paintings, sculpture and other objects, spanning from the medieval to the eighteenth century.[64]

The Castelvecchio is a sprawling object lesson in how visitors can be reconnected with artworks, architects with art and the public with the processes of both. Scarpa's careful use of materials, determined detailing, precise organization of gallery spaces and distinct methods of display mediate his interventions, the existing structure and artworks to orchestrate intimate interart encounters. As elsewhere, his Castelvecchio interventions required precise reference points to establish comprehensibility out of distinct parts: courtyard; entrance; the palace itself; *il Sacello* (small stone tiled cube protruding from the ground floor façade into the garden); the galleries; and the Cangrande equestrian statue; all organized along dynamic lines of movement, threading through the museum collection. The history and architecture of the Castle complex, and the specific character of Verona – medieval structure, especially walls, local forms and use of stone and marble – are the sources of the forms, materials and modes of construction he employed for his interventions in the pre-existing layered fabric of the museum precinct.[65]

Emplotment

Narrative emplotment of the Castelvecchio galleries encompasses architecture, art and display (morphology), in concert with detailing (syntax) and materials (semantics). Experience of the Museum is structured out of its 'diverse elements': historical references; existing structure and precinct; Verona; parts of the museum collection; and the materials and methods of construction. By organizing diversity 'into an imaginative order, in … the same way … the plot of a story' does, Scarpa convincingly configures multiple 'events, agents and objects', organizing the Castelvecchio in a manner that 'renders those individual elements meaningful as part of a larger whole in which each takes a place in the network that constitutes the narrative's response to why, how, who, where, when, etc.'[66] A complex, discontinuous, associative whole is assembled from distinct parts, drawn together by compelling spatial narratives, rendered comprehensible by material, detail, colour and display. Describing the Castelvecchio as emplotted derives from French philosopher Paul Ricoeur (1913–2005), whose preoccupation with time and narrative is suggestive of Scarpa's mode of thinking and working. *Emplotment* provides precise terms for describing Scarpa's work and method that extends beyond the limits of modernist architectural discourse:

> By bringing together heterogeneous factors into its syntactical order emplotment creates a 'concordant discordance', a tensive unity which functions as a redescription of a situation in which the internal coherence of the constitutive elements endows them with an explanatory role.[67]

Bodies in motion, through the time and space of the galleries, give form to Scarpa's narratives of experience. Despite some descriptions of his work as fragmented (as if anticipating some whole), or discontinuous (suggesting intermittence or inconsistence), *narrative emplotment* is more accurate, because it shifts attention from form, or formal coherence, to materials, unfolding embodied experience and use.

Figure 4.8 Museo di Castelvecchio (1957–64; 1968–69; 1973–75), Verona, Italy. Carlo Scarpa, Architect. [Photo: Nathaniel Coleman, 2007].

Castelvecchio magic

The temporal simultaneity of Scarpa's work and working methods is less a rejection of modernity and its trappings – technology and industrialization for example – than a means of recollecting the present as doubly anticipatory; of the future and the past as its ground. The richness of his formal, spatial and material encounters derived from a rhythmical cohabitation of past, present and future in his imagination, making it possible for him to be modern while embracing inheritances from the past, without directly copying elements or motifs. Although self-described as medieval, or Byzantine in temperament, his feeling for the antique was neither historicist nor revivalist, in large part because his surrealist habits of mind made literal reproduction impossible.

By operating within the *whole* of history – no matter how distant in time or space – Scarpa drew upon a general cultural inheritance as generative source material for interpretations in the present – liberated from the limitations of historicism, paralysing myths of progress and novelty. He borrowed freely; perhaps *justified* by his transcultural self-identity but more so because of shared spatiotemporal inheritances of the body. By excluding replication, Scarpa could make the foreign local, independent of claims to either authenticity or place of origin. Nevertheless, his acts of transliteration were bound to place (no matter how arbitrary). Past and elsewhere are never appropriated literally but together furnish contents of future imaginaries, which approximate an eternal present perpetually renewed.

Displaying machines

The Castelvecchio entry portal is one joint amongst many at the Museum; here between the galleries and garden enclosed within the precinct's heavy red brick defensive walls, which separates the inner sanctum from Verona. Once in the courtyard, Scarpa's material play begins in earnest: the green grass and shrubs; gravel; water elements reflecting light and building; stones of many types and colours; metal; and concrete, all form counterpoints to the bulk of the museum's stuccoed exterior walls. There are complex sequences of orientating devices, including an 'L' shaped tinted concrete wall edged with metal that extends outward from the building into the courtyard to draw visitors inward, towards the initial galleries, populated with medieval art, primarily statues.

Prepared by the preliminary complexities of the entry sequence, Scarpa makes the sculptures within the ground floor galleries come *alive*; refilled with the animating spirit they conceivably had when originally carved. The numerous wood and metal mechanisms of display he invented for presenting the artworks guides visitors through the galleries. Each displaying *machine* challenges the lifelessness of conventional displays by recollecting exertions ostensibly bound up with carving the sculptures, and the manual effort and mechanics required to position them, especially the combinations of metal hardware and wood. The implied and actual movement plotted by the galleries (signalled on the floor, ceiling and at thresholds), in combination with the display apparatus, renders the works dynamic.

Figure 4.9 Museo di Castelvecchio (1957–64; 1968–69; 1973–75), Verona, Italy. Carlo Scarpa, Architect. [Photo: Nathaniel Coleman, 2007].

To avoid temporal confusion, Scarpa always identifies his interventions as modern but tensions remain, especially where wood and metal join. A revivified medieval energy is conjured up throughout, characterized by a kind of pre-modern fascination with how things go together, how they operate and the materials out of which they are made, which returns palpable pleasure to them, especially the metalwork. The extruded, clipped together or glued, so common today, is not part of the story. Every connection is articulated. Every job presents an opportunity to invent another *machine*, primarily for displaying artworks but also to span voids, open and close doorways, suspend elements, or to attenuate light or produce it, amongst other mechanisms that intensify visceral encounters with materializations of human effort.

The avoidance of extrusion in favour of expressed connections makes Scarpa's details cognate with pre-modern craft. Despite overheated detailing and obsessive consideration of every element, Scarpa's settings are attuned to human rhythms, which makes them serene and encourages recollections of art's revelatory potential. Such composure is especially evident at the Brion Monumental complex, where tombs and other funerary elements are simultaneously sculptures in a tranquil garden of death and apparatus for conducting meaning, remembrance and contemplation.

Flying horses

The most audacious of the Castelvecchio's many magic moments is at the eastern end of the main museum block, closest to the medieval Ponte Scaligero, which crosses through the Castelvecchio site and then the Adige River. Here, Scarpa's surrealist logic explodes into view.

In a manner akin to the chestburster scene in Ridely Scott's film *Alien* (1979), the main ground and first-floor galleries *erupt* out of the main museum block at its eastern end, revealed as bodies within the host body of the existing structure. In this astonishing jointed moment, the foreign body of Scarpa's intervention subsumes the carcass of the existing building, producing a moment of dramatic juncture and *explosive* rupture. However, the threat of chaos is contained by the rough stone and brick wall in front (through which the *explosion* extends by way of wood, metal and concrete extensions), the adjacent concrete riverside wall and the courtyard garden moat to the side and below, which promises to contain any *scattered* fragments. The linkages here to the rest of the museum, on both ground and first floors, are like hinges and shots, especially the bridge at the first-floor level.

The intensity of this episode is orchestrated to produce a climax appropriate to one of the most prized objects in the collection: the fourteenth-century Italian Cangrande equestrian statue, originally part of the Veronese della Scala family tomb. Although numerous episodes at the Castelvecchio ensnare visitors within surrealist scenarios that collapse alienating distances, none is more powerful than the Cangrande display. Scarpa's unique solution hints at the original local importance of the family the statue represents, while heightening the thrill of the whole setting. The statue seems ready to take flight, to escape its podium and the walls of the museum, perhaps to rejoin the tomb from whence it came. With this joint, extravagant detailing is at a gargantuan scale, not typically associated with details, which are expected to be small-scale decorative, or technical, connections (Plate 2).

The explosive impact of the Cangrande installation is perpetually startling. In this imperishable event, the subversive atmosphere of the museum is confirmed. By stealth, the antique modern that builds up momentum through the succession of galleries reaches its climax, intensified by the orchestration of existing and new materials and elements, particularly the concrete additions and the shift in roof material from terracotta tiles to copper:

> The [Cangrande] figure, first of all placed almost out of reach, is presented to the viewer from the most unlikely angles, almost as a kind of demon, both familiar and disquieting, the pivot point of a dynamic, diffused, ragged, space … There is undeniably something 'surreal' in the apparition of Cangrande to the visitor of Castelvecchio, whether he reaches it along the catwalk crossing a sheer drop, or views it from below from one of the many other angles available. The passage to the other reality is simultaneously mediated by materials and forms … As is shown by the arrangement devised for Cangrande, Scarpa's respect for history by no means excludes his taking pleasure in playing with it.[68]

In the preceding passage, Tafuri outlines the unique character of the Cangrande installation, which illuminates aspects of Scarpa's exhibit work more generally. For example, artworks are ingenuously placed both within and out of reach, spatially and temporally, which intensifies the shock of encounters with them. In this instance, 'unlikely angles' and a 'catwalk crossing a sheer drop' dislocate visitor and statue alike. Cangrande becomes a flying 'demon', an 'apparition', 'familiar' through age but 'disquieting' because strangeness has been returned to it, making the whole experience – 'mediated by materials and forms' – 'surreal'. Waking reality slips into a dream realm, opened up, and joined, by a 'passage to the other reality'. As Tafuri observes, Scarpa could only have orchestrated this bewildering 'pivot point of' the 'dynamic, diffused, ragged, space' of the Museum by respecting 'history' while simultaneously 'playing with it'.[69]

Tafuri's further analysis of the Cangrande display clarifies it as a concentrated example of Scarpa's museum method: First; 'The sequence of materials in forms carefully studied so as to achieve effects of discontinuity always has a precise aim: the work is subtly, yet decisively "alienated" from its context, suspended in its own specific time, while snatched from spatial and temporal indefinition', which returns displayed artworks to their own time; transporting visitors there as well. Second; 'The measure used in the abstractions that give life to the mediating devices developed for the supports is the mark of Scarpa's profound respect for the work of art'. The distinctive detailing of the display apparatus contributes to its *time machine function* of transporting artworks back to their 'specific time', along with visitors. Third; 'Scarpa invites us to accept the discontinuity of historic time, to work with it, to "fashion" it by means of successive constructions'. He 'explored the limits of this game' by giving it 'free play within a careful reading of the works themselves …, involving the relation between the many kinds of time in the collective memory'. As such, Scarpa foregoes the *scientific* linear time of art history and museums in favour of more intimate temporal rhythms. Fourth; using the three 'instruments' just outlined, Scarpa achieved the following on multiple occasions: 'In some way, the works Scarpa installed in their places seem *liberated*: liberated from traditional bonds, set free for new interpretations, liberated as problematic images, stimulating us to wonder about their meaning'.[70]

Art, architecture, experience

The spatial, material and formal discontinuousness of Scarpa's architecture is counterbalanced by conceptual comprehensiveness, mediated by drawing and construction. He restored the Castelvecchio, determined the location of each object in the collection and invented the elements for hanging, mounting, housing and lighting them. All the physical and curatorial aspects of the museum emplot the displayed artefacts and visitors' experiences of the whole through its parts.[71] The overall effect intensifies object meaning, individually and collectively, facilitating vital experiences of them as *alive*.

If Scarpa's Gipsoteca Canoviano is – in its clarity – Neoclassically cool, his Castelvecchio smoulders, appropriate to the Medieval and Renaissance art it mostly houses. In every instance, his sensitivity to context – encompassing sociocultural temporalities, along with topography, and climate – greatly expanded conceptions of the origins of the works housed. Accordingly, he reveals *appropriate display* as above all else a matter of atmosphere, conceived of critically and historically, beyond simply emphasizing dramatic differences in mood. Scarpa's architecture is shaped around a different sort of functionalism, neither exactly technical nor exactly emotional but rather determined by profound empathy for the multidimensional specifics of each work and the place of his intervention. Emplotment in anticipation of visitor presence and experience of the art, building and display apparatus is key, with each a matter of material, making and conception.

Close the museums?

Scarpa's complex revelatory encounter with tradition was arguably a response to the new cultural conditions of Europe (and beyond) after the Second World War, during which mourning for what has been lost parallels museums' ascendance to secular temples, then entertainment complexes and subsequently shopping malls. Because of their sepulchral character, closing museums might seem promising, if doing so at least returned culture to the streets. However, almost contemporaneously with Scarpa's work on the Canoviano and Castelvecchio, Adorno cautioned against renouncing 'culture out of loyalty to it'; by closing museums, for example:

> The museums will not be shut, nor would it even be desirable to shut them. The natural-history collections of the spirit have actually transformed works of art into the hieroglyphics of history and brought them a new content while the old one shrivelled up. No conception of pure art, borrowed from the past and yet inadequate to it, can be offered to offset this fact.[72]

As anachronistic as it is paradoxical, Scarpa's excavation of lost associations between architecture and the arts intensifies the value of painting and sculpture (amongst other artefacts). He concentrates on the new content of art, rather than the shrivelled-up old one but never renounces 'culture out of loyalty to it'. His museums parallel Adorno in another way; they invite us to treat art with 'deadly seriousness'. For both, concentrated viewing is a form of meditation, while slowed movement can recuperate the *shock* of art by enabling its disclosure of other truths, inaccessible to either rationalism or science. As Adorno observes:

> it is no longer possible to stroll through museums letting oneself be delighted here and there. The only relation to art that can be sanctioned in a reality that stands under the constant threat of catastrophe is one that treats works of art with the same deadly seriousness that characterizes the world today.[73]

At the Castelvecchio, painting and sculpture are anything but adjuncts to architecture, rather, by being given a generous home within it, it is possible, if only for a moment, to steal access to art in a position of import far weightier than that of diversionary objects of entertainment, or instruments of investment, or aesthetic pleasure.

Scarpa and after

Although Scarpa's mode of practice seems defunct – eclipsed by the globalized building industry – it persists as a varied, refreshingly obsessive, model for alternatives. If his approach appears unviable, his artisans' organization survives as a robust countercurrent: less unsustainably heroic and uncritically global than typical practices; local but also more convincingly recession proof.

Tenuous traces of Scarpa's obsessions persist; in Zumthor's work, in one direction, in Williams and Tsien's in another, as well as in Miralles's. There is, however, no sense in attempting to identify literal continuances of his approach in the work of anyone. In the first instance, doing so is irrelevant; in the second, it is doomed to failure. Any convincing evidence would simply confirm dull derivativeness. Scarpa's legacy is a record of making that exists outside the narrow confines of industrialized building production, and the perishing expressions of so-called icon architecture. Material and making are his modes of articulation – from drawing to building, which only experience makes sensible. Scarpa's work reenchants architecture by way of material obsession, combined with an equal ardour for process, and modes of production. Encounters with his work set in motion imaginings that suturing past and present might actually make it possible to invent nontrivial architecture, despite ever diminishing prospects.

Notes

1. See, Giuseppe Mazzariol and Giuseppe Barbieri, 'The Life of Carlo Scarpa'; and Francesco Dal Co, 'The Architecture of Carlo Scarpa', in *Carlo Scarpa: The Complete Works*, Francesco Dal Co and Giuseppe Mazzariol (eds), Milano/New York: Electa/Rizzoli, (1984) 1985, pp. 9–23, 24–69.

2. Mazzariol and Barbieri, 'The Life of Carlo Scarpa', p. 20.

3. See, Paul Ricoeur, 'Universal Civilization and National Cultures', in *History and Truth*, Charles A. Kelbley (trans.), Evanston, IL: Northwestern University Press, 1965, pp. 271–84; Kenneth Frampton, 'Six Points for an Architecture of Resistance', in *The Anti-Aesthetic: Essays on Postmodern Culture*, Hal Foster (ed.), New York: The New Press, 1998 [1983], pp. 17–34; Fredric Jameson, 'The Constraints of Postmodernism', *The Seeds of Time*, New York: Columbia University Press, 1994, pp. 129–205.

4. Scarpa recollected; 1991 interview with his client, Aldo Businaro, quoted in Giuseppe Zambonini, 'Process and Theme in the Work of Carlo Scarpa', *Perspecta*, 20 (1983): 21–42 (p. 22).

5. Frampton, 'Carlo Scarpa and the Adoration of the Joint', in *Studies in Tectonic Culture*, pp. 299–332.

6. Louis I Kahn (1974), 'Forward', in *Carlo Scarpa Architetto Poeta*, London: Royal Institute of British Architects, unnumbered pages, reprinted in Louis I. Kahn, *Writings, Lectures, Interviews*, Alessandra Latour (ed.), New York: Rizzoli, 1991, p. 332.

7. Marco Frascari, 'The Lume Materiale in the Architecture of Venice', *Perspecta*, 24 (1988): 136–45; Frascari, 'A Heroic and Admirable Machine: The Theater of the Architecture of Carlo Scarpa, Architetto Veneto', *Poetics Today*, 10, no. 1, Art and Literature I (Spring, 1989): 103–26.

8. Ruskin, *The Stones of Venice* (1960 [1851–1853]), p. 13.

9. On surrealism, see: Phil Powrie, 'The Surrealist *Poème-Objet*', in *Surrealism: Surrealist Visuality*, Silvano Levy (ed.), Great Britain: Keele University Press, 1996, pp. 57–77.

10. See, Nathaniel Coleman, 'Is Beauty Still Relevant? Is Art? Is Architecture?', *Architecture Philosophy*, 1, no. 1 (2014): 81–95.

11. Manfredo Tafuri (1973), *Architecture and Utopia: Design and Capitalist Production*, Barabara Luigia La Penta (trans.), Cambridge, MA: MIT Press, 1975, pp. x, 182.

12. Tafuri, *History of Italian Architecture, 1944–1985*, p. 111.

13. Ibid.

14. Carlo Scarpa, 'Interview with Carlo Scarpa' (1978), in *Carlo Scarpa: The Complete Works*, p. 297.

15. Ibid., Scarpa, 'Can Architecture Be Poetry?' (1976), p. 283.

16. Ibid.

17. Ibid., Scarpa, 'A Thousand Cypresses' (1978), p. 279.

18. Ibid., Scarpa, 'Letter of the Venetian Rationalists' (1931), p. 287.

19. Ibid., Scarpa, 'Interview with Carlo Scarpa' (1978), p. 297.

20. Ibid., Tafuri, *History of Italian Architecture, 1944–1985*, note 01, chapter 6, p. 229. See, Francesco Dal Co and Giuseppe Mazzariol (eds), *Carlo Scarpa, Complete Works*, Milano: Electa/Rizzoli, (1984) 1985. More have subsequently followed.

21. For Tafuri's theorization of capitalism as 'total system', see Fredric Jameson, 'Architecture and the Critique of Ideology' (1982), in *Architecture, Criticism, Ideology*, Joan Ockman, Deborah Berke, and Mary McLeod (eds), Princeton: Princeton Architectural Press, 1985, pp. 442–61.

22. Frascari, 'A Heroic and Admirable Machine . . .', pp. 103–26 (p. 103).

23. Ibid., p. 104.

24. Ibid., p. 105.

25. Ibid., pp. 106–7.

26. Ibid., p. 108.

27. Ibid., p. 109.

28. Frascari, 'Review: *Carlo Scarpa the Complete Works*', *JAE*, 41, no. 1 (Fall, 1987): 54–6 (p. 54).

29. Frampton, *Studies in Tectonic Culture. . .* , p. 332.

30. Lyman Tower Sargent, 'Review: Is there only One Utopian Tradition', *Journal of the History of Ideas*, 43, no. 4. (October–December 1982): 687. See, Zambonini, 'Process and Theme in the Work of Carlo Scarpa', pp. 21–42; and, Frascari, 'A Heroic and Admirable Machine . . .', pp. 103–26.

31. Giuseppe Zambonini, 'Notes for a Theory of Making in a Time of Necessity', *Perspecta*, 24 (1988): 23.

32. Ibid., pp. 22–3.

33. Tafuri, 'Carlo Scarpa and Italian Architecture', in *Carlo Scarpa: The Complete Works*, p. 86.

34. Zambonini, 'Notes for a Theory of Making in a Time of Necessity', p. 13.

35. Livio Dimitriu and Mario Botta, 'Achitecture and Morality: An Interview with Mario Botta', *Perspecta*, 20 (1983): 126–7.

36. Tafuri, 'Cultura e Fanatasia di Carlo Scarpa', Paese Sera, 3 December 1978, reprinted in Zambonini, 'Process and Theme in the Work of Carlo Scarpa', p. 23.

37. Tafuri, 'Carlo Scarpa and Italian Architecture', pp. 85, 86, 92, 95.

38. Marco Frascari, 'The Tell-Tale Detail', *VIA* 7 (1984): 22–37 (p. 36).

39. Ibid.

40. Frampton, *Studies in Tectonic Culture. . .* , p. 310.

41. Tafuri, 'Carlo Scarpa and Italian Architecture', p. 95.

42. Frascari, 'A Heroic and Admirable Machine . . .', p. 110.

43. Ibid., p. 111.

44. Ibid.

45. Tafuri, *History of Italian Architecture, 1944–1985*, p. 114.

46. Ibid.

47. Zambonini, 'Notes for a Theory of Making in a Time of Necessity', p. 220.

48. See, Tafuri, *Architecture and Utopia*; Coleman, *Utopias and Architecture*; Coleman, *Lefebvre for Architects*.

49. For more on architectural drawing, see: Hubert Damisch, 'The Drawings of Carlo Scarpa', in *Carlo Scarpa: The Complete Works*, pp. 209–13; Robin Evans, 'Translations from Drawing to Building' (1986), in *Translations from Drawing to Building and Other Essays*, London: Architectural Association Publications, 1997, pp. 153–93; Frascari, *Eleven Exercises in the Art of Architectural Drawing: Slow Food for the Architect's Imagination*, London and New York: Routledge, 2011; Alberto Pérez-Goméz and Louise Pelletier, *Architectural Representation and the Perspective Hinge*, Cambridge, MA: MIT Press, 1997; Joseph Rykwert, 'Translation and/or Representation', *RES: Anthropology and Aesthetics*, no. 34 (Autumn, 1998): 64–70; David Ross Scheer, *The Death of Drawing: Architecture in the Age of Simulation*, London and New York: Routledge, 2014.

50. For a discussion on ornament relevant to the ornamental, or decorative, qualities of Scarpa's work, see, Anada K. Coomaraswamy, 'Ornament', *The Art Bulletin*, 21, no. 4 (December 1939): 375–82.

51. Paul Valéry, 'The Problem of Museums' (1923), in *The Collected Works of Paul Valéry Volume 12: Degas, Manet, Morisot*, Jackson Mathews (ed.), David Paul (trans.), London: Routledge & Keegan Paul, 1960, p. 206.

52. Although the proposition here is speculative, 'Museum Fatigue' was first diagnosed more than a century ago, and continues to be studied; one of the earliest studies, and a more recent overview, include: Benjamin Ives Gilman, 'Museum Fatigue', *The Scientific Monthly*, 2, no. 1 (January 1916): 62–74; and Gareth Davey, 'What Is Museum Fatigue?' *Visitor Studies Today*, 8, no. 3 (2005): 17–21.

53. Valéry, 'The Problem of Museums' (1923), pp. 203–4.

54. Ibid., pp. 203, 205.

55. Ibid., p. 202.

56. Theodor W. Adorno, 'Valéry Proust Museum' (1955), in *Prisms*, Samuel and Sherry Weber (trans.), Cambridge, MA: MIT Press, 1967, p. 175.

57. Valéry, 'The Problem of Museums' (1923), p. 203.

58. Adorno, 'Valéry Proust Museum' (1955), p. 175.

59. Valéry, 'The Problem of Museums' (1923), p. 206.

60. Adorno, 'Valéry Proust Museum' (1955), p. 175.

61. Ibid.

62. Ibid., p. 176.

63. Luciana Miotto, *Carlo Scarpa: I Musei*, Venezia: Marsilio, 2006, p. 90.

64. For more on the Castelvecchio Museum, see: Richard Murphy, *Carlo Scarpa and Castelvecchio Revisited*, Edinburgh: Breakfast Mission Publishing, 2017; Alba Di Lieto (ed.), *I disegni di Carlo Scarpa per Castelvecchio*, Venezia: Marsilio Editori, 2006. On the Museo Gipsoteca Canoviano, Possagno, see: Judith Carmel-Arthur and Stafan Buzas, *Carlo Scarpa. Museo Canoviano, Possagno*, Stuttgart and London: Edition Axel Menges, 2002. See also: Castelvecchio Museum, Verona official website, available from http://museodicastelvecch io.comune.verona.it/nqcontent.cfm?a_id=42555&tt=museo (internet accessed 02 February 2018). The Advent, *Catholic Encyclopedia*, on-line Catholic Encylopedia available from http://www.newadvent.org/cathen/03298b.htm (internet accessed 02 February 2018). Antonio Canova, Museo Gipsoteca, Possagno, official website, available from http://www.museocanova.it/menu.php?name=hom&lang=uk, internet (accessed 02 February 2018).

65. Much of this paragraph is indebted to, Miotto, *Carlo Scarpa: I Musei*, pp. 57–64.

66. Kim Atkins, 'Paul Ricoeur (1913–2005)', *The Internet Encyclopedia of Philosophy*. Available at: http://www.iep.utm.edu/r/ricoeur.htm (internet accessed 07 December 2018).

67. Ibid.

68. Tafuri, 'Carlo Scarpa and Italian Architecture', pp. 79, 81.

69. Ibid.

70. Ibid., p. 79.

71. Ibid., Atkins, 'Paul Ricoeur (1913–2005)'.

72. Adorno, 'Valéry Proust Museum' (1955), pp. 178, 185.

73. Ibid., p. 185.

CHAPTER 5
POOL AND CAVE: ZUMTHOR'S THERMAL BATHS AT VALS (1996)

Swiss architect Peter Zumthor's (b. 1943) preoccupation with the contribution of material to the creation of building atmosphere, and how architecture can respond to augment place, by producing desirable frameworks for inhabitation, suggests that he is the architect par excellence in the argument for material as reality preserve. However, since material is considered here as non-essentialist and non-foundationalist, in the hope of resisting a fall into what Adorno called 'the jargon of authenticity', Zumthor quickly becomes more problematic. On the one hand, he is an exemplary practitioner of material meaning in architecture; from the hard matter of concrete, stone, brick; to the liquidity of water; the more ambivalent matter of glass, or the non-matter of light, shade, air and temperature; all contribute to producible atmospheres. On the other hand, Zumthor's work perpetually drifts towards *foundations* and *essences*, with the risk of becoming a discernible *jargon of authenticity*. In much the way Scarpa's anachronistic work makes him problematic, Zumthor's apparent architectural essentialism conceivably problematizes the postulates developed in this book. It is in this spirit that his Therme building (1990–96) and renovations of the existing 1960s spa hotel complex, in Vals, Graubünden, Switzerland, are considered.

Producing place

The Therme Vals building is probably Zumthor's best-known work. Firmly establishing his reputation, the complex is a luxury spa, and a stop on an expanded architectural grand tour, a remarkable result for a project that began with reinvigorating municipal baths and subsequently updating the surrounding 1960s era hotels. Although most discussions of the Baths focus on the distinctive spa building, it is worth noting that its character and siting transformed the existing hotel structures surrounding it into a comprehensible complex. As municipal baths, they are open to all on a daily basis, whether a village resident or not, and whether staying at the hotel or not. Free and paid entry to the Therme continued in this manner from the time of its opening until at least 2012, when the local council sold off the complex to a private developer. Until then it had been managed by Zumthor's wife, Annalisa.[1]

Recollecting their long involvement with the Therme, Zumthor remarked: it 'was a social project, me and my wife lived there for almost 20 years with the community …, [who] owned [it,] and [it] was successful … It now belongs to a financial figure who bought all of it and destroyed it. The tragic thing is that it's an egotistical local guy that killed it all.'[2] Recollecting that the original motivation of the Therme Vals was to augment an existing village resource shifts perception to reveal a more altruistic civic programme, intended to dignify the municipal baths. Yet, the association of the Therme with its architect, along with the perceived super-refinement of his work, has obscured the inclusive social dimension of the project.

Surely welcoming, and a worthy enhancement of the special water filling the baths, and a social benefit for the community; nonetheless, the Therme has been identified with luxury and status from the start, inevitable considering the use, the architect's able orchestration of materials and details, and sensitive site emplacement. The qualities of the bath building and renovated spa hotel (guest rooms and public spaces), masterly managed by Annalisa Zumthor, ensured the enterprise's popularity beyond expectations, which guaranteed eventual maximum monetization of its qualities and success.

Only some firm covenant encompassing the entirety of the complex, when the baths received listed building status, could have protected the atmosphere. But as press materials from the period of the Zumthors' tenure attest; from the start, the project was bound by its predicted contribution to economic regeneration of the village: 'It is still a fragile success – it would only take a lack of confidence in the future of the valley of Vals for the [local] economy to potentially [crumble] again. But it shows what the Swiss

Figure 5.1 Vals Village, Graubünden, Switzerland. [Photo: Nathaniel Coleman, 2007].

mountain regions could be like with a masterpiece of architecture.'[3] The problem with such strategies is that continuing success depends on emphasizing destination appeal; places for visitors, rather than locals. Inevitably, the strategy was always speculative: 'Vals is off the main tourist trail, and has nothing noteworthy at first sight. It is a pretty village but there are many prettier in Switzerland.'[4]

Atmospheric roots

Located in a picturesque Alpine valley on the edge of a pleasant village, for most visitors, the onward journey (by car or bus) to the Therme Vals begins in Chur to the north and east, just over 50 kilometres away. Chur is the capital of the Graubünden canton, location of the main train and bus station, major services and three additional Zumthor projects. Some 30 kilometres from Chur, the road passes through the town of Ilanz, where travellers turn left for the final 20 kilometres to Vals along a much smaller

Figure 5.2 Vals Village Valley Entry, Graubünden, Switzerland. [Photo: Nathaniel Coleman, 2007].

road that winds its way along the mountains and through the valleys. Concentrating on the journey from Ilanz to the Therme is crucial for analysing Zumthor's building as it reveals many sources of the project's forms, materials, construction and details and atmosphere. Along the road from Ilanz to Vals, driving speeds are slower, especially where the road squeezes down to one lane without warning, or sides a vertiginous drop, edged only by flimsy wooden guard rails. For driver and passenger, the greater focus that comes with slowing down reveals the land's uniqueness, particularly negotiations with it by human inhabitation, which prepares visitors for the specifics of Vals and the Therme.

Along the way, mountains, fields, stone, streams, rivers, waterfalls, with water cascading down into valleys, come into view, as does a developing appreciation for how animals and humans have adapted to this terrain, demonstrated as much in the particularities of mountainside farming, as in the unique buildings bedded into the land. Of particular interest are the numerous small sheds that change ever so slightly from valley to valley. In these, something of Zumthor's architecture at Vals begins to emerge: hay lofts/feeding sheds, made with wood and stone and horizontal and vertical elements, assert permanence against inevitable transience. In every instance, human interventions are rooted, embedded within the place, by seeming appropriate but also more literally by being partly dug into the earth. Even the road infrastructure is topographically situated, thereby providing more source material for Zumthor's bath building.[5]

Figure 5.3 Road Infrastructure, outside Vals on road from Ilanz – farm buildings above, mountainside beyond. Graubünden, Switzerland. [Photo: Nathaniel Coleman, 2007].

Producing atmosphere

Throughout his writing, Zumthor uses the unfashionable word 'essence', or 'essences' (suggesting prelapsarian, or primordial wholeness), with its whiff of absolutes. But the drive from Ilanz to Vals, through the stark landscape, dotted with an abundance of traditional buildings, constituted from local materials, does seem to justify some talk of 'essences', no matter how *outré*. The remoteness and relative wildness of the landscape, especially the mountains and dramatic skies, conjure up the sublime, even though the land within view is largely cultivated. Upon arriving in Vals, its agreeable valley location is in parts domesticated and wild, severe and unpredictable. On more dramatic days, fog rises and clouds descend, thunder and lightning explode in the sky, the rain comes down hard, and, as a direct result, the electricity fails for a while. Then, the weather changes, the sun appears and the temperature rises; soon enough, it all changes again, as passing clouds roll across the sky.

The genius of the Therme building is its localness and the way this is communicated in siting, forms and materials. As with Scarpa, being rooted is achieved in a cosmopolitan manner. Amongst all of the locally sourced motifs in the baths building, mountains and sky are the boldest. Deployed as materials, mountains are *borrowed* as natural space-defining walls, delimiting an expanded perimeter. Mountain views are carefully framed, internally through large glazed openings, externally by large voids. The changeable sky is also pressed into service, especially as the *ceiling* for the outdoor pool and decks.

Although Zumthor asserts that in his work, material is not an end in itself, his preoccupation with atmosphere inevitably positions it at the centre of his method. Atmospheres in architecture are ultimately made out of material presences manipulated according to the intention of producing a particular effect, of light, sound, space, temperature or emotional association. At Vals, material is key to achieving perception of the desired mountain cave atmosphere, as the product of explicit authorial intent.[6] To realize it required orchestration of light, sound and temperature, amongst other palpable 'materials'. In this way, Zumthor's work gets to the heart of the matter of this book, including its central problematic: manipulating material is surely *essential* to preparing architecture for experience but when thought of as *essence*, in the sense of being either 'authentic' or 'original', material transforms into what Adorno described as a 'jargon of authenticity', a kind of specialized language intended to confirm authentic experience of the self and the world, especially in the absence of authenticity.

Zumthor's method[7]

Zumthor looks very closely all around at the setting of his future buildings. Local topography; land use, including farming; building materials; methods of building; types of building, vernacular or universal; climate; infrastructure; and so on, all provide the (material) sources of his work. His attentiveness establishes the unique lexicon of each project, at times affirmed at others negated, or even memorialized in negation. Once the lexicon is in place, the main function of the intended building is elevated to an honorific event; filtered through his self-conscious preoccupation with authorship, wholeness and the production of an *authentic original*. At its most extreme, Zumthor's *primordialism* verges towards being totalizing. The predisposition for control probably helps to explain one of the work's especially intriguing characteristics, which – when present – has a whiff of the perverse, or vaguely S&M: 'pain' as a counterpoint to 'pleasure'. In places, this comes across as almost punitive, which admittedly adds to the work's allure. The Therme dressing rooms are a multisensory example of this.

More generally, this punitive aspect is not only evident in how disciplined the bath building is, in conception and execution alike, but also in its planning, and through the imposition of atmosphere as a produced form of experience. In analogizing a series of pools within mountain caves, the claustrophobic qualities of a subterranean cave system comes across; like being in an underground labyrinth, which could produce anxiety, especially in the smaller set off bathing areas. Both small and enclosed, they are awkward when busy. Simply put, the architecture disciplines the movements of the body, mostly met by willing submission to this direction. In that moment, subject becomes object, another material at the architect's disposal. It is not so much that the architect is actively sadistic (or that inhabitants are necessarily masochistic); it is simply that this is the normal drift of things. Both architect and inhabitant could resist. Some do; most do not.

As important as material and its associative meanings are as sources of Zumthor's architecture, the result is a product of his distinct conceptualization of his role in the design and building process; in the organization of his studio, including his expectations of collaborators; his relationships with clients; and conservation of an optimum scale of practice to protect all of the modes of production required to achieve a narrowly defined outcome. All crucial for ensuring that Zumthor's 'authorship' is discernible, not only to critics, other architects and students but to *everyone*.[8] While it is surely reasonable for an architect to want to be recognizable as the author of his/her buildings, exaggerating this risks shifting emphasis from use to appearance, and therefrom to a form of exchangeable personal branding. Accordingly, cultivating *authenticity* of expression could be construed as *inauthentic*. Zumthor's preoccupation with the 'real'; 'wholeness'; and 'the inherent laws of concrete things' and the 'primal' or '"culturally innocent" attributes of elements' – their 'essence' – encourages this reading, as does his claim of 'developing an architecture that sets out from and returns to real things'.[9]

Above all else, Zumthor's appeal to Heidegger's essay 'Building Dwelling Thinking' alerts one to the darker horizons of his discourse of *authentic originals*. For example, he acknowledges: 'The concept of dwelling understood in Heidegger's wide sense of living and thinking in places and spaces, contains an exact reference to me as an architect.'[10] Developing on this, he explains:

When I try to identify the aesthetic intentions that motivate me in the process of designing buildings, I realize that my thoughts revolve around themes such as place, material, energy, presence, recollection, memories, images, density, atmosphere, permanence, and concentration ... Martin Heidegger gave the title 'Bauen, Wohnen, Denken' ('Building, Dwelling, Thinking') to an essay with his reflections on what it means to build homes and live in specific places. Building, dwelling, and thinking are activities which belong together and which men use as ways to learn about and be part of the world. Heidegger observed that our thinking, as abstract as it may seem, is closely connected with our experience of place.[11]

Although the problematic of the 'jargon of authenticity' is returned to later in the chapter, Adorno's following observation is worth noting now for the light it sheds on Zumthor's appeal to Heidegger:

> he did not foresee that what he named authentic, once become word, would grow toward the same exchange-society anonymity against which *Sein und Zeit* rebelled. The jargon, which in Heidegger's phenomenology of small talk earned an honored position, marks the adept, in their own opinion, as un trivial and of higher sensibility; while at the same time that jargon calms the constantly festering suspicion of uprootedness.[12]

For the moment, 'uprootedness' as a discomfiting condition of modernity that begs for attention, rather than calming, provides a lens for considering how Zumthor's Therme Vals might have grown 'toward the same exchange-society anonymity' it ostensibly disaffirms.

As a self-identified *auteur*, achieving 'the self-sufficient corporeal wholeness of an architectural object' is 'the essential ... aim of' Zumthor's 'work'.[13] Accomplishing this inevitably demands maintaining tight control over results by closely managing the numerous sorts of collaborations building production entails. Although work onsite can be a bit more difficult to command, doing so in the office is easier. As he describes it, 'This outfit is organized like a farmstead, like an old-style master class'. Clarifying further, he asserts: 'I paint the paintings, but I need others to contribute so I'm not alone. They have input, but it's my painting.'[14] Obviously, outcomes can only be guaranteed by tightly controlling – as much as possible – the modes of production onsite and in the office, not least by keeping it manageably small, even with the expanded geographical reach of his work.

In addition to maintaining as much control as possible over the design and production process, Zumthor is equally careful about the work he accepts. Although controlling input as the only sure way to control output might seem self-evident, most architectural practices feel compelled to grow and expand; the size of the office, the scale and scope of work taken on, as well as geographical reach. However, multiple scale shifts upward in operation all too frequently dissolve the very qualities that made expansion possible in the first place, which Zumthor fully understands, manifested in keeping the number of live projects small and by maintaining his studio's atelier scale.[15]

Stone and concrete

The most obvious material at the Therme is stone, which appears to cover nearly every surface of the structure, internal and external, other than the largely concrete ceiling and mountain meadow carpeted roof. The stone, locally quarried Valser quartzite, is emblematic of Zumthor's ethos of locking a building into the specifics of its place 'by endeavoring to answer the basic questions arising from the location of the given site, the purpose, and the building materials', as at the Therme Vals.[16] Here, the stone embeds the building in its site in at least three ways: its source is within walking distance of the building; it recollects the mountain into which the building is partly submerged; and it contributes to producing spatial effects, and an overall atmosphere, reminiscent of mountain caves and subterranean pools. Zumthor is at great pains to demonstrate how the use of the stone is structural, rather than either decorative, or cladding, in Loos's sense:[17]

> Although devoted to the truth of materials, Zumthor is rather coy in his explanations of structure. The Baths are in fact a composite of in situ concrete and load-bearing gneiss from a local quarry.

> None of the stacked stone is, in Zumthor's world, insulted by being merely applique.[18]

Arguably, initial encounters with the stone strips suggest that they are cladding, rather than structural. For Zumthor, misconstruing the composite structure (which he calls 'Vals Compound Masonry'), made up of the bands of stone upfront and concrete behind keyed together, must be evidence of 'theories detached from things'; disclosing a sort of academy bound abstract discourse disconnected from 'the reality of architecture' as building.[19]

Apart from proclaiming his position within architecture culture – not academic, *so* engaged in the *real* world of construction – Zumthor dodges how easily one might take for granted that the stone is cladding rather than structural, based on expectations developed over more than a century of modernist architecture, during which exterior and interior surface (facade/wall panel) was liberated from underlying structure (frame/support), to form independent elements, with skin usually either hung from structure, or as part of a layered system.

In Loos's view, cladding is no less dignified than some 'truth to material', or 'structural honesty', or at least need not be. Since lived experience is more valid than either, cladding is to a building, room or façade, what dressing is to a person. Moreover, following Loos, as the space-defining element in architecture, cladding is more significant than nearly all else. So, worrying about whether the quartzite slabs are perceived as structural or not is ultimately irrelevant, outside of some particularized modernist architectural discourse concentrated on 'truth', or 'authenticity'. The mood the quartzite contributes to producing, its appropriateness for the tasks set for it and its effectiveness in defining the space,

Figure 5.4 Stone and Concrete (and Water), Near Vals. Graubünden, Switzerland. [Photo: Nathaniel Coleman, 2007].

however, does matter. Accordingly, the crucial question is less one of structural 'honesty', than of whether or not the Therme is appropriately *dressed* for the bodily events it shelters.

As suggested by Loos, cladding is one thing, whereas the concealment of structure common to trivial architecture is another, even when apparently *necessary*. As such, knowing that the Valser quartzite forms a structural compound with the concrete can be culturally satisfying. But if possible confusion of this compound structure with cladding is problematic for Zumthor, surely there must have been a way to detail the hybrid (ancient Roman influenced) system to ensure less chance of misperception; to reveal seen and touched surface as *also* structural (Plate 3). The source of this confusion resides in the system itself: the stone is cut into shallow slabs (or strips) that have been layered one atop the other to produce a striated appearance, characterized by variations of grey. The overall effect is so taut as to invite perception of it as a skin; as a surface (membrane) concealing unseen structure (though in places the surface is uneven as if to produce the *illusion* of being loadbearing).

Renaissance architect and theorist Leon Battista Alberti thought of buildings as body-like: structure is akin to a skeleton; what is seen is akin to skin covering muscle, organs, arteries and so on, including the framework of bones (supporting and containing the whole bodily enterprise). Analogous to visible skin protecting unseen innards beneath it, Alberti conceived of beauty as an underlying idea that would otherwise remain invisible if not made tangible by ornament, as the necessary auxiliary 'light' illuminating it.[20] Perhaps it is possible to claim the same for the visible quartzite and invisible concrete structure behind it at the Therme.

By Loos's time, skeletal structure had become largely independent of both the muscle, etc., of a building and its skin. For him, necessary structure was subordinate to visible skin, transferring the former status of ornament to visible cladding. It is in this sense that US architect Louis Sullivan (1856–1924) – admired by both Loos and US architect Frank Lloyd Wright (1867–1959) – asserted that 'form ever follows function', which differs in two significant ways from the twentieth-century modernist phrase: 'form follows function', which suggests that building form should somehow be a literal expression of the activity housed.[21] Although somewhat related, Sullivan's proposition (primarily for tall buildings) was both more general and specific. General in the sense that the form of specific classes of use: entry (mercantile activities); mezzanine (including mercantile or professional activities); repetitive accommodation (offices in his thinking); and services (in the attic, or above) should each have a visibly distinct (interpretative) expression in the disposition of building form. His conception of form and function was specific in asserting that visible 'ornament should appear … as a thing expressing … the spirit of the structure', inventively, not literally.[22] Following a trajectory from Alberti, through Sullivan and Loos, Scarpa's emphasis on details (or joints), in concert with materials and colour, can be seen as comprising a method informed by all three. On the other hand, Zumthor's approach is stricter.

While layering the stone in the Therme surely takes advantage of its load-bearing qualities in compression, Zumthor's details do not show how this also forms part of a structural system combining the visual appearance of the stone with its compressive qualities, to provide the concrete concealed behind with a kind of permanent formwork:

> stone and concrete are combined in a special way: section by section, stone slices of different widths and lengths are stacked on top of each other, with concrete poured into the back creating a firm bond between the stone slices and the 'liquid stone' [concrete] … On the exposed side of the wall the slabs are stacked flush on top of each other but they are staggered in the back where the concrete is poured.[23]

Staggering the quartzite on the back formed a key for the poured concrete to lock into as it set, thereby producing an integral structure. In other places, the concrete is exposed. For example, 'all of the walls built into the mountainside' that the visitor comes into contact with, and 'where the concrete is pigmented'; including in pools without stone walls, and for the ceiling.[24]

The use of Valser quartzite also analogizes local construction. The same material – perceived as strips, or shallow slabs – is used to shingle roofs on a large number of structures in and around Vals, especially the small barn structures dotting the mountainside. As a distinctly local material, quarried close by, using quartzite strips for his building risks being overly literal. In this sense, the expression is direct, rather than metaphoric, essential or symbolic – though the overall material refinement at the baths abstracts and formalizes ordinary use, making it more knowing and modern. As alluring as this is, its directness might have benefitted from just one more step of poetic translation. What that might look like is difficult to say, no less so than knowing how the quartzite/concrete compound might have been expressed to avoid confusion.

While the combination quartzite/concrete load-bearing structure recollects local use of the stone for roof shingles, in its more common use, quartzite is seen in elevation, revealing sheet-like cuts of material. On residential, commercial and farm buildings in Vals, the gable ends of structures are visible, making the quartzite roof shingles appear as if in section, as strips. On sloping roofs, the shingles are placed almost flat, in a step-like manner, down the incline of the gable (Plate 4). Internally and externally, Zumthor's suggestive use of quartzite for the baths may recollect local use but clarifies – or modernizes – it, akin to his interpretation of the existing 1960s hotel buildings that revealed their unexpected elegance. Selection of a most local – even vernacular – material for the baths, made thoroughly modern through refinement, encourages perception of it as surface treatment, rather than as structural and loadbearing, other than of itself. Although perhaps obviously appropriate for this particular use and setting, Zumthor's specification of Valser quartzite made it locally visible again.

Water

After stone and concrete, water is the most important material (phenomenal and literal) in the Therme Vals. Phenomenally for its connotative qualities; literally for its properties, especially when in contact with the skin. Like Zumthor's quartzite/concrete compound system, the denotative and connotative aspects of water are intrinsic to one another, as much a matter of *fact*, as of cultural associations based in history and memory. But unlike the quartzite/concrete compound system, the distinctiveness of memory and experience is discernible. Such mutuality actually enhances the significance of each: the necessity of water for species survival is augmented by poetic reflection on it but only because such associations have a material basis.

From the outset, the Therme Vals was conceived of in full awareness of bathing as a fundamental part of being human, from our origins as fish-like tadpole creatures making their way towards the egg and the nine-month swim in amniotic fluid; our first bath, and all the baths after; trips to water (pool, lake, river, ocean), to ritual cleansings, including a final one after death. Bathing is a daily habit that confirms being cared for, of caring for oneself and of caring for others. Water is undoubtedly a powerful analogy of life, and the life cycle; it constitutes at least 60 per cent of each body, and is required to sustain life. Because water persists as the original source of planetary life, it is elementarily necessary for survival. Accordingly, water attains to a natural symbol of life.[25]

Water is to life, as is air. Perhaps more so. One breathes without thinking but health requires drinking water and bathing in it, entailing conscious effort. Required for farming, construction and cooking, water enables existence. Taking waters communally engages bathers – even if unbeknownst to themselves – in a shared experience of bodily care. At the Therme, stone and concrete provide solid counterparts to the liquidity of water, containing it, while providing surfaces for it to run over (calling to mind mountain streams coursing through rock channels, before falling into valleys) (Plate 5).

Cave

Throughout, the Therme analogizes a cave system, interspersed with grottoes and pools internally, and a pool with mountain vistas externally, organized around the bodily event of bathing, ostensibly recuperating primordial conditions. Organization, forms and use are enhanced by the key materials: stone, concrete (as a surrogate for stone); light (mostly filtered); water (in places still, in others flowing or moving, and of varying temperatures: from cold to hot); and metal. Distinctive acoustics augment the atmosphere of the baths with a myriad of suggestive sounds, including some composed especially for it. All of these elements seemingly derive directly from the local land, redirecting attention back to it. The almost overwhelming sensuality of the setting makes consideration of apparent place essences (*genius loci*) seem acceptable, perhaps appropriate, maybe even

Figure 5.5 Concrete Dam, with Mountain Behind, Upstream from Vals, Graubünden, Switzerland. [Photo: Nathaniel Coleman, 2007].

necessary. In the resonant architectural setting of the Therme Vals, talk of essences could be construed as fundamental to inventing its dramatically cultivated constructed atmosphere for bathers coming to take the waters.

Forms/proportion; circulation/organization; materials; construction; siting; framing views; sensitivity to the land, the existing hotel buildings, the town, and to the normal modesty of bathers; in concert with the details (elements, connections, hardware); surface/colour/finishing (walls, pavement, ceilings); lighting; and sound are all brought together to create a compelling atmosphere. Essences may be problematic but the Vals experience of water, striated slabs of quartzite stone, layered up, one upon the other in compression, bearing down towards the earth, in concert with the concrete, to support the vast volume of water contained therein, suggests that no other arrangement, or material, is imaginable. Producing an impression of perfection in every sense, this is ultimately a source of doubt at the Therme. Perfection – true perfection – is beyond human achievement. In the final analysis, the Therme is just too *smooth*, not just the confounding surface of the combinatory system of Vals quartzite and concrete, but in conception also.

Perfection?

In the pursuit of perfection: wholeness, authenticity, originality and produced atmosphere, Zumthor's Therme smooths over the natural and animalistic wildness (of the local roofing slates, for example) that would have made it more resistant to consumption, and thus closer to the primordial qualities it supposedly recuperates. Imperfection – roughness – is the correlate of human fallibility. Perfection of the sort Zumthor comes very close to realizing is achievable only if aims are limited by the tightest control. In relation to materials, it is not the desire for perfectibility, or even smoothness itself, that necessarily refuses fallibility. However, extreme precision, smoothness and slickness of finish surely tend to express denial of palpable failure. It is no wonder, then, that industrialized production is adept at producing precisely these qualities, with even apparent roughness often constituting just another expression of smoothness (of conception at least). Crucially, unmet desire for perfection must prevail, rather than perfection itself, as seemingly achieved.

In Ruskin's view, striving for the unachievable inevitably ends in failure but is evidence of a certain wildness of thought and imagination, which, because of its inventiveness, is more beautiful and noble: human because *bad* but perfect because of this, 'in its own bad way'.[26] Although Zumthor references both the natural and technological sublime (the surrounding mountain landscape and infrastructure), the work is constrained by his need for control and perfection, resulting in forms and finishes that are less rugged, rough or varied than might be expected. Rather than being vigorous – like the mountain terrain – the Therme is more subdued, making the whole also less powerful, or savage, than the mountain sublime suggests. And yet, Zumthor understandably avoided too picturesque a depiction of mountain wildness in the Therme, which would have simply replaced incipient slickness with bald-faced kitschiness.

Considered against the preceding chapters on Ruskin, Loos and Scarpa, Zumthor's work could be understood as aspiring to impossible perfection; a degree of closure or finality at odds with human ability and existence (apart from death); and a degree of continuous control that even in the absence of clocks is more directional than discontinuous. In relation to materials and finish, smoothness of conception and execution predominate, unlike the wildness of Scarpa's work which always threatens to exceed constraints. Loos's conception of material cladding as space defining surely confounds both senses of 'authenticity' in Zumthor's work: 'truth to materials', and 'honesty of structure and construction', in one direction, and *essential* experience in the other.

Despite its tendency towards slickness of conception and execution, when visited, depending on the time of day, the bathing experience in the Therme was occasionally funhouse-like, to the delight of children (over five) and adults alike. It was not characterized by a hushed silence, or aloofness (though that may have changed since Annalisa Zumthor no longer manages the complex). The mostly open to all visiting hours meant that the setting could be almost boisterousness. Children splashed about, couples embraced, individuals communed with their thoughts, and their bodies, in the various rooms attuned to varieties of sensory experience (augmented by light, sound, water and air temperature, colour and material). And yet, the experience is recollected as something of a seduction, less *authentic* than *beguiling*.

A jargon of authenticity?

In *The Jargon of Authenticity* (1964), Adorno criticizes German philosopher Martin Heidegger (1889–1976), amongst other German existential philosophers writing after the Second World War. In Adorno's view, central to their work was a philosophical position purporting to articulate a return to authenticity (perhaps desirable in the aftermath of catastrophe).

Trent Schroyer summarizes Adorno's argument as follows: 'His basic thesis is that after World War II this philosophical perspective became an ideological mystification of human domination – while pretending to be a critique of alienation.'[27] It could seem both extreme and unkind to assert that a 'mystification' of this sort operates throughout Zumthor's work. But rather than constituting evidence for why Zumthor's architecture should be denounced, this rather explains its appeal, especially the Therme Vals. Paraphrasing Adorno, Schroyer continues:

> Use of existentialistic terms became … a jargon: a mode of magical expression which Walter Benjamin called an 'aura'. In the aura of existentialism the historical need for meaning and liberation was expressed, but in a way that mystified the actual relation between language and its objective content.[28]

At the baths, this 'mode of magical expression' operates across two languages: the textual and the architectural; in statements about the work, and through the work itself.

The catastrophic bureaucratized and industrialized slaughter of the Second World War and the Holocaust confirmed the failure of modernity. Subsequently, the risks posed by technological progress to planetary survival have shattered any plausible assertion of continuity between European – Western civilization – before and after the War. The ensuing crisis largely persists as 'the need of meaning and liberation', which because impossible to satisfy, only mystification can recover. Zumthor's rhetorics of 'authentic' and 'original', combined with an emphasis on 'atmospheres', emerging out of primordial associations, arguably distorts 'the actual relation between language and its objective content'.[29] In this instance, these are the realities of post-Second World War alienation, reflected in equally alienated spatial practices and building-industry modes of production. Less an act of resistance than of mythification, Zumthor's Therme Vals is arguably more consolatory than emancipatory, obscuring actual conditions as a means for postponing transformative responses to them.

In architecture, 'the word' is multifaceted; it includes not only authorial intent, which is largely language based, but also materials, details, spatial practices and modes of production (including in the studio), all of which contribute to tensions between desires and results, and to the perceivable 'atmosphere' of a building. For Zumthor, 'atmosphere' is the most important thing in architecture. Form is not an end in itself. Materials are not ends in themselves. Function is not an end in itself. Construction is not an end in itself. According to him, somewhat echoing Loos, architecture is made up of many things; no one thing on its own can confirm architecture. Although multi-determined,

Figure 5.6 Farm Building, Mountainside above Vals, Graubünden, Switzerland. [Photo: Nathaniel Coleman, 2007].

in Zumthor's lexicon, 'atmosphere' represents an end that could organize all of the constituent elements of architecture. Conceptualized in this way, *atmosphere* risks quickly becoming *determinate*, while *use* could remain largely *propositional*. As represented by Zumthor, *atmosphere* is fixed, whereas *use* is almost always open, despite efforts to close it. Accordingly, *use* is a more realistic organizing principle than *atmosphere*, which, to be immediately perceptible, requires too much management of experiences.

Obviously, experience is crucial to architecture but is (spatially and temporally) situational, as is atmosphere, so long as it is perceived rather than dictated. Although situational, atmosphere in Zumthor's work is almost a substitute for *type*, or typologies, which, in their prescriptiveness, are ultimately sterile – kinds of *idea-fixe* that attempt to manage inhabitation, use and form as determinate. Although not definitively answered, the Therme Vals raises the question as to whether or not 'atmosphere' is for Zumthor a kind of *idea-fixe*?

The aim here is not to nullify the Therme Vals's architectural virtues but rather to clarify their philosophical context, while also illuminating Zumthor's method and attitude towards materials. Doing this requires highlighting the evident tensions within the architecture itself, including the *truth* it supposedly recuperates and embodies. According to Schroyer, 'Adorno's critique [of the jargon of authenticity] focuses on the jargon's incapacity to express the relation between language and truth, in that it breaks the dialectic of language by making the intended object appear present by the idealization inherent in the word itself.'[30] The correlate of this at the Thermae Vals is the range of primordial references represented as essences (land, local, national, vernacular or atmospheric): mountain (landscape, sublime); water (life origins, stream, waterfall, cleansing); rock (solidity, locality); cave (womb, chthonic); light (obscurity, clarity); temperature (cold, warm, hot); coalesced into an event of communal sensuality. All of these associations may be credibly linked to their sources and referents in the building but arguably presume a no longer (or never) alienated condition, for which there is no credible evidence.

More succinctly, at the Therme, 'the idealization inherent in the word itself' could be limited to 'authentic', 'original' and 'atmosphere', evident in declarations of authorial intent, manifest in the architecture itself.

'Authentic', 'original' and 'atmosphere' are represented as *fixed* (or at least as *fixable*), even though each is at best contingent. By representing the three terms, or characteristics, as factual, thus transposing them into forms of jargon, each becomes an example of how: 'The jargon, therefore, falls into an objectivism that conceals the difference between philosophical reflection and the in-itselfness of the object of reflection.'[31] All three terms ('authentic', 'original' and 'atmosphere') together constitute an assumed confirmation of 'authenticity' – 'in-itselfness' – whereas their provisionality is actually much better suited to 'philosophical reflection', as a limit, in the sense of: 'what is/what could be authentic/original/atmosphere'. The value of this reflection resides in illuminating possible methods for resisting rapacious consumption of otherwise laudable works that could become intrinsic to them. Otherwise, such works risk being exhausted by their remaking into commodity fetishes. Although this is the destiny of anything identifiable as *new*, there are tactics for resisting this, from modes of production in architects' offices to the building site, including how material is conceptualized and used.

Surrendering myths of achievable perfection, including reification of imperfection, suggests one such tactic for resisting being consumed. However, at the Therme Vals, just the opposite was pursued to its logical conclusion, arguably dooming it to inevitable fetishization. As Scheroyer's analysis of Adorno's *The Jargon of Authenticity* suggests, for Zumthor's Therme, this begins with the representation of 'authentic', 'original' and 'atmosphere' as objective: 'Such objectivism loses the intent of reflection to maintain a self-consciousness of the mediation of fact through the thinking subject.'[32] Most cynically, these otherwise laudable aspirations come to define Zumthor's *brand*.

Scheroyer continues: 'Consequently, in the jargon objective consciousness is compressed into self-experience, and an idealism results.'[33] With the advent of idealism, the apparently recuperating object of authentic experience (of bathing at the Therme Vals), risks coming to share 'with modern advertising the ideological circularity of pretending to make present, in pure expressivity, an idealized form that is devoid of content.'[34] Although a municipal baths, the Therme Vals is marketed as a destination spa hotel. While this has ensured its popularity, and with it financial security, it overwhelms the social content at its core, which, at any rate, would, one imagines, be largely irrelevant for most paying visitors. Without its civic dimension featuring prominently, and now without the special charm of being managed by Annalisa Zumthor, it risks being just another upscale destination, devoid of content. But this is not simply a product of success and the rapacious logic of the market destroying something otherwise perfect in every way. Rather, the idealized forms apparently made present by the 'pure expressivity' of the building always constituted an extremely fragile construct of apparent essential content: the bathing was never as primordial (authentic) as represented. The seeming experience of 'a nonexistent actuality' was, from the outset, largely produced by its 'mass media' presence.[35]

The significance of the Therme is, in equal measure, a construction of whatever it actually holds in reserve as a *work* (of art), confirmed by actual experience of the complex; Zumthor's verbal and textual framing of the building, including adoption of these claims by others; and its exposure in print and online, including in this chapter. Following Scheroyer's summary of Adorno's *Jargon of Authenticity*, the apparent 'essences' of the Therme could be read as a hasty 'attempt to achieve a reconciliation, irregardless of the objective processes of alienation which block meaning and autonomy', indicating 'only … awareness of the depth of the need' for recuperation of *authentic experience*.[36] As compensation, rather than transformation, the claims made for and by the Therme are emptied: 'expressions of authenticity, freedom, etc., is an attempt to actualize these ideals outside of the objective social context: to fulfill heroic cultural models independent of the society.'[37] Inevitably, fulfilment is at best momentary: 'Behind these empty claims for freedom the socio-economic processes of advanced capitalist integration continue, intensifying the dependence of all persons upon large organizational units for employment and welfare.'[38]

At one level, subjecting the Therme Vals to this sort of criticism might seem petty, excessive or simply irrelevant, a meaningless academic indulgence. But this would leave only two options: submission or delusion, because resistance of any sort must be out of the question. If this last assertion is at least considered – even for a moment – then despite its myriad virtues and charms, the Therme's '"blessings" conceal' the 'objective context of unfreedom' that dominates the current socio-economic and political context; 'and in the name of critical reflection the [baths, as permeated with the] jargon [of authenticity] joins hands with modern advertising in celebrating the meaningfulness of immediate experience.'[39] Zumthor and the Therme are surely not alone in this predicament. Architecture, more so than almost any other artistic activity, is entrapped within dominant modes of production, constrained to reproducing the spaces of globalized capitalism, determined by its spatial practices. Resistance is all but impossible, though by no means out of the question, even in built works.[40]

What about Scarpa?

As US architect Louis I. Kahn (1901–74) showed, renewal of any material, form, detail or institution requires reinvention out of its origins, intersected and/or bisected by present social, economic, political and cultural (artistic) conditions.[41] Perhaps this sheds light on how the Therme Vals suffers as an attempt to manifest a recuperation that cannot simply be desired, or wished for. To be had, it must be worked through, and out, in a more determined (philosophical/political) manner. In that sense, the Therme Vals is more myth than utopia, whereas Scarpa's work is more utopia than myth, akin to Kahn's, which is grounded in fairy tales.[42] As myth, the Therme Vals is a proposition of recuperation as if achieved; as if the authentic experience of bathing had actually been recovered. Original in terms of authorship, so *new*, but primordial in terms of activity – bathing – thus ancient. Echoing the objectives of Zumthor's Therme, Leonard Koren outlines some imagined optimum characteristics of baths:

> Baths are almost always rich in symbolic and metaphorical implications ... So how *do* I define a great bathing environment? It is simply, or rather not-so-simply, a place that helps bring my fundamental sense of who I am into focus. A place that awakens me to my intrinsic earthy, sensual, and paganly reverential nature. A quiet place to enjoy one of life's finest desserts amidst elemental surroundings. A profoundly personal place, even when shared with other people, suitable for the most intimate sacraments of bathing.[43]

According to Koren, most 'designer-created baths', individual or communal, are 'oppressively, sterile, boring, or mannerist caricatures of some historical model'. By the same token, he asserts that 'extraordinary sensitivity' is the most important qualification for a bath designer, which most lack. As a corrective, he argues for *undesigning the bath*:[44]

> The term 'undesign' has two simultaneous meanings ... One stresses the negative *un*, as in the 'reversal of design', 'release from design', or 'rectifying the problems

caused by design'. The other meaning suggests that which is unaffected by the industrial-designed civilization in a positive way, i.e., the elemental and evocatively primitive.[45]

The preceding quote illuminates yet another tension at play in Zumthor's Therme: he surely wants to rectify 'the problems caused by design' in most communal bathing environments; he also wanted to invent an 'elemental' setting embodying nearly all of the characteristics Koren argues optimum baths require. However, by using the methods and trappings of 'industrial-designed civilization' to escape from it, rather than collapsing the divide between the *new as desire*, and the *primordial as reclaimed*, in Zumthor's Therme, the *new* is represented as a pathway to accessing authenticity, which is ultimately unrecoverable; precisely because alienated by the very techniques deployed to retrieve it. In the end, origins can only exist as mental images, at best approximated in external reality, rather than being ever fully retrievable.

As outlined previously, Zumthor's more fundamentalist relationship to 'authenticity' and to the 'ancient', as compared with Scarpa's surrealistic approach, arguably opens up a greater divide between their work than the relative restraint, or economy of expression, of one, as compared with the more ornate, decorative or Baroque qualities of the other. Significantly, Scarpa's work is looser (in planning, conception and execution) than Zumthor's. Because its claims to *authenticity* are both more relaxed and arch, Scarpa's work is neither as literal nor 'compensatory', or perfectionist as Zumthor's; surely not in the same ways. Arguably, Zumthor and Scarpa stake out two sorts of *perfectionism*: for Zumthor, this desire translates into relative totality; for Scarpa, it is decidedly cultural.

In relation to their divergent attitudes to site and material, it might be possible to characterize Zumthor as engaging in excavation, whereas Scarpa is already embedded. In this sense, Zumthor's work is more alienated than Scarpa's, which is what makes it compensatory, an imagined recuperation. Scarpa cultivates, like a farmer, making due with existing conditions in an effort to transform them. Whereas Zumthor attempts to impose qualities upon a *fallen* world, Scarpa introduces them by stealth. Accordingly, Scarpa's work is sown, Zumthor's is reaped, or harvested. Because culture is always incomplete, and mostly operates at cross purposes to itself, an architecture of ostensive completeness, no matter how 'real', in the sense of being materially present, will ultimately be 'abstract', in the sense of attempting to manifest some preternatural ideal.

In contradistinction, an incomplete architecture, especially if materially present, will be more ordinary, and in this sense, 'concrete', even if it proposes, or is evidence of, a radical transformation, which, at any rate, will be propositional rather than ideal. In this sense, the realm of the 'concrete' is ultimately more 'propositional' than the 'ideal'. Both may be 'real', because they exist, but one represents abstract or hypothetical optimum conditions, whereas the other embeds within the realms of rhythmic time and everyday necessity; as rooted, rather than excavated. It would be untrue to describe Scarpa's work as disinterested in atmosphere but 'use' (in its broadest and deepest senses) seems to describe it better. As a production of material, construction, colour and use, atmosphere in Scarpa's work is propositionally experienced rather than determined; it is thus infinitely renewable, rather than exhaustible. But when 'atmosphere' is construed as analogous to 'intention' it becomes determinate, in a manner that imagines inhabitation, use and form as uncontaminated.

The 'authentic original' Zumthor strives to achieve can only ever be provisionally realizable but only if the original sources (eternal present) of institutions and construction are disobediently reimagined and reinvented in the present, as not entirely faithful interpretations of what already exists, or is already known. To resist their own exhaustion, architectural propositions must begin with the known, in order to reveal something otherwise unknown, or unexpected, about it; to surpass it through corrections, in the reinvention of institutions in the present. For example, the stacked stone construction and cave-like interiors of historic *hammam* (Turkish Bath) bathing structures in the Arab world, which are direct descendants of ancient Roman baths, surely provided a model for Zumthor's Therme but lost in translation from the ancient world to modern Switzerland is the 'sheen of antiquity', which Japanese author Junichiro Tanizaki (1886–1965) describes as:[46]

> the glow of grime … that comes of being touched over and over again, a sheen produced by the oils that naturally permeate an object over long years of handling – which is to say grime. If indeed 'elegance is frigid', it can as well be described as filthy … among the elements of the elegance in which we take such delight is a measure of the unclean, the unsanitary … Westerners attempt to expose every speck of grime and eradicate it.[47]

Not only is it impossible for the new to 'have the sheen' of antiquity, unless contrived, the silted-up grime associated with age and use is also a source of ambivalence. The allure of the old almost always loses out to hygiene. Even so, the smoothness of surface and technique produces interminably photogenic but equally antiseptic environments, inimical to life's inescapable untidiness.

Consuming the baths

The very aims and programme of the Therme (economic regeneration; spa) surely contributed to its ready consumption. But might it also be that the spa building – despite Zumthor's claims for its wholeness – presents itself more as a series of tableau too easily suggesting lifestyle settings, or backdrops, for fashion photography?[48] Its restrained beauty and simplicity make the Therme Vals inevitably alluring, in a particular way, connoting a certain luxury and status associated with high-end fashion. Its very simple clean lines show it as *elemental*, in an ostensibly pure and natural way (mirroring the same in the mountain landscape). However, this also makes appropriation easier, as does its relative smoothness. Inscribed in its fundamental simplicity is a drift towards branding, an inevitable by-product of the rhetoric associated with producing an authentic original, and wholeness. The degree to which this has been achieved introduces a range of characteristics to the work unable to resist consumption, or appropriation, by the 'culture industry', as a commoditized unique experience.[49]

The Therme building is indubitably seductively beautiful but this can also produce a queasy feeling that one has in turn been seduced, by an offer impossibly larger than the reality of itself. Comprehending the nature of this seduction is crucial to developing an understanding of Zumthor's baths and his work more generally. The benefit in this is to position Zumthor's work on one side of a negative dialectic, with its decisive opposite as a counterpoint, to reveal more precisely the nature of its inbuilt brand aspect, and therefrom to begin imagining how this might be recalibrated, to produce less consumable alternatives. Declaring that the baths take up residence on this side or that of a binary is ultimately of little use. But reflecting on Zumthor's Therme Vals as a an example of the 'jargon of authenticity', counterbalanced by its extreme opposite (perhaps the jargon of *inauthenticity*), suggests how something else could be identified: works able to resist their own consumption, and transformation into commodity fetishes, subsumed within the culture industry. Keeping hold of what is positive and desirable about the Therme building is key, despite any queasiness produced by its seductiveness, or precisely because of this. Rem Koolhaas might perhaps represent the extreme opposite of Zumthor. Paradoxically, the work of both intersects at the extremes of their respective rhetorics; at that point where the ultimate disposition of their architecture and ideas for consumption meet. For Koolhaas, who extols *opportunism*, it seems intentional. Perhaps for Zumthor, with his talk of *essences*, it is accidental.

Despite fondness for the Therme Vals, Zumthor's architecturally manifest 'jargon of authenticity' reveals apparent alterity as conformity to high-end fashion sensibilities. Ultimately, anything that in any way lends itself to being commoditized will be exploited accordingly. Paradoxically, the source of this is internal to the Therme, residing in precisely those qualities that make it distinctive: its overall precision; orchestrated atmosphere; generally hygienic conditions of smoothness; and readily comprehensible literalness. The spa programme itself and original conception of the building as a touristic destination, with a local economic regeneration agenda, contributed to its inevitable branding. The first evidence of this unfolding process was the early use of the Therme as a setting for fashion photography.[50]

While the isolated details of any building may lend themselves to being photographed, overall photogeneity of a project largely depends on its formal coherence, or assembly of tableaux suited to abstraction and display as framed. While most architects who build aim to produce agreeable settings, there is a difference between attractive photographic images and distracted lived experience. Project diffusion through print and electronic media is crucial for developing the reputation of architects and buildings but reproducible images are never a substitute for being there. Loos was well aware of the professional benefits of photography but rejected it anyway:

I am against photographing interiors. The results are always different from the original. There are architects who design interiors not so that people can live in them, but so they will look beautiful in the photographs ... Photographs *dematerialize* reality, but precisely what I want is for people in my rooms to feel the material around them ... So you see, photography says nothing. Photography produces pretty or not so pretty pictures. It diverts people from the object. It miseducates them ... Photography is a deceiver ... They [architects] make their reputation with pretty drawings and beautiful photographs.[51]

The preternatural quality of photographs, as Loos asserts, cannot replace bodily experience, especially of interiors. In the many decades since Loos wrote the passage cited here, the deceptions of photography have been fully naturalized, arrogating to images the status of being *more real* than lived reality. Before touch, lenses, viewfinders and screens often mediate first experiences of things, even actual bodily encounters with them. As a matter now of consciousness, rather than choice, it is difficult to imagine an architect who is not aware of the profound importance of mechanically and digitally reproduced images of architecture for shaping experience as much as reputations; or for illustrating books on architecture. Accordingly, no matter how disconcertingly essentialist Zumthor's writing might be, its manifestation as the work presents the greatest problem, not least by contributing to making the Therme more consumable than he probably hoped it would become.

Notes

1. Jessica Mairs, 'Peter Zumthor Says Therme Vals Spa Has Been Destroyed', *dezeen*, 11 May 2017. Available online at: https://www.dezeen.com/2017/05/11/peter-zumthor-vals-therme-spa-switzerland-destroyed-news/ (Accessed 06 March 2018).

2. Ibid., Zumthor quoted.

3. No Author, 'Summary: Visionary Policies Help Reverse Decline of Mountain Regions in Switzerland', *Therme Vals – Press Information*, Press-pack, Vals, 24 December 2003, p. 4 of 15.

4. Ibid.

5. Sigurd Hauser and Peter Zumthor, *Peter Zumthor Therme Vals*, Zurich: Scheidegger & Spiess, 2007.

6. Ibid.

7. For Zumthor's own statements on his method, see in particular: Peter Zumthor, *Atmospheres: Architectural Environments – Surrounding Objects*, Basel: Birkhäuser, 2006; Peter Zumthor, *Thinking Architecture*, Second, Expanded Edition, Maureen Oberon-Turner and Catherine Schoenberg (trans.), Basel: Birkhäuser, 2006; Hauser and Zumthor, *Peter Zumthor Therme Vals*; and Peter Zumthor, 'The Tension of Not Being Specific: Tod Williams and Billie Tsien in Conversation with Peter Zumthor', *2G:Revista ~Internacional de Arquitectura = International Architecture Review*, no. 9 (1999): 8–21.

8. Steven Spier, 'Place, Authorship and the Concrete: Three Conversations with Peter Zumthor', *arq: Architectural Research Quarterly*, 5, no. 1 (March 2001): 15–36 (p. 22).

9. Zumthor, 'The Hardcore of Beauty', in *Thinking Architecture*, pp. 29, 31–2.

10. Ibid., p. 37.

11. Peter Zumthor, 'Lightness and Pain', in *Peter Zumthor Works: Buildings and Projects, 1979–1997*, Basel: Birkhäuser, 1998, p. 7.

12. Theodor W. Adorno, *Jargon of Authenticity*, Knut Tarnowski and Frederic Will (trans.), London and New York: Routledge, 1964, p. xii.

13. Ibid., p. 32.

14. Ellen Himmelfarb, 'Inside Peter Zumthor's Mentor Program', *Azure Magazine*, 6 January 2016. Available at: https://www.azuremagazine.com/article/pritzker-architect-peter-zumthor / (Accessed 02 April 2019).

15. Peter Zumthor, Unpublished interview conducted by Nathaniel Coleman, Therme Vals Hotel, Switzerland 2007 (Digital voice recording). See also, Jessica Mairs, 'I'm Trying to Change My Mysterious Reputation, Says Peter Zumthor', *dezeen*, 12 May 2017. Available at: https://www.dezeen.com/2017/05/12/peter-zumthor-interview-trying-to-change-myste rious-reputation-architecture/ (Accessed 02 April 2019).

16. Zumthor, 'The Hardcore of Beauty', p. 31.

17. Peter Zumthor, Unpublished interview (2007).

18. Raymund Ryan, 'Primal Therapy', *AR* (*Architectural Review*), August 1997, pp. 42–9 (p. 44).

19. Hauser and Zumthor, *Peter Zumthor Therme Vals*, p. 101; Zumthor, 'The Hardcore of Beauty', p. 37.

20. Leon Battista Alberti, 'Glossary', in *On the Art of Building in Ten Books*, Joseph Rykwert, Neil Leach, Robert Tavernor (Trans.), Cambridge, MA: MIT Press, 1988 (1453/1486), pp. 420–8.

21. Louis H. Sullivan, 'The Tall Building Artistically Considered' (1896), in *Kindergarten Chats and Other Writings*, New York: Dover, 1979 (1918), p. 208.

22. Louis H. Sullivan, 'Ornament in Architecture' (1892), in *Kindergarten Chats and Other Writings*, p. 192.

23. Hauser and Zumthor, *Peter Zumthor Therme Vals*, p. 101.

24. Ibid.

25. Ibid.; Leonard Koren, *Undesigning the Bath*, Berkeley, CA: Stone Bridge Press, 1996.

26. John Ruskin, 'The Nature of Gothic', *The Stones of Venice* (1853), in *Unto this Last and Other Writings*, Clive Wilmer (ed.), London: Penguin, p. 92.

27. Ibid., Schroyer, 'Introduction', in Adorno, *Jargon of Authenticity*, p. xii.

28. Ibid.

29. Ibid.

30. Ibid.

31. Ibid., pp. xii–xiii.

32. Ibid., p. xiii.

33. Ibid.

34. Ibid.

35. Steve Parnell, 'Peter Zumthor's Therme Vals Baths in Print', *AJ*, February 2009. Available online at: https://www.architectsjournal.co.uk/culture/peter-zumthors-therme-vals-bath s-in-print/1990584.article?search=https%3a%2f%2fwww.architectsjournal.co.uk%2fsearcha rticles%3fqsearch%3d1%26keywords%3dZumthor's+therme+vals+in+print (Accessed 12 March 2018).

36. Schroyer, 'Introduction', p. xiv.

37. Ibid.

38. Ibid.

39. Ibid.

40. Coleman, *Lefebvre for Architects*.

41. Coleman, *Utopias and Architecture*, pp. 155–95.

42. See, Coleman, 'Fairy Tales and Golden Dust', in *Utopias and Architecture*, pp. 155–73.

43. Koren, *Undesigning the Bath*, pp. 10, 13.

44. Ibid., p. 10.

45. Ibid., p. 98.

46. Ibid., pp. 44–55, 72–83.

47. Jun'ichirō Tanizaki, *In Praise of Shadows* (1933), Thomas Harper and Edward Seidensticker (trans.), London: Vintage Books, 2001 (1977), p. 20.

48. See: Janet Jackson, *Every Time*, Official Music Video, Directed by Matthew Rolston, 1998. Available at: https://m.youtube.com/watch?v=4md2LqtNo-U (Accessed on 15 March 2018); 'Body Building', 10 Page Swimwear Feature shot at the Therme Vals, *UK Vogue*, July 1997; Paul L. Knox, *Cities and Design* (London and New York: Routledge), pp. 9–12.

49. Theodor W. Adorno, *The Culture Industry, Selected Essays on Mass Culture*, J. M. Bernstein (ed.), London and New York: Routledge, 1991.

50. For an overview of this process, see: Parnell, 'Peter Zumthor's Therme Vals Baths in Print'.

51. Loos, 'On Thrift' (1924), in *On Architecture*, Michael Mitchell (trans.), Riverside, CA: Ariadne Press, 2002, pp. 178–9.

CHAPTER 6
TERMINAL JEWEL: WILLIAMS AND TSIEN'S FOLK ART MUSEUM (2001)

A genuine curiosity for material animates the work of architects Todd Williams and Billie Tsien. Steeped in the forms, materials and construction methods of modernist architecture, their work hints at the spatial virtuosity of Le Corbusier; Wright's approach to material as the first point of contact between individuals and buildings; and Scarpa's conception of signification as primarily a matter of materials and details. Their intermixing of audacity and specificity, accomplished within building-industry limits, is cognate with Finnish-US architect Eero Saarinen (1910–61). A positive negation of Kahn's *degree-zero* monumentality also suffuses their work.

Williams and Tsien's joy in detailing and play with materials is more artistic than mystical and less mythical than poetic. Reminiscent of Scarpa but distant from Zumthor, their buildings are more *open* than *closed*. Openness derives as much from attitudes towards materials and construction, as from narrativity. *Truth, authenticity* and *wholeness* are not jettisoned but do not have a sacred status in their work, which distinguishes it from Zumthor's. Nevertheless, they share with him a sense of obligation to the tenets of twentieth-century modernist architecture theory and practice – rationalism, honesty of construction and the suppression of ornament – but with a uniquely relaxed attitude towards control and fallibility.

Truth to material may not dominate but matter's narrative possibilities do, evident in the impress upon it of intellectual and physical labour. Although such recollections of making by hand are suggestive of Ruskin, skill of execution somewhat obscures this. Material meaning is cultivated, rather than indwelling, though silted-up associations are acknowledged as accruing to elements and methods of construction through long use, making signification socially constructed and situational. In a territory triangulated by Loos, Scarpa and Zumthor, Williams and Tsien disobediently engage with fundamentalist modernist precepts.

American Folk Art Museum in New York City

Williams and Tsien's now-demolished former home of the American Folk Art Museum in New York City provides a portal into their work. Previously standing next to the Museum of Modern Art (MoMA), at 45 West 53rd Street, the building is remembered most for its nearly opaque facade of pockmarked white bronze panels.

The Folk Art opened to wide acclaim on 11 December 2001, three months to the day after the World Trade Center towers were destroyed. Timing lent the building a mystique as a New York Phoenix rising from the ashes and rubble of the Twin Towers. Architecture critic Herbert Muschamp believed it represented 'an opportunity [for the city] to restore its eroded sense of optimism about the urban future'.[1] Amongst other accolades, it was named 'Best Building of 2001'.[2] Its solid street wall distinguished the Folk Art from its Midtown Manhattan corporate neighbours dominated by glass and steel, apart from Saarinen's brooding stone-clad CBS Building across the street.[3] In response to spiralling debt, the Folk Art Museum relocated, selling its building to MoMA in 2011. By 2013 MoMA determined to demolish the building as part of its expansion plans, which it did in 2014.

The Folk Art Museum was a 30,000-square-foot, 'eight-level building' with 'gallery space for permanent and temporary exhibitions' on the upper four floors. Natural light filtered downward through a 'skylight above' the 'grand interior stair', and was introduced 'into the galleries and … the lower levels' through 'openings'. In addition to more conventional displays, 'niches' were 'built into the structure and circulation paths' to encourage 'informal interaction with a changing selection of folk art'.[4] A bijoux 'café overlooking 53rd street' and 'the two-story atrium' was on the mezzanine. The narrow 40-foot-wide building was 'surrounded on the front and back sides by sites owned by the Museum of Modern Art'.[5]

As is typical of their work, narrative was emplotted along multiple pathways through the building, augmented by material finish. Williams and Tsien conceived of visits to the museum 'as a personal journey composed of surprise encounters with … objects through the use of diverse paths ,… presented through traditional and non-traditional display spaces'.[6] Circulation narrativized use, enriched by material, volumes, forms and folk art, in support of memorable repeat visits.

Sensitive to the building's location in the shadow of MoMA, and at the behest of their clients: 'The facade … [was] designed to make a strong but quiet statement of independence.' It was 'sculptural in form', and supposedly recalled 'an abstracted open hand that folds slightly inward to create a faceted plane'.[7] Although surely faceted, the facade did not quite conjure up an 'open hand', but did offer a subdued welcome to the other world of folk art. The seams joining individual facade panels were emphasized to highlight their distinctiveness, also intensifying its faceted quality and modulating the sunlight. Like a patterned quilted blanket thrown over a bed, the facade naturally alluded to the domestic scale of the museum building and folk art within (Plate 6).

Williams and Tsien begin each project by identifying opportunities for developing loose narrative frameworks. Client and anticipated use are central, as are topography and milieu, furnishing clues to how a building could provide platforms for recursive experiences. Because they do not isolate architecture (as representation) from building (as construction), across a brainwork/physical labour divide, structure, construction and materials are considered from the start. Akin to Loos, material surface dominates volume and form as space defining and for establishing mood. Although material use, assembly and finish recollect the hand in making (recalling Ruskin), a principle of cladding dominates (reminiscent of Loos). The visible and the touchable are more important than hidden structure, or *concept*, as the facade confirmed.

Facade

Williams and Tsien were determined to make the facade panels clearly perceptible as cladding (truthful/honest), though mostly to intensify the made quality of the assembly. Revealing architecture as *made* is a rejoinder to the near-seamless extruded quality of typical glass and steel curtain walls. 'Metal panels of tombasil, a form of white bronze, clad the building. Spaces between each panel reveal the darkened wall of the weather barrier behind.'[8] Although they explored other materials and production processes, cast tombasil panels best satisfied their 'desire to clad the building in a material that was both common and amazing, and that would show a connection with the handmade quality of folk art'.[9] Tombasil is 'a commercially produced white bronze alloy used for boat propellers, fire hose nozzles, and grave markers (hence its name)'. When hung, the panels retained marks of the 'direct fabrication technique', including the impress of 'sand molds taken from concrete and steel', intended to reproduce the original pockmarked samples made 'by pouring the material directly onto the concrete floor of the foundry'.[10]

Muschamp described Williams and Tsien's design for the building as 'restrained but not impoverished', and as 'nearly abstract but' inviting 'a range of meaning', including the facade:

> The form holds many allusions …; to the importance John Ruskin gave to the craftsman's hand in *The Seven Lamps of Architecture*, and to the stylized hand used by … Le Corbusier to symbolize the mastery of tools. This is a modern building that embodies the strong continuities between modern architecture and the crafts tradition.[11]

Although a *modern* building, it was not an entirely *modernist building*. Indeed, negating orthodox modernist norms was its most risky aspect.

When discussing the sixty-three tombasil panels comprising the Folk Art Museum facade, Tsien emerged as more comfortable with 'the decorative' than Williams. For her, 'decorative is not a derogatory term', whereas for Williams it is 'not something that's good'.[12] Both were keen to distance their work from Scarpa's ornamental tendencies, which Tsien described as 'sort of beautiful, or precious' but 'brought in from the outside', because extrinsic to construction.[13] For them, any concession to 'the decorative' *must* be 'intrinsic to the building itself'; emerging directly out of its 'actual making', rather than applied, or ornamental.[14] In this regard, Tsien observed:

> I think particularly in some of our earlier projects, which were also smaller, people have talked to us … about Scarpa and our work, because we're very interested in [the] idea of detail. I think probably, though, that our sense of detail [is less]

something that's added or applied [than] it's revealing the material that is part of the building itself. So I think it has changed a little bit, particularly as we've worked more in buildings and less on interiors.[15]

Although differentiating themselves from Scarpa, Williams and Tsien acknowledged a shared care for 'how things are made'; as well as sharing a more subdued 'decorative thing' with Zumthor. In contradistinction, for them, Scarpa verged towards the excessive or extreme: 'fetishizing ... details', that are frequently unnecessarily 'decorative, or additive', particularly at the 'Brion Cemetery'.[16]

Decorative anxiety runs through the entire history of modernist architecture, from at least Loos's 'Ornament and Crime' essay to the present day. Because Williams and Tsien's Folk Art Museum facade was indubitably cladding; hung from the building but not intrinsic to it (other than as a symbolic, or emotional, identifying device), it was problematic for them. Tsien observed that because 'the ... façade' was not 'intrinsic to the ... [construction of the] building', it was 'literally decoration', or 'a giant piece of jewelry ... hung on the face of the building', like a 'black dress'.[17] Williams concurred. Though its boldness derived from not trying to be anything other than jewel-like.

Coming upon the faceted facade walking down 53rd Street, it held its own against the substantial bulk all around it, despite its small size. Its primary function was to draw you in, to be memorable and to put up valiant resistance to its dominant neighbours, MoMA in particular. When invited to consider the risks taken in their work as amongst its most engaging aspects, Williams and Tsien were initially incredulous but they could understand how the anomalous, faceted, jewel-like, sombre Folk Art facade might be construed as risky in Manhattan, amongst the emblems of power surrounding it. For Tsien, risk resides entirely in problems of construction, for example the difficulties of mounting the facade, including 'the last panel', which 'went up, basically the day the Museum opened'.[18]

At first, neither Williams nor Tsien welcomed the idea that risk is desirable, partly because they want to distance themselves from the sort of 'big bold' statements produced by 'Zaha Hadid' Architects, for example. Yet, the Folk Art Museum building facade was surely audacious.[19] Indeed, facade and interior were notable for the myriad chances taken with materials, forms, volumes and circulation, especially in architecturally conservative New York City. For Williams, problems of construction, including resolving new materials, are not risks but the boldness of the facade was: 'The risk to me is the fact that it ... is such a strong statement ... It actually also feels a little like the great ... [bronze women] in MoMA.'[20] For example, 'the River' (begun 1938–39; completed 1943; cast 1948) by French sculptor Aristide Maillol (1861–1944).

Although enthusiastic about the Maillol sculpture's power, Williams was discomfited by the Folk Art facade's assertiveness.[21] For Williams, 'the most worrisome thing' was its being 'a detached bold facade', which 'scared the hell out of' him. Although 'the construction, and ... putting together' the facade might have been 'a struggle', he did not see that as 'risk taking'.[22] But 'because façades come last', he 'worried it would be detached' and end up looking like a 'snowplow' hanging off the building. Even so, making it was less of a physical, expressive or theoretical problem than he imagined, apart from issues of manufacture and execution.

In the end, the facade's material presence and perceptible 'quiltness' satisfied the architects, clients and much of the public. Because Williams and Tsien do not want their work to be confused with the extravagant formal (branding) statements of so-called *icon* buildings, Williams worried that they had gone too far, producing a kind of museum logo – 'snowplow', or 'medallion' – in response to the clients' desire for a 'statement'.[23] As noted earlier, Tsien's 'fear' contrasts with Williams's by being concentrated on 'struggles' associated with production, including worrying that the 'the panels would never fit', or that 'like a jigsaw puzzle' some of the pieces – facade panels – would go missing. Although applied, rather than intrinsic, Tsien described the facade as 'grounded in … its relationship to … something … made by hand'.[24]

The moral of the facade story is that architectural risk is primarily of two sorts: *production* and *conceptualization*. While the former is rarely insurmountable, the latter casts lingering doubt. If Williams worries about exaggeration and trusting intuition too much, Tsien is more preoccupied with problems of construction. She is more relaxed about impurities of conception, including the decorative, while he is more at ease with technical problems. Their asymmetrical and mutual engagement with such differences contributes to the distinctiveness of their work.

Williams and Tsien resolved the Folk Art facade snowplough problem at their Skirkanich Hall, University of Pennsylvania Bioengineering Department, West Philadelphia (completed 2006). The cantilevered facade, overhanging the street 35 feet above it, effectively demarcates the entrance, while intensifying its presence. Although analogous to the Folk Art Museum, the amply glazed tall entry lobby – shielded by the outstretched welcome of the overhang – is more physically and perceptually permeable.

Materially, the most prominent feature of Skirkanich Hall is the suspended facade of cascading glass panels, against an expansive backdrop of hand-glazed brick (ranging from black to acid yellow, with mossy green as the centre point). Although neither is load bearing, because hung from the structure as at the Folk Art, the assemblage is more in keeping with modernist layered framed construction, made explicit by the cantilever (raising the bulk). Overall, the distinctive entry element (which enhances the street) is integral to the building's structure, without foregoing visual or physical impact.

When MoMA announced its intention to demolish the American Folk Art Museum, protest focused on the facade. Despite not being structurally intrinsic, preserving it as a disembodied object, or applying it to another structure, was generally rejected as pointless, confirming that in just a dozen years, use (familiarity and memory) made the facade, structure and interior indivisible. Skinning would have only emphasized erasure as a matter of power. Affection for the facade notwithstanding, the architects' profounder achievement resided within: materially; sectionally; volumetrically; and in the display of the artwork (developed with Ralph Appelbaum and Associates, exhibition designers).

Plate 1 Kärntner Bar (American Bar or Loosbar), (1908), Vienna, Austria. Adolf Loos, Architect. Materials: marble (coffered ceiling, pillars and floor), onyx (clerestory above entrance), mahogany (bar and other furnishings) and brass (accents). [Photo: Nathaniel Coleman, 2017].

Plate 2 Museo di Castelvecchio (1957–64; 1968–69; 1973–75), Verona, Italy. Carlo Scarpa, Architect. [Photo: Nathaniel Coleman, 2007].

Plate 3 Stone and Concrete (?) Render, above Vals, Graubünden, Switzerland. [Photo: Nathaniel Coleman, 2007].

Plate 4 Quarzite Roofs Slates, Vals, Graubünden, Switzerland. [Photo: Nathaniel Coleman, 2007].

Plate 5 Water and Stone, Vals, Graubünden, Switzerland. [Photo: Nathaniel Coleman, 2007].

Plate 6 American Folk Art Museum, NYC (1998–2001, Demolished 2014). Tombasil Façade, 53rd Street. Tod Williams and Billie Tsien, Architects. [Photo: Nathaniel Coleman, 2008].

Plate 7 American Folk Art Museum, NYC (1998–2001, Demolished 2014). Tod Williams and Billie Tsien, Architects. *Carceri* Qualities of Folk Art Museum. [Photo: Nathaniel Coleman, 2008].

Plate 8 Scottish Parliament, Edinburgh, Scotland (1999–2004). EMBT (Enric Miralles and Benedetta Tagliabue, Architects). Member of Scottish Parliament (MSP) Block ('Skating Minister'). [Photo: Nathaniel Coleman, 2012].

Plate 9 Scottish Parliament, Edinburgh, Scotland (1999–2004). EMBT (Enric Miralles and Benedetta Tagliabue, Architects). Debating Chamber. [Photo: Nathaniel Coleman, 2012].

Plate 10 Querini Stampalia Bridge (1961–63), Venice, Italy. Carlo Scarpa, Architect. Steel arch and structure, Istrian stone step/abutments, metal uprights, wood handrails with brass accents, wood. [Photo: Nathaniel Coleman, 2007].

Plate 11 Barbican Estate Housing (1969–76), City of London, United Kingdom. Chamberlin, Powell and Bon, Architects. Timber window frames make the flats more homelike, internally and externally. [Photo: Nathaniel Coleman, 2017].

Plate 12 Dulwich Picture Gallery (1811–17), Dulwich, London, UK. Sir John Soane, Architect. Altered, added to, damaged by Second World War bombing, rebuilt (as original) after the War, and altered later. A direct, almost ancient use of brick. [Photo: Nathaniel Coleman, 1999].

Plate 13 Town Hall, Hilversum, The Netherlands (1928–31). Willem Marinus Dudok, Architect. Early Modernist Civic Building. Yellow buff glazed brick; taut unbrick-like skin. Emphasis on forms, scale of individual material is revealed close-up. [Photo: Nathaniel Coleman, 2015].

Plate 14 Barbican Estate Housing (1969–76), City of London, United Kingdom. Chamberlin, Powell and Bon, Architects. Concrete Frame Construction with various finishes, from rough to smooth (and shapes); timber window and door frames, brick pavers, water, vegetation, variety of building heights, use and materials, produce an amenable setting. [Photo: Nathaniel Coleman, 2017].

Plate 15 Hubertus House (1973–81), Exterior, Amsterdam, Holland. Aldo van Eyck, with Hannie van Eyck, Architects. Coloured metal façade panels adorn (and gentle) concrete frame structure. [Photo: Nathaniel Coleman, 1999].

Plate 16 Pavilion Le Corbusier, Zurich (1960–67). Le Corbusier, Architect. Materials: metal, glass and concrete, designed according to LC's Modulor proportional system; also known as the Heidi Weber Haus – Centre Le Corbusier. © Nathaniel Coleman. © F.L.C. / ADAGP, Paris and DACS, London 2019. [Photo: Nathaniel Coleman, 2007].

Figure 6.1 Skirkanich Hall, Bioengineering Department, University of Pennsylvania, West Philadelphia (2006). Cantilevered Entry Façade. Williams and Billie Tsien, Architects. Materials: hand-glazed ceramic brick, mossy green colour centre in spectrum from overall acid yellow to black; cantilevered shingled-glass panes (partly etched); zinc panelling; Canadian black granite. Structural concrete frame, (visible in parts internally). [Photo: Nathaniel Coleman, 2008].

Fibreglass

Writing in the 1940s, Summerson raised a challenge to the orthodox modernist banishment of ornament, anticipating Williams and Tsien's attempts to resolve the problem by attending to material surface. According to Summerson, an 'architect's relation to the materials at his [her] disposal' has the best chance of being 'productive and happy ... when a strong will-to-form has to struggle with a relatively intractable vocabulary of means'. Summerson does not recommend a return to ornament but rather identifies 'the modulation of surface' as 'a teasing and embarrassing problem' that begs to be solved in a positive way; primarily through addition, rather than subtraction, in mastering surface.

Apart from echoing Ruskin, Summerson anticipates Williams and Tsien's use of each project as an opportunity to subject their powerful architectural imaginaries to a 'struggle' with the significant limits of the construction industry, through materials, finishes and forms. According to Summerson, 'the problem is not ... the purely technological one of finding the adequate materials, adequate finishes, revetments which "weather well". Rather, 'the problem of surface remains unresolved simply because architects in their anxiety to get rid of the clogging cloying legacy of the subjunctive, have surrendered themselves too blindly to … [eschewing] ornament'.[25]

Although use and section, in anticipation of experiencing bodies, are at least as important as form in Williams and Tsien's architecture, they are just one part of their struggle with material. While they aim for expression intrinsic to construction, to avoid confusion with ornament, mastering surface is embraced as a positive challenge. Their continuous effort to expand conceptions 'of the meaning and possibilities of architecture' is grounded by use and the realities of contemporary construction, which keeps them close to modernist architecture, even as they take material and decorative risks.[26]

By courting the tensions material and structural problems give rise to, Williams and Tsien make a place in their work for the decorative that derives from construction. Concentrating on colour, depth, shadow, solidity and texture (amongst other qualities) reintroduces architecture to the realm of fine arts, while the sensuousness produced by this invites bodily experience. The architects' multidimensional and multisensory approach to combining matter, colour, form and movement is how they work out integrated problems of bodily experience and material meaning in buildings: the made thingness of the work is a source of the sensory stimuli bodily desire responds to, while their buildings encourage imaginative engagement with them through use.

After the facade, the Folk Art Museum's most striking material element was a fibreglass panel dropping from the building's nearly full 85-foot height to the ground floor. Its colour, material qualities and dramatic fall made it unmissable. Moving downward through the building (the preferred path), or upward, climbing the stair wrapped around the panel revealed the formal and spatial distinctiveness of both.

The prominence of the sectional organization of volumes at the Folk Art – as in much of their work – constituted an additional *material*. Others included stone (Pietra Piesentina, quarried north of Venice) that largely clad the interior floors and walls; the mix for exposed 'poured-in-place concrete walls' included 'terrazzo ground to produce a smooth finish that' revealed 'the stone aggregate', and the walls were also 'bush hammered'. Daylight was also significant, particularly the inventive ways it was made to suffuse the largely windowless building. Steel (cold rolled: stair, interior; terne coated stainless steel: exterior), laminated insulated glass and wood (cherry and Douglas fir) were also used.[27] However, the resin fibreglass panel, with its standing seems, was especially distinctive. Recollecting their inclusion of the material and element, the architects noted:

We very much liked the translucency and its 'low tech' quality. Originally, we wanted to use a screen wall of fiberglass to shield the primary staircase …[to] create silhouettes of people walking up and down the stairs. We wanted the screen to be blue. However, since it was a permanent part of the building, the fiberglass needed to be fireproofed, a process that would have produced a murky brown tone. The samples show how the color changed as we worked with the fabricator to produce what eventually became the blue-green panels.[28]

Figure 6.2 American Folk Art Museum, NYC (1998–2001, Demolished 2014). Blue-green fibreglass panel. Tod Williams and Billie Tsien, Architects. [Photo: Nathaniel Coleman, 2008].

The sections of the fibreglass panel were bolted together, hung from above and dropped through the middle of the primary staircase as a single element. While distinctive, it was not obviously functionally or structurally *necessary*. Its material quality, use and placement were at odds with the tenets of orthodox modernist architecture: it was not essential (which distances it from Zumthor), and materially poor (which distances it from Scarpa). But it was neither an economizing compromise nor frivolous; its logic was experiential. As presence intensified, moving near the panel while descending, or ascending, the stair anchored the action while introducing a degree of mystery, making it narratively necessary.

The panel startled in the jewel-like building; however, this move decisively collapsed the divide between 'high' and 'low' culture, and between MoMA art and folk art. Reimagining offhand corrugated roofs – of the sort found all over the United States – as a carefully crafted panel, upended preconceived notions of folk art as *low*. With its prominent position at the narrative heart of the building, the fibreglass panel pronounced the architects' affinity for folk art as the equal of any other art, not some curiosity to be admired ironically, if at all.

Figure 6.3 American Folk Art Museum, NYC (1998–2001, Demolished 2014). Blue-green fibre-glass panel and stair. Tod Williams and Billie Tsien, Architects. [Photo: Nathaniel Coleman, 2008].

Tsien associated their material choice for the panel with earlier screens they produced for a travelling exhibition (Quiet Light, 1994) of Isamu Noguchi's (1904–88) Akari light sculpture lamps: 'fiberglass is something that is cheap and not a big deal.' Although you would not expect to find it 'within the body of the museum', they required 'something … [lightweight] and inexpensive … and also incredibly common. Because … folk art … is done by people who aren't trained as artists,' which is why they 'wanted to make [the] materials feel very common'.[29] Even if the panel is recollected as convincingly purposeful, and Tsien described it as thematically core to the Folk Art Museum, Williams saw it as risky.

Although they had good reasons for using the fibreglass panel, they struggled with it. Williams wondered if he should 'have done it', no matter how 'integral' its 'fabulous qualities' seemed at the time. In retrospect, he determined it was excessive, because it masked the 'interesting structure …, and … floating body of the stair'. However, even more importantly than its material commonness, they wanted to drop 'a virtual line of water right down through the building', where there was 'very little space'.[30]

Admittedly, the fibreglass panel did not quite call to mind a 'virtual line of water' driving downward from near the top of the building to just above the ground floor slab but it did emphasize the drop, while intensifying descending and ascending the stair. Although the panel did not exactly support authorial intentions for it, William's use of 'virtual' is significant. The colour, standing seams, height and vertiginous drop of the panel could conceivably analogize an abstracted line of water, legible as a kind of flow. Williams felt a structural rationale for the panel, as integral to the stair assembly, was necessary to justify it but above all else he wondered if 'one needed all that stuff'.[31] Was it too elaborate? It surely was not reductive, but was it 'actually essential?'[32]

Reiterating her greater tolerance for the decorative, Tsien asserted that although not strictly technically functional, or structurally necessary, the fibreglass panel was as 'essential' as the tombasil facade: 'I think if its stripped bare it's too bare,' suggestive of Loos's conception of material cladding as analogous to being appropriately dressed. Ultimately, the fibreglass panel was as risky as the facade was.[33]

Incompleting relationships

Williams and Tsien's work pushes the limits of technical functionalism by expanding conceptions of use to encompass bodily experience and emotional responses to the world of others and things; always grounded in the *facts* of construction. Despite preoccupations with structural rationality, suppression of ornament and resisting decorative excess in their work, emotional functionalism is clearly on an equal footing with technical functionalism.[34]

According to Adorno, supposed negations of the rational in architecture tend to translate into 'the restoration of an allegedly free fantasy ... of expression'. When technical, functionalism affirms the quantitative and predicable, the results are reductive.[35] The pervasiveness of reductive functionalism renders it largely invisible, whereas 'free fantasy' garners greater exposure. Though, as Adorno observes: 'If out of disgust with functional forms and their inherent conformism' one 'wanted to give free reign to fantasy', the work 'would fall immediately into kitsch'.[36] Treading a knife-edge between functionalism, or pure construction on one side, and fantasy – risking falling into kitsch – on the other, may make Williams and Tsien's work not only difficult to pin down but also more compelling.

Williams's description of how his and Tsien's practices differ from Zumthor's and Scarpa's provides insight into their negotiations of the knife-edge. For him, Zumthor reduces 'things down' as much as possible to 'squeeze ... the poetry' out of them. On the other hand, 'Scarpa [builds things] up.' Although Zumthor *subtracts* and Scarpa *adds*, Williams believes they all share an interest 'in the residual poetry of architecture', partly evident in a weightiness, achieved by 'clawing away' at the earth to make 'good marks on' it, with 'a kind of permanency'.[37] Also shared is a preoccupation with narratives of experience that buildings either facilitate or thwart, and enough complexity to hold things in reserve that bodily experience and memory partially disclose.

Because each building constitutes the primary source for nearly inexhaustible interpretations, written descriptions are no substitute for being there. As Williams put it: 'the result of anyone's work is actually the work itself, rather than what they say, or what even other people say'.[38] Although a presentation of itself, the work is not static, because each experience of it partly remakes it: 'architecture speaks for itself' through building, which speaks 'to each person [who] inhabits' it. Buildings are 'never exactly as you want them to be, they have their own life'; are not 'fixed' things, so are 'always changing'.[39]

Williams and Tsien's attitudes towards *wholeness* and *control* most separates them from Zumthor, whose preoccupation with formal coherence translates into attempts to regulate the total reality of his buildings. He achieves this by maintaining – as much as possible – a single theme in each. His expressed desire to produce an *authentic original* presumes a manifestly discernible constructed entity. A single idea dominating material in the service of a particular use makes it theoretically possible to achieve more complete control over final results. Also controlled is production of a specific atmosphere (or emotional response). Ultimately, limitations and boundaries are Zumthor's central preoccupations.

As Zumthor put it: 'I try to make something as whole and complete as possible … I always work on establishing one main theme for each building'.[40] In contrast, Williams observed: 'I think a project is not something I can fully control or fully know …; we accept the risk of elements getting out of control'. For him, 'relationships are more important … than control or containment'.[41] If Zumthor *condenses* and Scarpa *intensifies*, Williams and Tsien arguably construct a mean between the two extremes. In this regard, Zumthor's faith in diagrams is revealing, especially in contrast to Willaims and Tsien's doubts. For Zumthor, 'a good architectural idea' can always be diagrammed 'on the back of a matchbook cover', whereas Williams, will 'never be able to draw a diagram on the back of an envelope'.[42] Single authorship might be a contributing factor to the clarity of Zumthor's work, while Williams and Tsien's collaboration inevitably produces enticing hybridity. In differentiating himself from them, Zumthor proffered:

> I know I feel this passion for containment and space, a contained space, the intimacy of being protected by architecture … I still imagine you wandering around … Let me see if I can define how we differ. For example, I always work on establishing one main theme for each building, otherwise I don't know what I'm doing there … How do you know what you are doing? … Do you work with a main theme? Or, if not, what is your method to keep your ideas under control?[43]

Artists' descriptions of their own work are only useful if independently supported by the work itself. Authorial intentions at best only introduce initial terms of criticism. Accordingly, Tsien observes, even if an artist aims to avoid confusion, 'everybody, has their own truth about a space …, the perception of space is very personal … Architects … have their own truth about what they think about [a] space', thus, even with deeper understandings of 'how people really react to … buildings', the 'private experience of a space' will always confound such knowledge.[44] Mismatches between claims and results do not necessarily confirm artistic failure.

Open work

According to Williams and Tsien, only the experiencing subject can speak for his or her encounter with a building. Even so, they do not surrender intention. Rather, according to Williams, although he knows what he thinks the work is about, 'every person' who experiences the building will have something distinct to say. He asserts, 'if I talk about my work [it's] because it's in a state of flux.'[45] Such openness to nearly inexhaustible interpretations, built upon experience, imbeds Williams and Tsien's conceptions of architecture within the fine arts, rather than as primarily a commercial endeavour. The studio sensibility resists overdetermination through every project stage, which translates into suspending anticipation of others' experiences of completed buildings, or attempts to overdetermine them. Despite their reluctance to pronounce a theory, their work and statements verify each other as a practice method that is ultimately pragmatic. As Williams observes, building significance is 'embedded in … moments [of] experience' because uniquely individual attempts to 'separate … and intellectualize' experience are doomed.[46]

Italian novelist and critic Umberto Eco (1932–2016) theorized the poetics of open work, proposing: '(1) "open" works, insofar as they are *in movement*, are characterized by the invitation to *make the work* together with the author [artist, architect]', which mirrors Williams and Tsien's conceptions of their architecture, and actual experiences of it.[47] Eco continues: '(2) on a wider level (as a *subgenus* in the *species* "work in movement") there exist works which, though completed, are "open" to continuous generation of internal relations which the addressee [visitor, inhabitant] must uncover and select in his [her] act of perceiving the totality of incoming stimuli.'[48] Thus, while it would be inaccurate to describe the Folk Art building as having been incomplete, it was surely open to continuous reinvention, or recompletion, by visitors. Although perhaps not Williams and Tsien's precise intention, it is clearly relevant. Eco explains why this might be: '(3) *Every* work of art, even though it is produced by following an explicit or implicit poetics of necessity, is effectively open to a virtually unlimited range of possible readings [experiences], each of which causes the work to acquire new vitality.'[49]

Preparing their architecture for openness includes developing multidimensional conceptions of context, which encompasses adjacencies; intended use; individual or institutional aspirations; budgetary and other limitations; cultural or regional milieu; and topography. All of their projects are 'inspired by the context in which' they 'work'. For example, 'at the Neurosciences Institute [La Jolla, California] the inspiration was clearly the Salk [Institute by Kahn] but' their response was not direct. They looked at the Salk 'out of the corners of' their eyes and 'directly', to ensure it was 'embedded in' them. Such consideration did not prefigure duplication. Rather, it is a method for finding their 'own truth'. For the Folk Art, they identified some pre-existing details from their work that they felt were either 'appropriate to folk art …, or … indirectly' related to their 'interest in folk art', motivated by a desire to establish 'some relationship to the context'.[50] Such relationships are not necessarily affirmations, especially when negation reveals positive directions, as in their critical encounters with the Salk, which informed

Figure 6.4 Neurosciences Institute, La Jolla, California (1992–95). Tod Williams and Billie Tsien, Architects. [Photo: Nathaniel Coleman, 2004].

the Neurosciences Institute. Likewise in the way Williams and Tsien transformed the small scale of the Folk Art Museum (determined by factors beyond their control) into outsized virtues: opacity, extravagant sectional and volumetric arrangement and complex circulation countered the limitations of a restricted site and context of conventional Manhattan buildings.

If its expansive site meant Williams and Tsien could associate the Neurosciences Institute's three main buildings as loosely linked episodes along a variety of meandering paths, the Folk Art's compact site demanded different tactics. At about 40 feet wide, and no more than 100 feet deep, lateral movement along wandering paths just was not possible but compressed episodes exploding upwards was. Similarly, the less intense Skirkanich Hall is also a dynamic urban building on a compact site that imaginatively responds to context by emphasizing verticality.

Piranesi

Although the Folk Art Museum encompassed themes Williams and Tsien have explored in earlier and subsequent buildings, it remains unique within their *oeuvre* and for architecture more generally. Even the most ostensibly radical post-mid-twentieth-century architecture *must* conform to the building industry by limiting architecture to problems of technique, or appearance. Through impressive acts of will, drawing upon a wellspring of optimism and utopian imaginaries, the architects produced a veritably visionary work, except that it was actually built. Folk Art building project architect

Matthew Baird is quoted as saying: 'It was conceived as a house for art, that was partly inspired by [British architect] Sir John Soane's [1753–1837] Museum in London' (1808–09, 1812).[51] Inevitably, his observation brings to mind Italian draftsman, printmaker, architect and art theorist Giovanni Battista Piranesi (1720–78), who greatly influenced Soane, particularly his House Museum. If Williams and Tsien were thinking about the Soane Museum when designing the Folk Art building, Piranesi would have been inescapable. Soane's museum consists of three terraced house plots, has a distinctive central facade and is as cramped as it is organizationally adventurous. While domestic in scale like the Folk Art, Piranesi is the most important shared factor, particularly the 1761 Second State of the *Carceri d'invenzione* – *Imaginary Prisons* – suite of etchings, which have influenced architects since their publication. Of these, Plate VII, 'The Drawbridge', is most suggestive of the Folk Art Museum, which helpfully features on Williams and Tsien's firm website, along with another Piranesi etching and a few other visionary architectural drawings.[52]

The point of the website display is to pronounce their own vision as *not* visionary: 'The power of the drawn idea can be almost as irresistible as the sun ... Piranesi's dark, layered, mysterious drawings ... have ... reverberated in our collective architectural imaginations.' No matter how alluring, 'Visionary architecture achieves its greatest power as unbuilt work.' Inevitably, to build is to compromise, inescapably ensnaring work within the spatial practices and modes of production of global capitalism, no matter how reluctantly. For even the purest hearts, making architectural ideas into real buildings through construction entails varying degrees of dissolution: 'What is lost in the actual realization of the work? Is the thought more powerful when it is expressed without dilution than the ambiguity that results from responding to a complex series of factors so common and necessary as client, cost, code, and use?' With this, Williams and Tsien ask the profoundest question architects must daily consider. Clearly, they accept the inevitable impurity of realization but do not want to completely surrender their architectural vision: 'We are not visionary architects, but we are beginning to see more clearly.'[53] As visionary, the Folk Art Museum may have been an anomaly for its architects, which is perhaps also what made it a distilled manifestation of their core concerns, and why hindsight reveals demolition as inevitable.

Although the Folk Art Museum did not literally embody Piranesi's 'Drawbridge', the etching prefigures the building's unique circulation, volumes, lighting, sectional organization and somewhat labyrinthic character. Like 'Drawbridge', the Folk Art had multiple routes of circulation, including numerous stairways, and catwalklike pathways (Plate 7). Both also share an extreme interiority, claustrophobic in Piranesi's etching, mostly so in the Folk Art Museum. Considering the reference to Soane's Museum, and the presence of the 'Drawbridge' on the studio's website, these associations *must* be more than casual. In consideration of what they value most in the organization and experience of their buildings, the association transcends formal, or representational, similarities to be comprehensible primarily in terms of use and analogy. Piranesi's *Carceri* series may be torturous but this is multi-determined, not simply visionary, or depictions of sadistic incarceration fantasies.

In the *Carceri*, Tafuri identifies the articulation of a breaking point in Western civilization, one profound result of which is the disappearance of architecture in any traditional sense: 'Architecture might make the effort to maintain its completeness and preserve itself from total destruction, but such an effort is nullified by the assemblage of architectural pieces in the city.'[54] The concept of negation in Williams and Tsien's work was introduced earlier though they would probably distance themselves from Tafuri's declaration of architecture's death as inevitable in an epoch of capitalist expansion. Paradoxically, the Folk Art building was a stark materialization of the impossibility of architecture, which explains its sources in Piranesi's *Carceri* and how it could be Phoenix and terminal simultaneously. In short: *why* it could not survive.

Tafuri asserts that in responding to the end of architecture, Piranesi 'had, therefore, to limit himself to enunciating emphatically that the great new problem was that of the equilibrium of opposites, which in the city finds its appointed place: failure to resolve this problem would mean the destruction of the very concept of architecture.'[55] Precisely these tensions played out in the Folk Art Museum, all the more poignant in the light of its demolition, which relegated it to visionary status. As Tafuri observes, in the *Carceri* (and by extension the disappeared Folk Art Museum):

> the destruction of the very concept of space merges with a symbolic allusion to the new condition being created by a radically changing society. ... In these etchings the space of the building – the prison – is an infinite space. What has been destroyed is the center of that space, signifying the correspondence between the collapse of ancient values, of the ancient order, and the 'totality' of the disorder.[56]

There is perhaps no more apt location for playing out this drama architecturally than in the shadow of MoMA (with its undying faith in modernist rationality), in a building dedicated to the intuitive irrationalities of Folk Art. However, in this negation, a more fully human space is anticipated. One that acknowledges fallibility, drifting concentration and desires to wander, outside of the enclosing bureaucratic rationality of modernity. The same qualities Tafuri attributes to the *Carceri* proved fatal for the American Folk Art Museum building:

> But the prison, precisely because infinite, coincides with the space of human existence. This is very clearly indicated by the hermetic scenes Piranesi designs within the mesh of lines of his 'impossible' compositions. Thus what we see in the *Carceri* is only the new existential condition of human collectivity, liberated and condemned at the same time by its own reason.[57]

Inevitably, cities made in the image of bureaucratic rationality will not tolerate negations of their systematicity; less so assertions of the human condition of being 'liberated and condemned at the same time by its own reason'. Banality is okay, trivial architecture is fine, spectacle is encouraged and anything that smooths consumption or contributes to apparent efficiencies is applauded. In Tafuri's view, by the early twentieth century –

the period of greatest modernist strength on display at MoMA: 'The "loss" foretold by Piranesi has now become tragic reality. The experience of the "tragic" is the experience of the metropolis.'[58] Following Tafuri, this is the context of production that art now must respond to, not least in creative disaffirmations of it. Choosing not to build is one solution, capitulation is another but Williams and Tsien chart a third option by optimistically negating the supposed total 'system' that necessarily makes buildings like the Folk Art *impossible*. Accordingly, its destruction is less significant than that it ever existed at all.

By leaving much open to the interpretation of experiencing subjects, who become co-producers of a building's atmosphere through bodily movement, their work provides for unanticipated narrative possibilities. As the first point of contact between individual and building, material is crucial for establishing the open conditions of varied encounters. However, on its own, material is not significant enough to sustain improvised exploration,

Figure 6.5 Giovanni Battista Piranesi, Etching, Second State of the *Carceri d'invenzione*, or, *Imaginary Prisons* (1761); Plate VII, 'The Drawbridge'. Etching. Available online at: https://archive.org/details/gri_33125010859573 (Accessed: 22 July 2018). Publication date: 1761. Published in Rome. Not In Copyright. Courtesy of Getty Research Institute. Getty Research Institute, Research Library, 1200 Getty Center Drive, Suite 1100, Los Angeles, CA 90049-1688.

which is why the architects introduce multiple paths of circulation and vertiginous sectional arrangements into their buildings. Sectional arrangement of volumes most emphatically suggests bodily presence and movement, second only to stairs. Following stairs, ramps and catwalks most explicitly analogize movement by facilitating it. Views into, towards, downward, across and upward, through volumes, hint at the possible discoveries varied movement promises.

Stairs

The main stair at the Folk Art Museum recollected the character – material, details and atmosphere – of the primary stair in architect Marcel Breuer's (1902–1981) Whitney Museum building (1966), NYC. An association both Williams and Tsien invite, extending it to all of their work. For Tsien, 'It's always the model', likewise for Williams, who describes it as 'very important'. Although primarily a fire escape, Williams describes the Whitney stair as 'wonderful' and 'humane', noting that the 'change of cadence as you go up' makes it 'very easy … to walk up'.[59]

For Williams, the Whitney example highlights how 'terribly important' stairs are as the 'measure [of] a person' in buildings. Whether or not anyone is 'on the steps …, you feel the presence of … a person by virtue of the relationship of the foot to the risers, to the tread', which prefigures 'a person moving through space'. Although buildings are shaped around bodily activities, stairs declare this most explicitly. When 'properly done', stairs beg 'for a person to' inhabit them but when 'not properly done'; when 'just a continuous extrusion', they discourage inhabitation; experienced as an unwelcoming 'system' that cannot be entered, even if technically functional. A 'properly done' stair 'unfolds and allows you to find a place … as you move up; a bench to sit on, a change of cadence, of the width of the stair'.[60]

The Folk Art Museum calls to mind Piranesi's *Carceri*, not as simulacrum of the 'Drawbridge' but rather by being like it. In many parts of the museum, visitors came upon the art along divergent paths of movement, emphasizing bodily experience. Although this could seem to diminish the art's value, it actually augmented it. Challenging vitality draining conceptions of museums as educative, or quasi-sacred; displaying artworks as moments along multiple ways of coming and going, or drifting, enlivened the folk art on view.

The three staircases in the Folk Art connoted and denoted action. The architects' intensive concentration on anticipated bodies in motion translated into a setting that impelled museum visitors to involve themselves in reimagining the artworks and architecture. Tafuri identifies something similar in encounters with the *Carceri*: 'the spectator of the *Carceri* is obliged, more than invited, to participate in the process of mental reconstruction proposed by Piranesi'.[61] Whereas Piranesi lamented the loss of prior cultural conditions, more than 250 years later, this is the only knowable context. As such, Williams and Tsien share with Piranesi a now rooted 'systematic criticism of the concept of "center"'.[62]

Without a centre, of the sort 'classicist harmony' previously structured, architectural space unbound either disappears or opens towards subjective conceptions of the infinite.[63] For Williams and Tsien, this involves the inevitable tensions of relationships, fallibility and individual movement and experience; most effectively prefigured by stairs: 'the stair represents the energy of a person moving through space', a significance denied when 'an elevator or an escalator' displaces them. According to Williams, diminishing stairs communicates that the 'the body doesn't really matter'; flows of movement 'through space' might 'but not the … beat of the heart', or the 'feeling of the thigh or the foot, or' any other part of the body.[64]

Stairs anticipating bodily movement are directly related to the architects' delight in working sectionally. Accordingly, Williams noted: 'one of the very first things I draw is a person …, standing, and a person moving up a stair', which makes it possible to 'feel the dimension of the space … It's not so much necessarily finding the sectional space' but rather finding 'the person in the space and then … the section'.[65]

The introduction of multiple paths made up of discrete parts experienced along spines of movement displaces centre in Williams and Tsien's buildings. Once the authoritative hierarchies of centre are deconstructed, drifting becomes the method for constructing individual spatial narratives. In Williams's mind, associations between buildings and spaces are desirable but for them to be positive, 'they cannot be tightly connected'. Indeed, 'the more loosely connected the better'.[66] The aim is to confound prescribed perceptions by facilitating multiple experiences of relationships between spaces in a building. Recurrent themes perceived in distraction begin to preconsciously associate spaces, elements, materials or motifs. Although similar elements may silt up in the 'memory', recollections are not literal.[67] Motifs are not provided as road signs but as fodder for half-noticed recollections layered into fictional – subjective – memories of a dreamed-up whole, as a poetic shadow of the 'real' building.

Inevitably, writing about experiences of architecture portrays authoritative accounts that make explicit precisely the associations Williams believes *must* remain preconscious. The anticipated visitors to their buildings would be distracted, feeling their way along multiple paths without thinking too much about it. For Williams, 'there have been paths that have been suggested, and there are relationships that have been suggested but are … linked only by …memory.'[68]

The idea that bodily experiences of their buildings are individually constructed out of fallible memories collected in distraction, rather than directed, invites freely associated perceptions. Looseness is amenable to relationships (between people and things), including collaborations, because it tolerates difference. When internalized, the other is actively embraced as generative and dynamic. Accepting fallibility – that nothing can always be gotten right – is a prerequisite, which translates into a lot of *air* in Williams and Tsien's buildings. Only by trusting some measure of intuition can liveliness be introduced. In general, but particularly at the Folk Art Museum, this is construable as a ceaseless search for a different humanlike (imperfectible) order. The embrace of fallibility not only extends to their experimentations with materials, but is also central to it. For Williams, the impossibility of solving every materials problem is what makes working with 'different materials so exciting':

> These are complex three dimensional problems that penetrate through every fiber of the building …, so, the more you allow different things to come in; me to allow Billie into my life; the site to come into my life; … the client to come into our life; the more you are absolutely going to be forced to fail, but fail while struggling … for perfection. And to me that's what you want … And that's why success is such horseshit. Because success means you haven't failed.[69]

The virtue of the loose fit is that it makes perfection unachievable, which introduces possibilities for continuously enacted dramas, long after the architects have left the building to the occupants. Courting the unknowable animates the things and events that comprise their buildings. Acknowledging the fugitive qualities of their work, Tsien observed:

> there's a kind of complexity that is also withheld and is not absolute, … we really don't want the work to reveal everything right away. And, … it's only through habitation that you understand the layers. Which is not to say that it is just willfully complex but that there are perhaps episodes that you might miss … at first, … that after awhile you perceive. And ,… each person sees it in a different way; … it's not the same message for everybody.[70]

Tsien's reiteration of creative tensions between the openness of the 'withheld' and 'not absolute' and the desire for their buildings to still be 'knowable', including discouraging readings of them as simply 'willfully complex', outlines their method and artistic objectives. Their attention to use and construction is solid proof that the eccentric layered spaces they invent, which refuse to 'reveal everything right away', are more subtle than 'just willfully complex'. Embracing the full range of intricacies required to produce a more human order are matters of relationships and difference at every level. As Williams observed:

> I'm interested in relationships but I don't want to complete all the relationships, I'm not sure I want to complete any relationship. I want … the relationship to be … suggestive … If the work is too tidy [it will be less amenable to difference], so that's why we need to leave the story open, full of possibilities but incomplete so you can complete it in your way … Because our two ways will never complete perfectly …, because we're too different. And I'm not interested in being the same.[71]

Williams and Tsien make a virtue of the tensions inherent to split authorship by embracing their individual distinctiveness, as work and life partners. Accepting self and other as forever incomplete, thus never fully knowable, reveals relationships as perpetually in flux and always developing. Oscillating interactions, holding things in reserve, animates their work. Buildings (anyone, thing) are unknowable unless lived with, slowly unfolding through experience. In part because of its site – suggestive of Soane's House Museum – but also because of the intimacy of folk art, the Folk Art building was quite domestic, inviting accommodation and tensions of the sort one finds at home. As the great setting of intimacy and deceit, houses are intense stages of relationships. Tensions in the building were articulated materially; between light and dark; smooth and rough; open and closed; soft and hard; warm and cold; transparent and opaque; solid and void.

Buildings ought to analogize the untidiness of being human as rhythmic coherence, in otherwise atonal spatial arrangements that renounce centre. Though still comprehensible, such a setting would open to the peculiarities of individual experience.[72] As living, buildings are never completed. Each experience is unique. Only death – demolition – aborts the process. Written description, photographs and drawings are no substitute for bodily experience. No matter how much it satisfied the architects' intentions, clients' desires and visitors' expectations, destruction terminated the unfolding story of the Folk Art building too soon. Aware of the correlation between the liveliness of persons and buildings, Loos asserted: 'An apartment must never be completed. Are we human beings ever finished, complete in our physical and psychological developments? Do we ever come to a standstill?'[73]

Epilogue: Mourning a terminal jewel

Williams and Tsien's American Folk Art Museum was demolished because it did not conform to conservative conceptions of modernist architecture, originally codified by MoMA with the seminal International Style exhibition (10 February to 23 March 1932), organized by influential architect Philip Johnson (1906–2005), architectural historian Henry-Russell Hitchcock Jr.(1903–87) and art historian and first MoMA director Alfred H. Barr Jr. (1902–81), who coined the term.[74] A companion volume, *The International Style: Architecture Since 1922*, written by Hitchcock and Johnson, was published in 1932.[75]

Together, the International Style exhibit, catalogue and book defined the limits of modernist architecture: cubic ferro-concrete structures in one direction and structurally expressive glass and steel buildings in the other, with occasional hybrids, including the use of brick. The clearest overall example of all three in the exhibition was German architect Walter Gropius's (1883–1969) work. Founder of the Bauhaus (1919–28), he emigrated to the United States (1937), where he directed the Harvard University Graduate School of Design from 1938 to 1952, thereby extending his influence to the present.[76] The central aim of MoMA, and more so of the International Style exhibit, was to divest the *new* architecture of whatever politically transformative programme it might have had; recasting it as a problem of style, thereby rendering it consumable; for eventual ossification as the official style of bureaucratic modernity. Whether state capitalist or state socialist, corporate or institutional, International Style modernist architecture mostly produces empty signifiers. As defined by Barr in the exhibit catalogue, the new 'aesthetic principles' of the style were based primarily upon the nature of modern materials and structure and upon modern requirements in planning. Slender steel posts and beams, and concrete reinforced by steel have made possible structures of skeleton-like strength and lightness. The external surfacing materials are of painted stucco or tile, or, in more expensive buildings, of aluminum or thin slabs of marble or granite and of glass both opaque and transparent. Planning, liberated from the necessity for symmetry so frequently required by tradition is, in the new style, flexibly dependent upon convenience.[77]

Characterized by specific materials, structural systems and planning, intended, as much as possible, to reflect the logic of machines and machine production, in its purest form, International Style architecture would be structurally rational, lightweight, have an open plan and be wrapped by a taut skin. Ornament (or any perceived excess) would be stripped away. Outside of the ablest of hands, modernism is ruthlessly unforgiving, quickly becoming a caricature of the rationalist optimism it was meant to represent. Right from the start, *Style* consistency was violated, either by incompetence or by efforts to expand modernism's limited poetic capacities.

As the birthplace of the International Style, MoMA would have been unable to assimilate the dissonant Folk Art Museum building into its expansion plans. The *New York Times* reported the decision to demolish as follows: 'MoMA officials said the building's design did not fit their plans because the opaque facade is not in keeping with the glass aesthetic of the rest of the museum. The former folk museum is also set back farther than MoMA's other properties, and the floors would not line up.'[78] The impossibility of MoMA's institutional consciousness to accommodate architecture disobedient to International Style limitations on its doorstep sealed the fate of the Folk Art building. Early on, Muschamp outlined the specific virtues of the building that would have also made it unassimilable:

[Williams and Tsien] have made values associated with folk art – intimacy, companionship, aspiration – accessible to modern audiences. They do not crib folk art forms. They do not draw upon pop-culture kitsch. Rather they turned modern architecture inside out. In place of modernism's aesthetic of objective norms, they use abstract form to explore the emotional content of public space … Materiality always pulls Mr. Williams and Ms. Tsien back from the brink of pure abstraction. They treat pieces of translucent corrugated plastic, steel supports on a stair, and panels of polyurethane foam like artifacts of incalculable value, as if the building were the private scrapbook of industrial culture.[79]

In 2013, architect Aaron Betsky highlighted the paradoxical relationship between the building's uniqueness and the inevitability of demolition:

The former American Folk Art Museum is a stunning design, both in the way its façade abstracts and inflects the traditional brownstone row house, and in the intricacy of its interior spaces. Both achievements, however, also buttress an argument for tearing the building down.[80]

Condemned for the very qualities that made it significant, perception of it as 'bespoke' and 'obdurate' were pressed into service as explanations for its unassimilability, thereby justifying demolition as necessary, because out of step with MoMA's brand identity.[81]

By establishing a material and spatial rejoinder to trivial post-Second World War architecture, the Folk Art became decisively redundant; doomed for its specificity and strangeness because marketplace logic permeates culture. It is as if only generic buildings inline with modernist banality, extending from the Bauhaus to Koolhaas, are continuously reusable. Lefebvre identifies this as a legacy of orthodox modernism: 'When it comes to the question of what the Bauhaus's audacity produced in the long run, one is obliged to answer: the worldwide, homogeneous and monotonous architecture of the state, whether capitalist or socialist.'[82] With almost satirical perfection, then chief curator of MoMA's architecture and design department, Barry Bergdoll, is quoted as describing the decision to demolish the Folk Art in bureaucratic terms, as 'administrative'.[83]

Inevitably, the building was not esteemed by everyone. Some commentators blamed it for the Folk Art Museum's troubles that ultimately led to demolition. One observed: 'it is notable for a blank, vaguely lunar, metal-clad facade that is armored and fortresslike, positively foreboding … The most egregious touch is a broad stairway connecting the third and fourth floors that takes huge bites out of the narrow, already limited galleries.'[84] Denouncing the building, art critic Jerry Staltz rejected its every possible virtue as a litany of shortcomings.[85]:

> Despite the many rave reviews the 30,000-square-foot building received when it opened in December 2001, it was immediately clear to many that the building was not only ugly and confining, it was also all but useless for showing art … The inside was worse. Dominated by showy staircases of many scales going in different directions, ill-conceived nooks and niches, the galleries were long narrow corridors or landings, sometimes only a few feet wide, making it impossible to see the art.[86]

Stalz's frustration with the building's unexpected character made it incomprehensible to him, in anything but negative terms. His use of 'ugly', and exasperation with the building's most distinctive qualities, calls to mind Adorno's observation that: 'The prohibition of the ugly has become an interdiction of whatever is not formed *hic et nunc*, of the incompletely formed, the raw. Dissonance is the technical term for the reception through art of what aesthetics as well as naiveté calls ugly.'[87] In Adorno's terms, because dissonant, Staltz was compelled to call the Folk Art 'ugly' but this produces its own inversion to become a statement of the highest praise. It is precisely the malformed, the raw, the strangeness of Williams and Tsien's Folk Art Museum building that makes it a self-renewing event (even in its absence).

Although cramped with narrow galleries and too much stair, the building was distinctive, for NYC, and as museum architecture almost anywhere. As concrete evidence that nontrivial architecture is still possible, even in the twenty-first century, the building was incongruous. While Williams and Tsien's buildings are consistently adventurous, the Folk Art Museum was a concentrated manifestation of their artistic ethos. It ably housed the vital fragility of folk art, and was itself a work of misfit architecture, destined to be devoured by its establishment neighbour. Paradoxically, commissioning Williams and Tsien to make such a bold statement so close to MoMA entrapped the Folk Art Museum building's patrons in an unwinnable endgame: outsider art would never achieve insider status. The right building ended up on the wrong lot, built on the wrong street, in the wrong part of town. Commenting on the building's imminent demolition, Tsien observed:

> We feel really disappointed ... There are of course the personal feelings – your buildings are like your children, and this is a particular, for us, beloved small child. But there is also the feeling that it's a kind of loss for architecture, because it's a special building, a kind of small building that's crafted, that's particular and thoughtful at a time when so many buildings are about bigness.[88]

Figure 6.6 *Carceri*-like; possible partial source of Scarpa's Cangrande Installation at the Castelvecchio Museum. Nearby the Tomb of Cangrande I in the della Scala cemetery, fourteenth century; Church of Santa Maria Antica, 1185, Verona, Italy. Also reminiscent of aspects of Williams and Tsien's Folk Art Museum. [Photo: Nathaniel Coleman, 2007].

The fragmented pathways of Piranesi's 'The Drawbridge' and Scarpa's Cangrande installation at the Castelvecchio intersect in memories of the spatial logic of the Folk Art Museum. All three negate centre, not as tragedy but as an event of modernity. Dynamic experiences are emphasized by dramas of circulation, enacted through individual bodily movement, across vertiginous catwalklike pathways (or multiple stairways). Not surprisingly, the material palette in the Folk Art Museum building also recollected that astonishing moment at the Castlevecchio, not as simulacrum but as a nod to the particularities of a specific tradition (See Figure 6.6).

Notes

1. Muschamp, 'Fireside Intimacy for Folk Art Museum', 14 December 2001.

2. 'World Architecture ARUP Awards', Reported in *Architecture Week*, 21 August 2002. Available online at: http://www.architectureweek.com/2002/0821/news_1-1.html (Accessed 30 March 2018).

3. For an overview of the Folk Art Museum demolition, see Robert Beauregard, 'We Blame the Building! The Architecture of Distributed Responsibility', *International Journal of Urban and Regional Research*, First published 22 June 2015. Available online at: https://doi.org/10.1111/1468-2427.12232 (Accessed 02 April 2018).

4. Tod Williams and Billie Tsien, 'Museum Building', *American Folk Art Museum*, http://www.folkartmuseum.org/default.asp?id=875 (Three pages, downloaded: 7 January 2008. No longer available).

5. Ibid.

6. Ibid.

7. Ibid.

8. Ibid.

9. Ibid.

10. Ibid.

11. Herbert Muschamp, Critic's Notebook: 'Design for Folk Art Museum Points to the Future by Honoring the Past', *New York Times*, 29 October 1997. Available online at: https://www.nytimes.com/1997/10/29/arts/critic-s-notebook-design-for-folk-museum-points-future-honoring-past.html (Accessed 30 March 2018).

12. Billie Tsein, Unpublished author interview with Tod Williams and Billie Tsien conducted by Nathaniel Coleman, TWBTA Studio, New York, March 2008 (Digital voice recording).

13. Ibid.

14. Ibid.

15. Ibid.

16. Ibid., Williams, Unpublished author interview, March 2008.

17. Ibid.

18. Ibid.

19. Ibid.

20. Ibid.

21. Ibid.

22. Ibid.

23. Ibid.

24. Ibid.

25. Sir John Summerson, 'The Mischievous Analogy' (1941), in *Heavenly Mansions and Other Essays on Architecture*, New York and London: W. W. Norton, 1963, pp. 213–14, 215, 216–17.

26. Ibid., p. 2018.

27. Williams and Tsien, 'Museum Building'.

28. Ibid.

29. Williams and Tsein, 'Quiet Light' project description, *TOD WILLIAMS BILLIE TSIEN Architects | Partners*. Available at: http://twbta.com/work/quiet-light (Accessed 02 April 2018).

30. Williams, Unpublished author interview, March 2008.

31. Ibid.

32. Ibid.

33. Ibid., Tsien, Unpublished author interview, March 2008.

34. For a discussion of 'emotional functionalism' and other relevant concepts introduced by Dutch architect Aldo van Eyck (1918–1999), see Coleman, *Utopias and Architecture*. See also, Coleman, *Lefebvre for Architects*.

35. Adorno, *Aesthetic Theory* (1970), p. 44.

36. Ibid., p. 33.

37. Williams, Unpublished author interview, March 2008.

38. Ibid.

39. Ibid.

40. Peter Zumthor, 'The Tension of Not Being Specific: Billie Tsien and Tod Williams in Conversation with Peter Zumthor', *Williams and Tsien Works: 2G International Architectural Review*, 1, no. 9 (1999): 8–23 (pp. 8, 14).

41. Ibid., pp. 14, 15.

42. Ibid., p. 14.

43. Ibid., pp. 8, 11–12, 14.

44. Tsien, Unpublished author interview, March 2008.

45. Ibid., Williams, Unpublished author interview, March 2008.

46. Ibid.

47. Umberto Eco, 'The Poetics of the Open Work', in *The Open Work*, Anna Cancogni (trans.), Cambridge, MA: Harvard University Press, 1989, p. 21.

48. Ibid.

49. Ibid.

50. Williams, Unpublished author interview, March 2008.

51. Matthew Baird, quoted in Michael Webb, 'Outrage: MoMA is a Neighbourhood Bully in Dooming New York's Folk Art Museum', *The Architectural Review*, 10 May 2013. Available

online at: https://www.architectural-review.com/rethink/outrage-moma-is-a-neighbourhood-bully-in-dooming-new-yorks-folk-art-museum/8647819.article (Accessed 05 April 2018).

52. Sir John Summerson, 'Neo-Classicism: Britons Abroad', in *Architecture in Britain: 1530–1830*, London and New York: Pelican History of Art, 1983, pp. 377–437.

53. Williams and Tsien, 'Slowly (improving) Vision', *TOD WILLIAMS BILLIE TSIEN Architects | Partners*, Website. Available at: http://www.twbta.com/9090 (Accessed 05 April 2018). Originally published in, *Williams and Tsien Works: 2G International Architectural Review*, 1, no. 9 (1999): 138–43.

54. Tafuri, *Architecture and Utopia*, p. 14.

55. Ibid., pp. 15–16.

56. Ibid., pp. 16–17.

57. Ibid., p. 18.

58. Ibid., p. 78.

59. Williams, Unpublished author interview, March 2008.

60. Ibid.

61. Manfredo Tafuri, *The Sphere and the Labyrinth: Avant-Gardes and Architecture from Piranesi to the 1970s* (1980), Pellegrino d' Acierno and Robert Connolly (trans.), Cambridge, MA: MIT Press, 1987, p. 26.

62. Ibid., p. 27.

63. Ibid., pp. 31, 51.

64. Williams, Unpublished author interview, March 2008.

65. Ibid.

66. Ibid.

67. Ibid.

68. Ibid.

69. Ibid.

70. Ibid., Tsien, Unpublished author interview, March 2008.

71. Ibid., Williams, Unpublished author interview, March 2008.

72. The reading advanced here, of Williams and Tsien's work as *atonal*, was suggested by: Courtney S. Adams, 'Techniques of Rhythmic Coherence in Schoenberg's Atonal Instrumental Works', *The Journal of Musicology*, 11, no. 3 (Summer, 1993): 330–56.

73. Loos, 'On Thrift' (1924), p. 182.

74. Philip Johnson, et al., *Modern Architecture International Exhibition: February 10 to March 23, 1932*, New York: The Museum of Modern Art, 1932. Available online at: https://www.moma.org/documents/moma_catalogue_2044_300061855.pdf (Accessed 04 April 2018).

75. Henry-Russell Hitchcock Jr and Philip Johnson, *The International Style* (1932), New York: W. W. Norton, 1995.

76. For more on Gropius, the Bauhaus legacy, and the lasting influence of his Harvard tenure, see: H. F. Koeper, 'Walter Gropius', *Encyclopædia Britannica*, Encyclopædia Britannica, inc., 14 December 2017. Available online at: https://www.britannica.com/biography/Walter-Gropius (Accessed 27 March 2018); Sigfried Giedion, *Space, Time and Architecture: The Growth of a New Tradition* (1941), Fifth Edition, Revised and Enlarged, Cambridge,

MA: Harvard University Press, 1982, especially pp. 477–517; and Herdeg, *The Decorated Diagram*.

77. Alfred H. Barr, Jr, 'Foreword', in *Modern Architecture International Exhibition*, pp. 13–14.

78. Robin Progrebin, '12-Year-Old Building at MoMA Is Doomed', *New York Times*, 10 April 2013.

79. Herbert Muschamp, 'ARCHITECTURE REVIEW; Fireside Intimacy for Folk Art Museum', *New York Times*, 14 December 2001.

80. Aaron Betsky, 'The Case for Modernism MoMA American Folk Art Museum', *Architect*, 08 May 2013. Available online at: http://www.architectmagazine.com/design/the-case-for-modernism-moma-american-folk-art-museum_o (Accessed 06 July 2018).

81. Liz Diller, of Diller Scofidio & Renfro (MoMA's current expansion architects), said: 'It's a damn shame that the building is obdurate', quoted in Robin Pogrebin, 'In Rare Public Forum, Architect Defends Decision to Take Down Former Folk Art Museum', *ArtsBeat New York Times Blog*, 29 January 2014, 2:11 pm. Available at: https://artsbeat.blogs.nytimes.com/2014/01/29/in-rare-public-forum-architect-defends-decision-to-take-down-former-folk-art-museum/?mtrref=www.google.co.uk (Accessed 29 March 2018). Barry Bergdoll, current MoMA chief design curator, described the building as 'a bespoke suit for folk art', quoted in Robin Pogrebin, 'Architects Announce Opposition to MoMA Plan for Former Museum Site', *ArtsBeat New York Times Blog*, 22 April 2013, 6:46 pm. Available at: https://artsbeat.blogs.nytimes.com/2013/04/22/architects-announce-opposition-to-moma-plan-for-former-museum-site/ (Accessed 29 March 2018).

82. Lefebvre, *The Production of Space*, p. 124.

83. Barry Bergodoll, quoted in Virginia C. McGuire, 'MoMA the Demolisher', *Architect's Newspaper*, 16 April 2013.

84. Roberta Smithmay, 'Downsizing in a Burst of Glory', *New York Times*, 12 May 2011.

85. Martin Filler, 'MoMA: A Needless Act of Destruction', *New York Review of Books*, 23 May 2013. Available at: http://www.nybooks.com/articles/2013/05/23/moma-needless-act-destruction/ (Accessed 29 March 2018).

86. Jerry Saltz, 'Architecture Killed the American Folk Art Museum', *Vulture*, 11 May 2011. Available at: http://www.vulture.com/2011/05/saltz_architecture_killed_the.html (Accessed 28 March 2018).

87. Adorno, *Aesthetic Theory* (1970), pp. 45–6.

88. Billie Tsien, quoted in, Robin Pogrebin, '12-Year- Old Building at MoMA Is Doomed', *New York Times*, 10 April 2013. Available online at: https://www.nytimes.com/2013/04/11/arts/design/moma-to-raze-ex-american-folk-art-museum-building.html (Accessed 03 April 2018).

CHAPTER 7
TECTONIC SHIFTS: MIRALLES'S ARTS AND CRAFTS ECSTASY AT THE SCOTTISH PARLIAMENT (2004)

The new Scottish Parliament complex in Edinburgh (1999–2004), comprising up to ten discernible structures (most interlinked), was designed by Catalonian architect Enric Miralles (1955–2000), with his partner (in life and work), architect Benedetta Tagliabue, known collectively as EMBT. The Parliament vigorously engages a range of materials in the construction of an enthusiastic rejoinder to conventional political arrangements; counterbalanced by a somewhat more sober encounter with territory as culture. At the Parliament complex, land is acknowledged as the most explicitly local feature of a place. Here, the architecture is a topographical story developed out of interpretations of material and context that extends to the surrounding landscape, encompassing the city and Holyrood Park, including Salisbury Crags, and Arthur's Seat (an extinct volcano). Land, material, construction and history are the stuff out of which the Parliament's significance is construed. A key source of these characteristics in Miralles's work is the constellation of language, forms and architectural longings suffused with a spirit of cultural independence; inherited at least partly from Catalonian architect Antoni Gaudí (1852–1926), who constructed settings of, and for, an independent national identity.[1] Although Miralles's Parliament complex might be misconstrued as a so-called icon building, or as 'entertainment architecture' (participating in city-branding programmes), his was a much more serious enquiry into architecture as political.

Although expressed in very different ways, Miralles shared with Williams and Tsien, and Scarpa, a conception of buildings as landscape. As such, the Parliament fixes cultural imaginaries to the land; close at hand, further afield and mythical, coalescing into assertions of the uniqueness of Scottish national identity. By clarifying micro and macro conceptions of locale, the complex prepares a ground for new ways of being, individually, socially and politically. Like Williams and Tsien, Miralles engaged with the realities of contemporary construction as an opportunity to reflect on the ebbing of craft in building, alongside possibilities for its reinterpretation (akin to Loos). If the work of Williams and Tsien is part of a modernist tradition of US architecture rooted in the work of Frank Lloyd Wright (1867–1959), Louis I. Kahn (1901–74), Marcel Breuer (1902–81) and Eero Saarinen (1910–61); Miralles was steeped in the building traditions of Europe, Gaudí in particular but also Scottish architect Charles Rennie Mackintosh (1868–1928) and Swiss-French architect Le Corbusier (1887–1965).[2]

Figure 7.1 Scottish Parliament, Edinburgh, Scotland (1999–2004). EMBT (Enric Miralles and Benedetta Tagliabue), Architects. Entry Pergola. [Photo: Nathaniel Coleman, 2012].

Before opening his own studio, Miralles, like Williams, worked for a more *rationalist* architect than he would become. Williams worked in the NYC office of US architect Richard Meier; Miralles in the studio of Albert Viaplana and Helio Piñón, in Barcelona. In much the way Williams applies the discipline he learned from Meier in his own work with Tsien; Miralles's work never severed ties between architecture and building. His experiments with materials and forms may begin with Viaplana and Piñón but did not stop there. Analogously, Williams and Tsien might begin with Meier's precision but are disobedient in its application. Overall, Miralles's work is wilder than Williams and Tsien's. Artistic temperament is surely the primary determining factor, but the distinctness of regional and national architectural cultures, including the building industry, will have contributed. Miralles also shared with Williams and Tsien professional collaboration with his spouse; with his first wife, Carme Pinós and then Benedetta Tagliabue, his second wife.

Miralles's work implicitly critiques the main currents of twentieth-century techno-utopian modernism, without abandoning them. Although recollected as utopian, twentieth-century modernist architecture has more in common with scientific-management and myths of optimized progress, than with the nineteenth-century utopian socialists it is often associated with. If twentieth-century modernist architecture had a utopian precursor, it was a peculiar admixture of nineteenth-century engineering achievements and the eighteenth-century physiocratic and absolutist utopianism represented by French Neoclassical architects Étienne-Louis Boullée (1728–99) and Claude-Nicolas Ledoux (1736–1806); as well as Jeremy Bentham's (1748–1832) Panopticon project (1791).[3]

Conceived in the service of power, as exercises in discipline and control, in relation to industrial production and social organization, the developments outlined in the preceding paragraph anticipate the totalizing rigidities of capitalist realist (and state socialist) twentieth- and twenty-first-century city planning. As Tafuri observed, mainstream twentieth-century modernist architecture is better understood as 'forming part of the same phenomena one wishes to analyze by means of' nineteenth-century utopian socialist ideas, which it supposedly derives from.[4] Accordingly, it is all but impossible to reconcile the architecture and city planning of the twentieth and twenty-first centuries with the nineteenth-century utopian socialist visions of François Marie Charles Fourier (1772–1837), Ruskin, William Morris (1834–1896) or Ebenezer Howard (1850–1928), who were critical of the increasing influence of factory labour and industrialization on all aspects of modern life.[5]

Miralles's interest in Mackintosh and Gaudí situates him within the milieu of nineteenth-century utopian socialism by way of its association with Ruskin and Morris, who sought to reform art, architecture, design and life.[6] Although best known for beautiful objects, the Arts and Crafts' main project was reform of industrial society. In Miralles's work, Le Corbusier bridges Ruskin with the Bauhaus, though it is independent of both. The wildness of the Scottish Parliament is imbued with these myriad sources. Much more than simply self-indulgently wilful, or novel, the riot of forms and materials that shape it are expressions of social and political freedom (or at least their possibility). At the Parliament, Catalonian desires for statehood are analogous to Scottish self-rule, and the not yet closed question of independence, which also makes it a paradoxical prefiguration of a cosmopolitan *national style*.

The array of materials and forms, in particular the myriad smaller elements applied throughout the complex, inside and out, continuously reduce its scale to reassert the embodied individual as the chief constituent of any just human order. Constant reaffirmation of individuality analogizes the temporal emergence of a collective (See Figure 7.2). Rather than being an immediately comprehensible form, apparent scattering across the site prefigures the complex social and political order the Parliament could contribute to achieving. Affirmative of Not Yet political possibility, the complex is a negation of the bureaucratic rationalism orthodox modernist architecture frequently structures. It also opposes the Houses of Parliament in London (1840–70), including its formality, assertions of racial nationalism, the adversarial political theatre it encourages, identification with Empire and association with thwarting desires for self-determination. Although more subtle, the Miralles Parliament also counteracts the Palace of Holyrood House across the road, official residence of the British Monarchy in Scotland. Taken together, these negations constitute a critique of centre, necessary for cultivating Scottish culture and civic national identity.

In planning the Scottish Parliament, Miralles drew upon the multilayered record of city building from premodern to the present surrounding the site at the terminus of the Royal Mile, which runs from Edinburgh Castle (twelfth to eighteenth century and later) to the Palace of the Holyrood House (fifteenth to eighteenth century), on the edge of Edinburgh's Old Town, with its medieval street layout and structures mostly from the sixteenth century to the present. The Parliament complex encapsulates an enriched temporal frame, extending backwards and forwards, mediated by the land as precursor and ground of evident of human culture. Understood in this way, the complex is alive

Figure 7.2 Scottish Parliament, Edinburgh, Scotland (1999–2004). EMBT (Enric Miralles and Benedetta Tagliabue), Architects. Riot of Materials (former public entry). [Photo: Nathaniel Coleman, 2005].

to context as a human thing and a matter of the earth, having little to do with specific forms, decorative motifs or historic styles.

By recognizing the limits of technicity (conceived of as an ethically neutral good), Miralles's Parliament complex is postmodern, politically and philosophically, though not stylistically, except as a rejection of orthodox modernism and historical styles. Neither a simulacrum of optimistic modernity nor a pastiche of any past, authority is not sought directly in the material form or character of Edinburgh's stately buildings. The Parliament's apparent strangeness is its affirmation of alternatives to the limits of managerialism, and present social and political conditions. The assimilable peculiarities of formal novelty, overheated branding and imageability, typical of global architecture did not motivate the design or production of Miralles's project. Rather, following Adorno, Miralles produced a utopian architecture that thinks better of us than we are:

Architecture worthy of human beings thinks better of men than they actually are. It views them in the way they could be according to the status of their own productive energies as embodied in technology. Architecture contradicts the needs of the here and now as soon as it proceeds to serve those needs – without simultaneously representing any absolute or lasting ideology. Architecture still remains, as Loos's book title complained seventy years ago, a cry into emptiness.[7]

Knowing what the Parliament signifies, or how to use it, is an open question. The building refuses to represent ideologies of the sort embodied by the London Parliament, or US Capitol building. Instead, it embodies an absolute and lasting ideology of open-ended political processes, communicated by materials and forms that uncover void as possibility, in opposition to the conciliatory closure populism or bureaucratic rationality promise.

The Parliament no more concretizes Scotland as it is now, than it is a transparent reflection of the political activities unfolding within it today, nor is it dismissive of either. Rather, the complex portends how Scotland could be, in some possible future; distinct from its dominant neighbour to the south. Miralles's original Parliament competition text was explicit about the intersection between architectural and political forms: 'We imagine our proposal for the new Scottish Parliament as a subtle game of cross views and political implications. But the crucial idea that sustains that: THE PARLIAMENT SITS IN THE LAND, because it belongs to the Scottish Land.'[8] While the resulting complex makes the status of Scottish land as precedent quite evident, less obvious is the debt its planning owes to the pre-modern layout of the Old Town. Looking backwards is a significant source of the complex's radical programme; identifying how pre-capitalist urbanism is a concrete model of spatial alternatives to the banalities of the Bauhaus legacy.[9]

In his own words, Miralles believed 'the making of a project is a learning process' in which the participants 'learn to be together', mediated by mutual 'kindness' that makes it possible 'to hear from each other'. In this instance, the result was to have 'created a piece of Scotland', manifested in 'the way the building merges ... history with the landscape', though he imagined it could have been 'cheaper' and 'a bit smaller', he believed it was as fitting a counterform for Scottish courage, as of its land. Acknowledging the controversy the complex attracted and seemingly anticipating that he might not be around for the opening, Miralles counselled: 'do not be afraid' and hoped 'to be able to see you at the debate. And open the building together if God allows.'[10]

At first glance, the Scottish Parliament complex could be confused with an alien landscape but only if expectations are formed by literal representations of Edinburgh's historic fabric in one direction, and its largely banal and trivial newer (mostly post-1980) architecture in the other (while almost all of its other twentieth-century buildings are strangely invisible). Ultimately, the complex hopes to welcome, rather than alienate, despite security enhancements that thwart envisioned openness and inclusiveness; imposed during construction and after, subsequent to the 11 September 2001 destruction of the World Trade Center in Manhattan. The most recent of these is a security screening hallway for visitors, opened in 2013, which effectively breaks the flow of the building towards the landscape beyond. Despite rehearsing some of the materials and forms of the building at the time of completion in 2004, the protruding block demonstrates little understanding of Miralles's poetics.[11]

Reconstruction memory

Miralles's narratives for the Parliament are suggestive of what French philosopher Paul Ricoeur (1913–2005) describes as 'reconstruction-memory': welcoming the new 'with curiosity and with the desire to reorganize the old with a view to making room for this newcomer' but negative reception of it derives from 'repetition-memory', according to which, 'nothing is worth anything except the well-known, and the new is odious'.[12] Suggestive of Miralles, Ricoeur preferred 'reconstruction-memory': 'It is no less a question of de-familiarizing the familiar than of familiarizing the unfamiliar.'[13] The dialectical relationship of history to memory and expectation is simultaneously the most compelling feature of the Scottish Parliament complex and (for some) its most perplexing quality.

Although the *familiar* is the default expectation for architecture – the London Houses of Parliament over the Scottish Parliament, for example – Ricoeur argues that only by de-familiarizing the familiar is it possible to conceive of the unfamiliar as a valid possibility. He describes this as 'distanciation', which is the 'dialectical counterpart of the notion of belonging, in the sense that we belong to a historical tradition through a relation of distance which oscillates between remoteness and proximity'.[14] He continues, 'Distanciation … constitutes … the critical moment in understanding'.[15] Not least by destabilizing fixed senses of the self as unitary, making 'imaginative variations' tolerable; thereby responsive to multiple conditions of reality.[16]

Anti-authoritarianism is both figure and ground of Miralles's Parliament, analogizing conditions of distanciation to produce a setting that challenges assertions of ultimate origins. By establishing a model of 'imaginative variations', rather than a unitary image, the Parliament prefigures a more open democratic spirit. Opposing expectations is a crucial part of how the complex does this. As Ricoeur observes: 'all consciousness of meaning involves a moment of distanciation, a distancing from "lived experience" as purely and simply adhered to.'[17] In those moments, politics could transcend management through the lighting up of imaginaries of the future, at the limit edges of the presently possible. In that spirit, one commentator wonders: 'Can the Scottish Parliament now meeting at Miralles' building, at last rise to match the standards of its home?'[18]

(Re)Presentation

The Scottish Parliament invites myriad associations of the sort introduced so far, beyond the literal references, including the vaulted polished concrete Main Hall ceiling, embossed with Scottish Saltire crosses; Garden Lobby roof lights, and the Tower Buildings' roofs references to upturned boats found on Lindisfarne Island, Northumberland and elsewhere along the North Sea coast (all of stainless steel, which clads most roofs throughout, and glass) (See Figure 7.3); Member of the Scottish Parliament – MSP – Building bay windows (encompassing so-called Think Pods, contemplative areas for MPs), inspired by the painting of Reverend Robert Walker (1755–1808) *Skating on Duddingston Loch* (c. 1795; popularly known as *The Skating Minister*), by Sir Henry Raeburn (1756–1823), clad in stainless steel, screened by oak poles, with timber window frames. One side of each of the protruding MSP 'Think Pods' also includes an upside down crow-stepped gable, a near direct quote of Mackintosh. Otherwise, the MSP Building is clad in granite and stainless steel (Plate 8). The overall arrangement of the complex (analogizing leaves and twigs, according to Miralles) recollects Mackintosh's landscape and flower water colours, for example, *Mont Alba* (c. 1924 – 1927) (See Figure 7.4).[19]

Figure 7.3 Scottish Parliament, Edinburgh, Scotland (1999–2004). EMBT (Enric Miralles and Benedetta Tagliabue), Architects. Garden Lobby (upturned boats). [Photo: Nathaniel Coleman, 2012].

Figure 7.4 Scottish Parliament, Edinburgh, Scotland (1999–2004). EMBT (Enric Miralles and Benedetta Tagliabue), Architects. Roofscape (upturned boats). [Photo: Nathaniel Coleman, 2012].

A pergola at the main entrance constructed with concrete columns, metal tubular framing and oak poles, which are also used for screening glazing here and elsewhere, including lattices on many of the MSP office bay windows, is said to refer to twigs; reiterated beside the MSP Building as a Bamboo Garden.[20] Beyond the range of materials indicated in the preceding, there are more but the primary ones are concrete, oak, stainless steel and granite. Many, but not all, of the materials were sourced from Scotland. Though expedience may have been the factor, foreign materials and a Catalonian architect enact a productive tension between local culture and universal civilization, reflected also in the balance between industrial production and recollections of handwork.

Despite the variety and occurrence of scaling and softening devices throughout, concrete asserts itself as the dominant material externally (even when blocks are stone-clad), less so internally, especially where wood and light dominate. Nowhere is the presence of wood, metal and light more evident than in the Debating Chamber, with its nearly overwhelming roof structure, crafted from laminated oak beams supported by stainless steel joints. The light colour of the wood, and the fragility of the structure – made from so many parts, illuminated by an abundance of natural light – has produced a chamber decidedly different from the pious grandiosity of the all but hermetically sealed Commons Chamber in London. If the London Chamber is a post-Second World War simulacrum of Charles Barry (1795–1860) and Augustus Welby Northmore Pugin's (1812–52) nineteenth-century interpretation of fourteenth- to sixteenth-century English Perpendicular Gothic architecture, the Edinburgh Chamber is a unique vision of tradition and innovation; most explicitly demonstrated in the semi-circular seating arrangement, as opposed to the adversarial faceoff of benches in the Commons (Plate 9).

Even where most explicit, the references are reasonably subtle in expression, and abstracted enough, including the embossed Saltire Crosses in the vaulted Hall. However, the significance of the Scottish Parliament complex is not enhanced by knowing the sources of its references; they do not strengthen disruption of preconceived notions of what a serious institutional structure ought to be like. To some degree, knowing the motifs' origins, and what they refer to, diminishes the complex's dissonance by emphasizing whatever obvious pictorial qualities it might have. No matter how generative Scottish Crosses, upturned boats, skating ministers, flower and landscape paintings, or even the Scottish land, or Edinburgh itself might be, occupants and visitors need not be aware of these things, even if the architect absolutely required them.

The literal references fortunately stay on this side of kitsch; resisting becoming mawkishly representational, by being adequately abstracted. The significance of this

Figure 7.5 Scottish Parliament, Edinburgh, Scotland (1999–2004). EMBT (Enric Miralles and Benedetta Tagliabue), Architects. Vaulted Hall – Saltire Crosses. [Photo: Nathaniel Coleman, 2012].

cannot be overstated. One step too far, and the important work of the Parliament buildings would be crippled. As Adorno observes: 'Although kitsch escapes, implike, from even a historical definition, one of its most tenacious characteristics is the prevarication of feelings, fictional feelings in which no one is actually participating, and thus the neutralization of these feelings. Kitsch parodies catharsis.'[21] In contradistinction, Donald Campbell Dewar (1937–2000), inaugural First Minister of Scotland, and Miralles, did want the Parliament complex to facilitate a national catharsis of identity.

Although kitsch is identified with populism, some might argue that Miralles and his successors went way too far, without even achieving that. Or if they did, only by transforming the buildings into an entertainment complex. For example, from May 2014 through April 2015, there were over 300,000 visitors, in 2010 there were more than 400,000, though during 2017–18, visitor numbers were only 261,834.[22] The steady decrease inevitably relates to the age of the complex and the fact that the majority of visitors are from Scotland, which has a total population of just under 5.5 million.[23] A building-industry journal attributes this decline of visitor numbers to the complex's low image score:

> Image 2/5 In its prime duty to be a national icon, the exterior of the Scottish parliament building fails. It is an indecipherable jumble of forms, while the granite and fairface concrete are dark, gloomy and growing even more dingy with weathering. The main internal spaces, however, are furnished in natural timber and awash in daylight, and so remain exhilarating, inspiring and resplendent.[24]

This comment and the surveyed respondents who determined its conclusions have missed the point. As the Parliament grows gloomier 'with weathering', the more it adopts the atmosphere of Edinburgh's urban landscape. Its 'indecipherable jumble of forms' is intentional: it is not meant to be perceivable all at once like a nineteenth or twentieth-century monument, or twentieth-century or twenty-first-century spectacle building. Miralles's explicit aim was to not produce 'a landmark skyline to rival Big Ben', or a simulacrum of the London Houses of Parliament.[25] Actually, negative appraisals of the complex are testament to its continuing success in resisting consumption but might not bode well for its longevity. For now, the Scottish Parliament remains contentious by resisting easy comprehension; right at the heart of organizational tendencies towards inertia, and the impoverished imagination that dominates large bureaucratic institutions, especially politics.

From a material perspective, the scalar devices that render the expansiveness of the building comprehensible to individual persons – through analogy, or reference, rather than representation – animate even its most monolithic components. The overlay of elements that constantly recollect the size and dynamism of human figures makes the building intelligible as a proposition of alternatives. The most pervasive of these is a kind of upside down, reversed 'L', for which no explicit reference appears to have been declared. Described in an official guide only as a 'feature panel', some see it as simply a *curtain* (according to Tagliabue this is how Miralles saw them). For others, they are

Figure 7.6 Scottish Parliament, Edinburgh, Scotland (1999–2004). EMBT (Enric Miralles and Benedetta Tagliabue), Architects. Upside-down Reversed 'L's. [Photo: Nathaniel Coleman, 2012].

additional references to The Skating Minister, or to human figures as participants in the political process. The figure repeats so often as an applied element that they seem to be crawling across the complex. (The 'L' panel is only absent from the MSP Building, and the pre-existing, historic, though restructured, Queensberry House; parts dating from 1667). There are enough of these 'L' figures, made out of varied materials (oak, and grey, or black granite), for the group to constitute something of a community.

Politics of the future

As the detailed description of a possible Scotland; outlining as yet non-existent social systems in a space and time that can be experienced, the Parliament produces an 'anticipatory illumination' of the 'possibilities for rearranging social and political relations', necessary to engender 'built homecoming'.[26] Because it exceeds the limits of the presently knowable, the Parliament more effectively communicates to possible futures, than with the populist present. Since representing or realizing Utopia is impossible; building by building, block by block, incremental improvements could substantiate a possible future for architecture and cities, with the Scottish Parliament an early example of this. As such, the complex hints at potentialities of utopian accumulation over a long duration, across numerous sites, that could eventually establish more just and amenable cities, in contradistinction to the unwelcoming neoliberal settings constructed over substrates of orthodox modernism, and the ruins of traditional urbanism. In this regard, the new Scottish Parliament echoes Lefebvre's conviction that new spaces come first, preparing the ground for new ways of being.[27] Thus, what the complex hints at is crucial, even if how it is actually used comes up short. As architecture educator Alan Balfour observes:

> The Politics of the Miralles imagination has made the Parliament an informal, restless place, seeking an experience of continual change …, and anti-authority, continually open to new ideas and possibilities. It confounds expectations, it makes no predictions, suffers no illusion. It is architecture as landscape, not portrait … This is a thing shaped by the poetic.[28]

Institutional, public or civic structures offer the last opportunities for constructing more humane, body-centred, social environments than modernism generally could. Typically, architecture is constrained by the same dystopian Fordist and Taylorist frameworks modernist architecture aligned with; whether it lacks a social dimension, or asserts it; is ideologically neutral, or polemical; is determined by form, or by use; is a-tectonic, or tectonic. The relative freedom of Miralles's Parliament from such entrapment makes it unique. Although only relatively more free, he achieved a modicum of autonomy from the prevailing architectural consciousness to engage with given conditions negatively and dialectically, to produce something hopeful. By expanding the limits of modernism rather than abandoning it, Miralles's method – mediated by imaginative engagement with history and culture in its great setting and expression: the city – countered the habit of dominant spatial practices to ceaselessly erase distinctive qualities.

Future imaginaries

The alignment of orthodox architectural modernism with the technocratic and scientific rationality of modernity confounded its promises of better futures from the start. Modernist visions were never socially bold enough to cultivate adequately complex imaginaries. Accordingly, the city of modern architecture could not provide counterforms of renewed social life. The perceived need to be seen as technologically rational and scientific rendered many orthodox modernist architects incapable of exceeding the limits of the given. But even if the traditional city – wherever its traces survive – is a bridge between civic life in the present and its origins in the past, it is not quite a ready reservoir of radical spatial patterns, or renewed everyday life, for direct reuse in the present, no matter how robust. It is precisely this predicament – between the conceptual failings of modernism and the foreignness of the past – that the Scottish Parliament tangles with. Even if insurgent imaginaries of the future originate in the past – with premodern, pre-capitalist, spatial practices – translation is required; no matter how durable and supple the models.

Miralles's exploration of a possible architecture, impregnated with social and cultural imagination, rather than bereft of both, inaugurates concrete alternatives to the ideological crisis of architecture and urbanism persisting since Piranesi's day. His critique of twentieth-century orthodox modernist architecture and city planning employs its materials and methods of construction, as well as its conceptions, to effect dialectical engagement with its contradictory organizing myths. Architecture historian and theorist Colin Rowe (1920–99) and architect and educator Fred Koetter (1938–2017) outlined these myths in their influential book, *Collage City* (1978). They argued that these contradictions comprise a peculiar admixture of blind faith in techno-science combined with desires for a return to paradise; making orthodox modernist architecture pseudo-scientific *and* anti-urban simultaneously.[29] Juggled, rather than resolved, uncritical techno-utopian fantasies and half-baked instrumentalist fantasies of the built environment assured that twentieth-century modernist architecture – and much of its progeny – would be the enemy of urban life. But whereas Rowe and Koetter encouraged formalism – deploying collage techniques for using things (mostly borrowed from history) without believing in them, as a way to vacate ideological contents – Miralles pursued traces of modernist optimism about the possibilities of a political architecture.

By the time Miralles came to artistic maturity, the failures of modern architecture had been well-established, particularly its contributions to the destruction of urban life, even though its overall success maintained its status as something of an International Style. Because the spatial practices and modes of production of the globalized building industry largely determine architecture, architects have no choice but to subvert both. Thus, while preoccupation with materials, construction and use is central to Miralles's critique of orthodox modernist architecture, it is bound to the building industry. As with Scarpa, and Williams and Tsien, Miralles's subversion of modernist architecture turns on careful detailing, concern with construction, sensitivity to use and bodily experience, and attentiveness to material. All three acknowledge that in the epoch of modernity, architectural signification arises out of modes of thinking and doing that encounter the productivist myths of modernity dialectically, without requiring fantasies of escape.

Use

Because fulfilment can only ever be partial and temporary, experimenting with how to use the Scottish Parliament (structure and political body) as a *machine* for producing a better nation is open-ended. In its specificity, it confounds expectations of what a government building should be like. Beginning there, it undermines preconceived notions of architecture, especially its conventional divide from landscape. It even works against notions of so-called good taste, and contextualism, especially in its sensitive, and highly charged, historical milieu. Not surprisingly, this is most explicit in intersections between enlarged conceptions of use – its problematic organization, experienced in the circulation and loose association of accommodation – and in the ecstatic use of materials.

The varied material palette, deployed through construction, including detailing, challenges perceptions of the result as overwhelmed by decorative impulses taken to the extremes of an excrescence of ornament (for this writer at least). Crucially, the complex layers of material, structure and – yes – decorative diversity produce a dynamic condition that effectively analogizes the human assemblage that constitutes a democratic nation state, its political processes and parliamentary representatives. Moreover, excess here has an ethical dimension: countering conventional managerial politics of diminished expectations with capaciousness.

Conditions of diversity and liveliness, including momentary incomprehensibility or contradiction, constitute the possibilities put to work by the Parliament in cultivating imaginaries of the future, as desires for what is missing. However, to sustain its usefulness as a *hope machine* for producing alternatives, the Scottish Parliament must also negate itself. The relatively chaotic scattering of forms renders the Parliament generally unassimilable. In turn, this constitutes the explicit negation of centre effected by the complex, as a prefiguration of more human social and political orders. Taken together, these characteristics contribute to the structure's refusal, which constitutes its self-renewing potential.

By refusing to represent itself as a final form achieved (a thing, state or comprehensible form), the Parliament resists becoming compensatory image, or a necessary disappointment. Despite winning awards, or even functioning as a parliament, in concrete terms, the complex conditions of its realization separate it from the dominant spatial practices and modes of production it is nonetheless bound to, which is the surest evidence of the Parliament's persisting negation. The commitment required for it to come into existence was profound. Both its true patron, Dewar, who supported Scottish devolution, and Miralles, made the ultimate sacrifice, in the service of bringing the complex into being. Miralles died first, on 3 July 2000, followed by Dewar on 11 October 2000, years before the Parliament officially opened on 9 October 2004. Whatever their respective health problems, Miralles and Dewar's devotion to seeing the building through to completion must have taken a toll, as it did on others involved.[30]

For the complex to actually have been constructed, the intense commitment extended further. To Tagliabue, the EMBT studio; local partners RMJM; and many others as well.[31] The Parliament complex took more than six years to complete with a final cost of more than 430 million pounds, over ten times the originally anticipated amount. Intense debate surrounded the design and construction process, including being subjected to official inquiries.[32] As discussed elsewhere, the complex and its story are understandable according to Ruskin's 'Lamp of Sacrifice', in *The Seven Lamps of Architecture*, which in itself is unique for the twenty-first century.[33]

As forever *incompleting* itself – because a final fulfilment of longings is impossible – the Parliament discloses the missing as a permanent object of desire. But rather than dissipating hope, this intensifies it. Longing is self-renewing: frustrated desire refortifies hope; failure motivates subsequent attempts at fulfilment, no matter that final success is forever out of reach. The logic is human; rhythmic and cyclical, rather than instrumental, rational or linear. It is embodied, or concrete, rather than obscure, or abstract, even if hope accomplishes only its defeat and its reproduction: achievement of hope in some final form would either be the end of all possibility, or sure evidence that the desire was not bold enough. Accordingly, it is no wonder that throughout the process of realization, Miralles's Parliament complex was seen by many as a source of trouble, or utterly useless, surely profligate; precisely because it disrupted conventional fantasies of bureaucratic rationality.

The difficulty of the Parliament resides in its animation by a central paradox: to endure, it could not possibly succeed in answering infinitely open questions. Uncertainty and the embrace of unanticipated eventualities is the condition of life, as of politics. The very impossibility of realization or representation of some final ideal reveals desiring the new, rather than its fulfilment, as the vocation of art, politics and architecture. Perpetual rekindling of desire for the new is the *real* function of Miralles's complex; outlined by different sorts of logic; alternative notions of use; other ideas of making buildings and states; and extravagant materiality.[34]

Although difficult works of art can be assimilated over time, even domesticated as *classic* or as *heritage*, or as tourist destinations; so long as desiring rather than fulfilling prevails, something of their original disruptiveness can be kept in reserve. Thus, even if use subsumes the Scottish Parliament within the political morass, there is hope that something of its original otherness will persist. Anticipating this, Scottish author and artist Alasdair Gray (b. 1934) wrote:

> I ... think a new Scottish parliament will be squabblesome and disunited and full of people justifying themselves by denouncing others – the London parliament on a tiny scale. But it will offer hope for the future. The London parliament has stopped even pretending to do that. I believe an independent country run by a government not much richer than the People has more hope than one governed by a big rich neighbour.[35]

As Gray observes, the offer of 'hope for the future' is the central task of human institutions, a sentiment captured by his best-known motto, which adorns The Canongate wall of the Parliament complex: 'Work as if you live in the early days of a better nation.' The motto is cut into Iona Marble from the Isle of Iona, Argyll, Scotland, alongside additional quotations from Scottish writers and other sources, also cut into a range of native stone, including further stones adorned only with fossils. Miralles's building analogizes both Gray's motto, and his expectations for the Parliament. While the challenge is relevant for those working in the Parliament, the complex itself could be construed as the first setting of that better nation, no matter how far off it might be (See Figure 7.7).

Though somewhat different, Gray acknowledges his motto paraphrases Canadian poet Dennis Lee's long poem, *Civil Elegies*, especially: 'And best of all is finding a place to be in the early years of a better civilization.'[36] Beyond their similarity, the assertion of civic nationalism in both is most significant. In much the way Gray envisions Scotland independent from England, Lee imagines Canadian consciousness and culture liberated from US dominance. The choice of a Catalonian architect, rather than an English, British or even Scottish one is a corollary of both sentiments. As conceived by Miralles, the Scottish Parliament is far more cosmopolitan than the parochial Palace of Westminster, London (comprising the Houses of Parliament). Best known for its tower and clock,

Figure 7.7 Scottish Parliament, Edinburgh, Scotland (1999–2004). EMBT (Enric Miralles and Benedetta Tagliabue), Architects. Canongate Wall/Block. [Photo: Nathaniel Coleman, 2012].

and for asserting Englishness, by way of Pugin's distinctly native Perpendicular Gothic decorative programme – albeit on a Classical plan by Barry – the London Parliament is distinctly nationalist in character. Although bound to the Scottish land, Miralles's complex foregoes any discernible nostalgic vision of Scottishness, equivalent to the Englishness asserted by Pugin's decorative programme in London. The choice of a non-British architect has only deepened in significance since the complex was constructed.

No matter what happens to Scotland's relationship to the UK, or Catalonia's to Spain, the Parliament is a European building that pronounces Scottish independence, even if only as a thought experiment. As such, it is simultaneously a Scottish and a Catalonian building. The intensity of the complex – its exuberance – is national in character; of Scotland and Catalonia, beyond simply its architect's place of origin. For Miralles, this made sense architecturally, in the correspondences he could identify between Mackintosh and Gaudí, but also politically, and historically as well. Shared Celtic links being just one example.

Something missing

Although Miralles positioned himself within the tradition of modernism – late nineteenth- and twentieth-century architecture – he was reasonably successful in subverting the dominant procedures of the building industry; achieved through negative dialectical encounters with prevailing conditions. The strangeness of Miralles's work is as much an outcome of this as of individual artistic sensibilities. Outlining negation's promise, Adorno argues: 'Through the irreconcilable renunciation of the semblance of reconciliation, art holds fast to the promise of reconciliation in the midst of the unreconciled'.[37] The knot Adorno introduces not only captures the paradoxical relationship between architectural strangeness and modernism in Miralles's Parliament but also the tension between resignation and hope it materializes. In designing the Parliament, he set aside compensatory illusions for the project, and any idea that hope can be risk free. As German philosopher Ernst Bloch (1885–1977) argued, hope is risky:

> hope is the opposite of security. It is the opposite of naïve optimism. The category of danger is always in it. This hope is not confidence … If it could not be disappointed, it would not be hope … Otherwise it would be cast in a picture … Hope is critical and can be disappointed … Hope is … determined negation of that which continually makes the opposite of the hoped-for object possible … There would not be any process at all if there were not something that should not be so.[38]

Miralles's Parliament is animated by the spirit of Bloch's conception of Hope as process, rather than prediction (or picture), and as emerging from negation rather than blueprint. The disappointments here are orthodox modernism, and conventional parliamentary arrangements, architecturally and procedurally. The tangible hope for alternatives is the risk taken by the complex. For Miralles, as for Bloch, 'process' rather than 'picture' ('image', or 'form') is at the forefront of alternatives; with material imaginaries and use how this is communicated concretely.

Despite the impossibility of defining or depicting a realized Utopia, the Scottish Parliament complex is a situated example of other social, political and spatial possibilities. By pronouncing hope, the Parliament critiques the present but offers no fixed conception of Utopia achieved. In the short term, at least, association of the Parliament with Dewar's and Miralles's death, and with inevitably dashed hopes, compromises and endings, makes the complex poetically tragic. The Parliament is Miralles's last building, a marker of creative promise cut short; all the more poignant because neither he nor Dewar saw it completed. Death counterbalances all hope; sharpening the ultimate impossibility of realizing Utopia. Even so, longing is life's purpose. Adorno explains why Utopia can only be spoken about negatively – in terms of what is missing, rather than picturing its supposed achievement. Accordingly, the Parliament is a meditation on Utopia's desire, rather than a blueprint for it:

> One may not cast a picture of utopia in a positive manner. Every attempt to describe or portray utopia in a simple way, i.e., it will be like this, would be an attempt to avoid the antimony of death and to speak about the elimination of death as if death did not exist. That is perhaps the most profound reason, the metaphysical reason, why one can actually talk about utopia only in a negative way.[39]

As the vocation of utopia, negation is the language of hope. In organizing an affirmational complex of buildings, Miralles's Parliament is imbued with hopes beyond death that are impossible to satisfy in a single lifespan. It is only in this sense that the Parliament might be described as monumental.

As *process* rather than *picture*, the Parliament denotes desire rather than specific results. By enacting the prohibition on depictions of utopia realized, while embodying longing for it anyway, Miralles's complex is restless rather than settled. It articulates what it is not, and what it is against but as Bloch observes: 'every criticism of imperfection, incompleteness, intolerance, and impatience already without a doubt presupposes the conception of, and longing for, a possible perfection'.[40] Imaging perfection as a realizable concrete form can only ever be an approximation, a step towards some unachievable possible. The discontinuous, fragmentary, nature of the Parliament is more than a picture of Utopia; it embodies the indestructible desire for it. The distinct material and organizational qualities of the Parliament is the concrete presence of longing, free from illusions of centre.

Miralles's aversion to authoritarianism suffuses the concrete spatial arrangements he provided for renewed forms of social life. He described the work of architecture as an 'extended conversation inclusive of all involved'.[41] Antipathy towards unyielding systems of order is a first step to evading entrapment within them. Resisting propositions of definitive forms of spatial closure is pragmatic: any precise prescription for the new city, the new politics, a new way of being, can only ever be provisional. Imagining new spatial forms, analogizing renewed social forms and processes, is far more difficult than first imagining new social forms. Postponing authoritarian acts of closure is necessary to avoid the pitfalls of productivism that quickly shifts from theoretical concerns to impulsive construction; while realization nearly always neutralizes attempts to produce genuinely dissonant works of architecture.

Miralles's romanticist approach at the Parliament echoes nineteenth-century critiques of modernity, which concentrated on what had gone missing as industrialization took hold. Though he worked as a modern, he approached the homecoming Romanticism anticipates dialectically; as originating in the past but realized in the future, fully aware that return is, as Lefebvre observed, 'both impossible and inconceivable', because any wholesale 'return to the past' would offer little or nothing in the way of resolving the 'crisis of modernity'.[42] Materially, Miralles references the Old Town's medieval street pattern in the Parliament planning, while allusions to Edinburgh's gabled roofs make direct links with traditional Scottish buildings, without mimicking either.[43] Miralles's attachment to *his* Edinburgh, the land and the references he gravitated towards reveal a preoccupation with tradition and modernity.

By indefinitely postponing taking decisions on formal closure to construct a Parliament, before the new social forms it was intended to accommodate had taken shape, raised the risk that the new spaces will be perceived as incomprehensible, or ugly, because embodying dissonant future imaginaries. Such dissonant newness might also give way to attempts to transform it into something more institutionally or touristically consumable, as image or destination. Perhaps like Lefebvre, Miralles believed that new spaces prefigure new forms of social and political life. As Lefebvre put it: '"Change life!" "Change society!" These precepts mean nothing without the production of an appropriate space … To change life, … we must first change space'.[44] Whether Miralles would have made such a declaration is less relevant than the Parliament's potent romantic admixture of reform-minded idealism and optimism – extending from individual to state and place – fortified by stubborn impracticality.

As events have shown, Miralles was steely enough in his determination to shatter the bonds of restrictive realism; even *seeing* the Parliament complex through to completion after death. However one evaluates the Scottish Parliament, its cost not only to Dewar and Miralles but also to the public purse, sets it beyond purely practical, economic or technical criteria. By exceeding the limits of dominant categories of value, it anachronistically reaches beyond bureaucratic rationality towards poetic ideas of civic, or national, belonging. In this regard, following Ruskin, it bespeaks a 'desire to honour or please someone else by the costliness of the sacrifice.'[45]

Material can be a concrete manifestation of struggles against death, so long as a lack of care does not mark it as a sign of defeat. It can also evidence sacrifice; as an offer to some concrete good beyond the abstract measure of monetary cost as value. Material presence is not simply an assertion of wealth, status, luxury or power, it is primarily bound up with durability; not simply in relation to maintenance but that too. Durability, in the sense used here, suggests settings capable of containing death anxiety (amongst other worries), precisely because what is provided evokes timespans beyond one's own life. Simply put, solidity defies truncated life cycles of consumption, including the creative destruction associated with capitalist spatial practices and modes of production, which is how material can be a reality preserve.

As Miralles well understood, a structure too monumental in scale, material or form, would have been alienating not least because too similar to familiar parliament buildings and modes of governmental self-representations of centralized power. Lavishness of construction and detail communicate alternatives most effectively (so long as undergirded by wild enough conceptions). Although futile, Arts and Crafts artists' resistance to the solvent of machine production models this, akin to Loos's preoccupation with workmanship. In accordance with Ruskin, Miralles appears to have equated an 'increase in apparent labour as an increase of beauty in the building.'[46] It is in this spirit that the overabundance of elements (and materials) at the Parliament ought to be considered. Of these, the ones that could be handmade (even if not handcrafted) most humanize the structures, in terms of scale and also by recollecting human work dignified by individual effort, within collectivities. In this, the myriad elements, materials and excessive forms and details nourish desires for a fuller public life, in the urban realm and in politics. As the realities of digital technologies facilitate a mass turn inward, towards solipsistic relationships with the world, the physical audacity of the Scottish Parliament recollects our animal origins, our original home in nature and the association of sensual pleasure to survival. Moreover, aliveness to the world of people and things recollects the body as the instrument of knowing through experiencing; for relating to others, and for making contact with the world beyond the individual self.

By analogizing the vibrant urban qualities of Edinburgh's Old Town, Miralles's complex pronounces an alternative modern city and social possibilities. A reminder that for all its risks, everyday life encounters in the public sphere persist in providing the greatest opportunities for testing one's own humanity, and the possible good of civilization. The fallibility coursing through the Scottish Parliament complex opens it up as a platform for as yet unforeseen achievements beyond itself in the future; relative to it as a materially present work of architecture housing a political body and process.

Constructing difference

Constructing alterity is all but impossible, other than as unbuilt two- or three-dimensional representations of it. However, when an image is taken for the thing, when representations (abstractions) are misconstrued as actual substitutes for (concrete) reality, 'communication' is mistaken 'for revolution'. Because apparent *otherness* so quickly transforms into supposed rules for achieving alternatives, it is little wonder that Adorno, Bloch and Lefebvre cautioned against picturing Utopia, as an equivalence of it; as if achieved. And yet, architects require models of alternative practice. Arguably, the Parliament complex manifests possible Scottish difference.

Completed behind schedule and far exceeding its anticipated construction budget, the Scottish Parliament raises a multi-layered challenge to the London Houses of Parliament, especially the Commons debating chamber. More than insipid formalism, Miralles's complex demonstrates how alternative social and political practices are problems of form. Accordingly, contradictions are invited rather than expelled, as the only viable way of resolving them, to produce a more comprehensive beauty, of a sort Adorno describes in the following:

> Beauty today can have no other measure except the depth to which a work resolves contradictions. A work must cut through the contradictions and overcome them, not by covering them up, but by pursuing them. Mere formal beauty, whatever that might be, is empty and meaningless; the beauty of its content is lost in the pre-artistic sensual pleasure of the observer. Beauty is either the resultant of force vectors or it is nothing at all.[47]

Echoing this, Lefebvre asserted: 'Surely there comes a moment when formalism is exhausted, when only a new injection of content into form can destroy it and so open up the way to innovation.'[48] In its apparent strangeness, including resisting its own consumption, in part by not being amenable to postcard images, Miralles's Parliament complex exceeds 'mere formal beauty', not least in the fullness of the content suffusing its forms.

Conceived in terms of values other than money, symbolic rather than instrumental, and disobedient by confounding architectural and institutional expectations, the complex is as disruptive of conventions as a shelter for mainstream politics could hope to be. As a material expression of shared desire for self-rule, the Scottish Parliament – as a political body and as a structure – required necessary sacrifice to become a *machine* for achieving this. Sacrifice here is public in nature; an offering to honour the community.

The strangeness and excesses of the complex declares the audacity of the political project it could house. In achieving this, the Parliament counters what Ruskin described as the 'the prevalent feeling of modern times, which desires to produce the largest results at the least cost'.[49] Analogously, its vision of politics extends beyond matter-of-fact solutions to problems of instrumental necessity. One need not like the Parliament for its otherness to intrude upon consciousness, as it pries open cracks through which other perceptions and practices might be drawn. The complex is socially generative, not because it is novel, or only because it breaks expectation, but because it is interrogative; an evocatively vital setting for contemplating governance, national identify and conceptions of belonging.

In contradistinction to the Palace of Westminster and the other invited proposals for the project, Miralles's Parliament does not adhere to conventional architectural representations of capital buildings; it is not organized according to any specific national or historical style, or ideal geometry. It is decidedly anti-monumental, even as it attains the status of a monument. It is a heterogeneous setting that raises multifarious challenges; not least by disrupting established expectations. As much as possible, it is a counter-parliament, situated as distant from the London Houses of Parliament as is conceivable, while also asserting its difference from the nearby Queen's Palace of Holyrood House. Unconventionally contextual, the Scottish Parliament stakes out alterity less determined by the specifics of architectural style or taste than by the material manifestation of its bold assertions, making it available for continuous testing, and perpetual improvement through use.

Ultimately, the Scottish Parliament complex articulates 'another utopia', of a kind that facilitates imagining 'utopia otherwise'. Thinking with the Parliament makes it possible to construe 'a new intelligence of utopia', which – suggestive of Adorno – 'does violence to itself' by including 'the critique of utopia'.[50] A discipline through which hope (utopia), 'acquires the hardness necessary to destroy the myths that ruin utopia [hope]'.[51] As a hope *machine*, the Scottish Parliament complex opens up vistas 'far into the distance … in order to penetrate the darkness so near it of the just lived moment, in which everything that is both drives and is hidden from itself'.[52] Although not all readers will concur with the association of the preceding passage from Bloch with the Parliament, the argument here is that it is grounded in the pragmatics of the complex – how it is sited; its attentiveness to use – emotional and technical function; its elements and details; the materials out of which it is made; and the modes of production (including its extreme cost and construction delays) that make it concrete, rather than abstract.

Bloch asserts that 'we need the most powerful telescope, that of polished utopian consciousness, in order to penetrate precisely the nearest nearness'.[53] By making the familiar strange, Miralles's Parliament complex provides at least some of the optics for Bloch's telescope – mirroring, reflecting and refracting, to magnify desire: to illuminate 'the most immediate immediacy, in which the core of self-location and being-here still lies, in which at the same time the whole knot of the world-secret is to be found'.[54] Miralles's Scottish Parliament does this in two ways: by illuminating 'the direction of a retrieval of the multiplicity of cultures, forms of living and the different ways of survival invented by humanity in the course of its history' and by continuously returning attention to what is missing.[55]

Notes

1. Ignasi de Solà, *Gaudi*, Kenneth Lyons (trans.), Barcelona: Ediciones Poligrafa, S. A., 1984, pp. 5–11.

2. Alan Balfour, *Creating a Scottish Parliament*, Edinburgh: Finlay Brow, 2005, pp. 85–6; Sarah Lyall, 'Enric Miralles, 45, Who Designed Scottish Parliament's New Home', *The New York Times*, 07 July 2000. Available at: https://www.nytimes.com/2000/07/07/arts/enric-miralles-45-who-designed-scottish-parliament-s-new-home.html (Accessed 08 April 2018).

3. Coleman, *Utopias and Architecture*; Manfredo Tafuri, *Architecture and Utopia: Design and Capitalist Development*, Barbara Luigia La Penta (trans.), Cambridge, MA: MIT Press, 1976 (1973).

4. Tafuri, *Architecture and Utopia*, p. 44. See also: Joseph Rykwert, 'The Dark Side of the Bauhaus' (1968); and 'The Nefarious Influence on Modern Architecture of the Neo-Classical Architects Boullée and Durand' (1972), *The Necessity of Artifice*, New York: Rizzoli, 1982, pp. 44–9, 60–5. Mauro F. Guillén, *The Taylorized Beauty of the Mechanical: Scientific Management and the Rise of Modernist Architecture*, Princeton: Princeton University Press, 2006; Nikolaus Pevsner, *Pioneers of Modern Design: From William Morris to Walter Gropius* (1936), London: Penguin, 1991.

5. Coleman, *Utopias and Architecture*.

6. Lyall, 'Enric Miralles, 45'.

7. Adorno, 'Functionalism Today', Jane Newman and John Smith (trans.), *Oppositions*, 17 (Summer 1979): 31–41 (p. 38). Originally presented to the German Werkbund, 1965.

8. Enric Miralles Moya, 'Concept Design', Scottish Parliament Building Proposed Team: EMBT Architects Associates; RMJM; Ove Arup & Partners Scotland, p. 2. Available at: http://www.parliament.scot/visitandlearn/16080.aspx (Accessed 09 April 2018).

9. See, Lefebvre, *The Production of Space*; Henri Lefebvre, *Rhythmanalysis: Space, Time and Everyday Life*, Stuart Elden and Gerald Moore (trans.), London and New York: Continuum, 2004 (1992); Ernst Bloch, 'Building in Empty Places' (1959), in *The Utopian Function of Art and Literature: Collected Essays*, Jack Zipes and Frank Mecklenburg (trans.), Cambridge, MA: MIT Press, 1988, pp. 186–99; Coleman, *Lefebvre for Architects*.

10. Enric Miralles, Transcript of fax from Miralles, 28 March 2000, reprinted in Balfour, *Creating a Scottish Parliament*, pp. 57, 58.

11. No Author, 'The Scottish Parliament's New £6.5 million Security Gate will Open to the Public Today', *The Scotsman*, 23 August 2013. Available online at: https://www.scotsman.com/news/politics/scottish-parliament-opens-6-5m-security-gate-1-3059078 (Accessed 16 April 2018).

12. Paul Ricoeur, 'Architecture of Narrativity', *Études Ricoeuriennes / Ricoeur Studies*, 7, no. 2 (2016): 31–42 (p. 40). Available at: http://ricoeur.pitt.edu/ojs/index.php/ricoeur/article/view/378/196 (Accessed 16 April 2018).

13. Ibid.

14. Paul Ricoeur, 'Phenomenology and Hermeneutics' (1975), *From Text to Action*, Kathleen Blamey and John B. Thompson (trans.), Evanston, IL: Northwestern University Press, 1991, p. 35.

15. Ibid.

16. Ibid.

17. Ibid., p. 40.

18. Susan Bain, *Holyrood: The Inside Story*, Edinburgh: Edinburgh University Press, 2005, p. 293.

19. For an overview of these references and a brief discussion of the Scottish Parliament complex more generally, from inception to construction process, see: Murray Grigor and Enric Miralles, *Holyrood A New Parliament for Scotland*, Scotland: Scottish Parliament, 2001. Available at: https://vimeo.com/38038463 (Accessed 13 April 2018). See also, Various, *The Scottish Parliament: Official Guidebook*, Edinburgh: Scottish Parliamentary Corporate Body, 2009; and Charles Jencks, *The Scottish Parliament*, London: Scala Publishers, 2005.

20. In addition to the Grigor documentary (see n. 19), many of the intended references are identified in the various pages of the official Scottish Parliament website, 'Parliamentary Buildings', accessible from the 'Visit Parliament' subsection on the 'Visit and Learn' page. 'Parliamentary Buildings' page. Available at: http://www.parliament.scot/visitandlearn/15807.aspx (Accessed 13 April 2018).

21. Adorno, *Aesthetic Theory* (1970), p. 239.

22. No Author, *Scottish Parliament Statistics Volume 2017–2018*, SP Paper 465, Session 5, Scottish Parliamentary Corporate Body, 2019, p. 131. Available at: https://www.parliament.scot/ResearchBriefingsAndFactsheets/SPStatistics_17-18.pdf (Accessed 03 February 2019); No Author, 'Holyrood Visitor Figures Hit the Heights', *News Archive*, The Scottish Parliament, 04 January 2010. Available at: http://www.parliament.scot/newsandmedia centre/17720.aspx (Accessed 13 April 2018). Tom Gordon, 'Holyrood "Engagement" Strategy Overhauled as Visitor Numbers Hit Record Low', *The Herald/Sunday Herald*, 8 October 2016. Available at: http://www.heraldscotland.com/news/14790317.Holyrood__engagement__strategy_overhauled_as_visitor_numbers_hit_record_low/ (Accessed 14 April 2018).

23. No Author, 'Scotland's Population 2017', *National Records of Scotland*, Wednesday, 1 August 2018. Available at: https://www.nrscotland.gov.uk/news/2018/scotlands-population-2017 (Accessed 03 February 2019)

24. Martin Spring, 'Scottish Parliament: Miralles' Magnificent Mess Revisited', *Building*, 29 January 2010. Available at: https://www.building.co.uk/focus/scottish-parliament-miralles-magnificent-mess-revisited/3156995.article (Accessed 14 April 2018).

25. Ibid.

26. Jack Zipes, 'Toward a Realization of Anticipatory Illumination', in Ernst Bloch, *The Utopian Function of Art and Literature: Collected Essay*, pp. 11–43.

27. Lefebvre, *The Production of Space*, pp. 59, 190.

28. Balfour, *Creating a Scottish Parliament*, p. 84.

29. Colin Rowe and Fred Koetter, *Collage City*, Cambridge, MA: MIT Press, 1978.

30. For a compelling telling of the story of the New Scottish Parliament building, from its prehistory through opening, see: Stuart Greig, Producer/Director, *The Holyrood Files* (Documentary film), IWC; BBC Scotland; Scottish Screen, 2005. Available at: https://vimeo.com/185674169 (Accessed 10 April 2018).

31. Ibid., Greig, *The Holyrood Files*.

32. For more on the story of the New Scottish Parliament building, see the following: Bain, *Holyrood: The Inside Story*; Peter Lovat Fraser Baron Fraser of Carmyllie, *Spitting Tacks: Lord Fraser's Report into the Building of the Scottish Parliament*, London and New York: Tim Coates Books, 2004. Available online at: http://www.parliament.scot/SPICeResources/Hol yroodInquiry.pdf (Accessed 11 April 2018); Miles Glendinning, 'Towards a New Parliament',

The Architecture of Scottish Government: From Kingship to Parliamentary Democracy, Dundee: Dundee University Press, 2004, pp. 316–64.

33. Nathaniel Coleman, 'Architecture in the Material Space of Possible Transgression', in *Transgression: Towards an Expanded Field of Architecture*, Louis Rice and David Littlefield (eds), London and New York: Routledge, 2015, pp. 185–206.

34. Adorno, *Aesthetic Theory* (1970), p. 32.

35. Alasdair Gray, *Independence: Why Scots Should Rule Scotland*, Edinburgh: Canongate Press, 1992, p. 63.

36. For a good overview of this, see Harry McGrath, 'Early Days of a Better Nation', *Scottish Review of Books*, 28 March 2013. Available at: https://www.scottishreviewofbooks.org/2013/03/early-days-of-a-better-nation/ (Accessed 11 April 2018).

37. Adorno, *Aesthetic Theory* (1970), p. 33.

38. Ernst Bloch, 'Something's Missing: A Discussion between Ernst Bloch and Theodor W. Adorno on the Contradictions of Utopian Longing' (1964), in Ernst Bloch, *The Utopian Function of Art and Literature: Collected Essays*, pp. 16–17.

39. Ibid., p. 10.

40. Ibid., p. 16.

41. Miralles, 'Clip of Filmed Interview', in *Holyrood A New Parliament for Scotland*.

42. Henri Lefebvre, *Introduction to Modernity* (1962), John Moore (trans.), London: Verso 1995, p. 279.

43. Grigor, *Enric Miralles*.

44. Lefebvre, *The Production of Space*, pp. 59, 190.

45. John Ruskin, 'The Lamp of Sacrifice', in *The Seven Lamps of Architecture*, p. 11.

46. Ibid., p. 21.

47. Adorno, 'Functionalism Today', p. 41.

48. Lefebvre, *The Production of Space*, p. 145.

49. Ibid., p. 11.

50. Miguel Abensour, 'Persistent Utopia', *Constellations*, 15, no. 3 (2008): 406–21 (p. 415).

51. Ibid.

52. Ernst Bloch, 'Introduction', in *The Principle of Hope*, Volume I, Neville Plaice, Stephen Plaice and Paul Knight (trans.), Cambridge, MA: MIT Press, 1986 (1953/1959), p. 12.

53. Ibid.

54. Ibid.

55. Gianni Vattimo, 'Utopia Dispersed', Colin Anderson (trans.), *Diogenes* 53, no. 18 (2006): 18–23 (p. 22).

PART TWO
THE LONG VIEW OF MATERIALS IN PLAY

CHAPTER 8
HUMAN TOUCH: THE ENDURING WARMTH OF WOOD

Trees are perhaps the quintessential space-defining element. They create boundaries, allées, and may have been the source of ancient Greek columnar orders. Although stone was used simultaneously with – or even before – wood to create the earliest columns in the West, because analogous to upright bodies, tree trunks endure as putative models for columns, especially in relation to ancient Greek temple architecture.

Columns are the building element most explicitly body like. In origin myths, trees are the source of the first house: the primitive hut.[1] Every visible use of wood, whether or not intended, recollects the ancient place of trees and wood in the invention of architecture. When use reveals its source, wood, like other natural materials, leather for example, confronts us with the dual nature of human beings' as simultaneously of nature and apart from it. Wood can thus be as unsettling as it is comforting.

Reminding us of our own mortal form, wood rots but grows again. It disrupts desires to be denatured, or master nature. Its perishability underscores the folly of trying to overcome time and death. Wood's double valence, its embodiment of decay and rebirth simultaneously, increases its intensity, as does its double association with warmth.

In this chapter, wood in architecture is considered historically, theoretically and mythologically as an originary building element. Theorists, including Vitruvius, Laugier and Semper are considered, as are the ways architects, including Louis I. Kahn; Aldo van Eyck; Renzo Piano; and Peter Zumthor (amongst others) have used wood. Particular emphasis is placed on wood as equally at home when used for structural framing (as timber), exterior and interior cladding, decorative finish and as furniture; conceptually as much as technically. The transition from wood to stone in ancient Greek architecture is also considered, alongside its use in ancient, traditional and modern architecture.

The Barbican Estate, City of London, is referred to for the unconventional use of materials, including wood, in a complex of its size, scale and ambition at the time of its construction. It is distinctly modernist but has remained continuously desirable, despite pockets of disdain for it, including having once been voted the ugliest building in London. Because its particular character associates it with the sort of post-Second World War architecture often rejected as brutal, the Barbican's continuing appeal is somewhat curious. While its success is multi-determined (wealthy inhabitants, location in the City of London, good maintenance) it surely has something to do with its materials, form and construction. The Barbican's greatest virtue is its physical presence, balanced by the relative invisibility of its architects. Though by no means anonymous, it is unburdened by makers with overexposed reputations.

Wood and stone

Wood's pervasiveness and enduring desires to keep it close are matters of material science, evolutionary psychology and poetic associations. In material matters, French philosopher Gaston Bachelard (1884–1962) grounds poetic imagination in his scientific background.[2] He alerts us to how resonances of material science can reveal matter's latent poetry; having less to do with aesthetics or visual appearance than with deeper – more pragmatic – reasons why one material is selected over another, for its emotional charge, or usefulness for reverie. Bachelard helps recollect how human associations with materials through touch closely parallel their actual physical properties (as sources of significance). Accordingly, bodily experience of materials – touch – is more significant than their use as signs.

Amongst its other properties, like a tree bending in the wind, wood's tensile strength is self-evident. Talk of wood in architecture begins with the tree, encompassing meditations on its meaning in building. Although use of wood derives from its material properties, experiences of living with it and touching it determine its significance. Inherence is less influential than use. As with other materials, what is done with wood is more meaningful than its rareness, cost or any myths about inherent qualities. Bachelard alerts us to the vitality of materials that only physical encounters activate, including visual pre-figurations of touch:

> Where the dynamic imagination is concerned, there evidently exists a *super-object* above and beyond the object ... This block of wood which leaves me indifferent is only a thing. But if my knife begins to carve it, this same wood block suddenly becomes greater than itself, *a super-object*, taking on all the power of provocation in the resistant world, and admitting, naturally, all the metaphors of aggression.[3]

Doing anything in the world, to it, or with material, is aggressive. The earth – material, receives the impact of desire, or will, to shape the human habitat. Building a building – all architecture – is a struggle: making dependent on force. Equally for encounters with specific materials: 'If a worked material (wood for instance) reveals itself to contain an internal hierarchy of hardness, with its softer area and its harder knots, the reveries stimulated by work are multiplied.'[4] Engagement with material dialectics of hard and soft within wood (or analogous encounters with any material) encourages daydreams of possibility, as sources of inventiveness. Digitally simulated buildings and materials – determined by performance standards – reproduce the cultural dominant of products and consumption but deplete the world of intense encounters with objects that stimulate reveries:

> for anyone who has worked with wood, this piece of oak is a dynamic tableau: it offers a portrait of energy. Between the passages of soft, pale wood, and the dark, hard knots there is more than a mere contrast of colors. The material imagination perceives here a transposed version of the dialectic theory of form and substance.[5]

In harmony with Bachelard, throughout this book, the argument is that *material on its own has little intrinsic value, prior to the work that inscribes it with significance*. While that assertion might seem to work against another key argument: that *material constitutes a reality preserve in architecture*, human impress on matter is how the world is dreamed into existence. Or, as Bachelard argues:

> the material imagination engages us dynamically. In the realm of the imagination everything comes to life: matter is not inert and the pantomime that gives expression to it cannot remain superficial. For someone who loves the substances of the material world, simply to name them is already to have begun to work them.[6]

Nineteenth-century German theorist and architect Gottfried Semper (1803–79) sheds light on this apparent paradox; identifying the potential for confusion with a particular habit of mind that by emphasizing material in relation to construction, constricts architecture rather than unfettering it:

> In ancient and modern times the store of architectural forms has often been portrayed as mainly conditioned by arising from the material, yet by regarding construction as the essence of architecture we, while believing to liberate it from false accessories, have thus placed it in fetters.[7]

While acknowledging the laws of nature, including material science, Semper is certain that ideas (desire, will) come before material essence: 'Architecture like its great teacher nature, should choose and apply its material according to the laws conditioned by nature, yet should it not also make the form and character of its creations dependent on the ideas embodied in them, and not on the material.'[8] While value added through labour is the emphasis here, Semper augments it with *convenience*: the suitability of a particular material for expressing ideas. In developing this point, he explains that although we may admire ancient Greek temples for the austerity of their white marble, they were originally colourfully decorated; the stone was selected primarily for its suitability as a *canvas* for the paint, and secondarily for its availability.[9]

Even the fine white marble used to construct temples was chosen because 'it lent itself to the most perfect finish treatment and was very durable at the same time', making 'the stucco coating' previously necessary to prepare more porous stone for painting 'superfluous.'[10] Consequently, contemporary conceptions of a specific material as magnificent might simply be a backward projection of present values. Convenience also disrupts the idea that the shift from wood to stone in ancient Greek temples – during the sixth century BC – was progressive, rather than pragmatic.[11] Perhaps wood was originally used for temples because of its rareness but also because of the ease of working with it. Equally, 'marblelike limestone or porous shell-lime' in temples was likely used because they were more abundant. Topography and patterns of inhabitation make Greece largely unforested, so wood was used sparingly.[12]

For Deplazes, 'the transfer of timber to stone construction is' a 'fundamental topic' in the 'development of Western architecture', because 'the original timber structures remain visible' in the 'stone construction' of 'ancient temples ... as ornamental, stylistic elements'. Stone may have replaced wood in the development of ancient Greek temple architecture, but its traces remain (as evidence of 'recalcitrant cultural permanence', just as in the wood grain impressions left in concrete by formwork, which Deplazes believes is prefigured by the 'transitory and provisional character' of wood. But these traces also reveal human relationships with wood as participation in the 'transitoriness and constant renewal' of a growing world.[13]

In Semper's terms, 'Temple' is the idea for which convenient materials are selected; an issue of practicality related to expression and availability. According to him, a 'materialistic way of thinking ... allied with antiquarianism', is an obstacle to understanding because it overlooks 'the most important influences on the development of art': selection of 'the most suitable material' for embodying ideas. Aligned with this, he asserts: 'the ideal expression of building', gains 'in beauty and meaning by the material's appearance as a natural symbol' (of itself).[14] Fantasies about the past and myths about the intrinsic value of materials obscure how art actually develops. Despite differences, Semper's conception is reminiscent of Ruskin's 'Lamp of Sacrifice': building significance is in direct proportion to the quality and quantity of labour and costliness of material. However, the first *materials* out of which buildings are *constructed* are ideas, which precede matter, make their impress upon it and extend it. The apparent tension between value added to material through labour and material depth itself is, in each instance, either resolved or not. Human interaction with material – rather than the material itself – produces resonances. In the midst of this tension, material emerges as reality preserve. Its sheltering capacity depends on its aptitude for lighting up reverie. Bachelard touches upon this, wondering: 'If the material imagination is sometimes weak, shouldn't we fault the cheap veneer on our furniture that frustrates deeper dreaming? So many objects today are no more than surfaces! so many materials depersonalized by impoverished varnishes!'[15] Photorealistic depictions of wood, especially on work desks, are the mark of stultifying bureaucratic rationality.

Vitruvius, Laugier, Semper

As first century BC Roman architect and theorist Vitruvius recollected, the dwelling house, thus architecture, has three parallel origins. The first shelters were either 'green boughs'; 'caves' dug 'on mountain sides'; or built like swallows' nests, 'out of mud and twigs'.[16] In Vitruvius's first shelter myth, material drawn from trees predominates. Originary dwellings were either chthonic cave enclosures, or tectonic frames suggested by tree cover in the wood. If the solid enclosures of stone, brick and concrete buildings (masonry construction in general) recollect caves, or the underworld; wood construction – analogous to steel frames, or earlier iron – suggests nest-like grids.[17] While masonry wall structures may be decomposed by voids, the massiveness remains, in much the way the lightness of wood persists, even if only paradoxically, no matter how much is forced to become monolithic.

Vitruvius's description of the first huts, and traces of origins in later timber architecture, was picked up around 1,850 years later by French Jesuit architectural theorist Abbé Marc-Antoine Laugier (1713–69) in his influential *Essai sur l'Architecture* (1753) – *An Essay on Architecture*. Laugier sought to reform architecture during its post-Baroque splintering by returning to what he called its essences. He concentrated on the tree-like character of originary wood architecture. According to him, in fulfilling the basic need for shelter, the primitive 'wants to make himself a dwelling that protects but does not bury him': the desirability of trees over caves.[18] Laugier's primordial hut would be constructed out of 'four of the strongest ... fallen branches in the forest', raised upright and arranged in a square. Joining these would be 'four other branches' laid 'across their top', forming a singular post and beam cellular unit.[19] Branches surmounting this formed the gable ends of a pitched roof, covered with 'leaves so closely packed that neither sun nor rain can penetrate'.[20] The space between the upright branches would be filled in to protect inhabitants from the 'cold and heat'.[21]

According to Laugier: 'All of the splendors of architecture ever conceived have been modelled on the little rustic hut', described above.[22] He continues: 'It is by approaching the simplicity of the first model that fundamental mistakes are avoided and true perfection achieved.'[23] Just in case not already clear, Laugier reminds readers: 'The pieces of wood set upright have given us the idea of the column, the pieces placed horizontally on top of them the idea of the entablature, the inclining pieces forming the roof the idea of the pediment.'[24] To reform architecture, to keep it *true*, or to at least sharpen its aims, he asserts: 'Let us never lose sight of our rustic hut.'[25] He concludes: 'in an architectural Order only the column, the entablature and the pediment form an essential part of the composition.'[26] The veracity of Laugier's myth is less significant than its enduring resonance. As rejoinders to Baroque and Rococo excesses, his clarifications anticipated the reductive cellular character of industrially produced modernist architecture, initially worked out in the eighteenth-century Neoclassical architecture he influenced.

Although interrupted by nineteenth-century eclecticism, about 150 years later – fortified by Neoclassical models – Laugier's *Laws* took hold. Around 100 years after its publication, Laugier's *Essay* encouraged Semper's conception of a reformed architecture based on a primordial structure; a Caribbean hut he saw displayed at the Great Exhibition of 1851, in London, housed in the Crystal Palace (1850–51), by Sir Joseph Paxton (1803–65) and Engineers Fox & Henderson. Even more directly than Laugier, Semper's 'Four Elements of Architecture' (1851) continue to influence building design and construction.

Like Laugier, Semper located the origins of settlements with wood. In harmony with Vitruvius, he believed that 'the setting up of the fireplace, and the lighting of the reviving, warming, and food-preparing flame' was 'the first sign of settlement'.[27] Based on his observation of the Caribbean Hut, amongst other evidence, Semper divided architecture into four distinct elements: the hearth (the 'sacred focus around which the whole [building, settlement, community] took order and shape ...; the first and most important, the moral element of architecture').[28] He grouped 'the three other elements' around the hearth: 'the *roof*, the *enclosure*, and the *mound*'. Each identified with a specific material and skill in working it: 'ceramics and afterwards metal works around the *hearth*, *water* and *masonry* works around the mound, *carpentry* around the *roof* and its accessories.'[29] Significant here is that for each element, use (need *and* desire) precedes material. Material and technique follow in relation to their suitability for fulfilling specific requirements. Neither form, nor aesthetics, nor material inherence come first; use does. But this does not negate the sensuous pleasures of material; rather, it intensifies them by relating it directly to bodily experience.

According to Semper, fire is safely contained at the centre of dwellings; the mound provides a solid and defensive foundation from which the building rises. Of necessity, the roof must be light so it does not overburden the structure supporting it. Each element has an emotional and technical function; or more precisely, each is related to psychological well-being and biological survival. Although architects and theorists from Vitruvius onwards have understood this, Bachelard is especially adept at communicating the double nature of the material world.[30] In describing the 'poetry of houses', he oscillates between emotional and physical solidity as protecting and orientating the body and dreams alike:

> beyond all of the positive values of protection, the house we are born in becomes imbued with dream values which remain after the house is gone ... A house constitutes a body of images that give mankind proofs of illusions of stability ... A house is imagined as a vertical being. It rises upward. It differentiates itself in terms of its verticality ... Verticality is assured by the polarity of the cellar and attic ... Indeed, it is possible, almost without commentary, to oppose the rationality of the roof to the irrationality of the cellar.[31]

Read alongside Bachelard's observations, the impact of Semper's quadripartite conception of architecture is revivified, in particular the relation of the fourth, *enclosure*, to the other three elements.

Prefiguring Loos' concentration on cladding over structure – as the primary space-defining element, Semper argues that enclosure gives rise to 'the art of the wall fitter ... that is, the weaver of mats and carpets'. Moreover, 'the carpet in its capacity as a *wall*, as a vertical means of protection' has influenced 'the evolution of certain architectural forms.'[32] According to him, 'hanging carpets' were 'the true walls, the visible boundaries of space' which meant that 'the often solid walls behind them ... had nothing to do with the creation of space' but rather 'were needed for security, for supporting a load, for their permanence, and so on.'[33] As the wall-defining element, the carpet is much more important than the structure it hangs off of behind it. In this, Semper prefigures modern steel-framed construction, characterized by distinct cladding and curtain walls, hanging from or infilling, structure, to define enclosure. His description also brings to mind wood frame construction, which, after all, is a precursor of steel frames. That carpets are woven is significant because, according to Semper, weaving is coterminous with the earliest enclosures:

> The wildest tribes are familiar with hedge-fence – the crudest wickerwork and the most primitive pen or spatial enclosure made from tree branches ... The weaving of branches led easily into mats and covers then to weaving with plant fiber and so forth ... Wickerwork was the *essence of the wall*.[34]

The use of plant matter in building is as old as the first dwelling houses. But industrial production of building materials, synthetic laminates with photorealistic images of woodgrain, engineered wood, including glulam beams, disincorporate bodily memories of wood's origins in forests; as growing trees that are living plants. Even managed forests capitalizing on timber's renewability contribute to dissociation. The 'steps toward reforestation', through which 'the lumber industry' transformed 'from being an exploitation of natural resources into what' is 'in essence an agricultural enterprise' transforms wood into a simulacrum of itself; valued primarily for being an economical, easy to work, readily available resource.[35]

Natural symbols: wood

With almost no recourse to materialist fantasies of inherence, wood (timber) arguably attains to the status of a natural symbol. Considering the centrality of wood in the architectural origin myths of Vitruvius, Laugier and Semper and the axiality of fire and the hearth for Vitruvius and Semper, as expressing cultural currents traversing time and space, unsurprisingly: 'Timber makes a particular impact on people' in all of its forms, from 'solid construction' to '[t]hin surface veneers applied to reasonably priced wood-based products.'[36] If inherent meaning does not provide an answer as to why wood 'is', as Wright asserted, 'the most humanly intimate of all materials', liked for the way it feels and looks, more convincing is its renewability, pervasiveness, workability and association with both the earliest shelters, oneiric or otherwise and the acquisition and control of fire as the focus[37] of settlement and civilization.[38] As Bachelard argues, divisions between dream and reality are confounded by daydreams, with material providing richly generative fodder for structuring all three.

If the source of associations with wood – its meaning – derives from its pervasiveness and immemorial use, its significance – as with other materials – could be said to be simultaneously socially produced *and* natural.[39] But as suggested earlier, it is also a matter of material science. For example, the perception of wood as warm is most frequently attributed to its visible qualities, or texture, and to what is called its 'figure', encompassing the species specific distinctive characteristics of grain, growth rings, rays, knots; colour, or its workability by hand and the distinct smell of each species.[40] Also significant is constant awareness of wood's combustibility, which contributes to perceptions of it as a carrier of contained, or immanent, warmth. Although other fuels may be used, wood is *always* imagined as having kept the earliest controlled fires burning. Even in our epoch of gas or electric energy for warming or cooking, nothing compares to a living flame consuming logs, or to food cooked with charcoal. On the other side of the life cycle, trees and forests bring a sense of well-being to human beings that is as much psychological as biological, whether street trees, urban parks or woods. Echoing this, the following passage outlines the unique relationship between humans and wood:

> Timber is cut and machined from trees, themselves the product of nature and time. The structure of the timber of trees has evolved through millions of years to provide a most efficient system that supports the crown, conducts mineral solutions and stores food material. Since there are approximately 30000 different species of tree, it is not surprising to find that timber is an extremely variable material …Unlike so many other materials, especially those used in the construction industry, timber cannot be manufactured to a particular specification. Instead the best use has to be made of the material already produced… Timber as a material can be defined as a low density, cellular, polymeric composite, and as such does not conveniently fall into any one class of material, rather tending to overlap a number of classes.[41]

The diversity of wood and its suitability for myriad uses makes it as variable as human beings, who, it seems, locate something of their own tension between infinite possibility and finitude in the material. Trees analogize our own mortality but can outlive us as well. Deciduous trees in particular are constant reminders of rhythmic time, to which humans are better suited than the clockwork time of progress, or scientific management. In buildings, the use of wood encapsulates both ends of the lifecycle: the wood we see and live with is uniquely alive but we are aware of its vulnerability as well.

One may associate wood with warmth through touch, or in the caloric reserve captured within it, released by fire when it burns. But the experience of touching wood is ultimately determined by the quality of effort that has gone into preparing it for just such encounters. The cheap veneers Bachelard referred to in the quote earlier are less costly because they are easier to produce; not least because they require fewer hours of labour (or growth) to make. But the greatest appeal of wood (beyond even its texture and grain) is its warmth, though even in burning, not all fires are equal. Wood choice for burning is related to species' qualities; of smell; smoke, the character of the flame – its shape, intensity, caloric output; and duration of burning but significance derives from the epicurean delights (and heat) modern wood burning provides. Wood, its burning, the flame, or odour are meaningless without a warmed human body to enjoy them. No matter how elemental, significance comes with an experiencing subject. Nevertheless, 'the low thermal conductivity combined with high storage capacity' of wood are two of its most notable virtues.[42]

The attendant warmth of wood is not just a matter of future burning; it is also a fact of its material character: 'Wood draws little heat out of the human body when touched, and so is experienced as pleasant, sensual and warm.'[43] The warmth of wood is a material fact of it, but its potential as a natural symbol – in the way Semper intends – still depends on the ideas wood is deemed most suitable for expressing – ideas manifest in building form and material. As in the cheap veneers that Bachelard worries frustrate dreaming, not all wood is alluring or convincingly warm. While any material, including those discussed in the following chapters, may attain to the status of a natural symbol that does not confirm inherence.

For example, brick has a similar status to wood as captured warmth but not all brick confirms this assertion. Much contemporary brick is cold. Likewise, metals are generally cold, which is why Finnish architect Alvar Aalto (1898–1976) wrapped metal elements with leather where they would be touched. His motivations were as much practical as poetic: when the temperature is low enough, touching metal can be extremely painful, whereas leather, like wood, 'draws little heat out of the human body'. But like wood, when used structurally, metal suggests a skeleton: it is light and airy, so it need not in every sense be cold. The density and weight of concrete, unenhanced by resonant associations, might explain negative perceptions of it. The all-encompassing reach of Rome in its totalizing imperial phase is inextricably bound to concrete, which might also explain disagreeable associations with the material; as a figure of stifling bureaucracy. But concrete can also be used to great effect, by Le Corbusier, for example; or the Pantheon in Rome. Glass is perhaps the most problematic of all materials. It is the pervasive material of modernity. It is often associated with transparency, and transparency with democracy, or freedom but as discussed in a later chapter, its bizarre condition as 'an amorphous solid neither a liquid – supercooled or otherwise – nor a solid', thus existing in 'a state somewhere between those two states of matter', can make it terribly disorientating.[44] As equally associable with surveillance and affectless clockwork dystopias of surface, as with Fascism and illumination, the meaning of glass, like any material is contradictory (only more so). Significance depends first on ideas and then on what is done with the material, perhaps suggested by its dominant qualities.

Wood in architecture

As Wright observed: 'Wood can never be wrought by the machine as it was lovingly wrought by hand into a violin for instance, except as a lifeless imitation.'[45] Industrialization in modern architecture introduces tensions to wood use, between its natural symbolism and radical transformation by the mass production of nails and screws; the ever greater scale of its processing by timber mills; the developing ease with which it can be made into sheet materials, including plywood; the advent of engineered timber products, including glulam beams; and its transformation from found resource to managed crop.[46] Although Wright may have been overly optimistic in his conviction that 'the beautiful properties of wood may be released by the machine to the hand of the architect', he surely understood that success or failure was no more a matter of technique than of supposedly inherent aesthetic qualities. As he put it, the architect's 'imagination must use it [wood] in true ways – worthy of its beauty'.[47] While these 'true ways' may be a matter of contention, there are twentieth- and twenty-first-century examples of architects' compelling use of wood.

As Wright noted in 1928, apart from rare specialized work, 'carving has a small place', rather, when exposed, wood is valued primarily for its 'silken-texture or satin-surfaces', mostly in the form of 'flat-surfaces and rib-bands'; one need only think of veneered flatpack furniture, now rare panelling, or floor planks.[48] When used structurally, timber members are largely long and lightweight, or shorter lightweight pieces might be built up alone or in combination with longer lengths, for window and door frames, or structural framing, including trusses. The emergence of more rationalized uses of wood parallels the Industrial Revolution. Inevitably, the machine imposes its own economizing logic on material possibilities.[49]

Mathematical Bridge

The so-called Mathematical Bridge in Cambridge, UK – linking the old and new sections of Queen's College across the river Cam, is a single arch bridge 'composed of Timbers

Figure 8.1 Mathematical Bridge, Queen's College Cambridge, 1748–49, repaired 1866, rebuilt 1905. Designed by William Ethridge (1709–76). 'The Bridge ... may without Flattery, be esteemed one of the most curious pieces of carpentry of its kind in England' (Edmund Carter, *The History of the University of Cambridge, from Its Original, to the Year 1753*, p. 186). [Photo: Nathaniel Coleman, 1979].

curiously joined together.'[50] Apart from being made of wood, it is engineered, in the sense of having been assembled from a complex arrangement of straight pieces that together give the illusion of being curved. The Bridge is a compact expression of transforming building practices, including calculation and the assembly of pre-cut elements according to a clearly worked out design. Queen's College reports that the bridge was 'designed in 1748 by William Etheridge (1709–76), and was built in 1749 by James Essex the Younger (1722–84). It has subsequently been repaired in 1866 and rebuilt to the same design in 1905.'[51]

Confusion about its actual date of original construction; misattribution of its design to Sir Isaac Newton; and its repair and subsequent reconstruction, when teak was substituted for oak, and bolted connections for 'the original iron screws and oak pins', has done little to diminish perceptions of its 'authenticity'.[52] Although a twentieth-century replica, the Bridge is still considered 'a rare survivor of eighteenth-century tangent and radial trussing techniques', having been listed in 1950.[53]

Querini Stampalia Bridge

Carlo Scarpa's Querini Stampalia Bridge, 1961–63, Venice, Italy, is similar in scale to the Mathematical Bridge (both also include teak). Though separated by more than two centuries, like the earlier bridge, even at a glance, idea clearly preceded material, without the wood loosing its impact. The strength of the executed idea fortifies material significance. As with all of Scarpa's work, modern cohabitates with ancient, while surprising elements are always at hand. Although the arch of the Querini bridge is steel, resting on blocks of bright Istrian stone, with iron uprights and supports, the polished teak handrails, with luminous brass accents, and wood step and walkway are dominant.[54] On closer look, the less visible details are unpolished (in both senses), which makes crossing the bridge even more eventful (Plate 10).

Yale Center for British Art

Throughout the twentieth century to the present, wood has been used to gentle harder structures, most effectively when paired with concrete, as US architect Louis I Kahn (1901–74), and Dutch architect Aldo van Eyck (1918–99) have done in quite different ways. In Kahn's Salk Institute, La Jolla, CA (1959–65); Kimbell Art Museum (1966–72), Ft Worth, Texas; and the Yale Center for British Art, New Haven Connecticut (1969–74), wood is a material counterpoint to concrete. Kahn also uses travertine and water in places, as well as carefully managed lighting techniques, to counterbalance the cave-like tendencies of his work, influenced by Imperial Roman Ruins. The coolness and hardness of concrete dominate, which intensifies the warmth and softness of wood as its foil.

Figure 8.2 Yale Center for British Art, Yale University, New Haven, CT (1969–77). Louis I Kahn, Architect. Smooth white oak infill panels soften the concrete structural frame. [Photo: Nathaniel Coleman, 2001].

Hubertus House

In his Hubertus House shelter for single mothers and children, Amsterdam (1973–78), van Eyck follows Wright by using industrially produced sheets and sections of wood. Its agreeable properties introduce convincing domesticity to what could have easily been an anonymous, alienating and impersonal institutional setting.[55] While metal and concrete (block, columns, and slabs), are the other key materials; wood, light and protected vistas enhance the building's sheltering qualities. Used throughout for furniture, flooring and partitions, the wood ceiling panels perhaps go furthest in producing a welcoming – noninstitutionalized – atmosphere.

Figure 8.3 Hubertus House (1973–81), Dining Room, Amsterdam, Holland. Aldo van Eyck, with Hannie van Eyck, Architects. The wood ceiling panels counter typically banal dropped ceilings. [Photo: Nathaniel Coleman, 1999].

Barbican

If wood is a marker of domesticity that makes van Eyck's Hubertus House a counterproject to typical institutional buildings, the timber windows at Chamberlin, Powell and Bon's Barbican Estate (1959–82) are amongst its most distinctive feature. While the diversity of uses and materials, including brick, concrete and water and subtleties of planning, contribute to Barbican's appeal, timber windows are completely unexpected in a modernist megastructure – even for the residences. Although the rich material palette and varieties of spatial experience soften the concrete, nothing more effectively communicates 'home' in this traffic-free superblock than those timber frame windows (especially in an epoch of uPVC). But perhaps they signal to residents and visitors that only a project constructed in a place like the City of London (on a site levelled by Second World War bombing), at great expense, for affluent tenants, could possibly be built to such a high standard of specification.[56] The dark message in that would be the prospect that even 'home' has become the province of only the privileged few (Plate 11).

Tjibaou Cultural Centre

The Jean-Marie Tjibaou Cultural Centre, Nouméa, New Caledonia (1991–98), Renzo Piano Building Workshop, comes close to fulfilling Wright's hopes for beneficial encounters between wood and mechanized production mediated by architects.[57] At the

Figure 8.4 Tjibao Cultural Centre (1991–98), Nouéméa. New Caledonia Renzo Piano Building Workshop, Architects. Tjibaou Cultural Centre: Centre Culturel Tjibaou, Nouméa, New Caledonia - ADCK/Renzo Piano Building Workshop Architects (1991–98). [Photo: Nathaniel Coleman, 2004].

Centre, dedicated to Jean-Marie Tjibaou (1936–89), slain leader of the indigenous Kanak people, not only does wood dominate, it also has been brought up-to-date as a fully engineered construction material. Although there is a diversity of applications, curved glulam wood beams are the centre's most prominent feature, chiefly evident in the ten transpositions of traditional ceremonial Kanak houses ('Case'), each slightly different. Wood and other plant matter are dominant in the conical roofed Case, which conjure up the first shelters discussed earlier. Made from trees, the Case and the Tjibaou Cultural Centre appear to grow from the same forest.

The Case and Centre echo Nouméa's curving coconut palms and upright pine trees, which figure prominently in the Kanak people's myths and rituals.[58] In this instance, wood contextualizes the project on multiple social, spatial and temporal levels; softening the impact of the fully serviced modernist building, while adapting it to climate and community. The comingling of nature, culture and technology, mediated by wood, including engineered, establishes a dialogue with indigenous materials and methods of construction that outlines possibilities for encounters between tradition and innovation. Articulating how local and global can enrich each other is analogized in the modulating interplays between smaller and larger elements, as between wood and metal.[59]

Saint Benedict Chapel

Swiss architect, Peter Zumthor's (b. 1943) Saint Benedict Chapel (1988), Sumvitg, Switzerland, engages in a subdued dialogue with tradition and modernity and locality: (topography, nature, culture). His approach is similar to Piano's at the Tjibaou Cultural Centre, though at a much smaller scale. Whereas Piano's work is cosmopolitan, Zumthor's is ascetic. For example, while glulam is okay at the Tjibaou Cultural Centre, it would undermine Zumthor's chapel. Wood is used very directly, whether for structure, furniture, flooring, roofbeams or cladding. Apart from some metal hardware, lighting and roofing, there is only wood, augmented by limited clerestory glazing. Inside, the skeletal structure is fully exposed. The shingled exterior is familiar but taut; clearly legible as a modernist skin.

Topographically responsive, the chapel compliments its surroundings: mountain vistas, the land, local houses and nearby farm buildings. Nevertheless, its ovoid tower-like form makes it distinct. Although diminutive, its shape and negotiation of its sloping site accentuates its height, while the clerestory windows make it lighthouse-like, appropriate to its religious purpose and remote location. As a beacon, it is also sheltering, akin to the small farm buildings dotting nearby hillsides, which store livestock feed but reassuringly pronounce refuge. The chapel's lozenge shape, and visible ship-like structure within, is suitably nautical, given its expansive (almost oceanic) mountain location and liturgical purpose.

The material and structural directness of the chapel is modernist but reminiscent of traditional wood-framed buildings. Its relative *primitiveness* and the direct relation of frame to cladding recollects Semper's 'Four Elements'. Although the harmonious relation between material and idea make the chapel seem precise, some details are causally executed, which increases the building's appeal by tempering its intensity. At the level of production, this makes the chapel more intimately part of the landscape. Identifiable imperfections echo Ruskin, suggesting that Zumthor's ambition outreached achievable perfection. Relative flaws prevent the chapel from becoming oppressively perfect. Unselfconscious craft is more evident than the sometimes brittleness of his later work; demonstrating what a little uncertainty gains.

Barnes Foundation

There are numerous wood elements in Williams and Tsien's Barnes Foundation building, Philadelphia (completed 2012). Two in particular stand out: the stair to the basement from the main level, and the reclaimed wood floorboards in the central Light Court. Although stairs to secondary uses are usually considered unworthy of the attention Williams and Tsien lavish on them, the Barnes reconfirms their enduring concern for bodily experience.

For Williams, stairs always presume the presence of experiencing subjects. If a stair is inviting, even in the absence of anyone ascending or descending, bodily presence is perceptible.[60] Varieties of experience and opportunities to speed up, slow down, linger, stop, sit, or socialize, modulated by the stair itself (heights of risers, depth of treads, palette of materials), makes a welcome of it.

The material and finish of the Barnes stair invites climbers in a number of ways: the contrast of dark 'walnut and ipe' wood staircase, surrounded by 'Ramon gray limestone in linear hand chisel', and other lighter materials, illuminated by bright light coming through a large etched glass opening; eye level at the top of the stair but far above when at the second landing down. Because positioned above eyelevel, the light coming through glows but offers no views, thereby emphasizing bodily movement. A smaller glazed opening, above eyelevel at the second landing down, functions similarly. The stair experience is further enhanced by a luminous chandelier and a brass handrail.[61] A built-in alcove bench at the bottom of the staircase further accommodates the body. Nearly all of Williams and Tsien's memorable stairs, including at the Barnes, are characterized by a pronounced central element that rises from the bottom to the top, positioned within the gap between the two parallel runs. The decidedly vertical element analogizes ascending (and descending) and introduces wonder to climbing, by separating climbers at different stages of their journey, while offering partial views.

The wooden plank flooring in the Light Court was 'reclaimed from the Coney Island boardwalk', Brooklyn, New York, and is 'laid in a herringbone pattern', set within 'a gray limestone border'.[62] Knowing that the boards once graced the Coney Island boardwalk is alluring. The idea of using them came to the architects when recollecting their visit to 'the Iglesia de San Francisco', an early-seventeenth-century church in Santiago, Chile.[63] Although both stories will remain hidden from most visitors, the warmth of the wood

Figure 8.5 Staircase, Barnes Foundation (2012), Philadelphia, PA. Williams and Tsien, Architects.

floor introduces domesticity to the bright, albeit somewhat over-scaled, Light Court, which the architects claim 'is the living room of the Barnes Foundation.'[64] A proposition that returns consideration of wood to the assertion that its mindful use *always* references early shelters, domesticity and social life at many scales; making it – potentially – an immemorial symbol of human intimacy.

Notes

1. Joseph Rykwert, *The Dancing Column: On Order in Architecture*, Cambridge, MA: MIT Press, 1996; Rykwert, *On Adam's House in Paradise* (1972).

2. Roch C. Smith, *Gaston Bachelard: Philosopher of Science and Imagination*, Revised and Updated, Albany, NY: SUNY, 2016.

3. Gaston Bachelard, *Earth and Reveries of Will: An Essay on the Imagination of Matter*, Kenneth Haltman (trans.), Dallas: Dallas Institute of Humanities and Culture, 2002 (1947), p. 29.

4. Ibid., p. 40.

5. Ibid., p. 41.

6. Ibid.

7. Semper, 'The Four Elements of Architecture' (1851), p. 102.

8. Ibid., p. 102.

9. Ibid., p. 100.

10. Ibid., p. 98.

11. Spiro Kostof, 'Architecture in the Ancient World: Egypt and Greece', in *The Architect: Chapters in the History of the Profession*, Spiro Kostof (ed.), New York and Oxford: Oxford University Press, 1977, p. 16.

12. A. W. Lawrence, *Greek Architecture*, Revised with additions by R. A. Tomlinson, Middlesex: Penguin, 1983, pp. 19–34.

13. Andrea Deplazes, 'Concrete', in *Constructing Architecture: Materials Processes Structures*, Andrea Deplazes (ed.), Basel: Birkhäuser, 2005, p. 57.

14. Semper, 'The Four Elements of Architecture' (1851), p. 102.

15. Bachelard, *Earth and Reveries of Will*, pp. 41–2.

16. Marcus Vitruvius Pollio, *Vitruvius: The Ten Books on Architecture*, Morris Hicky Morgan (trans.), New York: Dover, 1960 (1914), Book. II, Chap. I, para. 1–7 (pp. 38–41).

17. Ibid., Book. II, Chap. I, para. 1–7; Manfred Hegger, Hans Drexeler and Martin Zeumer, *Basics Materials*, Basel: Birkhäuser, 2007, p. 33.

18. Marc-Antoine Laugier, *An Essay on Architecture* (1753), Wolfgang and Anni Hermann (trans.), Los Angeles: Hennessey & Ingalls, 1977, pp. 11–12.

19. Ibid., p. 12.

20. Ibid.

21. Ibid.

22. Ibid.

23. Ibid.

24. Ibid.

25. Ibid.

26. Ibid., pp. 12–13.

27. Semper, 'The Four Elements of Architecture' (1851), p. 102.

28. Ibid.

29. Ibid., p. 103.

30. Gaston Bachelard, *The Poetics of Space*, Maria Jolas (trans.), Boston: Beacon Press, 1964 (1958), p. 33.

31. Ibid., pp. 17–18.

32. Semper, 'The Four Elements of Architecture' (1851), p. 103.

33. Ibid., p. 104.

34. Ibid., pp. 103–4.

35. Cecil D. Elliott, *Technics and Architecture: The Developments of Materials and Systems For Buildings*, Cambridge, MA: MIT Press, 1992, p. 21; Hegger, Drexeler and Zeumer, *Basics Materials*, p. 33; John Dinwoodie, 'Timber', in *Construction Materials: Their Nature and Behaviour*, 4th Edition, Peter Domone and John Illston (eds), Abingdon, Oxon: Spon Press, 2010, p. 404.

36. Hegger, Drexeler and Zeumer, *Basics Materials*, p. 35.

37. 'Focus' derives directly from the Latin '*fŏcus*', meaning hearth, fireplace, altar, home, household, family, cook, stove.

38. Frank Lloyd Wright, 'In the Cause of Architecture IV: The Meaning of Materials – Wood', *The Architectural Record*, 63, no. 5 (May 1928): 481–8 (p. 481).

39. Elliott, *Technics and Architecture*, pp. 8–21.

40. Dinwoodie, 'Timber', pp. 418–21; Hegger, Drexeler and Zeumer, *Basics Materials*, p. 33.

41. Dinwoodie, 'Timber', p. 404.

42. Hegger, Drexeler and Zeumer, *Basics Materials*, p. 33.

43. Ibid.

44. Ciara Curtin, 'Fact or Fiction?: Glass Is a (Supercooled) Liquid', *Scientific American*, 22 February 2007. Available online at: https://www.scientificamerican.com/article/fact-fiction-glass-liquid/ (Accessed 09 June 2018).

45. Wright, 'In the Cause of Architecture IV: The Meaning of Materials – Wood', p. 488.

46. Pedro Guedes (ed.), *Encyclopedia of Building Technology*, New York: McGraw-Hill, 1979, pp. 228–36.

47. Wright, 'In the Cause of Architecture IV: The Meaning of Materials – Wood', p. 488.

48. Ibid., p. 486.

49. Ibid., pp. 481–8. See also Frank Lloyd Wright, 'The Architect and the Machine' (1894 speech); Wright, 'The Art and Craft of the Machine' (1901), Catalogue, 14th Annual Exhibition Chicago Architectural Club, March 1901; reprinted in *Frank Lloyd Wright Collected Writings: Volume 1, 1894–1930*, Bruce Brooks Pfeiffer (ed.), New York: Rizzoli, 1992, pp. 20–6; 58–69; Wright, 'In the Cause of Architecture I: The Architect and the Machine', *The Architectural Record*, 61, no. 5 (May 1927): 394–6.

50. For a historical overview of the Bridge, see: No Author, 'Mathematical Bridge', *Queen's College Cambridge*. Available at: https://www.queens.cam.ac.uk/life-at-queens/about-the-college/college-facts/mathematical-bridge (Accessed 10 June 2018). Edmund Carter, *The History of the University of Cambridge, from Its Original, to the Year 1753*, London, 1753, p. 186.

51. Ibid., 'Mathematical Bridge', *Queen's College Cambridge*.

52. No Author, 'Mathematical Bridge, Cambridge', *Engineering Timeline*. Available at: http://www.engineering-timelines.com/scripts/engineeringItem.asp?id=472 (Accessed 10 June 2018). See also: No Author, 'Cambridge Mathematical Bridge', *Cambridge Travel Guide*, 22 October 2012. Available at: http://cambridgetravelguide.bestcambridge.org/cambridge-mathematical-bridge/ (Accessed 10 June 2018).

53. 'Mathematical Bridge, Cambridge', *Engineering Timeline*; and Queen's College, Mathematical Bridge, *Historic England*. Available at: https://www.historicengland.org.uk/listing/the-list/list-entry/1125515 (Accessed 10 June 2018).

54. Sergio Los, *Carlo Scarpa: An Architectural Guide*, Venice: Arsenale Editrice, 1995, pp. 68–9.

55. Wright, 'In the Cause of Architecture IV: The Meaning of Materials – Wood', p. 488.

56. No Author, 'Our Archive', *Barbican*. Available at: https://www.barbican.org.uk/our-story/our-archive/construction (Accessed 10 June 2018).

57. Wright, 'In the Cause of Architecture IV: The Meaning of Materials – Wood', pp. 481–8.

58. Florence Klein, *Guide Mwakaa: The Pathways of Kanak Tradition*, Stéphane Goiran (trans.), Nouméa, Nouvelle-Calédonie: Agence de Développementde la Culture Kanak, 2000.

59. For more detailed information on Piano's Jean-Marie Tjibaou Cultural Centre, see Coleman, *Utopias and Architecture*, pp. 257–8, 281–96, 317–18.

60. Tod Williams, Unpublished author interview with Tod Williams and Billie Tsien conducted by Nathaniel Coleman, TWBTA Studio, New York, March 2008 (Digital voice recording).

61. Tod Williams and Billie Tsien, *The Architecture of the Barnes Foundation*, New York: Skira/Rizzoli, 2012, pp. 98–9.

62. Ibid., p. 112.

63. Ibid., pp. 112, 113.

64. Ibid., p. 113.

CHAPTER 9
FIRE AND WIND: THE APPEAL OF BAKING BRICKS

Bricks may be all too common but ordinariness situates them deeply in human associations with the built environment. As essential as daily bread, brickmaking conjures up domestic feelings analogous to baking. Analogies between baking bread and making bricks are considered in this chapter in relation to powerful human relations to fire. From its acquisition and control – including producing heat – brickmaking is charted through architectural treatises from ancient Roman architect, Vitruvius (active first century BC), to Italian Renaissance extensions by Filarete (1400–69), Leon Battista Alberti (1404–72), Francesco di Giorgio (1439–1501), and Andrea Palladio (1508–80) and nineteenth-century architect and theorist Gottfried Semper (1803–79). Although solid and cool, brick begins with clay to form a dough-like substance. Its subsequent material presence records the *captured* heat (of a kiln, or earlier, the sun), light and air required to harden it.

Firing the imagination

The origins of brickmaking, bound up with the size of hands (that form and lay bricks) and with baking (sun, fire, air), are recollected by receptions of the material as both warm and human-scaled. Bodily memories run deep in physique and psyche, despite technological progress and automated production processes. Handmade and machine-made bricks are qualitatively different, distinguished above all else by imperfection (that most human characteristic). Generally, the more perfection is achieved, the less humane the result; only paradoxical because education drives architects towards exactitude, in line with building-industry myths of faultless machine-made production. From a psychological perspective, flawlessness and alienation go hand in hand.

Especially since the Second World War, as architectural modernists' industrial aspirations progressed from fiction to reality – from rude approximations of machine-produced perfection to its relative achievement – the fragile character and quickly decaying bodies of fallible humans have become increasingly estranged from uncanny built environments – the appearance and organization of which feels better suited to the non-human. Until at least the 1950s, modernist architecture remained approximate (even handmade) compared to the mechanistic slickness of twenty-first-century production. Even later, the structurally expressive, so-called, high-tech Centre Georges Pompidou (1971–77), Paris, retains a crafted quality: its bespoke character a foil to otherwise overwhelming technical displays of structure and services. Tensions between its machine-like appearance and vaguely handmade character contribute to its status as amongst the most visited sites in Paris. As production values are perfected, industrialized building become slicker, rendering the constructed landscape stranger. Digital modes of representation communicate architects' ideologies of perfection to clients, developers, builders and the public. So long as drawings were rhetorical demonstrations of possible realities, their translation into buildings was approximate. Lack of fidelity between drawings and buildings did not make results unfaithful to the architect's vision. However, since engineering and architecture separated around 1750, representation as simulation has progressively replaced drawing as generative. Professionalization and digital developments parallel increasingly automated industrial production of materials and analogous building construction practices.[1] The production and use of materials mirror the transformation of representation. As the relationship between architectural drawings and built results becomes more exacting, the illusion of perfection becomes more seductive, alongside efficiencies of managed production.

Opportunities for embodied experience weaken as the built environment becomes a simulacrum of itself. A diminished human environment may be precise in execution but is an inadequate sheltering counterform of human fallibility, or emotion. As Ruskin observed: 'Of human work none but what is bad can be perfect, in its own bad way.'[2] Ideals of human rationality, encompassing aspirations to control nature and destiny, take shape with the Enlightenment, as the foundation of industrial production and modern bureaucracy (planning and managerialism). Inevitably, technocratic, bureaucratized building industries presume a likewise architecture, which education and practice contribute to reproducing.

Figure 9.1 Roman Forum (*Foro Romano*) (800 BC–A.D. 630); Basilica of Maxentius (A.D. 306) behind. Ancient Roman Brick. [Photo: Nathaniel Coleman, c. 1993].

Brick

Its humbleness, material qualities, finished size and relation to breadmaking make brick *manageable* physically and psychologically. Akin to bread, brick is a staple of building. Its enduring appeal is inseparable from its material properties: *terra-cotta*, cooked or baked earth; or its encompassing each of the ancient four elements: fire (hot and dry), air (hot and wet), water (cold and wet) and earth (cold and dry). As an immemorial companion in fulfilling basic human needs for shelter, brick predates recorded history – first made during the late Neolithic period (9,000–5,000 BC). The long use and humble character of brick recollects its earthy origins (*humus*, earth, soil, ground, floor). Moreover, it shares the same etymological root with *humanus* (human, people, human, cultured, refined). No wonder in myth, humans, like brick, begin as clay.

In describing the virtues of brick, Wright touches upon the elemental effect of the intermixing of fire and earth in its production:

> Perhaps you would make the walls of brick that the fire touched to tawny gold or muddy tan, the choicest of all earth's hues – they do not rise rudely above the sod ..., but recognize the surface of the ground on which they stand, gently spreading there to a substantial base that makes the building seem to stand more firmly in its socket in the earth.[3]

Earth (the earthy) dominates the other three elements that make up brick: Water (for producing the batter, or paste); Fire (spent light and heat for baking); and Air (cooling and curing). As the base of all things, Earth is the ground of foundations, farmland and culture. Water courses through the environment, including homes, and is essential for sustaining life (as rain; for drinking or cleansing; making up about 50–60% of the human body). The manufacture of brick depends on air (for curing), and the earth that forms it. Fire is warming, cooks food and bakes brick.

Thinking with brick

A range of buildings informs the discussion of brick developed here, including Sir John Soane's, Picture Gallery (1811–1817), Dulwich, London; Wright's Robbie House, Chicago, IL (1908–10); Finnish-American Architect, Eero Saarinen's (1910-1961) MIT Chapel (1955); Earl V. Moore Building (1964), University of Michigan; and Hill House (1958-1960), University of Pennsylvania; and Chamberlin, Powell and Bon's Barbican Estate (1959–82), London, UK – each is notable for a dynamic use of materials, including brick; complex spatial planning; and imaginative conceptualizations of hearth (even virtual) and home, even if mass housing (Plate 12; See Figures 9.2, 9.3, 9.4, 9.5, and 9.7).

Although brick can be used throughout buildings, its dominant physical and psychological presence is the fireplace, as the focus of dwellings. The word *focus*, Latin term for 'hearth' and 'fireplace', recollects the physical and perceptual centrality of fire

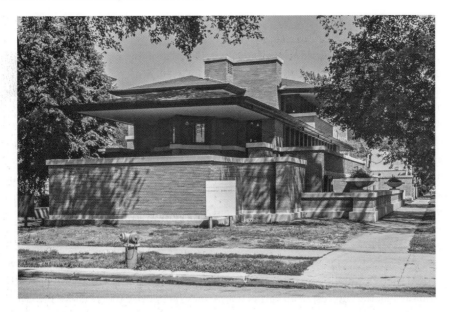

Figure 9.2 Robie House (1908–10), Chicago, IL, USA. Frank Lloyd Wright, Architect. The repose of Wright's horizontal work, and arrangement of volumes would have influenced Dudok's Town Hall – less so Sterling's History Faculty. Brick is used in a direct way, though inflected by the machine. [Photo: Nathaniel Coleman, 2003].

in domestic and social life, conjuring up the light and heat emanating from it, and the physical convergence of home and its inhabitants.[4] Fireplaces (even in their absence) persist as the psychosomatic centre of dwelling – recollecting the origins of architecture and the spent light and heat that bricks contain, which hearths retain. Accordingly, Bachelard observes: 'Fire is the ultra-living element. It is intimate and universal. It lives in our heart. It lives in the sky. It rises from the depths of the substance and offers itself with the warmth of love.'[5] Recollections of earth, fire and hearth are indwelling in perceptions of brick as *warm* – suggestive of the British English sense of *homeliness*, German *Gemütlichkeit* and Dutch *Gezelligheid*. By comprising all four of the ancient elements, brick is synonymous with a home on earth.

Vitruvius's *Ten Books on Architecture* (*De architectura*) is significant for being the only Western architectural treatise to have survived from classical antiquity. Although *lost* until the earlier part of the fifteenth century, *Ten Books* has greatly influenced architects since the Renaissance, summarized in the following by English architect Geoffrey Scott (1884–1929):

> Vitruvius provided the code ... Alberti founded his great work upon it ... The treatise which has so profoundly altered the visible world was indeed exactly designed to fit the temper of the Renaissance. It is less a theory of architecture than an encyclopedia of knowledge, general and particular, in easy combination.[6]

While architecture's own literature is a good place to start, myriad external sources support investigations into brick's persisting material meanings.

Figure 9.3 MIT Chapel (dedicated 1955), Cambridge, MA, USA. Eero Saarinen, Architect. [Photo: Nathaniel Coleman, 2003].

Figure 9.4 Earl V. Moore Building, School of Music, Theater and Dance (1964), University of Michigan, Ann Arbor, MI, USA. Eero Saarinen, Architect. [Photo: Nathaniel Coleman, 2003].

Figure 9.5 Hill House (1958–60), University of Pennsylvania, Philadelphia, PA, USA. Eero Saarinen, Architect. Saarinen was influenced by Finnish Architect Alvar Aalto (1898–1976), and by his architect father, Eliel Saarinen (1873–1950), in the direct use of materials, without portraying them as *essences*. [Photo: Nathaniel Coleman, 2003].

If bricks are earthy and warm and their manufacture is cognate with breadmaking, modern hermetic buildings obscure architecture's vocation for structuring the lifeworld. Air-conditioning, and climate control more generally, as well as structure concealed by surface treatments dissociate perception and bodily experience from the elements, including fire and wind. Buildings completely insulated from the environment are a relatively recent development. For example, Le Corbusier's *Cite de Refuge* in Paris, built for the Salvation Army (completed 1933), was the first hermetically sealed air-conditioned residential building.

Vitruvius

Brick can no more be isolated from fire, than bread can be from ovens. While the definitive origins of fire are elusive, this is less significant than its predating human beings and consciousness. As a species, we were thus born into a world of fire, amongst the other elements, which evolved into objects of consideration as their usefulness (technical *and* emotional) became known. For Sigmund Freud (1856–1939), inventor of psychoanalysis, the acquisition and control of fire is amongst the most significant events in human development:

> As regards ... civilization, there can be scarcely any doubt, if we go back far enough, we find that the first acts of civilization were the use of tools, the gaining control of fire and the construction of dwellings. Among these, the control of fire stands as a quite extraordinary and unexampled achievement.[7]

Like Vitruvius, Freud was a student of ancient Greek myth and culture, which explains the similarities between their origin stories of civilization. According to Vitruvius: 'The men of old were born like wild beasts, in the woods, caves, and groves, and lived on savage fare.' Their subsequent *discovery* and mastery of fire anticipates progress beyond that primordial state. First, a dense forest 'caught fire' during a storm, when high winds caused branches to rub together. Although initially 'terrified by the furious flame', once 'it subsided', people 'drew near' to it, because of the comforting warmth. Subsequently, 'they put on logs and, while thus keeping it alive, brought up other people to it, showing them by signs how much comfort they got from it.'[8]

The light and warmth introduced by domesticated fire became a natural *focus* of nascent community, and was a precursor of common language: 'In that gathering ..., from daily habit they fixed upon articulate words just as these had happened to come; ... in this chance way they began to talk, and thus originated conversation with each other.'[9]

In Vitruvius's telling, community depends on interchange and is itself a form of communication. Both derive from understandings (of things, virtues, principles, social dreams) held *in communi*. Language (in all its forms) structures sociability. For Vitruvius, not only does the acquisition and control of fire provide the focus necessary for the emergence of community and language, it is a precondition of architecture:

> it was the discovery of fire that originally gave rise to the coming together of men, to the deliberating assembly and to social intercourse. And so ..., finding themselves ... not being obliged to walk with faces to the ground, but upright and gazing upon the splendor of the starry firmament, and also being able to do with ease what ever they chose with their hands and fingers, they began in that first assembly to construct shelters.[10]

Drawn together by the warmth of communal fire (the sociability fostered by its literal heat), humans eventually acknowledged their unique capacities, which initiated self-consciousness, dreaming and the wonder of theoretical knowledge (*theōria*: contemplation, speculation). Imagining futures is a uniquely human capacity remarkably suited to political thought and architectural projection. As told by Vitruvius, the practical capacities afforded by agile hands and an opposing thumb join anticipation to making, which, in relation to material, reminds us that after conception, selection is as important as manipulation.

The earliest existent buildings were constructed of clay, mud, mudbrick and, finally, fired brick, as well as stone. The exceptionally long duration of masonry construction, from its most primitive forms to the most sophisticated, are as much a part of the human landscape as agriculture, art, cities and community. Building provides the physical enclosures of civilization within which social processes can unfold. When humans come together in communities and compare accomplishments, increasing sophistication ideally results. For Vitruvius, this is how building and knowledge advance. At first, shelters were made with found materials: 'green boughs', caves 'dug on mountain sides', formal and structural imitations of birds' nests and 'places of refuge' made 'out of mud and twigs.' Then,

> by observing the shelters of others and adding new details to their own inceptions they constructed better and better kinds of huts as time went on ..., they next gradually advanced from the construction of buildings to the other arts and sciences, and so passed from a rude and barbarous mode of life to civilization and refinement.[11]

Locating the beginnings of civilization around domesticated fire – coterminous with the social construction of community, language, building and then cites and culture – is the surplus significance residing in brick. *Every* use of brick recollects this, comments on it, interprets, or renounces this content – even when advanced technical modes of production scrub it clean of residual associations with the origins of culture. In such instances, the silted-up significance of brick returns as a spectre weighed down by human history and material culture. Brick's scale ensures its every use, no matter how slick (or nefarious), recollects *all* previous uses. Attempts to transform it into a modernist skin-like membrane are only desirable when contrasted to preconscious brick associations. The undesirability of the same also turns on association. Both are matters of attachment (Plate 13).

Filarete

Italian architect and treatise writer Antonio di Pietro Averlino, known as Filarete (1400–69), placed the origins of architecture at the moment Adam was expelled from the Garden of Eden:

> when Adam was driven out of paradise, it was raining ... he put his hands over his head to protect himself ... after Adam had made a roof of his hands ... he thought and contrived to make some sort of habitation to protect himself from the rain and also from the heat of the sun. When he recognized and understood his need, we can believe that he made some sort of shelter of branches, or a hut, or perhaps

some cave where he could flee when he needed. If such were the case, it is probable that Adam was the first [architect].[12]

Filarete identifies the origins of architecture with necessity – shelter for survival. His emphasis on use reminds us that architecture conceived in isolation from it is relatively new and arguably *meaningless*. Fantasies of liberating architecture from the burden of use portray each point of Vitruvius's triad in opposition with the other. When *Venustas* (beauty, delight, art), *Utilitas* (utility, function) and *Firmitas* (structural integrity, firmness, strength) are disincorporated, architecture's significance splinters. In the event, the humble brick is particularly well-suited to materially reunifying the elements of Vitruvius's triad.

Alberti

As engaging as Vitruvius's and Filarete's origin stories are, Italian architect Leon Battista Alberti (1404–72), author of the *Ten Books on Architecture* (1452), perhaps the most famous architectural treatise after Vitruvius's, challenges his predecessor's story of architecture's foundations:

> Some have said that it was fire and water which were initially responsible for bringing men together in communities, but we, considering how useful, even indispensable, a roof and walls are for men, are convinced that it was they that drew and kept men together.[13]

By asserting that 'a roof and walls' drew communities together, by giving society a place, Alberti suggests that building precedes civic life, rather than the other way around. The assertion is not as strange as it might at first appear: communities require spaces of appearance to flourish. Although Alberti diverges from Vitruvius's generally accepted account of the origins of building and civilization, he too places fire at its centre: 'How many respectable families ... throughout the world would have totally disappeared ... had not their family hearth harbored them, as it were, into the very bosom of their ancestors?'[14] Even today, the hearth (imaginaries) persists as a focal point of households.

Fire and home

In much the way the sun is at the centre of our solar system, fire is at the centre of architecture, with brick embodying both. According to Wright: 'Fire is the father-creator to them all [materials] – below ground.' While 'light is mother-creator to all that rise in air out of the ground.' For him, earthly materials may be born of fire but human 'creative power' transforms them – with fire – into beautiful and useful elements:

Anything permanent as a constructive material comes into man's hands by way of Fire, as he has slowly learned to approach in 'degrees' the heat in which his globe of the earth was formed – and courage to set what he has himself made, again at its beneficent mercy. He knows much. But fire knows more and has constant surprises for him.[15]

Though ancient in origin, the gendering of material creation may seem anachronistic but in a spirit of cultural evolution, more than anything, the procreative process is alluded to in relation to generative tensions between the earthy (ground) and the ethereal (sky and sun). The sun sustains planetary life, but would be of little consequence for humans without the earth. Imaginatively, fire is a child of the sun: focusing its rays quickly translates into flame. Fire's place at the heart of traditional (and modern) homes recollects the Vestal Virgins who tended the perpetual flame in their ancient Roman Temple, dedicated to the eponymous goddess of the hearth. The heart is associated with fire and flame. Life itself is flame-like, burning bright, until extinguished by death.

Wright's comments above encapsulate the layered richness of associations with fire, and with materials wrought by its complementary aspects of light (intellect?) and heat (emotion?) but not so much the obscuring smoke it produces when things burn, which is perhaps its most dangerous aspect. Although potentially terrifying and destructive (its demonic side?), fire is equally purifying and transformative (its divine side?). It is life-giving: encapsulating the warmth and generative power of the sun. Even when hidden from consciousness, these associations persist, which explains the enduring (elemental?) power of natural materials. As receptacles of mysteries, dreams, and creation, and the sources of the human-made world (in relation to nature), the visceral physicality of materials draws bodies close to them. Fire's dual qualities are a reminder that resisting essentialist claims reveals any material's significance as primarily deriving from what is done with it.

Food is still cooked over fire, and like God in 'Noah and the Flood', it is difficult to resist when cooked outdoors over an open flame. Eating and fire inhabit the centre of home, ritual and civilization. But the scale of society can obscure the cross axes between its smallest and largest units. For example, the earliest experiences of eating and dwelling occur within the womb. At the microscale, the home is womb-like; at the macro-scale, the planet is. As Bachelard shows, home and world are inevitably inflected by the imagined experiences of first dwellings. Fire may also remind us of the passion we imagine was present when we were brought into being.

Brick and the fireplace

As developed so far, the origins of architecture and civilization, dependent on the domestication of fire, inform the enduring appeal of brick. As a somewhat more technologically advanced form 'of the working of raw earth, bricks are a kind of artificial stone manufactured by mixing clay with water to make it moldable and elastic', subsequently baked in a kiln. Curing 'at high temperature hardens the clay', which makes bricks durable, while providing them with 'high mechanical resistance'. Their range of desirable material properties include 'lightness, elasticity, malleability, adaptability to stress, good aging', and 'thermal insulation qualities, and natural protection from environmental dampness.'[16] In addition to the straightforward methods of their production and beneficial material qualities, the manageable size and weight of individual bricks makes them especially well-suited to rapid construction.

Factual descriptions of brick's virtues provide access to its poetical material qualities, not just technical ones. Reverie is an effective way of gaining awareness of brick significance. As Kahn, echoing Wright and Bachelard, observes: 'It's important, you see, that you ... honor the brick and glorify the brick instead of shortchanging it or giving it an inferior job to do, where it loses its character ... Brick is a beautiful material because it's a completely live material.'[17] One of brick's most compelling, almost overdetermined, qualities is its suitability for containing the same fire and heat required to bake it, which is also a significant source of its liveliness.

Brick's scale recalls the hand, thus the body, and by extension, community. Their constitution and manufacturing process associate them with fire, thereby the beginnings of human civilization. Fireplaces, hearths, chimneys and smokestacks are amongst the most recognizable building elements constructed with brick. Hearths and fireplaces, at the home's heart; chimneys loom high above; smokestacks rising from factories: bricks are constant reminders of warmth and origins. Although more explicitly prosaic than poetic, fireplaces and hearths highlight associations of brick with warmth throughout the built environment. The main function of the hearth was to contain fire for cooking and produce heat. The centrality of food and warmth to human survival makes them analogous to one another. Hence the reasonableness of associating bricks with bread.

Palladio

Although there is mention of fireplaces and hearths in many architectural treatises, Alberti, Francesco di Giorgio and Palladio considered their placement and construction in greatest detail. While Vitruvius places fire at the evolutionary centre of civilization, he does not reflect on fireplaces in building, which di Georgio touches upon. Apart from setting his narrative at the dinner table, which suggests proximity to the symbolic hearth of the dining room and to the functional fireplace of the kitchen, Filarete notes the presence of a fireplace each time he describes a dwelling, though not technically, as its construction would have been a matter of habit.

Palladio is as famous for his influential treatise *The Four Books of Architecture* (1570) as for his buildings, mostly in the Veneto region of Italy. Unlike Vitruvius, he was not particularly interested in the origins of architecture or culture. He describes the chimneys of antiquity in straightforward language, noting: 'The ancients used to warm their rooms in this manner. They made their chimneys in the middle, with columns or modiglions that supported the architraves, upon which was the pyramid of the chimney from whence the smoke issued.'[18] He goes on to describe other methods of conducting warmth through a building, including via pipes in the thickness of walls, 'through which they conveyed the heat of the fire that was under those rooms, and which came out of certain vents or holes that were made at the top of those pipes.'[19] He does not, though, describe the symbolic function of the hearth in much detail. Palladio concludes his discussion of chimneys by describing how they should be constructed, emphasizing the importance of issuing smoke outward from the building.[20] His descriptions of ancient fireplaces, as well as his prescribed methods for conducting smoke out of buildings, generally conform to the drawings of the same in Francesco di Giorgio's treatise.

Alberti

In his description of fireplaces, Alberti was concerned with the practical considerations of where to locate them and how to properly convey smoke out of buildings. 'Fireplaces', he writes, 'need to be far away from any woodwork, less sparks or the heat of the fire set light to nearby beams and timbers'.[21] He was equally preoccupied with the ambient conditions of rooms in relation to optimizing comfort. Accordingly, seasonal dining rooms are quite important for him. As an example, he notes that the principal requirement of the room for winter eating is that it be warmed by a hearth. The character of this room (ambient conditions and architectural qualities) should be appropriate to its seasonal use, foremost of which is the requirement for the near constant presence of a fire – climactically beneficial but producing potentially damaging smoke.[22]

Like other treatise writers, Alberti's intended audience is as much patrons as architects. Steeped as he was in ancient learning (shared with treatise writers from Vitruvius to Palladio), Alberti suggests that we ought to live and build in moderation, including the use of fire.[23] Beyond sound advice about moderate use, and the consequences of overindulgence, he was quite specific about how and where to locate the hearth within a room to maximize its ease of use and benefit:

> the ... hearth ... should be prominent, it should be capable of warming several people at one time, and it should have sufficient light but no draft (although there must be an outlet to allow smoke to rise). The hearth, therefore, must not be confined to some corner or recessed deep within the wall; at the same time it should not occupy the most important position in the room, where the guest's table should be.[24]

For Alberti, position and propriety (usefulness) are on an equal footing with technical considerations. He also demonstrates awareness of the psychological aspects of doing both well. He begins with the practical but shifts to the psychological: 'If we are to build somewhere very cold, we shall need fires. There are different kinds of fires, but the most convenient is the bright, open hearth: fire from smoky, vaulted ovens pollutes the air, makes our eyes water, and dims our vision.' Moving to the emotional, he observes: 'the very sight of the light and flames of a live fire is a cheerful companion, they say, to old men chatting by the hearth.'[25]

Concentrating on fire and fireplaces recollects the perceived *warmth* of brick as associated with the modes of production that bring it into existence. Making brick – primarily mud (earth) and fire (heat) but also water (mixed with the mud) and air (to dry or cool them) – conjoins with the preconscious experience of them as spent or captured fire and heat, and earth (less so with water and air). The material meaning of brick is its nearly unique coalescence of the ancient four elements (earth, water, air and fire), thereby embedding it within the natural world, close to life and the body.

Francesco di Giorgio

Francesco di Giorgio communicates an easy combination of artistic and practical considerations in descriptions of ancient fireplaces that are concise but evocative. Even though archaeologists seem to agree that fireplaces with chimneys, as we know them, did not exist until the middle ages, di Giorgio based his descriptions on ancient examples he apparently discovered during his travels throughout Italy, though no traces have been found. Even so, he was surprised that Vitruvius made no mention of fireplaces.[26] As a military engineer, di Giorgio's technical specifications for fireplace designs are more detailed than the other treatise writers. Nevertheless, comfort and convenience are never far from his thoughts.[27] As reveries of brick and fire play out in material imaginaries, they illuminate how each could be an emblem of the other – as powerful markers of *heimat* (home):

> For most people fire has its pleasurable attributes. The joy of the open grate with its play of light and colour is without equal as a releaser of fantasy. Indeed the fireside is a marvelous place for reverie, even more so perhaps when the wind is howling outside, dashing the inhospitable rain or snow against the window. The fireside, too is a place for companionship, and for intimate conversation.[28]

When fireplaces are generously proportioned and the room well warmed by its heat, a homely atmosphere prevails, no matter the complexities of home life, or individual tribulations, or so goes the belief.

Baking bread and brick

Although other materials may be used, because of their association with fire, imaginary fireplaces are almost always made of brick. Like our daily bread – source of proverbial sustenance – the bricks surrounding us are captured fire. The hearth, fireplace leading to the chimney, rising behind the chimneybreast, to the rooftop chimney stack, are often enough made of terra-cotta (cooked earth); passed through fire to bake it into brick.

Although Filarete doesn't treat fire directly, the kitchens and fireplaces mentioned in his treatise suggest its presence. He does, however, consider fire in describing making and baking brick. In these passages, allusions to cooking up buildings and food meet. On the other hand, Alberti makes the brick – bread/bread – brick analogy explicit in his description of baking one or the other:

> whether by accident or by careful investigation, they [the ancients] discovered that fire strengthened and hardened bricks, ... there is no building material more suitable than brick, however you wish to employ it, though it must be baked rather than raw, and the correct methods of molding and firing must be strictly followed.[29]

In its earliest forms, brick was used *raw*, hardened only by the sun. By the time Alberti was writing, the best *recipes* required specific methods for shaping and curing:

> We know from experience that the same clay will produce a much stronger brick if it is allowed, as it were, to rise, as dough does in bread making, and then is kneaded several times, until it becomes as soft as wax, and even the smallest stones have been removed. Baking will so harden brick that, if it is left long enough in the oven, it will become as tough as flint, further more, as happens with bread, the bricks get a solid crust, either while they are baked in the oven or when they are left to dry in the open air. This is why it is better to bake them thin, so that there is more crust and less crumb. And if they are baked and polished, they may well prove impervious to the assaults of the weather.[30]

Alberti's description is as appetizing as it is informative. Echoing his observation that brick becomes 'hard as flint' when baked, Filarete describes it as 'making "stone" from terra-cotta':

> brick, which is made of earth prepared in a certain way to make 'stone' and then cooked in order to be good so that it can endure water and cold ... [T]o make good brick, you must be careful to have good earth ..., neither too lean nor too fat ..., if it is lean it will not make good brick ... If ... it is fat, it is heavy and breaks easily in the drying or in the firing and it is also more difficult to cut ... This is enough about making 'stone' from terra-cotta.[31]

As with other treatise writers, Filarete's discussion of brickmaking comprises specific recipes, including listing ingredients, their quality, measure and the best clays for making *batter*. Also specified are the proper treatment and preparation of the ingredients before the batter is made, the brick formed and finally fired. Even if the similarities between making bricks and baking bread are simply matters of necessity, the correspondences *fire* material imaginaries.

Francesco di Giorgio's discussion of bricks is similar to Alberti's and Vitruvius's, all of which differ from Palladio's more cursory treatment. Di Girogio asserts that to achieve 'perfection ..., artificial stone [*piettre artificiale*]', (formed bricks) should be kept as long as possible, before being cooked.[32] He also notes, '*modern* bricks are one foot long and half a foot wide', but does not indicate their height.[33] Vitruvius's treatment of brick is the most technical. He states in a proto-scientific manner that because fire, water, air and the earth makeup an infinite number of things, the balance between them determines character and make up.[34] The proportional relationship between each element is the crucial factor that distinguishes one body, or thing, from another but also associates them all. Each of the four elements must be properly controlled to guarantee optimum balance in a body (animate or inanimate), which ensures *proper* functioning, including brickmaking:

> Bricks should be made in Spring or Autumn, so that they dry uniformly. Those made in Summer are defective, because the fierce heat of the sun bakes their surface and makes the brick seem dry while inside it is not dry ... Bricks will be most serviceable if made two years before using; for they cannot dry thoroughly in less time.[35]

Although now mostly made in very different ways, reflecting on Vitruvius's advice on brick encourages meditations on the nature of materials and their enduring significance.

Figure 9.6 Barbican Estate Housing (1969–76), Arts Centre (1971–82), foreground, City of London, United Kingdom. Chamberlin, Powell and Bon, Architects. Although brick is used sparingly – for housing on lower levels, low-rise structures, landscape elements and paving – the humanizing effect is powerful. The brick paving in particular unifies the complex, softens the concrete as do the timber frame windows, water and vegetation; more so and more effectively than the variety of forms. The mix of uses and low- and high-rise structures also soften the complex. [Photo: Nathaniel Coleman, 2017].

Mechanized production of brick might make it more technically perfect but risks depleting its desirable characteristics. Brick may be common but its scale, ease of manufacturing, handling in construction and the way weathering mellows it through time ensure its persistence as potentially amongst the most humane basic units of building. Even so, how brick is used determines its qualities and what it signifies.

Despite immemorial associations, like other materials, on its own, brick is largely meaningless (though by no means empty) (See Figure 9.6). However, when no longer formed by hand, the potential richness derived from inconsistencies of surface, colour, texture and cut are diminished. Like mass-produced bread, brick is now rolled out factory style, extruded and machine sliced, rather than handmade. When *perfect* in colour and finish – machine cut, smooth and *flawless* – it becomes uniform to the point of monotony.

The *perfect* modern brick is unfit for purpose because it is largely emptied of those aspects that defined its warm, humane character – its *anima* (conjured up by memory and use). *Perfect* slab walls of uniformly cut and coloured bricks are more like taut skins, or membranes, than rough-hewn walls wrought by immemorial production and construction processes (See Figure 9.7). Less satisfactory are towers faced with brick to give the impression of a more traditional masonry building, betrayed by gaping expansion joints separating obviously apparent sections of veneer. Here, brick is a slip, cladding or mask, which may, in specific instances, be agreeable enough, except that the aim is mostly deception (usually fooling only the architect or client). Baking bricks

Figure 9.7 History Faculty Building (1963–68), Cambridge University, Cambridge, UK. James Sterling, Architect. Influenced by Dudok's Town Hall. The orange-red brick is a taut modernist skin; the scale of individual bricks is of secondary importance. [Photo: Nathaniel Coleman, 1979].

and bread form constellations of homely recollections (connoting warmth, protection, sustenance and care) that even *misuse* has not obliterated. However, the earthiness of bricks and bread is most satisfying when imperfectly produced.

Fire might occupy the symbolic (and actual) heart of civilization (encompassing home and architecture) but it can be turned against itself: used in structures dedicated to terminating civilization ensnare bricks in destruction. Twentieth-century Nazi concentration and death camps constructed with bricks (including Auschwitz, located in Oświęcim, Poland) are harrowing examples: all of the material's associations with baking, home, hearth and civilization are all but broken – forever. Arguments about material neutrality are thrown into question. The same enduring characteristics that make brick desirable, also made it a convenient material for constructing the camps – perverting its agreeable qualities (outlined in this chapter). Only force of will, degrees of delusion and the risk of hope can sustain tenuous bonds with material meaning broken by catastrophe and mostly abandoned by post-Second World War architects. Fire's destructive form is the machines of war. Its darkening aspects are never far from its luminous qualities. Yet, how it is used, rather than essence, determines significance – though memory and association taints it.

Francesco di Giorgio's treatment of the darker and more luminous character of fire in the same treatise covering architecture, engineering, and military arts on the one hand considers the origins and construction of fireplaces, as well as detailing which earthly materials go towards making the finest brick, including how to properly cook them. On the other hand, in a similar manner, he discusses how one goes about burning boats, villages and castles amongst other things. [36] For di Giorgio, there would have been no contradiction to outlining the construction and destruction of architecture in the same treatise. In doing so, he challenges us with fire's inherently contradictory nature: it sustains life but just as easily can snuff it out. It can warm a building or destroy it. Bricks can be used to construct the edifices of civilization, or death camps. Do either sorts of associations – constitutive or pathological – reveal brick's essence? Arguably not, since, as is argued throughout this book, significance is still a matter of use, notwithstanding the durability of connotations (positive or negative).

Notes

1. Scheer, *The Death of Drawing*. See also, Evans, 'Translations from Drawing to Building' (1986), pp. 152–93.

2. Ruskin, 'The Nature of Gothic' (1853), in *Unto this Last and Other Writings* (1862), p. 92. See also: Coleman, *Utopias and Architecture*, pp. 115–32.

3. Frank Lloyd Wright, 'Architect, Architecture, and the Client' (1896), in *Frank Lloyd Wright: Collected Writings, Vol. 1: 1894–1930*, New York: Rizzoli, 1992, p. 35.

4. 'Focus.' *Merriam-Webster.com*. Merriam-Webster, n.d. Web. 28 June 2017.

5. Gaston Bachelard, *The Psychoanalysis of Fire*, Alan C. M. Ross (trans.), Boston, MA: Beacon Press, 1964, p. 7.

6. Geoffrey Scott, *The Architecture of Humanism: A Study in the History of Taste* (1924), New York: Norton Library, 1974, pp. 146–7.

7. Sigmund Freud, *Civilization and Its Discontents* (1929), James Strachey (trans.), Norton: New York, 1989, p. 44.

8. Vitruvius, 'Origins of the Dwelling House', in *The Ten Books on Architecture*, Morris Hicky Morgan (trans.), New York: Dover Publications, 1960 (1914), Book II, Chap. 1, pp. 38–40 (p. 38).

9. Ibid.

10. Ibid., p. 38.

11. Ibid., p. 38–40.

12. Filarete, *Treatise on Architecture*, John R. Spencer (trans.), New Haven: Yale University Press, 1965, Book I, p. 10.

13. Alberti, 'Prologue', in *On the Art of Building in Ten Books*, p. 3.

14. Ibid.

15. Frank Lloyd Wright, 'In the Cause of Architecture V: The Meaning of Materials – The Kiln' (1928), *The Architectural Record* (June 1928), in *Frank Lloyd Wright: Collected Writings, Vol. 1: 1894–1930*. New York: Rizzoli, 1992, p. 284.

16. Francesca Prina, *Architecture: Elements, Materials, Form*, Princeton, NJ and Oxford: Princeton University Press, 2008, p. 234.

17. Louis I. Kahn, 'Lecture at Pratt Institute' (1973), in *Louis I. Kahn, Lectures, Writings, Interviews*, Alessandra Latour (ed.), New York: Rizzoli, 1991, p. 323.

18. Palladio, *The Four Books on Architecture*, Issac Ware (trans.), New York: Dover Publications, 1965 (1738), Book I, Chap. 27: 'Of Chimneys', p. 33.

19. Ibid.

20. Ibid.

21. Alberti, *On the Art of Building in Ten Books*, Book I, Chap. 13, p. 32.

22. Ibid., Book V, Chap. 17, p. 147.

23. Ibid., pp. 147–8.

24. Ibid., p. 148.

25. Ibid., Book X, Chap. 14, p. 355.

26. Francesco di Giorgio Martini, *Trattati Di Architettura Ingegneria E Arte Militare*, a cura di Corrado Maltese, transcritzione di Livia Maltese Degrassi, Milano: Edizione Il Polifilo, 1967), Book II, p. 333.

27. Ibid., Book II, p. 334.

28. Donald Scott, *The Psychology of Fire*, New York: Charles Scribner's Sons, 1974, p. 5.

29. Alberti, *On the Art of Building in Ten Books*, Book II, Chap. 2, p. 50.

30. Ibid., pp. 50–2.

31. Filarete, *Treatise on Architecture*, Book III, pp. 28–9.

32. di Giorgio, *Trattati Di Architettura Ingegneria E Arte Militare*, Book II, p. 314.

33. Ibid., p. 315.

34. Vitruvius, 'Origins of the Dwelling House', Book I, Chap. 5, p. 18.

35. Ibid., Book II, Chap. 3, p. 43.

36. di Giorgio, *Trattati Di Architettura Ingegneria E Arte Militare*, Book I, pp. 207, 229.

CHAPTER 10
WILD AT HEART: CONCRETE AS
LIQUID STONE?

Although the origins of concrete go back to ancient Rome, it is only since the later nineteenth century that its use in construction has become pervasive. The aspirations and shortcomings of modernist architecture are bound up with concrete. In the UK, for example, raw concrete, or *béton brut* (borrowed from Le Corbusier), lent its name to the much maligned loosely defined post-Second World War brutalism style. Over time, it has become interchangeable with the perceived failings of modernist architecture and city planning, as 'brutal'. However, *rawness*, rather than *brutality*, preoccupied adherents of brutalism. Rawness, in the sense of 'savageness' that Ruskin extolled, is closer to what Le Corbusier had in mind when referring to *raw concrete* (See Figure 10.1). Thinking of concrete as *raw* and *savage* bespeaks longing for the transcendental and forceful qualities of stone but it is modern, industrially produced, and achievable with semi-skilled labour. In use, concrete ranges from smooth to rough (raw to refined), and is either evocative (a 'work'), or empty (a 'product', in Lefebvre's terms).

Concrete: Connotative/denotative

Reflections on concrete's multifarious expressive capacities are developed through considerations of work by architects including Le Corbusier, Louis I Kahn, Rem Koolhaas, Eero Saarinen, Moshe Safdie and Aldo van Eyck. The sophisticated use of materials (including concrete) at the Barbican Estate also informs the discussion. The monumental vaulted architecture of Imperial Rome provides a framework for considering persisting concrete signification on the one hand, and its association with industrial production on the other.

Concrete conjures up the ancient in the modern, even though when exposed, it is a decidedly contemporary material. Its pervasiveness, suitability to semi-skilled industrialized production, and parallels between its engineered form and developments in modernist architecture, inextricably bind it to perceptions of modernity. Concrete is a proxy for stone, though when stone-clad, the distinctiveness of both materials tends to be confounded. When aggregates are extremely course and exposed, concrete begins to take on the quality of *actual* stone, as almost a surrogate for it, more so than revetment, which is defeated by necessary expansion joints. Moreover, the differing degrees of skill required for building with them separates the two materials. Cutting

Figure 10.1 Convent of La Tourette (1953–60), Eveux-sur l'Abresle. Le Corbusier. Rough exposed concrete as modern stone substitute. © Nathaniel Coleman. © F.L.C. / ADAGP, Paris, and DACS, London, 2019. [Photo: Nathaniel Coleman, 1999].

and laying for stone; whereas concrete's liquid state when poured allows it to take almost any possible shape. As Wright observed; because shapeless, it is 'without its own nature'; until casting artificially gives it 'form, texture, or color', imposed 'by human imagination.'[1] Its plasticity, however, can encourage expressive extremes verging towards kitsch.

Regular geometric forms (cube, cylinder, pyramid, rectangle, sphere), emphasize concrete's solidity, whereas free-flowing organic shapes suggest its original viscosity; recollecting primordial states of chaos, or an alternative order – perhaps of nature (lava flows, maybe), as opposed to (the delimited spatial arrangements of) culture. Such dichotomies have value only when they contribute to understanding: more fluid shapes challenge associations of concrete with simple geometric forms. Alternatively, the virtuosity of concrete shells emphasizes human capacity, augmented by techno-science (no matter how 'organic' the resulting form). Significantly, the Pantheon in Rome expresses order and virtuosity but not primordial chaos. Unsurprisingly, amorphous shapes emerge parallel with the ascendency of globalization, alongside

Figure 10.2 Pantheon Dome (ca. A.D. 118–128), Rome, Italy. Built during the reign (117–A.D. 138) of Emperor Hadrian (76–A.D. 138). [Photo: Nathaniel Coleman, 1989].

intensification of the creative destruction native to capitalism. The more audacious the form, the greater the affinity with infrastructure, bureaucratic rationality and products.

Even when posthuman forms of concrete expression disrupt millennial orders established by geometric associations; the communicative capacity of cubes, cylinders, pyramids, rectangles and spheres will remain legible long into the future. Cubes analogize stability, the earth or 'the material world of the four elements': earth, water, fire, air.[2] Cylinders (pillars, posts or columns) analogize uprightness, human figures, and bearing weight but also 'the world-axis,' akin to posts, masts, and trees.'[3] Pyramids analogize the *axis mundi* – the World Centre, hierarchy and ascent; denoted and connoted by various mountain-temples found across cultures. Pyramids also conjure up stairs and ladders; or the pathway from the earth (square base) towards the sun, or heavens (three-angled sides, signifying resolution, denoted by the singular point of the apex).[4]

In their association with horizontality, rectangles connote repose, making them inextricably bound to inhabitation. Rectangles are the 'most rational, the most secure and regular ... [o]f all geometric forms,' which 'is explained empirically by' use: 'at all times and in all places, it has been the shape favoured' for 'preparing any space or object for immediate use in life', including: 'house, room, table, bed'. In comparison, squares imply 'tense domination born of an abstract longing for power, whereas the circle avoids all earthly associations by virtue of its celestial symbolism.' Other 'less regular shapes than the rectangle', including 'the trapezium or the trapezoid, are abnormal or dolorous forms, expressive of suffering and inner irregularity.'[5]

The forms introduced above derive meaning from use, in relation to the body (kin of *all* previous and future bodies), thereby contributing to making sense of existential predicaments, inflected by earth, sky, boundary, expanse, gravity, birth and death. The significance of each attains to a kind of natural symbol, no matter how a culture transforms them situationally. The association of rectangles with repose and inhabitation, with beds and horizon, also associates them with mounds of earth, thus with death and burial. Nevertheless, building significance is not automatic. No matter how powerfully associative, meaning can be confounded, whether a geometric form or a material. Imagination and ability enriched by poetic sensibility is paramount, which no seductive story, or amount of technique, can make up for.[6]

As three-dimensional projections of circles, spheres suggest eternity; a realm beyond human finiteness. In architecture, the association of spheres with the infinite takes shape most powerfully as domes, analogizing, the universe or 'the vault of heaven'; the sky:[7]

Figure 10.3 Kimbell Art Museum (1966–72), Ft Worth, Texas, USA. Louis I. Kahn, Architect. Materials: concrete structure; travertine infill; mill finished steel (interior and exterior); white oak (interior); lead roof. [Photo: Nathaniel Coleman, 2007].

in the geometrical symbolism of the cosmos, all circular forms relate to the sky or heaven, all squares to the earth, and all triangles (with the apex at the top) to fire and to the urge towards ascension inherent in human nature. Hence, the triangle also symbolizes the communication between earth (the material world) and heaven (the spiritual world).[8]

Although modern techno-scientific rationality obstructs direct comprehension of the forms outlined above, their meaning is still felt because the associations are bodily. For example, the increasing rareness of domes actually intensifies encounters with them; including with Michelangelo's remarkable St. Peter's cupola, or the Pantheon (both in Rome). Vaults are equally rare, making Kahn's transposition at the Kimbell Museum, Fort Worth, Texas, United States, noteworthy. Although modern, the Kimbell recollects vaulted Imperial Roman monuments with almost equal grandeur to ancient ruins. Unlike omnidirectional domes, vaults are directional. Both, however, connote the heavens. Or, at the very least, microcosms of secular sky (See Figures 10.2 and 10.3).

Concrete dialectic

Materially and formally, concrete is identified with solidity. Negative perceptions associate it with the overbearing bureaucratic landscape of modernity, whether state socialist or state capitalist. As quintessentially modern, it is identified with industrialization, mass production, building science and engineering. Its links with administrated life make it shorthand for the failures of orthodox modernist architecture. Expanses of parking lots and highway infrastructure, the muteness of the modern city and the brutality of much social housing, undergirds Lefebvre's association of concrete with the dominant dominated space of modernity:

> Now let us consider dominated (and dominant) space, which is to say a space transformed – and mediated – by technology, by practice. In the modern world, instances of such spaces are legion, and immediately intelligible as such: one only has to think of a slab of concrete or a motorway. Thanks to technology, the domination of space is becoming, as it were, completely dominant... [I]ts origins coincide with those of political power itself. Military architecture, fortifications and ramparts, dams and irrigation systems.[9]

The correlation of concrete with technological progress in the modern world, with infrastructure, and with the military-industrial complex, pronounces its central role in materializing dominance. Lefebvre clarifies the relation between particular spatial practices and productions of space with concrete as a material manifestation of 'dominant space' and 'the realization of a master's project.' More than any other material, concrete is associated with the spatial practices and power aspirations of modernity's dominant systems of economic and political organization: fascist, communist or capitalist.

For Lefebvre, the imposition of power makes modern space resistant to group appropriation, materially and formally: 'In order to dominate space, technology introduces a new form into a pre-existing space – generally a rectilinear or rectangular form'.[10] Modern concrete construction presupposes certain processes and forms; prefabricated or standardized, repetitive and often gridded, which makes the built environment less amenable:

> A motorway brutalizes the countryside and the land, slicing through space like a great knife. Dominated space is usually closed, sterilized, emptied out. The concept attains its full meaning only when it is contrasted with the opposite and inseparable concept of appropriation.[11]

Because the architectural 'slab of concrete' is interchangeable with concrete roadworks, the logic of its forms, materials and modes of production empties both of the lived. Arguably, this begins to explain why these *new* forms so stubbornly resist appropriation by individuals and groups. Concrete's formlessness, its malleability or liquidity, connoting a shape-shifting lack of specificity, conjured up the abstractness of modernity for Lefebvre, particularly in materializations of post-Second World War new towns:

> modernity opens its pages to me … Here I cannot read the centuries, not time, nor the past, nor what is possible. Instead I read the fears modernity can arouse: the abstraction which rides roughshod over everyday life – the debilitating analysis which divides, cuts up, separates – the illusory synthesis which has lost all ability to reconstruct anything active – the fossilized structures, powerless to produce or reproduce anything living, but still capable of suppressing it.[12]

As the quintessentially modernist material of new towns, concrete is a trope for the hope followed by dread these developments invoked. Although it would be too much to diagnose concrete as the cause of social dissolution, as generally used, it is surely symptomatic of it.

British architectural historian Adrian Forty closes in on a dialectical understanding of the material, observing that 'concrete is not immune to meaning' but although it has 'an iconography' it is 'unlike so-called "traditional" materials, whose meaning used to be thought inherent and embedded in them'. Instead, because it is 'fluid and mutable', its significance is 'made by the circumstances of history'. Accordingly, concrete communicates its unique set of meanings 'through paradoxes and contractions'. Therefore, 'whatever concrete strives to do, it almost invariably manages at the same time, to achieve the opposite.'[13] However, concrete does not strive to do anything. No matter what charge it carries – poetic or banal – is introduced to it by the conceiving architect, inflected by dominant modes of production, spatial practices and use.

Forty appears to have wanted to dissociate concrete – as one industrialized building material amongst many – from any supposed 'inherent or embedded' value or significance accruing to it as a virtuous emblem of modernity. But he confounds this by attributing *resistance* and *striving* to it, rather than emphasizing, as US architectural theorist David Leatherbarrow does, that the treatment of materials is the central issue, because none 'possesses any essence or "truth", nor' is 'singularly apposite to our time.' Leatherbarrow continues: 'the whole matter rests on the ways the materials are shaped and transformed, the way they become what they had not been before, the ways they exceed themselves.'[14] Leatherbarrow follows a line from Ruskin through Loos, who emphatically distinguished between negligible inherent material value, and the value added by mastering a 'material in such a way that' the 'work is independent of the value of the raw material.'[15]

Although Loos believed 'all materials are equally valuable', a work's worth does not simply rise in direct relationship to 'the quantity' of labour: 'the quality of labor' contributes most to the 'value of an object.' Nevertheless, he observes: 'We are living in a time which lays greater emphasis on the quantity of labor', because quantity is easier to measure and manage than quality.[16] But 'in the old days art, that is, the quality of the work, was more highly valued than today'; summarized by Loos as: 'Human labor, skill and art.'[17]

If Loos's emphasis on quality is combined with Lefebvre's 'fears of modernity', (in response to the role concrete played in the 'post-war boom'), the material emerges as more an ideological expedient than a structural one.[18] For this reason, concrete can seem permanently identified with paving over of the world, countryside and traditional city alike. The intensifying process of forcing modernity to take flesh confirmed fears of it. Uniformity is concrete's most obvious characteristic, what Forty describes as '*monolithism*'. According to him, 'the original and most common' expression of 'the modernity of reinforced concrete', is the creation of 'one continuous structure, dissolving the traditional distinction between load and support'.[19] Its malleability effectively mimics industrial processes of extrusion, even when poured on site. The overall effect of monoliths is abstraction, which drains concrete of its *concreteness* by emphasizing indeterminate malleability – a perfect resource for the social alienation of bureaucratic organization. Unconvinced by its plasticity, Lefebvre questions concrete's expressive potential:

> To build a few blocks of flats that are spiral in form by adding a handful of curves to the usual concrete angularities is not an entirely negligible achievement – but neither does it amount to very much. To take inspiration from Andalusia, and demonstrate a sensual use of curvatures, spirals, arabesques and inflexions of all kinds, so achieving truly voluptuous spaces, would be a different matter altogether.[20]

The key words in the above are 'sensual', 'inflexions' and 'voluptuous', all of which relate to the body's corporeality, to desire and to the rhythmic erotics of social intercourse and everyday life; precisely what technocratically rational angular modern concrete landscapes thwart (or erase). As transposed by Italian Baroque architect Francesco Borromini (1599–1667), Imperial Roman vaulted concrete architecture already suggests alternatives, which need not intensify fears of modernity bound up with the material. Only achievable if a pragmatic approach, of the sort Leatherbarrow recommends, prevails over ideologies of material essences, or 'truths':

Architecture can be eloquent if the designer first recognizes the preliminary poverty (thus also the potentials) of unfinished materials – not their (natural) richness. If a preconception of quality prevents the free exercise of finishing, the result will lack the rich specificity that makes work wonderful.[21]

At first glance, concrete confounds Letherbarrow's approach. Firstly, what possible 'natural richness' could concrete have? Without this, how could preconceptions of 'quality' be disregarded in favour of 'preliminary poverty'? With only a gloopy amalgam to work with, inventive possibilities for the free exercise of finishing are difficult to imagine. Secondly, concrete is already pure poverty, enriched by the constitution of the mix; the quality of the shuttering, pouring and curing; the care taken to remove the formwork;

Figure 10.4 Morse and Ezra Stiles Colleges (1958–62), Yale University, New Haven, CT, USA. Eero Saarinen, Architect. Cesar Pelli, Chief Designer. Materials: poured concrete combined with cut stone; reinforced rubble aggregate concrete. Liquid Stone: According to Saarinen, modernist architecture eschews heavy masonry walls because constructing them requires anachronistic craft methods. He described the Ezra Sitles' walls as 'masonry walls without masons, masonry walls which are "modern"' (Eero Saarinen, *On His Work*, A. B. Saarinen (ed.), New Haven: Yale University Press, 1968, p. 92). [Photo: Nathaniel Coleman, 2003].

or surface treatments once set. The liquidity of concrete and its capacity for monolithic smoothness have been confused with some 'natural richness', which obstructs attending to its 'preliminary poverty'. Conceptualizing it as 'liquid stone', or as inherently *modern*, and thus progressive, is equally unrevealing. Even though, as Wright observed: 'Cement may be, here as elsewhere, the secret stamina of the physical body of our new world' – 'an ancient medium' given 'new life, new purposes, and possibilities' by machine-made 'steel-strands' that have given 'concrete the right-of-way'.[22] Ease of production and malleability has made concrete pervasive but attending to labour and conceptions exceeding execution – over material essences – hint at resolutions to the problematics of concrete, including its bad reputation (See Figure 10.4).

Opus caementicium

Imperial Roman architecture was civic, largely provided for the benefit of the commonweal. Rome was a mass society with a far reach, which made it multicultural. Its expansive domain seemed all encompassing; projecting a putatively eternal order. Roman space was produced as enclosure; pronouncing universality. Imperial Roman conceptions of globalization, centre and periphery, are – as Loos observed – more credible precursors of the modern world than ancient Greece. Two interrelated factors enabled Imperial Rome to shape space around the conditions of citizenship: concrete construction and vaulted architecture.[23] As architectural historian William L. Macdonald observes: 'In many respects', for Imperial Roman monumental architecture, 'design and structure cannot be separated. The way Roman vaulted buildings were erected resulted in specific technical features and in stylistic characteristics as well.'[24] The Roman building process was inherently social, ensuring that the architecture produced would be as well. Basing almost every significant structure on vaulted concrete construction made it possible to build a variety of 'functional, permanent structures' in more places, from centre to periphery. Economical methods of construction producible by semi-skilled labour were uniquely suited to a vast empire with a preference for cities and great civic structures.[25]

A singularly economical system of construction was used to produce a specific formal language manifesting an analogous spatial conception as a microcosm of Imperial Roman world order. Encompassing, extensible and reproducible, Rome established a template for fulfilling the infrastructural requirements of emergent mass-society and the rise of national identities during the nineteenth century:

> the Roman experience of architecture and building in the High Empire was more like our own than that of any other age. Both periods are marked by a drive to surpass the old ... Even the smallest town was given some architectural token to represent the imperial peace. In general the Romans built more slowly and more permanently than we, but they had the same compulsion to make their cities conform, in their public buildings at least, to the modern age.[26]

A modernist error was to identify concrete with *modernity* rather than with mass society and bureaucratization, whether state socialist or state capitalist. Concrete was the most economical and efficient way to remake the world in the image of techno-scientific rationalism, nascent since the eighteenth century, which the crucible of Second World War established as the dominant order. Renewed 'interest in calcium silicate-based cements' leading to 'significant developments', did not take shape 'until the early stages of the Industrial Revolution in the second half of the eighteenth century'.[27] Unshackled from essentialist associations with modernity (as progressive), concrete could be addressed in terms of potential qualities; of conception, construction, execution and finish. Imperial Rome assists by modelling a hybridized approach, free from ideologies of concrete purity. Concrete construction in Imperial Rome consisted of pouring the mortar and aggregate between brick walls, or other permanent formwork, to produce an exceptionally durable integrated system of construction (akin to Zumthor's hybrid structure at the Therme Vals):

> Facing materials grew thinner and progressively less structural, and cores became increasingly able to bear heavier loads. This evolution intersected the discovery of pozzolana mortars, and later, the quantity production of high-quality kiln-fired brick; the builders of the imperial age made the most out of combining tradition and invention. The multiplicity of functions assigned to brick facing, which in some cases included a purely aesthetic and visual role, is typical of the economy of vaulted design.[28]

Above rock-solid walls rose arches, vaults, and domes: 'the dominant theme[s] of Roman architecture'. Making a virtue of its lack of independent qualities other than plasticity, in Imperial Rome, concrete mix was poured into wooden formwork and left 'until it developed sufficient strength to stand alone.'[29] The key difference between Imperial Roman concrete and current practices is the relationship to formwork, even though 'the Roman system of constructing molds in the form of the building has continued.'[30] Although conceived of in much the way it still is, the Romans did not expose concrete, so – in most instances – the formwork was integral, while malleability was fully exploited.

Despite being temporary, formwork still has a determining influence on the character of exposed concrete structures. The monolithic, banal, character of so much post-war concrete construction, and its association with totalizing systems of bureaucratic rationality, derives at least in part from modernist use of (exposed) concrete as a sign of modernity, economy, efficiency and productivity; as though these things are its inherent virtues. While analogous economic and productive characteristics made concrete useful for the production of space in Imperial Rome, these were secondary to its usefulness for producing the 'space-shaping ... forms and effects' of 'monumental interior[s]' (achieved with the 'omnipresent, generative force' of the 'circular curve', especially in 'vaulted spaces'), which were 'space-bordering' in themselves, and as microcosms of the empire.[31]

As Lefebvre observes, 'In the case of Rome, organization, thought and the production of space went together, indeed almost hand in hand. And they did so not under the sign of the Logos but under the sign of the Law.'[32]

The Pantheon is the most compelling existent manifestation of monumental Imperial Roman architecture. It pronounces the coming together of 'organization, thought and the production of space'.[33] Best known for its remarkable unsupported (unreinforced) coffered concrete dome, which remains the largest of its kind in the world, the Pantheon analogizes Roman world order as an enclosed space, subject to the rule of its law. According to Lefebvre, 'the erection of the Pantheon in Rome pointed not only to a comprehension of conquered gods but also to a comprehension of spaces now subordinate to the master space, as it were, of the Empire and the world.'[34] Elsewhere, he notes:

> The interior reproduces the world itself, as it emerges in and through the city, opening to the celestial powers, welcoming all gods and embracing all places. ... What Rome offers is an image that engenders (or produces) space. What space? Specifically, the space of power. Political space is not established solely by actions (with material violence generating a place, a legal order, a legislation): the genesis of a space of this kind also presupposes a practice, images, symbols, and the construction of buildings, of towns, and of localized social relationships.[35]

It is impossible to imagine present-day architects producing architecture as sophisticated as the Pantheon; especially the interplay it articulates between individual, community, and state, and between city, state and world. Present realities make it exceedingly unlikely that such interrelationships could be rendered intelligible through material and form, organized by coherent spatial practices and modes of production, capable of achieving multiple complex aims. The lesson of Imperial Roman concrete construction for architects now is to surrender fantasies about 'truth to materials', taking instead a pragmatic approach to concrete as *substance*, not *presence*:

> An amorphous material, concrete takes the shape given it by temporary forms of wood or, in the case of much Roman imperial wall and pier construction, of relatively thin shells of brick which upon the drying of the whole mass, become inextricably bonded into it. The Pantheon rotunda walls were built by pouring concrete into low, wide trenches formed by the inner and outer brick wall, the trenches rising precisely one upon another until the dome terrace level was reached. The dome was poured over an immense hemispherical wooden form, supported by a forest of timbers and struts, upon which the negative wooden molds for the coffers were fixed.[36]

MacDonald notes, 'the Pantheon' probably could 'have been made from cut stone' but 'poured concrete was a more suitable structural material for ... a monumental interior space vaulted over.' The suitability of concrete for the job was a matter of malleability and economy, inflected by modes of production:

> By using structural materials that were in themselves insignificant and anonymous – lime, sand, and bricks – the organization of workmen and their relationship to the flow of materials and the timing of pouring concrete was brought into line with the Roman predilection for clearly defined and efficient organization.[37]

In Imperial Rome, pragmatics joined poetry with economy to render useless things (the raw material of concrete) almost unimaginably evocative.

Concrete expression

German philosopher Ernst Bloch (1885–1977) asserted that modernist architecture had almost no capacity for prefiguring Utopia (as hope). He argued, 'true architecture' is impossible to produce, because it is far more 'a social creation ... than the other fine arts', which accounts for its enervating entrapment within 'the late capitalist hollow space'.[38] Bloch's 'social creation' echoes Lefebvre's alignment of 'spatial practices' with dominant 'modes of production', alongside prevailing imaginaries; globalized capitalism, for example.[39] Accordingly, Bloch asserts, 'Only the beginnings of a different society will make true architecture possible again, one that is filled at the same time constructively and ornamentally by its own artistic volition.'[40] By which he means the dream of a socialist Utopia: a unified society with common modes of political and artistic expression, including architecture. For Bloch, the more distant the possibility of achieving Utopia, the more intensely it is desired, risking cultural self-deceptions, prompting (false) assertions of alterity achieved, misconstrued as confirmation:

> The abstract engineer style [of orthodox modernist architecture] will not ... become qualitative, ... despite the deceptive freshness of 'modernity' with which the polished-up death is presented like morning glory. Today's technology, which is itself still so abstract, does [not] lead out of the hollow space, even as it is fashioned as an aesthetic one, as an artistic substitute. Rather this hollow space penetrates the so-called art of engineering (*Ingenieurkunst*) as much as the latter increases the hollowness by its own emptiness.[41]

Architects' complicity in producing (often abstract and concrete) so-called icons, integral to city-branding schemes, is just one manifestation of what Bloch outlines in the quote above. While not hopeless, the situation is extraordinarily unpromising. Consequently, anticipating alternatives must begin with a shift in emphasis, away from *gestures of difference* towards recollecting that '[a]rchitecture ... is and remains the attempt to produce the human home'.[42] Will is not enough, which could make achieving such deceptively simple objectives seem impossible. In this spirit, Bloch argued:

When a lifestyle is as decadent as the late bourgeois one, then mere architectural reform can no longer be shrouded but must be without soul. That is the result when between plush and tubular steel chairs, between post offices in Renaissance style and egg boxes there is no third thing that grips the imagination.[43]

Overcoming the elusiveness of that 'third thing' requires the sort of analysis of present conditions outlined by Lefebvre in *The Production of Space*. Simply shifting emphasis from 'exchange', including of images, towards 'use' would be a start. Adorno's 'negative dialectics' could help make Lefebvre's analysis operative in the production of different spaces. But because inescapably a social creation, more so than most other forms of artistic expression, architecture is largely incapable of negation, without also negating itself. As US cultural theorist Fredric Jameson observes:

what we think of as a radically different space from our own is little more than a fantasy projection of difference, it is the same masquerading itself as difference ... From within the system you cannot hope to generate anything that negates the system as a whole or portends the experience of something other than the system, or outside of the system.[44]

Even if desires for difference are frustrated by the conditions that feed those very desires, this is the coefficient of hope: the more desires for alternatives are frustrated the more force they will have, which keeps hopes for 'something other than the system' alive as an insatiable imperative, eclipsed only when reproduction is misconstrued as difference.

Despite architecture's entrapment within the cultural dominant, the brief considerations of some predominantly concrete buildings that follows shows how promising initial responses to the conundrum outlined in the preceding paragraphs begins with mindfully reimagining material choice, the actual conditions of construction, use and location. Although reproducing prevailing conditions of alienation is inevitable, architectural reality preserves nourish hope by holding fast to utopian desires.

Arches, vaults, domes and shells

In spaces based on the geometry of the sphere, or some fraction of it, volume predominates, or at least suggestion, or illusion, of it does. (See Figures 10.2 and 10.3: Pantheon and Kimbell). By accentuating volume, domes emphasize enclosure and interiority but also the world and the infinite. As the quintessential example of vaulted space, the Pantheon influences all subsequent domes, including Michelangelo's St Peter's cupola, which has extended the influence of the originator into the present, though now usually constructed with glass and steel, rather than concrete (thereby defeating perceptions of volume and interiority).

By recollecting domes, arches and vaults also suggest the space-defining character of ancient architecture (Figure 10.5). Thin shells are something of a hybrid between the two, whether or not the surface material is concrete. If domes analogize enclosure and totality, concrete shells recollect the liquid quality of pouring concrete. Such shapes, including more recent freeform constructions, are representations of liquescence that reference organic substances, slime mould perhaps (Figure 10.6). In its more extravagant forms, concrete becomes a vehicle of seemingly automatic processes, techno-scientific progress, or virtuosic technique, to produce spectacular buildings, or elements (Figure 10.7). When liquescency dominates – at least representationally – it takes precedence over concrete being 'a mass-material', 'impressionable', or 'continuous or monolithic'. Yet, recollecting original liquidity emphasizes concrete as 'a willing material', while its lack of 'tensile strength' is confounded.[45]

Figure 10.5 Amsterdam Orphanage (1955–60), Amsterdam, The Netherlands. Aldo van Eyck, Architect. Interior Prefabricated Shallow Concrete Dome. Pantheon on a Budget? [Photo: Nathaniel Coleman, 2004].

Figure 10.6 Trans World Airlines (TWA) Flight Center (1956–62), JFK International Airport, Idlewild, NY, USA. Eero Saarinen, Architect. Roman ruins were on Saarinen's mind (see Eero Saarinen, *On His Work*, 1968, p. 68). Zoomorphic/Organic Shell. [Photo: Nathaniel Coleman, 2003].

Column, beam, frame, wall

If concrete was the most convenient way for Imperial Rome to produce monumental vaulted buildings, since becoming the 'building material of choice – and the symbol of unbridled building activity' during the twentieth century, it is valued as the most convenient way to produce 'relatively inexpensive' buildings, without the requirement of 'highly qualified specialists'.[46] Its close association with the conception and production of modernist architecture highlights the double nature of concrete on a number of levels: 'It is an ambivalent material: used in liquid from, it is valued for its strength as artificial stone. Outwardly it shows the formwork rather than its own structure. Some people like concrete for its purist aesthetic, others find it brutal and inhuman'[47] (Figure 10.8).

Although concrete can be (literally) pressed into representing 'expressionist heroism' or 'monotonous mass production', and can express 'change' and 'stubborn stasis' simultaneously, while being 'alternatively hyped and maligned', depending on one's

Figure 10.7 Millstein Hall, Cornell University, College of Art, Architecture, and Planning (2006–11), Ithaca, NY. OMA (Rem Koolhaas), Architects. *Liquid* Concrete. Main materials: concrete and steel. [Photo: Nathaniel Coleman, 2017].

own philosophical bent, its identification with 'scientifically grounded production', rather than with 'coarse handiwork', dominates.[48] Such perceptions are unsurprising, considering modernist architecture's long association with industrial production, and the inconceivability of concrete's re-emergence and development, particularly reinforced, apart from engineering and advancing manufacturing processes[49] (Figure 10.9).

The greater part of concrete architecture is *down-to-earth*, foursquare and solid, rather than overheated 'vulgar historicizing', 'monumental rhetoric', or explicitly expressionist zoomorphic or biomorphic shapes.[50] Characterized by three-dimensional grids, or frames, traditional architectural elements are still discernible in the cubic forms that dominate. Columns, beams and walls, may be in evidence, though their structural role is often obscured by the monolithic effect of apparently continuous structure, or they are streamlined by combining two elements into one; mushroom columns, for example, that do away with the need for beams, thereby increasing available floorspace while enhancing perceptions of expansive enclosure.

Figure 10.8 Habitat 67 (1963–65), Montreal, Quebec, Canada. Moshe Safdie, Architect. Modularized Concrete Construction: Several Hundred Stacked Modules Fabricated Onsite. [Photo: Nathaniel Coleman, 2014].

Despite myriad approaches to building with concrete, more often than not, the results are banal. Whether taking advantage of the production benefits and expressive possibilities of concrete cast in-situ, or the controlled results of either precast, or post tensioned concrete, or the factory-based serial production of cast panels, or larger building elements, or simply using concrete as hidden structure, or for cladding, the strongest examples embrace the material's emptiness; so aptly described by Frank Lloyd Wright in 1928, who found it difficult to 'see … a high aesthetic property … in this conglomerate', which is an 'amalgam, aggregate, compound', with 'cement', its 'binding medium … characterless in itself'. Accordingly, 'The net result is, usually, an artificial stone at best, or a petrified sand heap at worst. … It is a mixture that has little quality in itself. … Is it stone? Yes and No.' Although often described as 'liquid stone', for Wright, and in use, 'the essential difference between stone and concrete … is the plasticity of

Figure 10.9 Dulles Airport (1958–62), Dulles, VA, USA. Architect, Eero Saarinen. Less explicit than TWA building but more figurative. Expressive of engineering above all else (and concrete structure). [Photo: Nathaniel Coleman, 2003].

the material as distinguished from natural stone which has none at all.' Wright asserts that concrete's 'aesthetic value' resides in its 'plasticity' but as 'artificial stone, concrete has no great, certainly no independent aesthetic value whatsoever.' For Wright, 'it has neither song nor story.'[51] The key point is this: whatever virtues any example of concrete architecture might embody, only 'human imagination' can have put them there. On its own, the material has no independent (artistic) value[52] (Plate 14).

Notes

1. Frank Lloyd Wright, 'In the Cause of Architecture VII: The Meaning of Materials – Concrete', *Architectural Record* (August 1928), pp. 98–104 (p. 102). Available online at: https://www.architecturalrecord.com/articles/11507-in-the-cause-of-architecture-vii-the-meaning-of-materialsconcrete (Accessed 16 July 2018), p. 102.

2. J. E. Cirlot, *A Dictionary of Symbols, Second Edition*, Jack Sage (trans.), London: Routledge, 1971 (1962), p. 74.

3. Ibid., pp. 16–17, 60, 255.

4. Ibid., pp. 15–16, 267.

5. Ibid., p. 272. See also, pp. 182–3, 219.

6. Wright, 'In the Cause of Architecture VII: Meaning of Materials – Concrete', p. 99.

7. Cirlot, *A Dictionary of Symbols* (1971), p. 13.

8. Ibid., p. 16.

9. Lefebvre, *The Production of Space*, pp. 164–5, see also pp. 549.

10. Ibid., p. 165.

11. Ibid.

12. Henri Lefebvre, 'Notes on the New Town' (April 1960), in *Introduction to Modernity* (1962), pp. 119–20.

13. Adrian Forty, *Concrete and Culture: A Material History*, London: Reaktion Books, 2012, p. 223.

14. David Leatherbarrow, 'Material Matters', in *Architecture Oriented Otherwise*, New York: Princeton Architectural Press, 2009, p. 91.

15. Loos, 'Building Materials' (1898), p. 37.

16. Ibid., pp. 37–8.

17. Ibid.

18. Forty, *Concrete and Culture*, p. 279.

19. Ibid., p. 34.

20. Lefebvre, *The Production of Space*, p. 397.

21. Leatherbarrow, 'Material Matters', p. 81.

22. Wright, 'In the Cause of Architecture VII: Meaning of Materials – Concrete', p. 99.

23. William L. MacDonald, *The Architecture of the Roman Empire, Volume I: An Introductory Study*, Revised Edition, New Haven and London: Yale University Press, 1985.

24. Ibid., p. 164.

25. Ibid., p. 166.

26. Ibid., pp. 181–2.

27. Peter Domone, 'Part 3 Concrete', *Construction Materials: Their Nature and Behaviour*, p. 83.

28. MacDonald, *Roman Empire*, p. 157.

29. Elliott, *Technics and Architecture*, p. 167.

30. Ibid., p. 197.

31. MacDonald, *Roman Empire*, p. 167.

32. Lefebvre, *Production of Space*, p. 246.

33. Ibid.

34. Ibid., p. 111.

35. Ibid., pp. 244–5.

36. William L. MacDonald, *The Pantheon*, Cambridge, MA: Harvard University Press, 1976, p. 38.

37. Ibid., p. 42.

38. Ernst Bloch, 'Building in Empty Spaces', pp. 189–90.

39. Lefebvre, *Production of Space*.

40. Bloch, 'Building in Empty Spaces', p. 190.

41. Ibid., p. 190.

42. Ibid., p. 198.

43. Ibid., p. 187.

44. Fredric Jameson, 'Is Space Political?' *Anyplace*, Cynthia Davidson (ed.), Cambridge, MA: Anyone Corp/MIT Press, 1995, p. 197.

45. Wright, 'In the Cause of Architecture VII: The Meaning of Materials – Concrete', p. 301.

46. Andrea Deplazes, *Constructing Architecture: Materials, Processes, Structures – A Handbook*, Andrea Deplazes (ed.), Basel: Birkhuser, 2005, p. 57.

47. Hegger, Drexeler and Zeumer, *Basics Materials*, p. 42.

48. Jean-Louis Cohen, 'Modern Architecture and the Saga of Concrete', in *Liquid Stone: New Architecture in Concrete*, Jean-Louis Cohen and G. Martin Moeller, Jr (eds), New York: Princeton Architectural Press, 2006, pp. 29–30.

49. Sigfried Giedion, *Building in France, Building in Iron, Building in Ferro-Concrete* (1928), J. Duncan Berry (trans.), Santa Monica, CA: The Getty Center, 1995; Guillén, *The Taylorized Beauty of the Mechanical*; Coleman, *Utopias and Architecture*, Coleman, 'Building Dystopia', *Rivista MORUS—Utopia e Renascimento*, 4 (1997): 181–92. Available online at: http://www.revistamorus.com.br/index.php/morus/article/viewFile/180/157 (Accessed 17 May 2018).

50. Kenneth Frampton, 'Louis Kahn and the French Connection', *Oppositions*, no. 22 (1980): 20–53, reprinted in *Labor, Work and Architecture: Collected Essays on Architecture and Design*, London and New York: Phaidon, 2002, p. 179.

51. Wright, 'In the Cause of Architecture VII: Meaning of Materials – Concrete', pp. 99, 102, 103.

52. Ibid., p. 104.

CHAPTER 11
IMAGING RATIONALITY: THE RESOLUTE MODERNITY OF STEEL

Steel, and metal, more generally, are used in architecture mostly for structural framing, exterior cladding and for fixings, including hardware, hinges, handles and taps. Although metals have been worked for millennia, their use now is primarily associated with modern building, particularly framing and cladding skyscrapers. Increasing use of iron in building construction during the nineteenth century, and then steel, originates with the mass production of rails for expanding railways. Prior to the twentieth century, iron and steel were mostly identified with conservatories, bridges, including suspension bridges and trainshed roofs (Figure 11.1). Beyond structure and cladding in high-rise construction, steel and metal can be used quite eloquently in smaller-scale buildings, especially for details and joints, including hardware and decorative elements, as in Carlo Scarpa's work.

But, as with all of the materials discussed in this book, steel has no essence. What is done with it determines its value, more so when conception exceeds execution. Supporting this reading of steel, Frank Lloyd Wright asserted: 'In itself it has little beauty, neither grain, nor texture of surface. It has no more "quality" in this sense than mud. Not so much as sand. It is a creature wholly dependent upon imaginative influences for "life" in any aesthetic sense at the hand of a creator.'[1]

Wrought modern

During the nineteenth century, individual and collective self-understanding transformed alongside changes already underway (in the West and beyond). Two forms of revolution ushered in these shifts in consciousness and practice: the Industrial Revolution (1750 onwards), beginning in Britain; and political revolutions (including, 1775–83, American; 1789–99 French; 1848, European; 1917, Russian). The sources of modern political and Industrial Revolutions can be traced to changing ideals originating with the Enlightenment (1685–1815).[2]

Characterized by belief in progress, borne of self-reliant reason cognate with the methods of modern natural science, the Enlightenment ultimately aligns human will with machines. Particularly by liberating desires for transforming nature and culture from obligations to the ancients. Encompassing secularization and emergent individualism, including conceptions of human agency, the Enlightenment

Figure 11.1 Palm House (1844), Kew Gardens, Kew, London Borough of Richmond upon Thames. Richard Turner, Manufacturer; Decimus Burton, Architect. Primary materials: wrought iron and glass. [Photo: Nathaniel Coleman, 1979].

loosened tradition, including the authority of religion, while raising questions about the divine right of monarchs. As such, it was the theoretical precondition for late-eighteenth-century political revolutions, particularly the ideas of moral good underpinning the American and then French Revolutions. Convictions that progress is a gift humanity could give itself fortified both and was a prerequisite for the Industrial Revolution.

Political revolutions, the rise of industry, and with it machines and machine production, disrupted the existing political order and seemingly eternal patterns of human existence and production. Until the end of the eighteenth century, building was almost exclusively a *craft* process but industrialization and rationalization of construction transformed it into a calculable process. Construction evolved into onsite assembly of prefabricated parts, made in laboratory-like factories. New materials and methods of construction altered long-held notions about the art of building, which dramatically transformed traditional cities. The theory and practice of architecture began to be reconceptualized in response to so much change. The French Abbé Marc-Antoine Laugier (1713–69), author of the *Essai sur l'Architecture* (1753), was amongst the most influential eighteenth-century theorists. In his book, Laugier, built upon the proto-rationalist ideas of French physician and architect Claude Perrault (1613–88) but was more intent on establishing rules for the 'lawful' practice of architecture, based on his conception of its *essences*:

In the *Essai*, Laugier traced the origin of architecture back to simple, primitive conditions and to simple ideas imitated originally from nature. He maintained that modern architecture should retain these qualities. For example, an order of architecture was essentially a column, an entablature or beam, and a pediment, and thus it should remain, recalling the primitive shelter.[3]

'Modern' above refers to Laugier's reform-minded hopes for the architecture of his own time. According to him, the closer architecture came – in conception and execution – to its 'natural' origins with the 'primitive hut' in the wood, including living tree trunks for columns, the more 'lawful' it would be. The prelapsarian primitiveness of Laugier's conception anticipates the ideology of renewal central to the development of modernist architecture. The purity of steel frame construction owes as much to Gottfried Semper's 'Four Elements of Architecture', as to Laugier's Primitive Hut; German architect Ludwig Mies van der Roe's (1886–1969), Barcelona Pavilion (1928–29, demolished 1930, rebuilt 1986), for example.

Perrault (introduced above), destabilized the ancient authority of Vitruvius, by revealing that the Classical Orders of Architecture lacked a consistent rule, which motivated Laugier's quest for an architectural prototype preceding such relativity:

> Perrault could not accept complete dependence upon those recognized as authorities ... He pointed out ... the extreme differences between the proportions set up by various so-called authorities, and how the buildings of antiquity failed to show the same proportions called for by the authorities.[4]

Significantly, Perrault's disruption of tradition laid the groundwork for modernist architecture, which evolved into suppressing Classical ornament, in proportional relation to the ascendency of engineered, assembled, and industrialized building (dominated by concrete, steel and glass). The unanticipated outcome of Perrault's challenge is the 'conventionalized, schematized' modernist building constructed everywhere – notable for simple forms and a reduction of elements; combining rationalist ideas of 'function' and 'truth to materials'.[5]

Once Perrault had concluded that premodern inheritances of architectural theory and practice contained 'no sure guides, no fixed rules; only custom', he proposed that such 'arbitrary beauty' ought to be counterbalanced by 'positive beauty'.[6] 'Founded on prepossession and prejudice', arbitrary beauty 'depends entirely on ideas derived from custom, usage, mode.' Whereas positive beauty, 'founded on solid, convincing reason', is characterized by 'richness of material, grandeur and magnificence of structure, exactness and neatness of workmanship, symmetry, and general proportions'.[7] Perrault's conception of qualitative (arbitrary) beauty introduced a relativist strain that continues to dominate architecture.

Although a precondition of modernist architecture, arbitrary beauty undermines the possibility of an International Style, apart from limited conceptions of production-related positive beauty. If myths of quantifiability persist in justifying the greater part of trivial practice, Rykwert summarizes Perrault's disruption of the status quo as follows: 'since the positive beauties of architecture require no particular skill to be appreciated but lie in the domain of common sense, their presence in a building is not due so much to the architect's particular skill'.[8] Instead, whatever ability an architect might have, resides 'in the operation of imagination, which deals with arbitrary beauty: it is in the realm of the irrational, in the realm of taste.'[9]

The peculiar relationship between 'positive' and 'arbitrary' explains much about architecture post-Perrault, and therefore informs the discussion of steel in this chapter. Wright's observations about the transformative effect of steel (and reinforced concrete) on architecture reveals the paradox introduced by Perrault as more opposition than dialectic. In rehearsing the positive virtues of steel; its uniformity, calculability, ductility, and strength (amongst others), Wright asserts that because it has little if any qualitative ones, it is 'wholly dependent upon' the imagination of the architect who uses it.[10]

Modern metal

Despite undermining it, Perrault believed the Classical language of architecture would persist as a matter of custom (or habit), even if arbitrary. It is thus unlikely he imagined his challenge to the Vitruvian inheritance would lead to its collapse. Subsequently, arbitrary has translated into novelty but positive beauty dominates. Over time, the clarity of steel frames, identified with high-rise construction methods, has become a prevalent source of quantitative value portrayed as qualitative. The Eiffel Tower (1887–89), Paris comes to mind but so do most tall buildings (Figure 11.2).

Designed by French engineer Gustav Eiffel (1832–1923), the eponymous Tower was constructed for the Paris Exhibition, as part of the 100th anniversary commemorations of the French Revolution. At 1,024 feet, it was the tallest building in the world from its completion until surpassed by the Chrysler Building, NYC (completed 1930), by architect William Van Alen (1882–1954) (Figure 11.3). Best known for its shiny metal pinnacle, it remains a striking presence on the skyline. Its automobile inspired materials and motifs are apt emblems of Chrysler cars. Prior to the Eiffel Tower, exposed metal – mostly iron – was used primarily for engineered infrastructure projects – bridges, hothouses and train sheds – or was largely concealed, as in the first steel frame tall building (which included cast and wrought iron), the Home Insurance Building (1884–85), Chicago, IL, designed by architect William Le Baron Jenney (1832–1907). In contradistinction, the Eiffel Tower pronounced metal on the skyline as exceeding the symbolic limitations of engineering, to become emblematic of the event it represented, of Paris, and the future. Earlier, Eiffel designed the armature for the equally bold 305-feet-tall Statue of Liberty (1865–86), in New York harbour.

From the dark Eiffel Tower to the present, metal has been used for modern monuments; partly to intensify prominence in the landscape – through sheen, reflection and size – and to emphasize apparent scale. Eero Saarinen's (1910–61) 630-foot-tall stainless steel Gateway Arch in St Louis, MO (1963–65) is a striking example (Figure 11.4). Before

Figure 11.2 Eiffel tower (1887–89), Paris, France. Alexandre-Gustave Eiffel, Engineer. [Photo: Nathaniel Coleman, 2006].

the Eiffel Tower, Joseph Paxton's epoch-making Crystal Palace (1850–51), London (discussed in the next chapter), was constructed of iron and glass (as well as timber), to house the 1851 Great Exhibition. It was a singularly important early example of industrialized building production, which has influenced modernist architecture from its nineteenth-century beginnings until today.

Metallic ends

If nineteenth-century transformations to architecture are traceable to three main causes: the Enlightenment, and its effects on all areas of knowledge, production and everyday life; the Industrial Revolution; and developments in architectural theory from the late seventeenth century onwards, reflecting newfound confidence that 'the moderns' could

Figure 11.3 Chrysler Building (1930–31), New York City. William Van Alen, Architect. Brick-clad steel-framed building, capped with stainless steel–clad crown and spire. The silver building in front of the Chrysler Building is the former Mobil Oil Corp. Headquarters (1956). Harrison & Abramowitz, Architects. Clad with pleated chromium nickel stainless steel panels. [Photo: Nathaniel Coleman, 2010].

surpass 'the ancients'; a fourth development, as an outgrowth of the others, was the decisive split between architecture and engineering around 1750. Frampton argues: the 'necessary conditions for modern architecture' took shape between Perrault's 'early awareness of cultural relativity' in the 'late 17th-century' that led him to challenge 'the universal validity of Vitruvian proportions ...', and the definitive split between engineering and architecture which is sometimes dated to ... 1747.'[11]

Although concrete is as central to the conceptualization and production of modernist architecture as steel (framed construction and reinforcement); when paired with glass, steel is more emblematic of capitalist realism and bureaucratic rationality. Accordingly, architecture culture mirrored nineteenth-century developments (with eighteenth-century origins), stimulated by intensifying manufacture and use of iron – in tandem with social and political changes. As a product of modern science in harmony with ideas of expansion, speed, time and motion and transparency, expanding use of

Figure 11.4 Gateway Arch (1963–65), St Louis, MO, USA. Eero Saarinen, Architect. Inverted Catenary Curve. Materials: stacked double-walled, triangular sections. Outer Skin, Stainless Steel; Inner Skin, Carbon Steel. Reinforced concrete between the two (up to 300 feet height). [Photo: Nathaniel Coleman, 2003]. [Photo: Nathaniel Coleman, 2003].

metal in architecture, primarily steel, is an enduring trope for industrialization and mass production.

Much like reinforced exposed concrete, and sheet glass, steel is a significant metonymy for modernity. As Wright observed, 'Steel has entered our lives as a "material" to take upon itself the physical burden of our civilization.' Its versatility, matching the kineticism of machines, is surely a reason for this but so is its suitability for manifesting techno scientific imaginings: 'Now ductile, tensile, dense to any degree, uniform and calculable to any standard, steel is a known quantity to be dealt with mathematically to a certainty to the last pound; a miracle of strength to be counted upon! ... A material that in the processes already devised not only takes any shape the human brain can reduce to a diagram but can go on producing it until the earth is covered with it'; best of all, it is relatively 'cheap'.[12] Wright saw 'concrete combined with steel strands' (reinforcing) as 'a new dispensation. A new medium for a new world' that would 'probably become the physical body of the modern, civilized world', as indeed it has.[13]

Interestingly, for all of their ingenuity, Imperial Romans did not develop tensioning elements for their vaulted concrete architecture.[14] Although like the Greeks before them, and builders after, they used iron to assist other structural materials, including 'dowels and cramps in their masonry' that is about as far as it went. 'Only later did' iron 'production advance sufficiently for it to become a major material for building.'[15] It was not until the emergence 'of English textile mill construction at the end of the eighteenth century' that 'metal-framed buildings' began to be developed in earnest.[16] Before buildings could go tall, iron and steel members needed to become calculable, and the passenger elevator had to be invented.[17] High-rise commercial building first took hold in the United States, along with the use of metal on facades, including cast iron.[18]

Despite steel and concrete sharing a relative absence of inherent qualities (other than what, as Wright observed, is 'artificially ... given to' them 'by human imagination') and because it is heavy and compressive, concrete is more obviously associated with the earth (subterranean and chthonic) than steel, which is light and tensile.[19] Concrete always presumes the water required to make it into 'paste' in Bachelard's terms. On the other hand, steel is associated with fire (ore extracted from the earth's crust, wrought by fire), and air (perceived lightness – ductility – steel frames reaching towards the sky). If the description of concrete as 'paste' (before hardening), and as combing earth and water – akin to bricks – is entertained, Bachelard's assertions about 'the combination of water and earth that is "realistically" presented under the guise of "paste," (*la pâte*)' become compelling: 'Paste (*la pâte*) is thus the basic component of materiality; the very notion of matter is, I think, closely bound up with it.'[20]

According to Bachelard, distinctions between (the four) elements remain significant because perceived oppositions between them are incompatible. For example: 'Fire and water, particularly, remain enemies even in reverie, and the person who listens to the sound of the stream can scarcely comprehend the person who hears the song of the flames: they do not speak the same language.'[21] Even completely dissociated from any symbolic resonances, fire and water could not be more opposed. The first burns, dries, devours; the second douses, wets, engorges. The first heats, the second cools. But water also mediates: 'Water is truly the transitory element. It is the essential, ontological metamorphosis between fire and earth.'[22] Bachelard's observation calls to mind the evaporation of water in the hardening process of concrete as it dries. He also associates the coolness of water with the coolness of air: 'Thus, each adjective has its privileged noun which material imagination quickly retains. Coolness, accordingly, is an attribute of water. Water is, in a sense, embodied coolness. It is indicative of a poetic climate.'[23]

Paradoxically, although the upward reach of steel (the lightness of skeletal steel frames, and its typical association with glass), suggests air, or the *airy*, in the sense of clarity (more so dematerialization), Bachelard observes, 'coolness is often applied negatively in the realm of air images. A cool wind implies chilling. It cools enthusiasm.'[24] Apart from the wind tunnel effect produced by tall buildings, the chilling cool wind might be the dominance of city centre space by corporate and bureaucratic spatial practices that inscribe midtowns of the mind with disorientating qualities, from outright alienation, to touristic feelings of being a stranger there oneself. De Certeau catches just this sensation in 'Walking in the City'.[25] Koolhaas in *Delirious New York* does the same, but backwards, by mistaking Midtown Manhattan for New York City; something New Yorkers, native or naturalized, would never do.[26]

Using steel

Not surprisingly, Koolhaas' misconception has won out and cities everywhere now want to *Manhattanize*, which simply means to build tall buildings, mostly unnecessarily, largely constructed with steel frames and a preponderance of glass.[27] So strong is the

Figure 11.5 Jewish Museum Berlin (1989–99), Berlin, Germany. Daniel Libeskind, Architect. Material: non-oxidized zinc panels, intended to encourage weathering. [Photo: Nathaniel Coleman, 2003].

steel imaginary of Chicago and Manhattan skyscrapers, even when a concrete frame is used, the association is with steel, especially if the building houses corporate tenants (less so if residential or institutional). Forgetting material for a moment, Rykwert observes that there is an 'association of very high building with recession and' with 'the impotence of corporate capital to generate a socially cohesive environment.'[28] But of course, steel, and metal more generally can be used for highly evocative structures, whether engaged with social renewal or in creating coherent social environments. The exterior cladding of Daniel Libeskind's Jewish Museum Berlin comes to mind (2001), as does Williams and Tsien's demolished Folk Art Museum façade, and Scarpa's more Medieval-like use of metal, especially ironmongery and manipulations that recollect it (Figure 11.5).

On rust

Though not an architect, US sculptor Richard Serra often uses large sheets of Cor-Ten to produce building-scaled works. Cor-Ten is a weathering steel notable for 'the oxidized steel coating, or "patina"' that forms on its surface 'when exposed to the atmosphere over a period of time', which 'inhibits further corrosion.'[29] The patina is a reddish brown colour on account of the higher than normal copper content in the steel. The brown can be quite uniform, almost paint-like, as at John Deere & Company Headquarters, Moline, Illinois (1963), designed by Eero Saarinen (1910–61). In other instances, the rusty aspect is more emphatic, as at the European Solidarity Centre, Gdańsk, Poland (2014), by local firm, FORT Architects. British sculptor Anthony Gormley's supersized Angel of the North (1994–98), Gateshead, England is also fabricated with Cor-Ten.

The short list of works in Cor-Ten above highlights either the ambivalence of the material, its dialectical character or both. If stainless steel – Saarinen's Gateway Arch, for example – is most notable for its reflectivity, or sun-like gleam (under optimum conditions), Cor-Ten is most notable for its rusty patina. If stainless steel is specified because it does not rust, Cor-Ten is selected because it does. But why? In the first instance, it has maintenance benefits. Once it has rusted over, its protective coating renews itself by regenerating continuously. The benefit of this is that no periodic protective recoating is required. Nevertheless, choosing rust has surprising resonances, even if selected for unambiguously positive reasons.

Rust inevitably conjures up, well, rust. A rusty nail threatens tetanus. When a car rusts out, it is ready for the scrap heap. In the United States, post-industrial regions, including, but not limited to, the Great Lakes and Midwest, once identified with factories and steel manufacturing, are now called the Rust Belt, connoting abandoned factories falling into ruin, crumbling along with the communities surrounding them; emblems of false promises and broken dreams wrought by globalizing footloose capital. Rust also conjures up abandoned farms, corroding machinery, a much diminished auto industry, and shut shipyards. Against this backdrop of decay, staking the material presence of the John Deere Headquarters, the Angel of the North sculpture, and the Solidarity Centre on Cor-Ten might seem peculiar. While its use is for the Deere Headquarters is probably earnest (associated with the endurance of steel and machines, as with the earth and moving it, including getting at ore); its use for the Angel and the Solidarity Centre is at worst problematically ironic, at best engaged in a negative dialectic of decay and rebirth.

Angel

The outspread wings of Gormley's Angel of the North (with a span approaching that of a Boeing 747), signposts the North East England region, including County Durham, Tyne and Wear and Northumberland.[30] The original brief called for the creation of 'an ambitious artwork that would become a landmark of the region's character'.[31] Gormley's sculpture appears to have revealed the subtlety of that simple requirement. Although the Angel's gargantuan scale (175-foot-wide wingspan, 20 metres tall) might connote triumph, the rusty Cor-Ten denotes the region's decline, with the loss of shipbuilding and coal mining. Actually, the material bespeaks both: deciding whether the Angel is a Phoenix or a tombstone is a matter of inclination. What it communicates directly to experiencing subjects at the moment of perception is altogether more ambiguous.

Although it is possible to park beside the Angel and walk around its ankles, while looking up towards the buttocks, wings and its head, the figure is mostly seen through passing vehicle windows, which explains why it is 'one of the most viewed pieces of art in the world ..., seen by more than one person every second'.[32] The statistic's significance

Figure 11.6 Angel of the North (1994–98), Gateshead, North East England. Antony Gormley, Sculptor. Material: Cor-Ten steel. [Photo: Nathaniel Coleman, 2010].

extends beyond its emptiness: whatever its merits, the Angel of the North is a roadside sign. As such, it is available for projections. It can be whatever one wants it to be. Since its erection, the regional narrative has largely been one of rebirth (albeit on the back of the service economy, and its adjuncts), based on the much admired Northern spirit. Accordingly, the material means nothing, likewise the sculpture itself. Akin to an advertisement meant to appeal to the broadest demographic, the Angel is a cipher, making it different from the sort of mindful use of material this book encourages. But achieving cipher status is the Angel's genius and its sculptor's. As an object of mass communication, the sculpture must have mass appeal. It is a testament to Gormley's gifts that he accomplished this adroitly; rescuing the work from the banality and apathetic reception that so often afflicts public art. Paradoxically, in its emptiness, the Angel is full.

And yet, the Angel's mass appeal has much to do with its scale, its nomination as an Angel (of Light, rather than Darkness), and the degree to which this is in tune with populist cultural narratives of rebirth, which is a more comforting story than stubborn decline but provides a cover for the creative destruction and entrepreneurialism of capitalism. In this instance, Cor-Ten seems almost calculated to introduce nuance to the work; lest the loss of shipbuilding and coal mining be forgotten amidst shopping and the tide of night-time economies, service industries, arts-led regeneration, and knowledge transfer. By putatively recollecting the history of a place, rust is a simulacrum of cultural memory, offering up myths of *closure*, by seeming to gentle the pain of loss.

Solidarity

Although of a different order than the Angel, the European Solidarity Centre structure can be read in practically the same way, despite doing triple duty as an events centre, location of the Solidarity museum, and housing a library. the Centre occupies a site just inside the gates of the Gdańsk Shipyard, famous as the birthplace of the Solidarity movement and strikes that spread nationally throughout Poland for eighteen months beginning August 1980. Ultimately, Solidarity took power in Poland shortly before the Fall of the Berlin Wall in 1989. A statement by one of the Centre's architects reasonably convincingly explains their selection of Cor-Ten but neglects the inevitable association of rust with decay:

> The use of this material is consistent with the aesthetic and symbolic concept of the ECS [European Solidarity Centre] project. Cor-ten is to refer to the landscape of the shipyard which is adjacent to the building of the ECS. After all, its raw, industrial terrain used to be strewn with similar rusting sheets. Reaching slightly deeper, this kind of material is a reference to the simplicity and austerity of the idea of Solidarity, which originated in this shipbuilding landscape.[33]

While the Cor-Ten no doubt recollects the adjacent shipyard, more precisely, the material out of which ships are constructed, or the industrial activity taking place there,

Figure 11.7 European Solidarity Centre (2014), Gdańsk, Poland. FORT Architects. Interior Event Space. Material: Cor-Ten steel. [Photo: Nathaniel Coleman, 2017].

its 'reference to the simplicity and austerity of the idea of Solidarity' is more problematic. Not only is the association abstract and unexpected but the Solidarity movement itself – its achievements and legacy – are not uncontested. Like political movements everywhere, it is anything but *simple*.[34] Equally problematic is the Solidarity Centre itself. Although the Solidarity museum and library give it cultural credibility, both seem ancillary to its apparently main programme: hosting events in a well-appointed setting with good auditoria, cafes, a restaurant, gift shop, temporary exhibition spaces, and ample 'breakout' spaces. Most importantly, its location encourages self-congratulation: the former Lenin Shipyard's more than three decades identification with Solidarity and the beginning of the end of the Soviet Union. As noted in relation to the Angel of the North, Cor-Ten is significant here. By participating in narratives of labour, industrial action, decline and rebirth; cultural memory is packaged, free of risk or any particular effort. As such, like the Angel, the Solidarity Centre, is something of a cipher, an advertisement for renewal that in itself purports to be the only proof required.

Paradoxes of Deere

In contradistinction to the Angel and Solidarity Centre, Saarinen's Deere Headquarters is convincingly experimental, at least according to the logic of this book, even if self-contradictory, and problematic for being a corporate headquarters. It is sensitively sited as part of a subtle landscape design by Hideo Sasaki (1919–2000) that takes full

Figure 11.8 John Deere & Company World Headquarters (1963), Moline, Ill, USA. Eero Saarinen, Architect. Looking north towards main building. Material: Cor-Ten steel. [Photo: Nathaniel Coleman, 2003].

advantage of the rolling hills and the main building fronting one of two artificial lakes; the larger lower one for flooding overrun and part of the cooling system, the smaller one closest to the building reduces the structure's bulk while providing a calming and cooling feature just outside the cafeteria.

The Deere building is significant for two reasons. First, as recollected by architect Kevin Roche, Saarinen's principal design associate and successor: 'This was the first time Cor-Ten steel was used in a building'. Accordingly, 'In a way it was a test, somewhat of an experiment.'[35] The decision to use Cor-Ten was encouraged by then Deere & Company Chairman, William Hewitt, though not directly stipulated by him. His conviction was that the building 'should be modern in concept, but at the same time down to earth and rugged.'[36] In tune with these aims, Saarinen observed:

> Deere & Company is proud of its mid-western farm-belt location and of its handsome farm machinery. The proper character for its headquarters' architecture would reflect the big, forceful, functional character of its products. Its architecture should not be a slick, precise, glittering glass and spindly metal building, but a building which is bold and direct, using metal in a strong basic way.[37]

Unlike the TWA Flight Center, where Saarinen verged towards kitschy explicitness by producing a big concrete bird, the Deere Headquarters is more sophisticated. The transposition of company values and activities, including the main materials and character of its signature products is surely communicated but so is a degree of benevolence, towards customers, employees and the community, who are invited to enjoy the park-like grounds during work hours. Distinctively, the aims for the building and the results are close enough to being directly perceived at the moment of experience, without the need for much talk about how 'x' refers to 'y', by way of some abstract and unexpected association.

At the Deere Headquarters, steel analogizes the farming machines, while Cor-Ten brown analogizes the dirt they move. The largess of the Headquarters makes it a bit like a Renaissance palace but its domination of the landscape also makes it a bit like the Palace of Versailles. Though a capitalist workplace within, caught in divisions of labour and exchange; farm machines, even non-cultivating earth moving equipment, are bound to use: using machines and making use of the land (for better or worse), in support of species survival. Stainless steel was not suitable; here, the lightness of steel turns downwards, from air to earth. Hewitt and Saarinen's descriptions of what they hoped to achieve would be meaningless if not confirmed by the building itself, in particular the Cor-Ten. In this instance, Saarinen's attempt 'to use steel to express strength' and 'to get into the buildings the character of John Deere products' is persuasive because the existent building is convincing on its own. In that light, his straightforward description of the use of steel for the Deere building is credible:

> Having decided to use steel, we wanted to make a steel building that really was a steel building (most so-called steel buildings seem to me to be more glass buildings than steel buildings, really not one thing or another). We sought for an appropriate material – economical, maintenance free, bold in character, dark in color.[38]

In almost all of his buildings, Saarinen used material in a remarkably direct way, as a form of 'material imagination', in Bachelard's terms, even at the TWA building. By using material as potentially meaningful in itself, he liberates it to its own poetic urgency, without asserting essences. Accordingly, the materials are almost always more evocative than the details, or the buildings themselves. In Saarinen's work, *gestalten* does not prevail. The whole is surely inferior to the sum of its parts, which his early death puts into perspective. Even without knowing his biography, his buildings are hasty, as though produced in a mad rush to get it all done before too late.[39] Although perhaps asking too much, reflecting on Saarinen's buildings with a sensibility inflected by the discontinuousness of Scarpa's work, and the openness of Williams and Tsien's, might begin to reveal its specificities amidst banalizing tendencies towards generality, which he perhaps pursued in an effort to achieve monumental effect, or declare a form.

Steel and concrete

In much the way steel requires concrete to fireproof it, concrete requires steel for reinforcing. Consequently, perception of a building as either steel or concrete depends on outward emphasis; on dressing or cladding (unless brick, wood, stone or glass predominate). In terms of bodily associations, steel is tensile, concrete compressive;

the first lighter, the second heaver. Steel recollects the additive process of wood frame construction, whereas concrete recalls load-bearing (or carved) stone construction. Concrete is cave-like, steel hut-like. The first is more closed (or enclosing), suggesting carving, or excavation – the deduction of material – to produce a volume. The second is more open, suggesting the accretive assembly of frames. Steel is additive, rather than subtractive; emphasizing open structure and assembly rather than wall, plane or volume, in the way concrete does.

The lingering presence of absent concrete formwork, left by impressions when removed, is explicitly subtractive. It is also potentially a source of the material's greatest communicative capacities. If a significant challenge of working with concrete is to confound its association with modernist banalities, the correlate for steel would be to use it for more domestic, civic or emotionally charged buildings. But steel is difficult to conceptualize beyond its association with managed production, touched upon by Wright in his considerations of the material. Because of this, the most compelling steel buildings are either paeans to the positive and quantifiably calculable, or must work very hard to confound associations by shifting them away from expectations; perhaps from work to play, from corporate offices and engineered achievements to recollections of climbing bars and roller coasters, as at Richard Rogers and Renzo Piano's Centre Georges Pompidou, Paris (1971–77) (Figure 11.9). For all of its productivist optimism, the Pompidou confounds association of steel with the managed world of corporate bureaucracies; even as it wallows in engineering and industrial production. Or perhaps the lightness of steel and its association with the self-abnegation of reflections (of mirrored glass or polished stainless steel) ought to be countered with the character of heavy machinery, as at the Deere Headquarters.

Obviously enough, the initial use of steel in railroad buildings and infrastructure projects makes it cognate with managed production and capitalist expansion; with business and exchange. Thus, while concrete's more obvious association with the earth, gravity, enclosure and the weight of stone suggests its use for high-rise and mass housing, and civic buildings, steel imaginaries are limited by its precise production, especially suited to structurally framing skyscrapers.

If usual associations between glass and steel call to mind mute, self-abnegating, buildings, perfectly suited to the bureaucratic deflection of responsibility identified with big business and big government alike, Saarinen's Deere & Company problematizes expectations. While expressing processes of assembly, it is decidedly not reflective. It would be incorrect to describe the building as anything but a corporate headquarters. Accordingly, it reproduces the association of glass and steel with the private sector and corporations, though Saarinen confounded this association at the University of Chicago Law School (1958–59), where glass predominates in the main building, which nonetheless has a concrete frame.

Saarinen's assertion that most steel buildings are actually glass buildings is telling. Apart from modernist obsession with transparency, as a trope for dynamism, enhanced by glass reflectivity, steel structure is usually enclosed within concrete for fire protection.

Figure 11.9 Centre Georges Pompidou (1971–77), Paris, France. Studio Piano + Rogers, Architects. Peter Rice, Engineer. Engineering as play. [Photo: Nathaniel Coleman, 2010].

Consequently, the material expressiveness of the structural frame must be reproduced decoratively on the façade. For example, the ornamental bronze I-beams applied to the bronze and glass clad exterior of the Seagram Building (1958), NYC, reassert the building's hidden concrete-protected steel structure. Designed by Ludwig Mies van der Roe (1886–1969) and Philip Johnson (1906–2005), the brown, silky smooth, colour of the building connotes slickness, rather than the relative roughness of the Deere building. The Seagram Building is the more self-consciously corporate of the two, revelling in its aloofness. A condition intensified by the expansive plaza fronting it, as sure evidence of wealth and power (Figure 11.10).

Stainlessness and rust

Perhaps Saarinen had the Seagram tower in mind when he declared that the Deere building would be anything but 'a slick, precise, glittering glass and spindly metal building'.[40] More likely, he was thinking of the building Mies and Johnson were competing with, the Lever House (1952), designed by Gordon Bunshaft (1909–90) for SOM, diagonally across from the Seagram, on the northwest corner of 53rd Street and Park Avenue. Here, two corporate headquarters face off: whisky and rum (Seagram brown), against soap (sparkling Lever Brothers). The Lever House is 'one of the first glass-walled International Style office buildings in the [United States, notable for] its facade made of blue-green glass and stainless steel mullions'[41] (Figure 11.11).

Saarinen's own CBS Building (1960–64), also in Midtown Manhattan, affectionately known as 'Black Rock', is his only skyscraper and drives home his point about steel as glass. It is decidedly the antithesis of Lever House and the Seagram Building, and as close as one could get to 'bold and direct' in the lonely corporate headquarters zone of Midtown. Clad in near black granite, the tower, with defensive triangular piers (from ground to full height) modulate the façade; producing anything but a 'neutral curtain of glass'. It was the first post-Second World War New York City skyscraper built 'with

Figure 11.10 *Modernism* appropriated: Seagram Building (1958), Manhattan, NY, USA. Ludwig Mies van der Roe and Philip Johnson, Architects. [Photo: Nathaniel Coleman, 2003].

Figure 11.11 *Modernism* consumed: Lever House (1952), Manhattan, NY, USA. Gordon Bunshaft, Architect (Skidmore, Owings & Merrill). [Photo: Nathaniel Coleman, 2008].

a reinforced concrete frame', and remains one of very few.[42] In arriving at 'a masonry building: concrete, clad in granite' Saarinen aimed to produce a tower that would 'weather well', and respond to his concern that 'too much modern architecture is flimsy looking'[43] (Figure 11.12).

Although there are many gradations, stainlessness and rust appear to be the endpoints of steel imaginaries in architecture, colour is a third, though less typical, option. Examples include the colour-coded service ducts at Pompidou; the colourful façade panels at Aldo van Eyck's Hubertus House, Amsterdam (1973–78); and the colourful panels of Le Corbusier's Pavilion, Zurich (1960–67) (Plates 15 and 16).

Figure 11.12 *Modernism* subverted? CBS Building (1960–64), Manhattan, NY, USA. Eero Saarinen, Architect. [Photo: Nathaniel Coleman, 2003].

Stainless steel may aptly project the gleam of automotive production and industrial progress, as at the Chrysler Building but once myths of infinite expansion, endless progress and open-ended opportunities for resource exploitation are no longer sustainable, post-industrial rust replaces stainless shine as suasive expression of prevailing conditions. Despite Saarinen's use of the material for the Deere Headquarters, Cor-Ten in particular lights up post-industrial imaginaries, even when it celebrates manufacturing and working the earth. While rust is the way Cor-Ten protects itself from decay, the quality of the condition, and its colour, suggest hard work, unemployment, the earth and ruin simultaneously. Using Cor-Ten risks garbling communication, but doing so opens up surprising material possibilities.

Notes

1. Frank Lloyd Wright, 'In The Cause of Architecture III: The Meaning of Materials – Steel', *Architectural Record*, August 1927, pp. 163–6 (p. 163). Available online at: https://www.arc hitecturalrecord.com/articles/11513-in-the-cause-of-architecture-iii-steel (Accessed 18 July 2018).

2. Peter Gay, *The Enlightenment: The Rise of Modern Paganism*, New York: W. W. Norton, 1966; Peter Gay, *The Enlightenment: The Science of Freedom*, New York: W. W. Norton, 1969.

3. Edward Robert De Zurko, *Origins of Functionalist Theory*, New York: Columbia University Press, 1957, p. 157.

4. Ibid., p. 69.

5. Joseph Rykwert, *The First Moderns: The Architects of the Eighteenth Century*, Cambridge, MA: MIT Press, 1980, p. 115.

6. Robin Middleton and David Watkin, *Neoclassical and 19th Century Architecture: The Enlightenment in France and in England*, New York: Electa/Rizzoli, 1987 (1980), p. 8. See, Claude Perrault, *Ordonnance For the Five Kinds of Columns after the Methods of The Ancients* (1683), Indra Kagis McEwen (trans.), Santa Monica, CA: Getty Center, 1993, especially pp. 47–63.

7. De Zurko, *Origins of Functionalist Theory*, p. 71.

8. Rykwert, *The First Moderns*, p. 115.

9. Ibid.

10. Wright, 'In The Cause of Architecture III: The Meaning of Materials – Steel', p. 163.

11. Kenneth Frampton, *Modern Architecture: A Critical History*, Forth Edition, London: Thames & Hudson, 2007, pp. 8, 14.

12. Wright, 'In The Cause of Architecture III: The Meaning of Materials – Steel', p. 163.

13. Ibid., p. 165.

14. MacDonald, *Roman Empire*, p. 165.

15. Elliott, *Technics and Architecture*, p. 68.

16. Ibid., p. 70.

17. Ibid., pp. 106–7.

18. Ibid., pp. 67–108.

19. Wright, 'In the Cause of Architecture VII: Meaning of Materials – Concrete'.

20. Bachelard, *Water and Dreams*, p. 13.

21. Bachelard, *The Psychoanalysis of Fire*, p. 89.

22. Ibid., p. 6.

23. Ibid., pp. 31–2.

24. Ibid., p. 31.

25. de Certeau, 'Walking in the City', pp. 91–110.

26. Rem Koolhaas, *Delirious New York: A Retroactive Manifesto for Manhattan* (1978), New York: Monacelli Press, 1994.

27. Joseph Rykwert, *The Seduction of Place: History and Future of the City*, New York: Vintage Books, 2002, p. 89.

28. Ibid., p. 227.

29. Peter Domone (revised by), Bill Biggs, Ian McColl and Bob Moon (previous authors), 'Iron and Steel', *Construction Materials Their Nature and Behaviour*, p. 74.

30. No Author, 'The History of the Angel of the North', *Gateshead Council*. Available at: https://www.gateshead.gov.uk/article/5303/The-history-of-the-Angel-of-the-North (Accessed 28 May 2018).

31. No Author, 'Angel of the North', *Gateshead Council*. Available at: https://www.gateshead.gov.uk/article/3957/Angel-of-the-North (Accessed 28 May 2018).

32. Ibid.

33. Wojciech Targowski, FORT Architects quote, Culture.pl, 'The European Solidarity Centre', *Culture Poland*. Available at: https://culture.pl/en/work/the-european-solidarity-centre (Accessed 28 May 2018).

34. Jan Repa, 'Analysis: Solidarity's Legacy', *BBC News*. Available at: http://news.bbc.co.uk/1/hi/world/europe/4142268.stm (Accessed 28 May 2018); Agata Pyzik, 'Poland Must Rediscover the True Meaning of Solidarity', *The Guardian*, Friday 13 September. Available at: https://www.theguardian.com/commentisfree/2013/sep/13/poland-union-solidarity (Accessed 28 May 2018). Adrian Karatnycky, 'Poland's Long Fall From Grace', *The Atlantic*, 29 February 2016, Available at: https://www.theatlantic.com/international/archive/2016/02/lech-walesa-law-and-justice-poland/471366/ (Accessed 28 May 2018).

35. Kevin Roche, quoted, Jennifer DeWitt, 'Deere World Headquarters building in Moline Turns 50 Years Old', *Quad City Times*, 16 June 2014. Available at: http://qctimes.com/business/deere-world-headquarters-building-in-moline-turns-years-old/article_06381862-a057-5c8e-ade8-b01744cf22ec.html (Accessed 28 May 2018).

36. William Hewitt, quoted, *Deere & Company Administrative Center*, Moline, IL: Deere & Company, No Date, No Page.

37. Eero Saarinen, quoted, *Deere & Company Administrative Center*, Moline, IL: Deere & Company, No Date, No Page.

38. Eero Saarinen, *Eero Saarinen on His Work*, Revised Edition, Aline B. Saarinen (ed.), New Haven: Yale University Press, 1968, p. 82.

39. Peter Blake, *No Place Like Utopia: Modern Architecture and the Company We Kept*, New York: W. W. Norton, 1993, pp. 255–61.

40. Saarinen, *Eero Saarinen on His Work*, p. 82.

41. No Author, SOM, 'Lever House'. Available at: https://www.som.com/projects/lever_house (Accessed 29 May 2018).

42. Saarinen, *Eero Saarinen on His Work*, p. 16; Jayne Merkel, 'CBS / "Black Rock"', *The Skyscraper Museum*. Available at: http://www.skyscraper.org/EXHIBITIONS/FAVORITES/fav_cbs.htm (Accessed 29 May 2018).

43. Saarinen, *Eero Saarinen on His Work*, p. 16.

CHAPTER 12
TRANSPARENCY: A DARKER SHADE OF GLASS

Although Frank Lloyd Wright considered both (reinforced) concrete and steel to be quintessentially modern materials, glass probably surpasses them as the foremost material of modernist architecture. He observed: 'the greatest difference eventually between ancient and modern buildings will be due to our modern machine-made glass. Glass, in any wide utilitarian sense, is new.' Although associations with glass as historically 'a precious substance limited in quantity and size' linger, as it has become cheaper to make, and 'perfect clarity' more easily achievable, its desirability has increased exponentially, such 'that our modern world' has drifted towards 'structures of glass and steel'. But 'as glass has become clearer and clearer and cheaper and cheaper from age to age, about all that has been done with it architecturally is to fill the same opening that opaque glass screened before, with perfect visibility'.[1]

In the preceding, Wright articulates the conundrum of glass in architecture: its pervasiveness, and association with myths of progress and sociopolitical fantasies of transparency, counterbalanced by the banalities of application, demands attention. Glass significance, from preciousness to ubiquitousness, and from biblical associations with crystal to perfect transparency, provides the pathway. Once associated with transcendence, glass is now mostly identified with transparency, encompassing publicity, consumption, office buildings, modern bureaucracies and views. Dubiously, glass transparency is also portrayed as a metonym for democracy. Unsurprisingly, expanding use of glass in building since the nineteenth-century parallels intensifying administration of individual life, alongside increasing exhibitionism, which obscures its earlier associations with revelation. Although ostensibly a natural symbol of openness, current usage renders glass *opaque*.

In *Notes from the Underground* (1864), Russian author Fyodor Dostoevsky (1821–81) intuited that Sir Joseph Paxton's (1803–65) Crystal Palace (1850–51) presaged absolute rationalism. In *We* (1924) (the first totalitarian dystopian novel), Russian author Yevgeny Zamyatin (1884–1937) expanded Dostoevsky's trope into a transparent state. Twentieth-century attempts to re-establish the phenomenal transparency of glass – analogizing revelation as translucence and refraction – were outdone by overuse and visuality; of picture window views and mirrored glass reflections. For example, German expressionist author Paul Scheerbart (1863–1915) and German Expressionist architect Bruno Taut (1880–1938) made unsuccessful early-twentieth-century challenges to modernist glass tendencies.

So pervasive is the logic of display that it obscures other possible meanings of glass. Transcendence cannot compete against modern associations of glass with loss of privacy, the panoptic sweep of bureaucratic systems and the spectre of totalitarianism.

Highlighting this, Benito Mussolini (1883–1945), Italy's Fascist leader from 1922 until 1943, described Fascism as a 'glass house'. A metaphor regime architect Giuseppe Terragni (1904–43) materialized in his Casa del Fascio (1932–36), Como, Italy, by confounding surveillance with freedom, under the sign of glass transparency.

Used uncritically as a trope for political transparency (when not simply a window), glass connotes exposure, vulnerability, control or consumption; more so than freedom. Accordingly, reflections on glass in this chapter are organized around buildings that attribute greater significance to glass and transparency than simply providing see-through membranes that seal voids against the elements. No matter its clarity, glass is never quite as neutral as it appears.

Transparency of reason

Transformation of glass (cognate with crystal and gems), from a precious element (when difficult to produce) into a pervasive building material, invites thinking about how its latent mystery and wonderment could be reactivated.[2] In Christianity, the crystalline qualities of glass were emblems of 'purity, spiritual perfection and knowledge', analogizing the 'light [wisdom] of God'; subsequently transposed as its most practical attributes: the gaze drifts freely inward and outward; daylight illuminates interiors; and sunlight warms.[3] Literal transparency aligns with the dominant technical characteristics of glass but has also become its dominant metaphor, transforming it into a generic sign, easily appropriated by Fascists, democrats and technological Utopians.

Although Wright could wax poetic on glass, he was disappointed by typical modern applications: 'What is this magic material, there but not seen if you are looking through it? You may look at it, too, as brilliance, catching reflections and giving back limpid light … as a material we may regard it as crystal – thin sheets of air in air to keep air out or keep it in.'[4] Perhaps, but as he observed, a 'sense of glass as crystal has not yet to any extent entered into the poetry of architecture'. Seemingly anticipating Wright's lament, during the pre-First World War period, Scheerbart and Taut, sought to recuperate the crystalline qualities of glass with their attempts to secularize its spiritual associations as utopian instruments of social enlightenment (especially with the *Glashaus*, 1914).

Beginning with the Crystal Palace, glass transparency became especially pronounced during the post-Second World War building boom, making Zamyatin's cautionary glass world into the stark reality of new, rebuilt and modernizing cities.[5] According to Mexican architect Louis Barragán (1902–88): 'it has been an error to replace the protection of the wall with today's intemperate use of glass windows' – transparency is disconcerting because it dissolves the emotional security of solid walls.[6]

Terragni's use of transparency as a trope for a merging of individual and regime under Fascism complicates non-critical suppositions about its interchangeability with glass and with democracy. Foster's Berlin Reichstag glass dome is a glaringly naïve example of this; raising doubts about the suitability of glass transparency as a symbol of post-World War Two German democratization (or post-Wall unification).

The predominant material qualities of glass – admitting, reflecting or refracting light – are suggestive, but neither transparency nor crystalline shimmer are natural symbols of transcendence, revelation or democracy. Material meanings develop associatively through making and use but are not fixed. Defunct, or lingering, associations do not confirm the eternity of connotations. Shifting emphasis from spiritual signification towards performance criteria during nearly 300 years of developments has given precedence to the practical, commercial or aesthetic values of glass over its emotional, or poetic, qualities. While the psychological benefits of natural light are unquestionable, room atmosphere is determined by more than outward views.[7] Diminished privacy, mirroring individuality flattened by bureaucratic rationality, and mass consumption are just some modern conditions affiliated with overuse of glass.[8]

Industrial production of glass transformed it from analogical figure to constructed reality: 'from the medieval idea of something to look at, to the modern one of something to look through'.[9] It now more persuasively reflects streamlined building practices (positivism) than transparent social or political processes (democracy). From transcendence to extreme reason, or simply introducing natural daylight, glass significance is more a matter of *situation* than *essence*, determined by what is done with it.

Suger

Drawn directly from biblical sources, Gothic cathedrals gave pre-modern crystal/glass symbolism its greatest architectural expression. Dematerialization of wall mass opened cathedrals to divine light, rather than views; made possible by transferring downward thrusting loads away from enclosing walls to exterior buttresses perpendicular to them. Pointed arches and ribbed vaults also contributed. These structural features made possible the soaring heights and openness principally associated with twelfth and thirteenth church building in France. Largely freed of load-bearing necessity, walls could tolerate large voids filled with expanses of precious glass (usually coloured), resulting in luminous interiors articulated by lucid structure.[10]

A jewel-like interior was the objective, not transparency, illumination or radiant heat. The view was towards the New Jerusalem; the light's warmth was analogous to God's love; the mysterious illumination of the stained glass confirmed Christ as the *new light*. The stained glass also illustrated stories from the Bible, about the cathedral's location, and its construction. The dynamic relationship of structure, world and revelation made Gothic cathedrals into eloquent promises of a better world to come; as the 'symbolic interconnection between cosmos, Celestial City, and sanctuary'.[11]

Associations with crystal glass and precious stones fill St John the Divine's descriptions of the Celestial City of the New Jerusalem in Revelation 21-22, which became the model of church building richness.[12] Bejewelled churches offered a foretaste of the New Jerusalem as a possible reality; not as representation, or substitution but as windows on to it, pathways towards it, as precincts of the Heavenly City (Figure 12.1).

Figure 12.1 Chartres Cathedral (Notre-Dame d'Chartres) (1194–1260), Chartres, France. [Photo: Nathaniel Coleman, 2003].

As anticipatory prospects onto the New Jerusalem, stained glass lifted the veil between earthly hardship and divine promise. Material richness was not profligate but a *transcendence machine*, as Abbot Suger (1081–1151) describes:

> Marvel not at the gold and the expense but at the
>   craftsmanship of the work.
> Bright is the noble work; but, being nobly bright, the work
> Should brighten the minds, so that they may travel,
> through the true lights,
> To the true light where Christ is the true door,
> In what manner it be inherent in this world the golden
>   door defines:
> The dull mind rises to truth through that which is material
> And, in seeing this light, is resurrected from its former submersion.[13]

Suger's restructuring of the abbey church of St Denis (1135–44), north of Paris, established the key features of Gothic cathedrals, particularly in the ambulatory, where the church opened towards the divine[14] (Figure 12.2).

The richness of Revelation's New Jerusalem informed Suger's conviction that bejewelled churches facilitate transcendence. Despite Taut's attempts to close the gap between sacred symbolism and modernist glass, medieval understandings of material – as form and content joined – is just too removed from separation of the two by modern consciousness:

> To the medieval thinker beauty was not a value independent of others, but rather the radiance of truth, the splendor of ontological perfection, and that quality of things which reflects their origin in God. Light and luminous objects … conveyed an insight into the perfection of the cosmos, and the divination of the creator.[15]

For Suger, church decoration was immanence: precious elements would convey believers from earthly care towards the divine as proximate. By guiding worshippers' spiritual attentions away from the mundane towards the sacred, the properties of glass (crystal and other precious materials) are reflections of hope:

> the loveliness of the many-colored gems has called me away from external cares, and worthy meditation has induced me to reflect, transferring that which is material to that which is immaterial, on the diversity of sacred virtues: then it seems to me that I see myself dwelling, as it were, in some strange region of the universe which neither exists entirely in the slime of the earth nor entirely in the purity of Heaven; and that by the grace of God, I can be transported from this inferior to that higher world in an anagogical manner.[16]

All the ornaments of the church pry open windows onto a divine promise. Although Wright still sensed the magic of glass; liberated from their anagogical vocation, Gothic Cathedrals are little more than models of rational structure with lots of glazing (ostensibly prefiguring glass and steel skyscrapers).

But even in a secular age, as Bachelard reminds us, reverie endures, augmented by the scientific qualities of materials. Wright's observation of glass 'as there but not seen' highlights its anticipatory – dreamlike – character, as perhaps recoverable even after technological advances eclipsed its semi-preciousness, which previously analogized the revelatory qualities of jewels and gems. Once glass became more widely available; first the powerful, then the wealthy, appropriated it's transcendent associations, mainly entranced by the reflectivity of good quality mirrors – the Hall of Mirrors (*Galerie des Glaces*), Palace of Versailles, France, 1678–84, for example. Paralleling secularization and technological progress, the primary function of glass shifted from figurative vision to literal viewing (Figure 12.3).

Figure 12.2 Abbey Church of St-Denis (façade: 1135–40). Apse: 1140–44; Abbot Suger's creation is pictured. Other parts of the church: 1230–80, St Denis, Paris, France. [Photo: Nathaniel Coleman, 2003].

Figure 12.3 Hall of Mirrors (*Galerie des Glaces*), Palace of Versailles, Versailles, France (1678–84). Jules Hardouin-Mansart, Architect. [Photo: Nathaniel Coleman, 2003].

Van Nelle factory

Expanses of glass in early modernist functionalist buildings were associated with instrumental reason, modern techno science and scientific management. An example is the Van Nelle factory in Rotterdam (1927–30), The Netherlands, designed by Johannes Andreas Brinkman (1902–49) and L. C. Van der Vlugt (1894–1936). In 1932, Le Corbusier described it as 'the most beautiful spectacle of our modern age that I know'.[17] The 'structure and movement systems [of the factory] were explicitly revealed', constituting an 'open and dynamic expression' of the industrial processes contained within.[18]

With its exposed reinforced concrete structural frame and dramatic glass curtain wall, disclosing both its mushroom columns and work-related activities within, the Van Nelle exalts the quantifiable practicalities of engineering and industrial production. And does so at an intersection between Taylorist Scientific Management, 'to produce efficient, worker-amenable production spaces', and 'the universalist, spiritual and transcendental nature of Theosophical belief'.[19] Overburdened by such collisions (invited by client and architect), glass at the Van Nelle factory achieves a state of confused signification; faithfully embodying the crises of tradition and ideology underpinning modernity and modernist architecture.

Figure 12.4 Van Nelle Factory (1927–30), Rotterdam, The Netherlands. Johannes Andreas Brinkman and L. C. Van der Vlugt, Architects. [Photo: Nathaniel Coleman, 2015].

A glass city

A precursor of the Van Nelle factory and Taut's *Glashaus* was the Crystal Palace, built for the 1851 Great Exhibition, Hyde Park, London, designed by gardener and glasshouses maker Sir Joseph Paxton, assisted by Charles Fox.[20] Over time, it has become the most influential nineteenth-century building, prefiguring assembly as the dominant mode of construction, eclipsing craft. The structure is recollected as 'the first ever example of prefabrication and large scale industrialized building'; 'not so much a particular form as it was a building process made manifest as a total system, from its initial conception, fabrication and trans-shipment, to its final erection and dismantling'.[21]

A 1965 report on prefabrication in Britain outlines various milestones of the building: it was a 'mixed construction of wrought and cast-iron prefabricated and repetitive structural units manufactured' offsite; it influenced 'the principle of repetitive component'; was 'transportable to one site and removable for re-erection to another'; and the whole process was fast: 'the working drawings were completed in seven weeks and the manufacture of and erection in nine months'. The Crystal Palace defeated poetic wonder with statistics: '1848 ft long, 408 ft wide at the base and 135 ft high at the transept'. The structure was infilled with 'about a million square feet of glass … in something like 300 000 standard-sized panels (about one third of England's glass production ten years earlier)'. Until at least 1965, it remained singular: 'probable that such an achievement in office, works, and site organization has never been equaled in the field of building in' the UK.[22]

As a great early achievement of economical and efficient prefabrication, and assembly at a large scale, the Crystal Palace anticipates the post-Second World War building industry. Though when constructed, it was *simply* the most practical solution to a particular set of problems. Maybe, but its vast expanse of glazed framing introduced a new space conception, characterized by 'perspectives whose lines diminished into a diaphanous haze of light', making it also an early revelation of *bigness*, spectacle architecture and super modernity. Qualities that associate it with darker sides of progress and transparency.[23] Acknowledging this, and its profound influence on architectural developments since it appeared, German philosopher Peter Sloterdijk argues that the Crystal Palace is emblematic of the capitalist production of space:

> From that point on, a new aesthetics of immersion began its triumphal march through modernity. The psychedelic capitalism of today was already a *fait accompli* in the almost immaterialized, artificially climatized building. … With its construction, the principal of the interior overstepped a critical boundary: from then on, it meant neither the middle- or upper-class home nor its projection onto the sphere of urban shopping arcades; rather, it began to endow the outside world as a whole with a magical immanence transfigured by luxury and cosmopolitanism. Once it had been converted into a large hothouse and an imperial culture museum, it revealed the timely tendency to make both culture and nature indoor affairs.[24]

In its immersiveness, global capitalism can seem total. Psychedelic (hallucinatory and mind altering) states nudge consciousness inward, away from external experiences of reality. The abundance of lightly framed transparent glass, enclosing a vast space, produced a kind of ecstatic disorientating effect of interiority, well-suited to the limitless insubstantiality of capitalism and consumption. The Crystal Palace transformed glass into a myth, not of transcendence but of proximity, enclosure and control.

Dostoevsky and the Crystal Palace

The Crystal Palace is a protagonist in Dostoevsky's *Notes from the Underground*, which influenced Zamyatin's later novel, *We*. Both consider the problematic of modern glass architecture as product and expression of instrumental reason (prefiguring pervasive glass transparency of later twentieth- and twenty-first-century abstract and reflective architecture). Anticipating Sloterdijk, the Crystal Palace of *Notes from the Underground* expands in *We* to become a determining glass world. For Dostoevsky, the Crystal Palace was a metaphor for the closure of capitalism and utopianism alike. For Zamyatin, glass society analogized intensifying state invasiveness in Soviet Russian, after the 1917 Revolution, including expanding control of individual thought and action. For both, glass transparency was a trope for the predicament of individuals within increasingly totalizing systems.

Its vast interior space, minimal structure and abundance of glazing made the Crystal Palace glow, while aligning it with technological society, and the display of products. Its enduring significance mostly turns on its prefiguration of building reduced to problems of managing timescales, quantities and performance. As an analogue of enclosing the world, the Crystal Palace was for Dostoevsky a marker of Western spiritual decline.

Narrativized as an 'epoch-making' image of process and progress (factory-made parts assembled on site), the Crystal Palace remains influential because its *best solution* was modelled on hothouses.[25] Echoing Dostoevsky, Sloterdijk summarizes the levelling aftereffects of the Crystal Palace as housing 'the world interior of capital';

> not an agora or a trade fair beneath the open sky, but rather a hothouse that has drawn inwards everything that was once on the outside. The bracing climate of an integral inner world of commodity can be formulated in the notion of a planetary palace of consumption.[26]

If Gothic cathedrals were metonyms of the New Jerusalem, for Dostoevsky, the Crystal Palace was an emblem of worldly attainment associated with solitude and the illusory promises of European capitalism.[27] His treatment of it and Zamyatin's glass dystopia were preceded by *What is to be Done?* (1863), written by Russian revolutionary novelist Nikolai Chernyshevsky (1828–89). The novel's main character dreams a perfect socialist Utopia achieved, set in a Crystal Palace as a kind of secularized New Jerusalem.[28] To

Figure 12.5 Crystal Palace (1850–51), Hyde Park, London. Sir Joseph Paxton, Designer, with Charles Fox. The transept, inside Crystal Palace, Hyde Park. Dickinsons's comprehensive pictures of the Great Exhibition of 1851. Dickinson, Brothers, Her Majesty's Publishers, 1852. doi: 10.5479/sil.495268.39088008102741. *Courtesy of the Smithsonian Libraries.* (Out of Copyright, US; Public Domain Mark 1.0; UK).

shelter the collective within, Chernyshevsky's fictional Crystal Palace is even vaster than the second state of the London original. Suggestive of Sloterdijk's perceptions, Chernyshevsky describes an 'outer building, of crystal and wrought iron' that 'is merely a case', containing an inner building notable for its expansive glazing, with 'immense and wide … windows' that 'stretch from floor to ceiling!'[29]

Described as revealing 'the horror of a secular utopia, the sort of "brave new world" where the individual is absorbed and lost in the machinery of technological and social progress'; Chernyshevsky's novel is a strange intersection between Christian millennialism and positivist optimism of the sort that Dostoevsky believed the Crystal Palace affirmed, which repulsed him.[30]

As 'an icon of industrial capitalism', Dostoevsky, saw the Crystal Palace as 'a man-eating structure, … a modern Baal – a cult container in which humans pay homage to the demons the West: the power of money and pure movement, along with voluptuous and intoxicating pleasures'.[31] For Sloterdijk, this is what makes it the great model of 'the world interior of capital'. The building's origins in the controlled environments of hothouses, dedicated to cultivating often alien plant life, suited it to its original use and Dostoevysky's poetic aims, embodying the unsettling and depersonalizing aspects of 'industrial capitalism, scientific rationality, and any sort of predictive, mathematical model of human behavior'.[32] Although not all architecture is dominated by glass, nearly all of it *is* assembled according to the logics of economy and efficiency introduced by the Crystal Palace. Though destroyed by fire in 1936, Dostoevsky was correct in believing it presaged permanent conditions of modernity.[33]

We

Although Zamyatin initially supported the Russian revolution, he became a fierce critic. The cautionary tale of *We* elaborates on the implications of the Crystal Palace outlined by Dostoevsky and Chernyshevsky, reflecting on the increasing totalitarianism of post-revolutionary Soviet Russia.[34] Zamyatin adopted Dostoevsky's portrayal of individual struggle against an extensively rationalist society, alongside his glass architecture metaphor. Whereas Dostoevsky indicts utopian socialism and European capitalism, Zamyatin targets Russian communism and English capitalism (he had worked in Newcastle upon Tyne, UK, as a naval engineer).[35]

Set in the twenty-sixth century, *We* describes a state where *everything* is glass, organized according to the Cartesian logic of orthogonal grids and multiplication tables. Zamyatin's future world looks to the theory and practice of Taylorism for clues to the prehistory of its well-oiled machine-like precision.[36] Named after US engineer Frederick Winslow Taylor (1856–1915), Taylorism is a system of industrial organization (scientific management) intended to maximize production through a range of efficiencies including the standardization of products and specialization of tasks. In *We*, Taylor is shorthand for modern conditions of routinized life and labour. Scientific management permeates all aspects of life, mirrored by transparent architecture, which analogizes likewise human relations. The extreme clarity of glass dissolves privacy and *murky* individuality, while exposing the dangers of an imagination. Glass heralds the dark promise of absolute transparency, analogous to the perfect organization only possible when individual and state merge.

Known by letters and numbers, people in *We* must not obscure anything. As literally windows upon an ideally transparent soul, eyes must be devoid of guile, intrigue or emotion. The presence of these are signs of being sick with an imagination or a soul – dangerous hindrances to optimized efficiency, in the effectively wall-less glass state of *We*. In Zamyatin's novel, the extreme reason Dostoevsky feared becomes the sum total of life, under the ever-watchful gaze of the 'great benefactor'.[37] Individual life is totally organized; as if the Crystal Palace now encloses everything. Although blithely used as a marker of freedom, there is no more natural trope for a totalitarian surveillance state than the permanent exposure of glass transparency: subversion and insurgency require solid walls to shield schemers.

Modernists

Early modernists, including, Walter Benjamin (1892–1940), embraced transparency as an ideal uncannily similar to Zamyatin fears. Just as Zamyatin conflated architectural with social, political and individual transparency, negatively, Benjamin imagined crystal-clear buildings would expose bourgeoisie decadence. Display through glass walls would ostensibly reveal class contradictions. But judgements through glass are bidirectional. Whereas glass in *We* enforces conformity, Benjamin believed that 'living in a glass house' is 'a revolutionary virtue' capable of transforming private life.[38]

The modernist promise of openness and infinite extension – transparency – never materialized in the ways imagined. Although exposure through glass, and its reflectivity, confuses more than it configures, transparency persists as a lazy mythologized metaphor of infinite reason (or disclosure) extending to all facets of life. While the transcendent promise of Gothic glass is irrecoverable, the challenge is to emphasize the luminosity and figurative transparency of glass, without surrendering to extreme exposure, display or specular disorientation. Doing so begins with negating the Crystal Palace's continuing

Figure 12.6 One of the many *children* of the Crystal Palace. A perpetual exhibition of manufactured goods. Toronto Eaton Centre (1977–81), Toronto, Ontario, CA. Eberhard Zeidler & B+H Architects. [Photo: Nathaniel Coleman, 2007].

sway over glass imaginaries and applications. But as Marshall Berman observed, its twentieth-century incarnations are pervasive:

> in the generation after World War Two, Paxton's ... building would emerge, in ... recognizable form, endlessly and mechanically reproduced in a legion of steel and glass corporate headquarters and suburban shopping malls that covered the land.[39]

In recognizing the Crystal Palace as the source of key architectural symbols of capitalism and anti-urbanism, Berman acknowledges 'how good a prophet Dostoevsky really was'[40] (Figure 12.6).

Scheerbart and Taut

Despite the dominance of literal transparency, Taut and Scheerbart envisioned a glass-crystal Utopia evoking the phenomenal transparency of Gothic cathedrals.[41] The communal effort that gave rise to Gothic cathedrals, encompassing qualitative uses of glass, convinced Scheerbart and Taut that they must be forerunners of a true glass architecture; combining pre-modern transcendent light with a form of transformative socialism. Scheerbart's promotion of dematerializing architecture made this explicit:

> If we want our culture to rise to a higher level, we are obliged ... to change our architecture. And this only becomes possible if we take away the closed character from the rooms in which we live. We can only do that by introducing glass architecture, which lets in the light of the sun, the moon, and the stars, not merely through a few windows, but through every possible wall.[42]

Chronologically, Scheerbart's *Glass Architecture* (1914) follows Dostoevsky's suspicion of glass transparency (1864) but precedes Zamyatin's (1924) outright fear of it. Accordingly, Scheerbart's pre-First World War glass vision is closer to Chernyshevsky's (1863) imagined socialist utopia sheltering in a Crystal Palace than to Dostoevsky's or Zamyatin's worries. While Scheerbart gave literary expression to the transcendent possibilities of modern spiritualized glass architecture, Taut attempted to give it architectural form, first in his *Glashaus* Pavilion (built for the 1914 Werkbund Exhibition in Cologne), then in his glass Utopia, *Alpine Architecture* (1917), a profusely illustrated book with brilliantly coloured renderings of crystalline Alpine cities.[43]

Despite subsequently designing more convincingly socially engaged buildings, Taut's long-demolished Glass Pavilion remains his most famous work.[44] Some of Scheerbart's slogans venerating glass were applied to each of the fourteen sides of the Pavilion, including: 'Happiness without glass How crass!'; 'Coloured glass Destroys Hatred' and 'Without a glass palace Life becomes a burden'.[45] Because conceived of as facilitating transcendence rather than providing views, there were no direct visual

Figure 12.7 *Glashaus*, Pavilion, Cologne Werkbund, 1914 Exhibition. Glass Stairway. Architect Bruno Taut. *Jahrbuch des Deutschen Werkbundes 1915*, München: Verlegt Bei F. Bruckmann A.-G., 1915 p. 82. (Out of Copyright). Courtesy of the University of Toronto.

links out from the *Glashaus*, nor into it. Any incoming natural light would have been heavily filtered.

The Pavilion concentrates glass' paradoxical material qualities, especially dematerialization of mass, which Taut believed would be inspirational. As a form of structural negation, dematerialization alleviates uneasiness associated with building as vainglorious expressions of worldly materialism, while analogizing self-abnegation. Renouncing one's own corporeality ostensibly establishes a pathway of transformation. In this regard, Taut and Scheerbart recovered an architectural paradox: great material expense is justifiable only if the results guide attention towards something higher.

At first glance, Scheerbart and Taut might appear to have successfully recuperated glass from its dissolution at the Crystal Palace (which apparently inspired them) but the Pavilion was sponsored by German glass industries.[46] By using the language of advertising to promote their crystal-glass Utopia, Taut and Scheerbart highlight the nearly insurmountable difficulties of shifting traditional metaphors to secular commercial contexts. Though Scheerbart's *Glashaus* aphorisms must have been partly whimsical, promoting glass as an available decorative and constructive material more convincingly aligns the Pavilion with industry than with quasi-religious attempts to transcend materialism by using a dematerializing material.[47]

Although more instrumental science fiction than programme for social transformation, Scheerbart and Taut's engagement with traditional glass-crystal associations remains of interest.[48] Despite their laudable aims, German philosopher Ernst Bloch (1885–1970) identified the futility of Scheerbart and Taut's attempt to combine modern glass and iron architecture with traditional sacred associations; so long as the 'hollows of late capitalism' entrap architecture.[49] Technological production of consistent, exquisitely transparent expanses of glass prohibits it from embodying divine light, revelation or humanity's hope for liberation from *corrupting* materiality. Rather, it is most readily associable with publicity and commercial architecture: plate glass shopfronts; self-abnegating mirrored glass corporate headquarters; and product-oriented glass pavilions.

As an almost natural symbol of exposure, surveillance, totalitarianism and Taylorism, liberating glass from identifications with industrialization, technology and rationalized production is as difficult to imagine as redeeming its transcendent potential.

'Fascism is a glass house'[50]

Terragni's Casa del Fascio (House of Fascism; or Casa) in Como, dedicated to transmitting the ideals of Italian Fascism, is a peculiar modern attempt to rejuvenate crystal-glass symbolism. Architectural theorist and historian Joseph Rykwert describes it as 'the only memorable monument to fascism, one which still retains what there was of the universal in its appeal.'[51] Understanding that appeal begins with accepting that its dedication to a demoralizing and brutal regime is *permanent*, despite attempts to depoliticize it as a key monument of modernist architecture.[52] For Tafuri, 'Italian criticism' either 'finds itself in difficulty with … Terragni' or 'desperately attempts to bring his work within the reassuring fold of the Modern Movement'.[53] Although formalist criticism empties the Casa of its 'highly explicit political agenda', its enduring appeal testifies to Terragni's success in 'reconciling two aspects of a new order: art and politics', by grounding his building 'in the new life praxis that he believed fascism provided'.[54]

Mussolini[55] envisioned an all-embracing totalitarian state that by filling the secular void would ameliorate the predicaments of modernity – the alienation of mass society exacerbated by industrialization and capitalism. He portrayed Italian Fascism as a glass house where individual and state fuse.[56] As a loyal regime architect, Terragni endeavoured to concretize the amalgamating aspirations of the state, including its social and political project to eradicate the 'danger of loneliness', 'rootlessness and homelessness' and 'dehumanization' symptomatic of 'mass society' and modernity.[57]

Figure 12.8 Casa del Fascio (1932–36), Como, Italy. Giuseppe Terragni, Architect. Exterior: Entry Façade. [Photo: Nathaniel Coleman, 2004].

The association of literal transparency with totalitarianism may be self-evident but the Casa enjoys its status because it faithfully embodies Fascism's universal appeal – a legitimate claim on an 'authentic … ground of the human condition on earth' (no matter how putrefied).[58]

To make the Casa fit for its ideological purpose, Terragni effectively collapsed phenomenal and literal boundaries. 'The guiding metaphor behind the design, as Terragni explained, was Mussolini's concept that "Fascism is a house of glass into which all can look."'[59] For all its subtleties, exposure and dissolution of privacy dominate; out of loyalty to the mystical glass-symbolism of the regime. Appropriately, its multiplicities manifest Fascism as a largely empty signifier: a screen for adherents' projections. The propagandist function was to shape perceptions of Italian Fascism as genuinely open to citizens. But physical openness was a ruse veiling unfocused darker aims.[60] Literal transparency is cloaked in phenomenal dress, though the latter is usually emphasized.[61]

Transposition of the Casa from Fascist monument to modernist exemplar (or idealized vision of a fictional Fascism) necessitates isolating it from politics but depends on inaccurate readings of Italian Fascism as 'anti-modern'. As a product of modernity (not a negative response to it), Italian Fascism aligns with vanguard aspects of modernism, including strains of anti-Enlightenment, primitivist, anti-rationalist and anti-capitalist sentiments, which contribute – beyond errors of judgement – to Fascism's enduring appeal.[62] Tradition and innovation (antiquity and modernity) are confounded in the recognizably purist Casa, which recollects temples. Like Le Corbusier, Terragni was influenced by Greek and Roman Temples and ancient Roman houses (amongst other Mediterranean sources).

Figure 12.9 Casa del Fascio (1932–36), Como, Italy. Giuseppe Terragni, Architect. Interior: Entry Lobby. [Photo: Nathaniel Coleman, 2004].

Although the many overlapping layers of structure previewed on the exterior continue inside – drawing the eye (and body) inward and upward, through the concrete grid frame – glazing behind does not allow visual access. Only the *idea* of openness is encouraged. Seeing into the building from outside is impossible on all sides, particularly through the eighteen fully glazed entry doors fronting the piazza, supposedly proving institutional transparency by apparently providing open access. However, inside their shadowy recess, the doors appear opaque at most times, exacerbated by differentials between interior and exterior illumination. All of the openings at the Casa are recessed which implicitly pushes interior volumes through the surface. While this controls sunlight and heat gain, it places most glazing in shadow, further prohibiting visual access, whereas views outward are facilitated throughout.

Glass block infill throughout the Casa signs transparency but is not. More than other glazed, or reflective, materials, it has all the characteristics of glass except actual transparency. Although a virtue for Taut, here it confounds access. Contradictory rather than consistent, the Casa is not so much phenomenally transparent as deceptive:[63]

> Fascism was spatially interpreted as a transparent system which invited the people to validate it by giving them access to it, indeed by being part of it; yet … its transparency annihilated any individuality. There was no inside, no private dimension: the system was transparent to the individual as the individual was transparent to the system.[64]

Materials throughout the interior, including marble floors, glass block, glazed tiles, polished metal and transparent window glazing, refer to reflectivity and transparency but are mostly signs of it.

Terragni was not alone in believing Fascism could redeem Italy by returning Italians to their ancient civilizing purpose, which is why the Casa embodies an ingenious synthesis of progress and tradition. As promised by the regime this was portrayed as rebirth and renewal, analogized by the Casa as a crystalline modernist prism recalling ancient Roman atrium houses enlarged to shelter the whole community. But because modern and progressive, this was analogized by glass and reflective surfaces within. Its taut marble skin marks the Casa as simultaneously rationalist and templelike.

> The 'glass house of Fascism' was not only meant to represent the party's qualities but also to embody and visualize the spiritual values associated with the new Fascist civilization and to insert it into a millenary tradition in virtue of its orderly structure, which was meant to correspond to the legacy of classicism.[65]

Terragni ably captured the intriguingly paradoxical dimensions of Fascism's pretentions: simultaneously progressive and conservative, modern and traditional. Embodying supposedly permanent and refreshing Mediterranean values embeds it within a specific ideology of history, while employing modern means and methods of construction associates it with progressive European architectural modernism; tempered by conservative nods towards Italian craft traditions.[66]

Transparent glass, the layered concrete structural frame and walls, and finishes, craft illusions of seamless progression inward from the exterior fronting the Piazza del Popolo, through the bank of glass doors, into the skylit central hall, and therefrom into the building's inner reaches. No matter how apparently literal the transparency, physical and visual access are largely false promises.

Throughout, voids; plate glass windows; glass block; and glass balustrades, amongst other materials and techniques, concoct perceptions of the Casa del Fascio as a *glass house* – as figuratively transparent, though it is solid and defended, even labyrinthic. Polished, reflective and transparent materials in the building do not spiritualize crystal/glass. Rather, the phenomenon of transparency is illusory; a deception concordant with the emptiness of Fascism's third way promise to resolve the crisis of tradition and modernity (typical of populist and totalitarian regimes generally, and a source of their enduring appeal).[67]

The Casa's continued use is pragmatic but does not cleanse its history. Nevertheless, formalist aesthetics oppose memory, as with US architect Peter Eisenman's apology: 'this work deserved to be situated outside the historical context' because it is a 'beautiful, pristine white cube that has a certain aura', locating it 'between classical and something else'.[68] But these estimable qualities are precisely what makes the Casa a lasting emblem of the *eternal return* of Fascist mythologies.

Transparency = Democracy?

Paradoxically, because it ably manifests the confused messages of Fascism, the Casa del Fascio more convincingly expresses the individual, social and political virtues of transparency than most generalized interpretations of it by liberal democracies. Least convincing are fictions of the interchangeability of transparency with freedom; as if shop window displays of choice and consumption were pathways to liberty. British architect Norman Foster's (b. 1935) glass dome (or cupola), topping the restructured Reichstag, Berlin (1993–99), for the reunified German Parliament, is s striking example of such fictions.

Tensions between democratic claims for the Reichstag Dome and its extension of the world interior of capital (a space of consumption to be consumed, and spectacular ornament of the branded city) are unresolvable. Intended to symbolize representative democracy, it is more Crystal Palace than Athens Acropolis, or US Capital. Relatively speaking, Terragni's Casa is figuratively transparent; whereas Foster's Reichstag dome is literally so. The first is partly a critique of capitalism and the crisis of tradition that marks modernity. The second recollects regimes of display established by the Crystal Palace. As a vehicle of spectacle and consumption, and a matter of technique rather than intention, Foster's dome rekindles the anxieties Zamyatin and Dostoevsky had about glass transparency.

The Casa del Fascio and Crystal Palace are compelling evidence for the *transparency trope* as spent, because hopelessly contradictory. Terragni's Casa problematizes the metaphor beyond resolution, especially as a trope for democracy. Literal or phenomenal, glass transparency can represent almost anything *but* freedom or democracy. The relationship of glass transparency with dystopic visions of modernity reveals the falsehood of portraying it as a natural symbol of liberal progressive values.

Built as a symbol of empire in 1897, the original Reichstag glass dome symbolized modernity, not democracy.[69] Set alight in 1933, as a precursor to Hitler's consolidation of power, fire transformed it into a symbol of Germany and Europe's slip into darkness. After the Second World War, despite attempts to recuperate the building as a symbol of West Germany's democratic rebirth, it remained largely unused until reunification with East Germany in October 1990. In 1995, artists Christo and Jeanne-Claude wrapped the building with fabric; a prefigurative act of unification notable for its relative opacity. A perhaps necessary 'papering over' of the past, making way for architectural and national renewal.

Although Foster's dome depends almost entirely on literal transparency to symbolize democracy, the workings of the Parliament remain mostly hidden.[70] No matter, since the 'mythical association of transparency with democracy' dominates, making the dome the nexus of internal contradictions throughout the restructured Reichstag[71]: 'tourists are attracted to the roof deck [and dome] but not the plenary chamber; they are interested in the vistas from above [across the centre of Berlin] but not the workings of German democracy'.[72]

The chilly atmosphere of the building and lack of physical – or visual – access to the workings of governance must encourage apathy. Because it is neither transparent nor 'transparent to views into the parliament', even if the dome symbolizes 'the building … as a civic presence, … it is hard to argue, as Foster and others do, that it symbolizes transparent government'.[73] While 'limited views' are provided from the cupola floor 'down through reflective glass into the … Bundestag (parliamentary chamber)' below, most visitors choose 'the ramps that spiral around the shell of the cupola, offering views out over the city'; preferring to 'look out rather than in upon each other, much less down' into 'the Bundestag'.[74]

Two ramps ascend the dome's perimeter in opposite directions. They may facilitate touristic panoramas but the crystalline optimism verges on the ironic. The fiction portrays transparency as quieting residual fears of an unresolved past that threatens always to bubble up from historical depths; and as allaying lingering doubts fed by the contradictions of capitalism, including its transformation of politics into management, and citizens into consumers.

The 'technologically generated imagery' of Foster's architecture may be rooted in the 'innovative engineering' of the nineteenth century, especially 'Joseph Paxton's Crystal Palace' but the Reichstag dome is no 'powerful reprise of Taut's proposed city crown' (which his 'glashaus' partially realized). Foster's dome is absent of both an explicit industrial programme and implicit transcendental one.[75] Although financed by industry, Taut's *Glashaus* was visionary (prefiguring a universal socialist Utopia); Foster's dome is prosaic and commercial.

If the glass house myth of Fascism Terragni articulated at the Casa del Fascio taints phenomenal glass transparency with spectres of totalitarianism; conflation of literal glass transparency with progressive modernity always recalls the Crystal Palace. Nevertheless, display window transparency, mythologized as a natural symbol of democracy, accurately expresses modern states as primarily *consumption machines* that transform citizens into shoppers. From the 1950s onward, transparency myths have fused economic progress with democracy, and then to capitalism as the guarantor of freedom, which makes display and consumption the proper habitus of the world interior of capital.

Best known for high-spec commercial buildings, and some equally well-serviced institutional ones, Foster's work is summarized as 'British' exemplars 'of technocratic prowess in a globalized culture', notable for 'clarity, computer-age craftsmanship, and industrial perfection'.[76] Accordingly, the renovated Reichstag – including the dome – recollects corporate offices, high-end hotels or luxury department stores, less so than democratic ideals: a precise emblem of global capitalism. As a techno-scientific idealization of consumer culture, it ends up highlighting governance as managing the economy. Despite the taint bureaucratic rationality carries after two world wars, Foster's dome is unabashedly technocratic, an assertion of naïvely instrumentalist beliefs in stated intentions, as if that were enough to banish doubts.

By transforming glass ideology into myth, the Reichstag dome attempts to resolve 'formally a fundamental contradiction'.[77] Glass ideology portrays itself as confirming institutional transparency at a functional level; as supposedly verifying the democratic (or some other) ideal as operative. In most instances, glass is represented as a natural

Figure 12.10 Reichstag Dome (1993–99), Berlin, Germany. Foster + Partners, Architects. [Photo: Nathaniel Coleman, 2003].

symbol, as if its own self-display is all that is required to confirm transparency myths. But its nefarious associations introduce too many contradictions to ignore. By supposedly resolving the mystical and transcendent aspects of crystal glass by identifying liberty, freedom and democracy with literal transparency – in a quasi-religious manner – ideology transforms glass into an essentialist association of its material property of transparency with virtuous conditions that only process and action (use) could actually confirm.

Other stories

Peter Zumthor's Kunsthaus Bregenz (Contemporary Art Museum), Austria (1990–97) articulates possible alternatives to uncritical shorthand use of glass. At the Kunsthaus the use of glass is as paradoxical as it is shocking: the literal transparency that dominates building construction is almost completely denied. There are no great views into or out from the building. Conventional emphasis on only one side of glass' paradoxical nature is reversed. If glass' non-material, or anti-material, character – its 'there not there' quality – is usually disregarded in favour of clarity, transparency and reflectivity, the exact opposite prevails at the Kunsthaus. Substantiality is emphasized; revealing glass' typical self-abnegation as undermining the solidity and concreteness of building materiality (whatever they are made out of).

As liquid in suspension, glass invites denying its material presence. But in most instances, this is simply lazy, innocent of any meditation on its central problem: its self-denying conundrum of being absent and present simultaneously. Examples include bulletproof glass, birds flying into glazed building facades, and mirrored reflection. However, when birds fall dead to the ground, after crashing into walls of reflected sky taken for the real thing, glass' solid nature is reasserted: it is as unforgiving as any stone wall.[78]

Zumthor's recuperation of the suspended liquidity of glass' goes some way in recollecting the mystery it derives from a shared genus with crystal. His simultaneous re-liquefication of it is not literal but challenges unexamined transparency. Inside, the building is like being underwater, perhaps submerged in Lake Constance, a few hundred metres away. When churned up, sand in water, out of which glass is formulated, obscures vision. A cloudlike condition predominates the glass use at the Kunsthaus: it is obscuring and suggestive, rather than transparent or explicit. Perhaps suggestive of the experience of being within Taut's Glashaus.

The otherworldly, undersea-like, atmosphere of the Kunsthaus is achieved with interior walls of either concrete or obscured glass (or glass block in the basement), the beach-like character of the polished concrete floors, and the elaborate built-up ceiling membrane of etched glass that filters indirect light (and air) from the exterior (introduces hints of the lakeside atmosphere). The materials, assemblies and colours produce the evocative interior atmosphere. The glazed ceiling membrane is a surrogate for the sky, or the water's surface from below. Zumthor's reclamation of glass's materiality and its immaterial mystery simultaneously discloses the banality of using glass as literal transparency. Appearing to follow Loos, Zumthor engages glass usage through precise understandings of 'its own' unique 'vocabulary of forms' that 'develop out of the way' it 'is produced and the ways ... it can be worked', developed 'with and out of the material' itself.[79]

On the exterior, glass is cladding rather than curtain wall. The bidirectionality of the effect produced is unique. Inside the building, the exterior cladding introduces a soft filtered light, so that whatever possible reading of it as decorative, in a negative sense of applique, is quieted by its emotionally functional necessity (for producing the desired atmosphere of the galleries and other spaces). Externally, the scale-like waves of architectural glass are true to its industrial production in sheets.

The wall-defining solidity of the exterior glass panels dramatically transforms the streets and spaces beside the Kunsthaus into outdoor rooms. The function of the glass panels as cladding is unmistakable; gaps between each sheet make it impossible to confuse them with the intricate supporting steel structure they mostly conceal. As with the exterior, internally, the armature can be glanced through gaps between the individual glass ceiling panels. In both instances, the dressing conceals a somewhat messy assembly.[80]

Although glass is generally smooth and usually deployed to produce a smooth membrane, at the Kunsthaus, it is *imperfectly* installed to create the scale-like faceted effect of the facade, enhanced by its translucency. The open joints between the glass panels throughout the building explicitly counter the technicity of typical glass construction as hermetically sealed membrane. The relative rawness counters the uniformly flat or smooth surfaces of conventional (paradoxically) airless sealed glass buildings. In conception and in its internal climatic conditions, air and light are filtered through the Kunsthaus facade, keeping the largely windowless interior fresh.

The open joints gesture towards mysteries out of reach (structure in this instance); thereby keeping enough in reserve to introduce a degree of satisfying tension to the building. Its full complexity as a *light machine* is hinted at but never fully revealed, because largely concealed behind the faceted facade panels externally, and the internal concrete gallery walls, and dropped glazed ceiling panels internally. Glass – transparent or otherwise – is disclosed as hiding at least as much as it discloses (exactly the opposite of the Crystal Palace).

As introduced earlier, Zumthor uses glass as space defining and atmosphere producing at the Kunsthaus, akin to the capacities Semper attributed to hanging carpets and rugs.[81] Although all four of the building's cladded facades are nearly identical (save for the clear glass doors and windows of the demarcated main entrance portal on one, and a service, or security entrance, on another), each adorns Bregenz by contributing to the overall civicness of the exterior spaces the Kunsthaus fronts. An ancillary building, distinctly different in character, houses administrative offices on the first floor, with a café at ground level spilling out onto an urban square defined by the two buildings. Together, they gesture outward towards Lake Constance and a number of historic squares nearby, which the ensemble completes. Whereas glass is anything but transparent (literally or figuratively) at the Kunsthaus, the much more explicitly solid structural concrete administrative building is permeable, largely opened to its surroundings on two sides, by large operable wall like windows.

If the Crystal Palace was the first unit of the world interior of capital – sharing its form, materials and controlled internal environment with nineteenth-century hothouses – Zumthor's Kunsthaus challenges its dominance. As a building in-between implicitly and explicitly open to the elements – air, spray off the lake, the smell of earth and the borrowed light of the sun – the structure contrasts with typical air-conditioned glass and steel buildings. Although largely opaque, the building's atmospheric openness – and limited translucence and transparency – makes it far less anti-urban than most literally transparent modern glass buildings. Unlike those buildings, its permeability is climatic above all else.

By working against the material's most obvious associations, Zumthor has partially recuperated the mysteries of glass at the Kunsthaus, without fully obscuring its most desirable quality: a play with light that has little to do with transparency or view. In this, Zumthor reveals light as his primary material, rather than any specific ideological claim for glass, or its transparency. Here, the primary task of glass is disclosed as the manipulation of light as a material substance, no matter its ephemerality: glass and the light it reshapes are not metaphor but presence.

Notes

1. Frank Lloyd Wright, 'In the Cause of Architecture: VI The Meaning of Materials – Glass', *The Architectural Record*, July 1928, pp. 11–16 (p. 11). Available at: https://www.architectural record.com/ext/resources/news/2016/01-Jan/InTheCause/Cause-PDFs/In-the-Cause-of-Architecture-1928-07.pdf (Accessed 28 June 2018).

2. Rosemarie Haag Bletter, 'The Interpretation of the Glass Dream – Expressionist Architecture and the History of the Glass Metaphor', *Journal of the Society of Architectural Historians*, 40, no. 1 (March 1981): 20–43.

3. J. C. Cooper, *An Illustrated Encyclopedia of Traditional Symbols*, New York: Thames and Hudson, 1978, p. 48.

4. Wright, 'In the Cause of Architecture: VI The Meaning of Materials – Glass', July 1928, p. 11.

5. On glass and iron, as industrialized building materials, see: Walter Benjamin, 'Paris Capital of the Nineteenth Century', and 'Karl Kraus', in *Reflections*, Edmund Jephcott (trans.), New York: Schocken Books, 1978, pp. 146–62, 239–73; Nikolaus Pevsner, *Pioneers of Modern Design from William Morris to Walter Gropius*, London: Penguin Books, 1975; Giedion, *Space, Time and Architecture, The Growth of a New Tradition* pp. 163–290; Frampton, *Modern Architecture*, pp. 29–40.

6. Louis Barragan, quoted in Emelio Ambasz, *The Architecture of Louis Barragan*, New York: Museum of Modern Art, 1976, p. 8.

7. For technical discussions of glass, see: Garham Dodd, 'Part 9 Glass', in *Construction Materials: Their Nature and Behaviour*, pp. 507–26; G. D. Taylor, '5 Glass in Construction', *Materials in Construction: An Introduction*, Harlow, England: Longman, 2000, pp. 163–73; and Hegger, Drexeler and Zeumer, 'Glass', in *Basics Materials*, pp. 62–5.

8. Janine Chasseguet-Smirgel, 'The Theme of Transparency', in *Sexuality and Mind, The Role of the Father and the Mother in Psyche*, New York: New York University Press, 1986, pp. 99–104.

9. Christopher Hall, *Materials: A Very Short Introduction*, Oxford: Oxford University Press, 2014, p. 75. Pedro Guedes (ed.), *Encyclopedia of Architectural Technology*, New York: McGraw-Hill, 1979, p. 283. For more on glass as industrial material and exposure, see Pierre Missac, 'Glass Architecture', in *Walter Benjamin's Passages*, Shierry Weber Nicholsen (trans.), Cambridge, MA: MIT Press, 1995, pp. 147–72.

10. Otto von Simpson, *The Gothic Cathedral*, Princeton: Princeton University Press, 1962, pp. 3–58. See also, Erwin Panofsky, *Gothic Architecture and Scholasticism*, New York: Meridian, 1985.

11. Ibid., p. 37.

12. Attributed to St. John Divine, 'Revelation 21–22', *New American Bible*. Available Online at: http://www.vatican.va/archive/ENG0839/_P134.HTM (Accessed 26 June 2018).

13. Abbot Suger, *On the Abbey Church of St.-Denis and Its Art Treasures*, Erwin Panofsky (ed., trans.), Second Edition, Gerda Panofsky-Soergel, New Jersey: Princeton University Press, 1979, pp. 47, 49.

14. Ibid., p. 63.

15. von Simpson, *The Gothic Cathedral*, p. 51.

16. Suger, *On the Abbey Church of St.-Denis and Its Art Treasures*, pp. 63, 65.

17. Le Corbusier, quoted, Cultural Hertiage Ministry, Netherlands webpage on UNESCO World Heritage status of the Van Nelle factory, Rotterdam (Van Nellefabriek). Available Online at: http://culturalheritageagency.nl/en/news/van-nellefabriek-in-rotterdam-is-unesco-world-heritage-site (Accessed 13 March 2016).

18. Frampton, *Modern Architecture*, pp. 134–5.

19. Graham Livesey, 'The Van der Leeuw House: Theosophical Connections with Early Modern Architecture', *Architronic*, 7, no. 2 (1998): 3. Available Online at: http://corbu2.caed.kent.edu/architronic/v8n1/v8n105.pdf (Accessed 13 March 2016).

20. See: Kenneth Frampton, *Modern Architecture, 1851–1945*, New York: Rizzoli, 1981, pp. 1–13; Roger Dixon and Stefan Muthesius, *Victorian Architecture*, London: Thames and Hudson, 1978, pp. 94–8; and Middleton and Watkin, *Neoclassical and 19th Century Architecture*, pp. 368–74, 378.

21. John Fleming, Hugh Honour and Nikolaus Pevsner, *Penguin Dictionary of Architecture*, Fourth Edition, London: Penguin, 1991, p. 17; Frampton, *Modern Architecture*, p. 34.

22. R. B. White, *Prefabrication: A History of Its Development in Great Britain*, National Building Studies, Special Report 36, London: Her Majesty's Printing Office, 1965, p. 17.

23. Frampton, *Modern Architecture*, p. 34.

24. Peter Sloterdijk, *In the World Interior of Capital* (2005), Wieland Hoban (trans.), Cambridge: Polity, 2013, pp. 169–70.

25. Frampton, *Modern Architecture, 1851–1945*, pp. 10–13; Fleming, Honour and Pevsner, *Penguin Dictionary of Architecture*, p. 327.

26. Sloterdijk, *In the World Interior of Capital*, p. 12.

27. Fyodor Dostoevsky, *Complete Works, Volume V*, Leningrad: Nauka, 1972–90, pp. 69–70, reprinted in W. J. Leatherbarrow, 'Introduction: Dostoevskii and Britain', in *Dostoevskii and Britain*, W. J. Leatherbarrow (ed.), Oxford and Providence: Berg, 1995, p. 8.

28. Nikolai Chernyshevsky, *What is to Be Done?*, Benjamin R. Tucker and Cathy Porter (trans.), London: Virago, 1982, p. 319.

29. Ibid.

30. Leatherbarrow, 'Introduction . . ', p. 8.

31. Ibid.; Sloterdijk, *In the World Interior of Capital*, p. 12.

32. Maynard Mack, 'Introduction', Fyodor Dostoevsky, 'Notes from the Underground' (1864), in Constance Garnett (trans.), Maynard Mack (general ed.), *The Norton Anthology of World Masterpieces*, New York: W. W. Norton & Co., 1987, p. 1850. David Denby, 'Can Dostoevsky Still Kick You in the Gut?' *New Yorker Magazine*, 11 June 2012. Available online at: http://www.newyorker.com/books/page-turner/can-dostoevsky-still-kick-you-in-the-gut (Accessed 21 March 2016).

33. See: Marshall Berman, 'The 1860s: The New Man in the Street', in *All That Is Solid Melts Into Air*, New York: Penguin Books, [1982] 1988, pp. 212–48. See also, Sloterdijk, *In the World Interior of Capital*. Dostoevsky, 'Notes from the Underground' (1864), p. 1874.

34. Yevgeny Zamyatin, *We* (1924), Mirra Ginsburg (trans.), New York: Avon Books, 1972. For the relationship between *We*, Aldous Huxley's *Brave New World* (1932), and George Orwell's 1984 (1949), see Berman, *All That Is Solid . . .* , 1988, n. 45, pp. 364–5. See also: Editors of Encyclopaedia Britannica, 'Zamyatin, Yevgeny Ivanovich', *Encyclopedia Britannica Online*. Available at: http://www.britannica.com/biography/Yevgeny-Ivanovich-Zamyatin (Accessed 22 March 2016).

35. 'Zamyatin, Yevgeny Ivanovich', *Encyclopedia Britannica Online*. For Dostoevsky influence on the 20th, see Gary Saul Morson, 'Fyodor Dostoyevsky Russian Author', *Encyclopedia Britannica Online*. Available online at: http://www.britannica.com/biography/Fyod or-Dostoyevsky (Accessed 9 April 2016). Zamyatin's motto (quoted): 'There is no final revolution. Revolutions are infinite', Mirra Ginsburg, 'Introduction,' *We*, New York: Avon Books, 1972, p. v.

36. Zamyatin, *We*, p. 23.

37. Dostoevsky, 'Notes from the Underground' (1864), p. 1868; Zamyatin, *We*, p. 66.

38. Walter Benjamin, 'Surrealism', *Reflections*, Peter Demetz (trans.), New York: Shocken, 1978, p. 180. On Benjamin's reflections on glass architecture, particularly Scheerbart, see: Detlef Mertins, 'The Enticing and Threatening Face of Prehistory: Walter Benjamin and the Utopia of Glass', *Assemblage*, no. 29 (1996): 6–23.

39. Berman, 'The 1860s', p. 247.

40. Ibid., pp. 246, 248.

41. On Scheerbart and Taut, see: Ufuk Ersoy, 'To See Daydreams: The Glass Utopia of Paul Sheerbart and Bruno Taut', in *Imagining and Making the World: Reconsidering Architecture and Utopia*, Nathaniel Coleman (ed.), Oxford and Bern: Peter Lang, 2011, pp. 107–37; Ersoy, 'Glass as Light as Air, As Deep as Water', in *The Material Imagination: Reveries on Architecture and Matter*, Matthew Mindrup (ed.), Surrey, England: Ashgate, 2015, pp. 155–67; and, Ersoy, 'The Fictive Quality of Glass', *ARQ*, 11, no. 3/4 (2007): 237–43.

42. Paul Scheerbart, *Glass Architecture*, James Palmes (trans.), in Paul Scheerbart and Bruno Taut, *Glass Architecture and Alpine Architecture*, Dennis Sharp (ed.), New York: Praeger Publishers, 1972, p. 41.

43. Bruno Taut, *Alpine Architecture* (1917), Shirley Palmer (trans.), in *Glass Architecture and Alpine Architecture*, pp. 75–127.

44. Ulrike Altenmüller-Lewis and Mark L. Brack, 'Afterword: *The City Crown* in the context of Bruno Taut's Ouevre', in *The City Crown by Bruno Taut*, Matthew Mindrup and Ulrike Altenmüller-Lewis (eds), Surrey, England: Ashgate, 2015, p. 162.

45. Paul Scheerbart's glass couplets for Bruno Taut's Glass Pavilion (1914) reprinted in, Scheerbart and Taut, *Glass Architecture and Alpine Architecture*, p. 14.

46. On Taut's Glass Pavilion and Scheerbart's *Glass Architecture* see, Frampton, *Modern Architecture, 1851–1945*, p. 188; Frampton, *Modern Architecture*, pp. 116–22; William J. R. Curtis, *Modern Architecture Since 1900, Third Edition*, London: Phaidon, 1996, pp. 106, 183–4; and Rosemarie Haag Bletter, 'Paul Scheerbart's Architectural Fantasies', *Journal of the Society of Architectural Historians*, 34, no. 2 (May 1971): 83–97.

47. Scheerbart's glass couplets for Bruno Taut's Glass Pavilion, *Glass Architecture* (1914), p. 14.

48. Scheerbart, *Glass Architecture* (1914), James Palmes (trans.), and Bruno Taut, *Alpine Architecture* (1919), Shirley Palmer (trans.), 1972, pp. 41–127. Dennis Sharp, 'Introduction', in Scheerbart and Taut, *Glass Architecture and Alpine Architecture*, pp. 8–29. Taut, 'A Programme for Architecture' (1918), Michael Bullock (trans.), in Ulrich Conrads (ed.), *Programs and Manifestoes on 20th-Century Architecture*, Cambridge, MA: MIT Press, 1970, pp. 41–3.

49. Ernst Bloch, *The Principle of Hope,* Volume 2 (1959), Neville Plaice, Stephen Plaice, and Poaul Night (trans.), Cambridge, MA: MIT Press, 1986, p. 737.

50. Metaphor widely attributed to Mussolini, including by, Emelio Gentile, *The Sacralization of Politics in Fascist Italy*, Keith Botsford (trans.), Cambridge, MA: Harvard University Press, 1996, p. 125. For more on Terragni's Casa del Fascio see: Curtis, *Modern Architecture Since 1900*, pp. 364–7; Frampton *Modern Architecture, 1851–1945*, pp. 384–5; Frampton, *Modern Architecture*, pp. 203–9, Richard A. Etlin, *Modernism in Italian Architecture, 1890–1940*, Cambridge, MA: MIT, 1991, pp. 439–80.

51. Joseph Rykwert, 'The Modern Movement in Italian Architecture' (1955), *The Necessity of Artifice*, New York: Rizzoli, 1982, p. 19.

52. Westin: 'the defining achievement of Italian Rationalism', Richard Weston, *Plans, Sections and Elevations: Key Buildings of the Twentieth Century*, London : Laurence King, 2004, p. 74; Frampton: 'the canonical work of the Italian Rationalist movement', Frampton, *Modern Architecture*, p. 205; and Zevi: a 'milestone of European modern architecture', Bruno Zevi, *Giuseppe Terragni*, Balogna: Zanchelli, p. 70 (translation by author).

53. Manfredo Tafuri, 'Giuseppe Terragni: Subject and "Mask"', Diane Ghirardo (trans.), *Oppositions*, 11 (1977): 1–25 (p. 3).

54. Ghirardo, 'Italian Architects and Fascist Politics: An Evaluation of the Rationalist's Role in Regime Building', *Journal of the Society of Architectural Historians*, 39, no. 2 (May 1980): 109–27 (p. 127); Ghirardo, 'Terragni, Conventions, and the Critics', in *Critical Architecture and Cotnemporary Culture*, William J. Lillyman, Marilyn F. Moriarty and David J. Neuman (eds), New York and Oxford: Oxford University Press, 1994, p. 100; Giuseppe Terragni, 'L Contruzione della Casa del Fascio di Como' ['The Construction of the Casa del Fascio in Como'], *Quadrante* 35/36, no. 8 (1936): 6, reprinted in Ghirardo, 'Terragni, Conventions, and the Critics', pp. 97, 100.

55. For the paradoxes of Italian Fascism, see: Ronald S. Cunsolo, *Italian Nationalism: From Its Origins to World War II*, Malabar, Florida: Robert Krieger, 1990; Roger Eatwell, *Fascism: A History*, London: Penguin Books, 1995; and Alexander Stile, *Benevolence to Betrayal*, New York: Summit Books, 1991.

56. For 'Fascist Religion', see: Gentile, *The Sacralization of Politics in Fascist Italy*; Mark Antliff, 'Fascism, Modernism, and Modernity', *The Art Bulletin*, 84, no. 1 (March 2002): 148–69.

57. Hanna Arendt, 'On the Nature of Totalitarianism: An Essay in Understanding', in *Essays in Understanding, 1930–1954*, Jerome Kohn (ed.), New York: Shocken Books, 1994, p. 360.

58. Terragni, 'La Costruzione Della Casa del Fascio Di Como', pp. 5–27, Debra Dolinski (trans.), reprinted in Thomas L. Schumacher, *Giuseppe Terragni: Surface and Symbol*, New York: Princeton Architectural Press, 1991, pp. 157, 159. Ibid., Arendt, 'On the Nature of Totalitarianism', p. 338.

59. Etlin, *Modernism in Italian Architecture, 1890–1940*, p. 439.

60. Terragni, 'The Construction of the Casa del Fascio in Como', p. 143.

61. Frampton on the Casa del Fascio's 'metaphysical spatial effect': *Modern Architecture*, p. 205–6; on its, 'literal and phenomenal mirror effects': *Modern Architecture 1851–1945*, p. 385. See: Schumacher, *Giuseppe Terragni*, pp. 139–70.

62. See: Antliff, 'Fascism, Modernism and Modernity'; Charles Burdett, 'Italian Fascism and Utopia', *History of the Human Sciences*, 16, no. 1 (2003): 93–108; Emilio Gentile, 'Fascism, Totalitarianiusm and Political Religion: Definitions and Critical Reflections on Criticism of an Interpretation', *Politics, Religion & Ideology*, 5, no. 3 (2004): 326–75; Jeffrey T. Schnapp, 'The People's Glass House', *South Central Review*, 25, no. 3 (2008): 45–56; Imona Storchi, '"Il Fascismo É Una Casa di Vetro": Giuseppe Terragni and the Politics of Space in Fascist Italy', *Italian Studies*, 62, no. 2 (2007): 231–45. See: Rykwert, 'The Modern Movement in Italian Architecture' (1955), p. 19.

63. Imona Storchi, '"Il Fascismo É Una Casa di Vetro"', p. 233.

64. Ibid., p. 241.

65. Ibid., p. 245.

66. Antliff, 'Fascism, Modernism and Modernity', p. 152.

67. Hanna Arendt, *The Portable Hanna Arendt*, Peter Baehr (ed.), New York and London: Penguin Books, 2000.

68. Peter Eisenman quoted, Hugo Lingren, 'Architecture: A Little Fascist Architecture Goes a Long Way', *The New York Times*, 12 October 2003.

69. Kathleen James-Chakraborty, *German Architecture for a Mass Audience*, London and New York: Routledge, 2000, p. 176.

70. See: Deborah Ascher Barnstone, *The Transparent State: Architecture and Politics in Postwar Germany*, London and New York: Routledge, 2005, pp. 175–208; James-Chakraborty, *German Architecture*, pp. 120–6; Michael J. Wise, *Capital Dilemma: Germany's Search for a New Architecture of Democracy*, New York: Princeton Architectural Press, 1998, pp. 121–34. For an official perspective on Foster's renovations, see Norman Foster, *Rebuilding the Reichstag*, Overlook Press: Woodstock, New York, 2000.

71. Barnstone, *The Transparent State*, p. 175.

72. Ibid., p. 207.

73. Ibid., pp. 205–6.

74. James-Chakraborty, *German Architecture*, p. 124.

75. Ibid., p. 124.

76. Wise, *Capital Dilemma*, pp. 133–4.

77. See: Louis Marin, 'Utopic Degeneration: Disneyland', in *Utopics: The Semioological Play of Textual Spaces*, R. A. Vollrath (trans.), Amherst, New York: Humanity Books, 1984, pp. 239–59.

78. Lisa W. Foderaro, 'A City of Glass Towers, and a Hazard for Migratory Birds', *The New York Times*, 14 September 2011.

79. Adolf Loos, 'The Principal of Cladding' (1898), in Adolf Loos, *On Architecture*, Michael Mitchell (trans.), Riverside, CA: Ariadne Press, 1995, pp. 42–3.

80. Ibid., p. 44.

81. Semper, 'The Four Elements of Architecture' (1851), p. 104.

CHAPTER 13
FORMS OF A CONCLUSION

As introduced in an earlier chapter, first century BC Roman architect and theorist Vitruvius believed the acquisition and control of fire fostered social assemblies that led to the invention of language, beginning with pointing out things of interest, therefrom to inventing shared names for them – initially as a matter of convenience then habit. Naming things in community makes them comprehensible by way of agreement. According to Vitruvius's schema, communication precedes architecture; coming together around the warmth and security of domesticated flame was a precondition of community and dwelling houses. In his conception, the arbitrary relation of signifier to signified was secondary to facilitating social interaction. Naming things was a matter of agreement necessary for communication enabling group survival, including conserving the hospitable flame. Use established a common language forming a precondition for building, which improved incrementally as desire became speakable and reality describable.[1]

Beginning with gestures, social communication prepared the ground for (non-theoretical) sheltering and then (more considered) architecture, as collective activities.[2] In much the way letters form words, words sentences and assemblages of sentences carry significance, (dependent on shared understanding), meaning in architecture hinges on intelligible elements. As used here, 'elements' refer to the individual architectural components out of which buildings are assembled – including columns, walls, stairs and so on, as well as materials. Within a culture, the 'connotative' and 'denotative' meanings of architectural elements become intelligible through long use and association.[3] Shared understanding developing out of relatively arbitrary initial associations transforms architectural materials and forms into felt meaning.

As the first point of contact between individuals and buildings, materials and assemblages of architectural elements are the most direct expression of architectural significance – matters of physical experience more than of sight. Initial structural elements become meaningful through use but associations with other elements augment their meaning. Nascent in this are alternatives to the banality of repetitive construction, suggesting how considerate assemblies of parts and materials could counteract dullness but only if meaning is conceptualized as a matter of relation, rather than of essence.

Shaping reality

The poetic immediacy of material assemblies is comprehensible through embodied experience – something dissociated theoretical texts struggle to account for by disavowing use, material and bodies. As physical presence, dematerializing architecture – even conceptually – is a form of escape. Despite the intellectual allure of pure theory and paper architecture, an architecture of words deemphasizes building, achieving little more than repressing the painful compromises of construction. Although buildings are determined by forces largely beyond architects' control, realization and utilization challenge and extend intention: use is the drama that gives architecture its purpose, which embodied experience renders intelligible. Because use is the source of meaning in building, words can create problems for architecture but dislocating it from language's worldmaking capacities risks severing it from stories that could make it sensible – notwithstanding the apparent compensations of theory mythologized as autonomous.

Disheartened by the brutal compromises of construction, some architects are compelled to decouple architecture from building. In this regard, it is possible to chart the ascendency of visionary representations following Piranesi (post-1750) as compensation for the continuing decline of architects' authority and architecture's social function. Similarly, the ascendency of the neo-avant-garde in architecture during the 1960s and 1970s encompassed a so-called 'theory explosion' of texts and images imagined as ameliorating the painful failures of orthodox modernist architecture; symptomatic of its all but total post-Second World War capture by the building industry.[4] In response, academic architects either rejected building as impossibly compromised, or saw it as an unfortunate necessity for developing professional credibility. American architect Lebbeus Woods (1940–2012) rejected building almost completely; Austrian architect Raimund Abraham (1933–2010) built very little; and American architect Peter Eisenman (b. 1932) has confessed to pursuing building out of *necessity*.

> I'm not interested in … people who spend their time worrying about the details or the grain of wood … or the color of material on the surface, etc. I could care less. That having been said, it is still necessary to build … Manfredo Tafuri once said …, 'Peter, if you don't build no one will take your ideas seriously. You have to build because ideas that are not built are simply ideas that are not built.' … Tafuri said history will not be interested in your work if you haven't built anything.[5]

Following Eisenman's logic, and architects pursuing autonomy more generally, projects are freed from results.[6] Instead, texts and drawings as theoretical stories of self-justification are pressed into the service of unbuilt projects as ends in themselves. Such divisions impoverish the physicality of buildings, because bodily experience is disavowed. But the link between language and architecture (in relation to experience) is less casual than fictions of autonomous theory suggest. Architecture *must* escape language and reality but would do well to get closer to both. Although buildings either do, or do not, satisfy emotional function and unexpected and improvised occupation may, or may not, renew them through time, they are continuously inflected by shadows of their architect's material intentions.

Individual self-understanding is informed by linguistically mediated conceptions of the world because language registers and shapes perceptions of reality that architecture structures. Architecture's task is to provide for the variety and vicissitudes of life. Language shapes conceptions of this vocation through descriptions of how buildings ought to shape reality – cognizant of successes and failures. Although meaning is a matter of bodily experience, significance is inextricable from language, which records and communicates encounters with the material assemblies constituting architecture. In their mutual shaping of reality – as conception and frame – architecture and language cohabitate in the mind as memories of the world and its making. Their interdependent correspondence makes it all but impossible to conceive one in isolation from the other. The authoritative status of language in shaping reality derives from its capacity for explaining experience through the communication of inner sates, and for its influence on recollected and subsequent experiences. The work of American linguist Benjamin Lee Whorf (1897–1941) supports developing this topic in an architectural context. As an example, Whorf's conception of language, thought and reality influenced Dutch architect Aldo van Eyck's (1918–1999) 'Steps Toward a Configurative Discipline', put into practice in his architecture.[7]

Language reality architecture

A pre-verbal architecture is, as Vitruvius suggests, a near impossibility, as much because linguistic communication facilitates collective work, as because language provides access to the vital desires around which buildings are shaped. Before it can be pronounced, mental images mediate desire, though language presents it most precisely by giving thought structure. Words provide access to the unconscious, to longings, more directly than images can. Sentences impose an order on words. Reflections constitute cosmologies generally held in common by speakers of a shared language – as intelligible representations of the apparent order of things constituting reality. Shared language and cultural experiences outflowing from it ensures that representations of reality can be communicated amongst group members with a fair degree of mutual understanding.

Constellations of conceptual differences between England and the United States, for example, begin with language, confirming Whorf's conception of the interrelationship between language, thought (mind) and reality.[8] Cultural context changes language and with it mind, such that even speakers within a particular linguistic sphere may struggle to understand each other if the reality it shapes is not mutual. While this might suggest the relativist cacophony of Babel, Whorf, followed by van Eyck, was convinced that sensitivities cultivated by encounters with multiple language realities contribute to fuller understandings of the world (as speakers of multiple languages can attest).

Within a specific group, sharing a language may provide the most direct route between internal and external reality but it is precisely the looser fit between architectural forms and comprehended significance that makes it possible for building meaning (as with art generally) to remain comprehensible across long arcs of time and space. The strangeness of Ruskin's language compared to the durable legibility of the architecture he loved is evidence of this. Both speak from their respective moments to the present but Ruskin's struggle to communicate with the present is more pronounced than for the architecture he wrote about. Nevertheless, longing verbalized suggests how it might be assuaged. Language shapes desire – how it is communicated but also its contents. Without shared language, desire would remain unspoken, thus unfulfillable. Mindfully assembling the constituent components of architecture, including materials, mimics dramas of cultivating individuality in a communal context.[9] The social production of language, its relativity and reality (of individual self-identity and common understanding) reinforces the case against essential content – of ideas and materials. Material meaning shares with reality the condition of being constructed. Understandings of both begin with articulations of desire, while bodily experiences of them are mediated by language.

Although meaning can be felt, the capacity to share its significance depends on language. Verbalization exteriorizes internal reality of felt meaning by giving it a communicable structure. The prefigurative mental images of designs, preceding exteriorizations of them as drawings (or other representations), are initially rendered through language before subsequent visualization. Architectural drawing is a form of translation – as architectural historian and theorist Joseph Rykwert observes:

> The passage from the mental conception to the built form involves a double translation therefore: first from the architect's mind to the graphic presentation initially his own – and secondly, from the drawing to the building, through the collaboration of those craftsmen who, like Alberti's carpenter, would act as his 'hands'.[10]

No matter how pictorial the 'mental conception' of a design might be, structuring the desire of authorial intentions requires language to render it knowable. While the architect can draw what he or she wants to do, prior to representation, only language makes desire comprehensible, in common and to the self.

When making architecture adopts the rules of language literally, its own modes of signification are excluded. Mental images and described intentions are isolated from the material reality of building, which breaks down bodily experience as the source of architectural meaning. Revealing how disconnected this is, Eisenman professes to having no interest in 'details or the grain of wood ... or the color of material on the surface'.[11] Moreover, he rejects 'the experience of the subject in architecture, the experience of materiality, of light, of colour, of space and so on'.[12] Rejection of these things – especially banishing the correlation between bodies, experience and signification – so schematizes architecture as to empty it of almost everything. While language is used to communicate the record of some thought, the result is split off from reality as a more than less shared event. Exiling the subject from architecture inevitably empties it of communicable significance. But the claim must also be read against Eisenman's perceived reputational requirement to build.

All buildings surely presume the presence of bodies, even if against the wishes of some architects. The irreconcilability of the competing aims asserted by Eisenman confound understanding because split off from shared conceptions of the reality of architecture in relation to building and experience. His claim that preoccupation with bodily experience characterizes 'architecture as a phenomenological enterprise' antithetical to 'architecture as a conceptual, cultural and intellectual enterprise' is ultimately nonsensical.[13] In all but the most trivial instances (and even then), architecture is *always* in parts conceptual, cultural and intellectual, comprising the theoretical, historical and structural – organized around conceptions of possible accommodations of bodily experiences. No matter how unconvincing they can be, self-identified phenomenological approaches to architecture are still 'conceptual, cultural and intellectual'. The crux of Eisenman's proposition equally confounds language, thought and reality. He argues: 'The "real architecture" only exists in the drawings. The "real building" exists outside the drawings. The difference here is that "architecture" and "building" are not the same.'[14] Apart from the fairly conventional split between building as utilitarian, and architecture as exceeding necessity, the claim that so-called 'real architecture only exists in the drawings' and 'real building' always 'exists outside the drawings' dematerializes architecture to the point of non-existence, while reproducing hidebound divisions of labour and significance.

Eisenman wants to remove architecture from external reality as material presences inviting shared bodily experience. The drawing becomes the thing of value; an autonomous text uncompromised by negotiations with the world (of construction), or shared bodily experiences of buildings. The thing built, as building, is severed from the drawing, as architecture. Since the architect's concern is with the supposedly 'real architecture', which 'only exists in the drawing', and Eisenman only builds to secure worldly credibility – as a requirement of others – the success or failure of his buildings (emotionally or technically) is of no concern, because it is ultimately of no interest to him. And, as he suggests, not his responsibility anyway, because someone else built it.[15] The point is that while language can exist in isolation from reality, as a situated shared creation of mind, this would produce a kind of nonsense confounding shared expectations, by renouncing commonality.

Despite Eisenman's confusing emphasis on turns of phrase, architectural aims confound realization when not thought through and made manifest by assemblages of words. Speaking desire inaugurates ways of fulfilling it by initiating its organization. Desire – hope, authorial intent – only becomes knowable through verbalization and visualization, which makes making possible. Eisenman's aim thus appears to be to confound comprehension by isolating architecture from building and bodily experience, perhaps to make it *autonomous*. Nevertheless, if invention and making take shape within a horizon of graspable shared experience that language organizes and communicates, comprehensibility of the constructed environment remains a real possibility – textually, visually and architecturally, in the form of materially present constructions, without necessarily becoming a *jargon of authenticity*.

The relative stability of the human body as model and reference extending backwards (and forwards) through innumerable generations of people links utility and meaning almost structurally to architecture. As such, the denotative and connotative significance of elements remains reasonably fixed over a long duration, within a culture but across them as well. Even if the original relation between signifier and signified in architecture may be arbitrary, use is so bound to the body, psyche and gravity that immemorial habit takes on an almost law-like quality, through the perseverance of cultural memory, no matter how foreign the past may be. Obviously, there is near limitless scope for experimentation, but to paraphrase Loos, climbing makes the stair.[16] Bodily, cultural and individual memory intersect in recollections of the meaning silted up in architectural elements.

The dominant spatial practices and modes of production that have developed since Piranesi's eighteenth-century discovery of drawing as compensation for the *impossibility* of architecture has loosened the ties between the linguistic universe and the material reality of building.[17] The paradoxical condition produced by this makes language – interpretation – necessary for recuperating reality, by identifying what is missing as the content of hope. Pursued through negation of the conditions that frustrate desire, hope longs to overthrow what *is* in attempting to establish conditions of homecoming.[18] The reality of architecture obscured by nearly three centuries of intensifying alienation and the associated catastrophes of the twentieth century could make the disconnect Eisenman wants to naturalize seem the only reasonable possibility. Yet, the obscured material reality of architecture is conceivably recuperable by language that could render it knowable, again. The buildings discussed throughout this book share an evident conviction that architecture is manifestly real – a matter of material, construction and bodily experience – that lends itself to description, in social and emotional terms, as much as in technical, formal or theoretical ones.

Relativity

Whorf's conceptualization of independent language groups as thinking differently from one another anticipates each inhabiting a different reality, structured by a worldview determined by the particularities of situated language:

> Just as it is possible to have any number of geometries other than the Euclidean which give an equally accurate perfect account of space configurations, so it is possible to have descriptions of the universe, all equally valid, that do not contain our familiar contrasts of time and space.[19]

His idea of linguistic relativity underpinned van Eyck's conviction that all building traditions are equally valid because each makes unique contributions to fuller understandings of the world. If the partial understanding of the world unique to the thinking and experiencing of each language group (in relation to the totality of possible language groups) was joined with the worldviews of *all* other language groups (or even a few), a fuller understanding of reality would emerge, at least potentially, a conception van Eyck welcomed into his architecture.

For van Eyck, Whorf's linguistic relativity suggested methods for enriching modernist architecture. Looking beyond the West and the present to other language realities and alternative spatial conceptions, and building traditions, enhanced van Eyck's understandings of human reality and enriched his architecture with expanded social conceptions of buildings and cities. For him, these augmented perspectives suggested how the limitations of industrially produced architecture could be overcome to provide settings for what he called 'built homecoming'. Van Eyck's Whorf-influenced architecture becomes felt meaning – expression rather than representation – because emerging out of fuller comprehension of varied human experiences.[20]

The relativity of multiple language realities, rituals and spatial practices suggests how rigid oppositions could be collapsed into parts of more complex wholes. Embracing relative patterns of relations, modelled by the parallel realities of diverse architectures and diverse languages, could inform the invention of rooms, buildings and cities better able to accommodate human emotion and desire. Alternative materials, forms and assemblies (or simply using them differently) could expand the limited poetic capacities of reductive modernist architecture.

As one element in a culture's expression of its reality, architecture is akin to the design of sentences, organized according to the spatial rules of the language group within which it is designed. As suggested by Whorf, ordinary individual architectural elements gain in meaning through configuration into comprehensible assemblages:

> patterns [of cultural organization] are not like the meanings of words, but they are somewhat like the way meaning appears in sentences. They are not like individual sentences but like SCHEMES of sentences and designs of sentence structure ... Sentences, not words, are the essence of speech, just as equations and functions, and not bare numbers are the real meat of mathematics. We are all mistaken in our common belief that any word has an 'exact meaning' ... That part of meaning which is in words, and which we may call 'reference,' is only relatively fixed ... Reference of words is at the mercy of the sentence and grammatical patterns in which they occur.[21]

In an architectural context, elements and materials are something like words, but their meaning only appears as parts of an overall scheme, or structure. The intersection between language and architecture is explicit.[22] An initial structural element may carry a silted-up charge of meaning on its own (a column for example, or marble), but gains in significance through association with other equally charged elements. The assemblage of a whole from these individual elements could reveal a configured pattern, far denser in expressive potential (and cultural significance) than any single element on its own. In this view, patterned structuring of discrete parts provides opportunities to construe architectural signification abundant enough to sustain curiosity and improvised inhabitation, despite the enforced limits of industrialized production.[23]

In Scarpa's work, whole parts are constituents of a discontinuous order, which differs from Zumthor's classical conception of wholeness as a kind of perfection, confirmed when nothing may be added nor taken away without compromising the work. However, as Williams and Tsien observe, a conception of what they want to achieve – as comprehensible – is necessary but without the degree of control Zumthor requires. In comparison, Miralles's work is loosest of all – to such a degree that it is convincingly episodic, rather than fragmented, discontinuous or emplotted, which also sets it apart from the patterning that characterizes van Eyck's work.

Social hieroglyphs

Architecture is not as nuanced as language; its elements are expressively more limited but potentially more immediately powerful. Architectural elements including materials, details, and forms constitute a series of hieroglyphic characters available for a kind of physical writing that through use speaks directly to the body. More explicit links between architecture and language could take shape at those junctures where material and form analogize some describable social idea. Here, social is intended to encompass individual and group experiences of being in the world, individually or collectively, from the uprightness of a body to the character of a community. The difficulty modernist architecture has in locating points of intersection with language arises, at least in part, from the tension between exaggerated individual artistic expression in one direction and trivial practice in the other, with both dominated by a more than less universal building industry that demands standardization.

While intelligible meaning depends on shared experiences of the world shaped by common languages, struggles for extreme expressions of individuality are confounded by relatively uniform spatial practices and modes of production, determined by globalization, which frequently translates into relative incomprehensibility, by reproducing the conditions supposedly surpassed. The possibility of more thoroughgoing negations, of the sort discussed in the first half of this book, become possible when the restrictions of dominant spatial practices and modes of production are acknowledged, as the first step to mastering, or transcending them, at least partly.

A more general obstacle to producing evocative architecture turns on what associates it with language while simultaneously separating the two. Although *abstract*, language can describe concrete experience with some precision; architecture, which is *concrete*, configures an abstract language of forms in attempts to analogize experience (use). Language is ephemeral and fleeting but its communicative role is more pronounced. Architecture is a fixed and static physical presence, which locates it in the background of life, so it must be more open.

At its best, architecture provides settings where it is good to do a specific thing, or a number of things generally. Language can establish terms of criticism for identifying this by informing on architecture, to reveal whether it does or does not accomplish its tasks. But language can also obscure the potential of practice by limiting its range of concerns and possibilities – for example, by opposing architecture to building, drawing to construction or image to material. Paradoxically, the more distant from use (experience) the conception (however communicated), the more conservative the resulting architecture will be, because abstract, or academic, in negative senses. Attempts to symbolize modes of thought and writing without reasonable points of reference to the physical elements of architecture (including material) and use, limits results to representation, rather than figuration, expression or analogy.

Throughout this book, use value (conceptualized as openly as possible) has been postulated as a non-negotiable criterion for defining architecture *as* architecture, in opposition to either pure technicity, or pure fantasy, which are forms of representation that either reject the burden of use, or so reduce its conception that it becomes all but useless (emotionally and technically). The relevance of material in this is that what is done with it signals the conceptions of use operative within a building (enriched, augmented or impoverished, reduced). Details and the methods of construction do the same but could do nothing without materials. Equally, as the first point of contact between experiencing subjects and buildings, material is more significant than either overall form or image in communicating underlying ideas of use, or facilitating it.

Architectural writing

Although writing about architecture risks dissociating buildings from bodies, the physicality of words, such as horizontal, vertical and escalate (amongst others) could also recuperate the poetry of beams, column, arches and stairs (to name just a few architectural elements), as a language of bodily experience.

Architectural language, the meaning of architectural elements, is not as mysterious as it might seem. The parts of structures that architects fit together to form buildings contributes to overall meaning, while the individual elements are units of signification in themselves. Bodily experience of connotative (emotional) and denotative (technical) function is how architectural meaning becomes knowable. In designing buildings, mental images of qualitative actions are given a prefigurative form as possible architecture. Architectural elements could be construed as mental images organized and initially configured by language, translated by drawings into instructions for builders to execute, who further translate these through the processes of construction. Each of the multiple exercises in translation interprets and abstracts the initial conception. Realization contributes to a living process of invention continued through (anticipated and transforming) use. When construction is complete, buildings are offered for inhabitation. If signification is direct and rich enough, there is greater likelihood that it will effectively pronounce itself directly to the body when experienced. Language can communicate what this is like but also prefigures its materialization.

Architecture anticipates, recollects and analogizes the body and conditions of being in the world. While *every body* is preconsciously aware of this, layered construction largely conceals building significance from perception by diminishing opportunities for expressive detailing – likewise the space defining, sensuous, qualities of materials, except where cladding is positive in Loos's sense. The tendency to hide structural elements beneath continuous surfaces, of plasterboard for example, alienates bodily reference. Although much building since the Second World War frustrates desires for resonant constructed environments, new and old examples still exist that recollect 'our responses to materials, to our most favoured or most loathed surfaces, textures and grains, and the associations they arouse' as 'keys to the inner life':

> Our relationship to structures is infused with bodily expectations – of weight, tension, impetus and rest. The joined members of a frame, the posts of a truss, the joists, beams and purlins reproduce for us our skeletal meaning. There are secret satisfactions in good timberwork: it answers the desire for structural logic and emphatically reinforces the sense we have of ourselves as being coherent bodies.[24]

Architecture makes little worlds, analogizes the one it sits within, and gains in meaning by echoing our own drama of being alive in it as 'coherent bodies', in motion or at rest, with 'skeletal meaning', external skin and the certainty of ageing, falling into ruin, and finally disappearing, forever. The passage quoted above reintroduces mindfulness of what is missing and might be possible in architecture as conceivable only in language, even if the hoped-for condition could only be satisfied by the material reality of building; a confluence of words, buildings, and dreams Bachelard perceived:

> Thus, very quickly, at the very first word, at the very first poetic overture, the reader who is 'reading a room' leaves off reading and starts to think of someplace in his own past … In short, the house we were born in has engraved within us the hierarchy of the various functions of inhabiting. We are the diagram of the function of inhabiting that particular house, and all the other houses are but variations on a fundamental theme. The word habit is too worn a word to express the passionate liaison of our bodies which do not forget, with an unforgettable house.[25]

Simultaneously real and imagined, the 'unforgettable house' rises at the intersection of memory and desire that only concrete evidence can confirm. For Kahn, 'The wish of a fairy tale is our inheritance of first desires. When you have a desire but you have no means, all you can do is wish, and it is still a fairy tale.' Yet, 'It is the wish which drives us forward, not know-how, not technology. What drives us is the yet unmade thing'; not the essences of materials but their possibilities, not technique but conception.[26] As the immemorial constant companion of human being – from birth to death, and all that lies in-between – the wonder is not that 'our relationship to structures is infused with bodily expectations' but that reductive methods of construction have been permitted to so utterly frustrate them.

Notes

1. Marcus Vitruvius Pollio, *The Ten Books on Architecture (1st C. BC)*, Book II, Chap. 1:7, pp. 38–9. See also, Rykwert, *On Adam's House in Paradise*, 2nd edn.
2. Ibid., Vitruvius, *Ten Books on Architecture*, Book II, Chap. 1:2, pp. 38–9.

3. Eco, 'Function and Sign: The Semiotics of Architecture' (1997), pp. 173–93.

4. See: K. Michael Hays, *Architecture's Desire: Reading the Late Avant-Garde*, Cambridge, MA: MIT Press, 2009; Joseph Rykwert, *The First Moderns: Architects of the Eighteenth Century*, Cambridge, MA: MIT Press, 1984; Tafuri, *Architecture and Utopia*; Tafuri, *The Sphere and the Labyrinth*, 1987.

5. Peter Eisenman, 'Interview: Peter Eisenman', Iman Ansari, *The Architectural Review*, 26 April 2013. Available at: https://www.architectural-review.com/view/interviews/interview-peter-eisenman/8646893.article (Accessed 24 April 2018).

6. For more on the topic of autonomy in architecture, see Nathaniel Coleman, 'The Myth of Autonomy', *AP* (*Architecture Philosophy*), 1, no. 2 (2015): 157–78. Available at: https://ojs.library.okstate.edu/osu/index.php/jispa/article/view/6099/5702 (Accessed 24 April 2018).

7. Benjamin Lee Whorf, *Language Thought & Reality, Selected Writings*, John B. Carroll (ed.), Cambridge, MA: MIT Press, 1956. van Eyck, 'Steps Towards a Configurative Discipline', reprinted in *Architecture Culture 1943-1968, A Documentary Anthology*, Joan Ockman and Edward Eigen (eds), New York: Columbia/Rizzoli, 1993, pp. 348–60 (pp. 327–43).

8. Note: Garson O'Toole, 'Britain and America Are Two Nations Divided by a Common Language George Bernard Shaw? Mallory Browne? Raymond Gram Swing? Apocryphal?', *Quote Investigator*, 03 April 2016. Available at: https://quoteinvestigator.com/2016/04/03/common/ (Accessed 24 April 2018). A traceable version of the phrase can be found in a novella by Oscar Wilde as follows: 'Indeed, in many respects, she was quite English, and was an excellent example of the fact that we have really everything in common with America nowadays, except, of course, language' (*The Canterville Ghost* (1887), Surrey: Alma Classics, Ltd. 2016, p. 5).

9. Jonathan Culler, *Ferdinand De Saussure*, New York: Penguin, 1976, p. 82.

10. Rykwert, 'Translation and/or Representation', pp. 64–70 (p. 66).

11. Ibid., Eisenman, 'Interview: Peter Eisenman'.

12. Ibid.

13. Ibid.

14. Ibid.

15. Ibid.

16. For further discussion on the topics introduced here, see Ferdinand De Saussure, 'Nature of the Linguistic Sign', from *Course in General Linguistics* (1916), Wade Baskin (trans.), New York: Philosophical Library, 1959, reprinted in *Contemporary Critical Theory*, Dan Latimer (ed.), New York: Harcourt Brace Jovanovich, 1989, pp. 3–16 (p. 11); Joseph Rykwert, 'Meaning and Building', *Zodiac* 6 (1957). Reprinted in *The Necessity of Artifice*, New York: Rizzoli, 1982, pp. 9–16; Rykwert, *The Dancing Column: On Order in Architecture*, 1996.

17. Tafuri, *Architecture and Utopia*; Lefebvre, *The Production of Space*.

18. Bloch, *The Utopian Function of Art and Literature: Collected Essays*.

19. Ibid., Whorf, 'An American Indian Model of the Universe', *International Journal of American Linguistics*, 16, no. 67–72 (1950): 57–64 (p. 58).

20. Aldo van Eyck, Various Titles and Dates, reprinted in *Team 10 Primer*, Alison Smithson (ed.), Cambridge, MA: MIT Press, 1968. See also, van Eyck, *Collected Articles and Other Writings: 1947-1998*.

21. Ibid., Whorf, 'Language Mind and Reality', *Theosophist* (Madras, India), January and April (1942): 246–70 (pp. 253, 258, 259).

22. Ibid., van Eyck, 'Steps Towards a Configurative Discipline', pp. 348–9.

23. Ibid., pp. 348–60.

24. David Brett, *C. R. Mackintosh: The Poetics of Workmanship*, Cambridge, MA: Harvard University Press, 1992, p. 75.

25. Bachelard, *The Poetics of Space*, pp. 14, 15.

26. Louis I. Kahn, 'Lecture to Towne School of Civil and Mechanical Engineering, University of Pennsylvania, Philadelphia, Pennsylvania, 19 November 1968', reprinted in *What Will Be Has Always Been, The Words of Louis I Kahn*, Richard Saul Wurman (ed.), New York: Access and Rizzoli, 1986, pp. 33–5 (p. 33).

SELECT BIBLIOGRAPHY

Abensour, Miguel.'Persistent Utopia'. *Constellations*, vol. 15, no. 3 (2008): 406–21.

Adams, Courtney S. 'Techniques of Rhythmic Coherence in Schoenberg's Atonal Instrumental Works'. *The Journal of Musicology*, vol. 11, no. 3 (Summer 1993): 330–56.

Adorno, Theodor W. *Aesthetic Theory* (1970), translated by Robert Hullot-Kentor. London and New York: Continuum, 1997.

Adorno, Theodor W. *The Culture Industry, Selected Essays on Mass Culture*, edited by J. M. Bernstein. London and New York: Routledge, 1991.

Adorno, Theodor W. 'Functionalism Today' ('Funktionalismus heute') (1965), translated by Jane Newman and John Smith. *Oppositions*, 17 (Summer 1979): 31–41.

Adorno, Theodor W. *Jargon of Authenticity* (1964), translated by Knut Tarnowski and Frederic Will. London and New York: Routledge & Kegan Paul, 1973.

Adorno, Theodor W. *Negative Dialectics* (1966), translated by E. B. Ashton. London: Routledge, 1973.

Adorno, Theodor W. 'Valéry Proust Museum' (1955). In *Prisms*, translated by Samuel and Shierry Weber, 173–85. Cambridge: MIT Press, 1967.

Alberti, Leon Battista. *On the Art of Building in Ten Books*, translated by Joseph Rykwert, Neil Leach and Robert Tavernor. Cambridge: MIT Press, 1998.

Altenmüller-Lewis, Ulrike and Mark L. Brack. 'Afterword: *The City Crown* in the context of Bruno Taut's Ouevre'. In *The City Crown by Bruno Taut*, edited by Matthew Mindrup and Ulrike Altenmüller-Lewis, 149–76. Surrey: Ashgate, 2015.

Ansari, Iman. 'Interview: Peter Eisenman'. *The Architectural Review*, 26 April 2013. Available online at: https://www.architectural-review.com/view/interviews/interview-peter-eisenm an/8646893.article (Accessed 24 April 2018).

Antliff, Mark. 'Fascism, Modernism and Modernity'. *The Art Bulletin*, vol. 84, no. 1 (2002): 148–69.

Arendt, Hanna. 'On the Nature of Totalitarianism: An Essay in Understanding'. In *Essays in Understanding, 1930–1954: Formation, Exile, Totalitarianism*, edited by Jerome Kohn, 328–60. New York: Shocken Books, 1994.

Arendt, Hanna. *The Portable Hanna Arendt*, edited by Peter Baehr. New York and London: Penguin Books, 2000.

Augé, Marc. *Non-Places: Introduction to an Anthropology of Supermodernity* (1992), translated by John How. London and New York: Verso, 1995, p. 79.

Bachelard, Gaston. *Earth and Reveries of Will: An Essay on the Imagination of Matter* (1947), translated by Kenneth Haltman. Dallas: Dallas Institute of Humanities and Culture, 2002.

Bachelard, Gaston. *The Poetics of Space* (1958), translated by Maria Jolas. Boston: Beacon Press, 1964.

Bachelard, Gaston. *The Psychoanalysis of Fire* (1938), translated by Alan C. M. Ross. Boston: Beacon Press, 1964.

Bachelard, Gaston. *Water and Dreams: An Essay on the Imagination of Matter* (1942), translated by Edith R. Farrell. Dallas: The Pegasus Foundation, 1983.

Bain, Susan. *Holyrood: The Inside Story*. Edinburgh: Edinburgh University Press, 2005.

Balfour, Alan. *Creating a Scottish Parliament*. Edinburgh: Finlay Brow, 2005.

Banham, Reyner. *Theory and Design in the First Machine Age*, Second Edition. New York: Praeger Publishers, 1967.

Select Bibliography

Barnstone, Deborah Ascher. *The Transparent State: Architecture and Politics in Postwar Germany*. London and New York: Routledge, 2005.

Barr, Alfred H., Jr, Philip Johnson and Henry-Russell Hitchcock, Jr. *Modern Architecture International Exhibition: February 10 to March 23, 1932*. New York: The Museum of Modern Art, 1932. Available online at: https://www.moma.org/documents/moma_catalogue_2044 _300061855.pdf (Accessed 26 April 2018).

Beauregard, Robert. 'We Blame the Building! The Architecture of Distributed Responsibility'. *International Journal of Urban and Regional Research*, vol. 39, no. 3 (May 2015): 533–49.

Benjamin, Walter. 'Karl Kraus' (1931). In *Reflections: Essays, Aphorisms, Autobiographical Writings*, edited by Peter Demetz, translated by Edmond Jephcott, 239–73. New York: Schocken Books, 1978.

Benjamin, Walter. 'Paris Capital of the Nineteenth Century' (1935). In *Reflections: Essays, Aphorisms, Autobiographical Writings*, edited by Peter Demetz, translated by Edmond Jephcott, 146–62. New York: Schocken Books, 1978.

Benjamin, Walter. 'Surrealism: The Last Snapshot of the European Intelligentsia' (1929). In *Reflections*, translated by Peter Demetz, 172–92. New York: Shocken Books, 1978.

Benjamin, Walter. 'The Work of Art in the Age of Mechanical Reproduction' (1936). In *Illuminations*, edited by Hanna Arendt, translated by Harry Zohn, 217–64. New York: Schocken Books, 1969.

Berman, Marshall. *All That Is Solid Melts Into Air* (1982). New York: Penguin Books, 1988.

Blake, Peter. *No Place Like Utopia: Modern Architecture and the Company We Kept*. New York: W. W. Norton, 1993.

Bletter, Rosemarie Haag. 'The Interpretation of the Glass Dream – Expressionist Architecture and the History of the Crystal Metaphor'. *Journal of the Society of Architectural Historians* (March 1981): 20–43.

Bletter, Rosemarie Haag. 'Paul Scheerbart's Architectural Fantasies'. *Journal of the Society of Architectural Historians*, vol. 34, no. 2 (May 1975): 83–97.

Bloch, Ernst. 'Building in Empty Places' (1959). In *The Utopian Function of Art and Literature: Collected Essays*, translated by Jack Zipes and Frank Mecklenburg, 186–99. Cambridge: MIT Press, 1988.

Bloch, Ernst. *The Principle of Hope*, Volume I (1953/1959), translated by Neville Plaice, Stephen Plaice and Paul Knight. Cambridge: MIT Press, 1986.

Bloch, Ernst. *The Principle of Hope*, Volume II (1959), translated by Neville Plaice, Stephen Plaice and Paul Knight. Cambridge: MIT Press, 1986.

Bloch, Ernst and Theodor Adorno. 'Something's Missing: A Discussion between Ernst Bloch and Theodor W. Adorno on the Contradictions of Utopian Longing' (1964). In Ernst Bloch, *The Utopian Function of Art and Literature: Collected Essays*, translated by Jack Zipes and Frank Mecklenburg, 1–17. Cambridge: MIT Press, 1988.

Brett, David. *C. R. Mackintosh: The Poetics of Workmanship*. Cambridge: Harvard University Press, 1992.

Burdett, Charles. 'Italian Fascism and Utopia'. *History of the Human Sciences*, vol. 16, no. 1 (2003): 93–108.

Burke, Edmund. *A Philosophical Enquiry into the Origin of Our Ideas of the Sublime and Beautiful* (1779), edited by James T. Boulton. Notre Dame: University of Notre Dame Press, 1958.

Carmel-Arthur, Judith and Stafan Buzas. *Carlo Scarpa: Museo Canoviano, Possagno*. Stuttgart and London: Edition Axel Menges, 2002.

Chasseguet-Smirgel, Janine. 'The Theme of Transparency'. In *Sexuality and Mind, The Role of the Father and the Mother in Psyche*, 99–104. New York: New York University Press, 1986.

Chernyshevsky, Nikolai. *What is to Be Done?* translated by Benjamin R. Tucker and Cathy Porter. London: Virago, 1982.

Cirlot, J. E. *A Dictionary of Symbols*, Second Edition, translated by Jack Sage (1962), 74. London: Routledge, 1971.

Cohen, Jean-Louis. 'Modern Architecture and the Saga of Concrete'. In *Liquid Stone: New Architecture in Concrete*, edited by Jean-Louis Cohen and G. Martin Moeller, Jr, 20–33. New York: Princeton Architectural Press.

Coleman, Nathaniel. 'Architecture in the Material Space of Possible Transgression'. In *Transgression: Towards an Expanded Field of Architecture*, edited by Louis Rice and David Littlefield, 185–206. London and New York: Routledge, 2015.

Coleman, Nathaniel. 'Is Beauty Still Relevant? Is Art? Is Architecture?' *Architecture Philosophy*, vol. 1, no. 1 (2014): 81–95.

Coleman, Nathaniel. 'Building Dystopia'. *Rivista MORUS—Utopia e Renascimento*, vol. 4 (2007): 181–92. Available online at: http://www.revistamorus.com.br/index.php/morus/article/view File/180/157 (Accessed 17 May 2018).

Coleman, Nathaniel. *Lefebvre for Architects*. London and New York: Routledge, 2015.

Coleman, Nathaniel. 'The Myth of Autonomy'. *AP (Architecture Philosophy)*, vol. 1, no. 2 (2015): 157–78.

Coleman, Nathaniel. *Utopias and Architecture*. London and New York: Routledge, 2005.

Coomaraswamy, Ananda K. 'Ornament'. *The Art Bulletin*, vol. 21, no. 4 (December 1939): 375–82.

Coomaraswamy, Ananda K. 'Saṁvega, "Aesthetic Shock"'. *Harvard Journal of Aesthetic Studies*, vol. 7, no. 3 (1943): 174–9.

Coomaraswamy, Ananda K. 'Saṁvega, "Indian Art"'. *Studies in Comparative Religion*, vol. 15, no. 3/4 (Summer-Autumn 1983): 1–11. Available online at: http://www.studiesincomparativ ereligion.com/Public/articles/Indian%20Art-by_Ananda_K_Coomaraswamy.aspx (Accessed 26 April 2019).

Cooper, J. C. *An Illustrated Encyclopedia of Traditional Symbols*. New York: Thames and Hudson, 1978.

Culler, Jonathan. *Ferdinand De Saussure*. New York: Penguin, 1976.

Cunsolo, Ronald S. *Italian Nationalism: From Its Origins to World War II*. Malabar: Robert Krieger, 1990.

Curtis, William J. R. *Modern Architecture Since 1900*, Third Edition, London: Phaidon, 1996.

Dal Co, Francesco. 'The Architecture of Carlo Scarpa'. In *Carlo Scarpa: The Complete Works*, edited by Francesco Dal Co and Giuseppe Mazzariol, 24–69. Milano and New York: Electa/ Rizzoli, 1985.

Damisch, Hubert. 'The Drawings of Carlo Scarpa'. In *Carlo Scarpa: The Complete Works*, edited by Francesco Dal Co and Giuseppe Mazzariol, 209–13. Milano and New York: Electa/Rizzoli, 1985.

de Certeau, Michel. 'Walking in the City'. In *The Practice of Everyday Life*, translated by Steven Rendall, 91–110. Berkeley: University of California Press, 1984.

Debord, Guy. *The Society of the Spectacle* (1967), translated by Donald Nicholson-Smith. New York: Zone Books, 1994.

Deplazes, Andrea (Editor). *Constructing Architecture: Materials Processes Structures – A Handbook*. Basel: Birkhäuser, 2005.

de Saussure, Ferdinand. 'Nature of the Linguistic Sign,' from *Course in General Linguistics* (1916), translated by Wade Baskin. New York: Philosophical Library, 1959. Reprinted in *Contemporary Critical Theory*, edited by Dan Latimer, 3–16. New York: Harcourt Brace Jovanovich, 1989.

de Solà-Morales, Ignasi. *Gaudi*. Barcelona: Ediciones Poligrafa, S. A., 1984.

de Solà-Morales, Ignasi. 'Weak Architecture' (1987). In *Differences: Topographies of Contemporary Architecture*, edited by Sarah Whiting, translated by Graham Thompson, 57–71. Cambridge: MIT Press, 1996.

Select Bibliography

De Zurko, Edward Robert. *Origins of Functionalist Theory*. New York: Columbia University Press, 1957.

Di Lieto, Alba (Editor). *I disegni di Carlo Scarpa per Castelvecchio*. Venezia: Marsilio Editori, 2006.

Dinwoodie, John. 'Timber'. In *Construction Materials: Their Nature and Behaviour*, Fourth Edition, edited by Peter Domone and John Illston, 403–506. Abingdon: Spon Press, 2010.

Dixon, Roger and Stefan Muthesius. *Victorian Architecture*. London: Thames and Hudson, 1978.

Dodd, Garham. 'Part 9 Glass'. In *Construction Materials: Their Nature and Behaviour*, Fourth Edition, edited by Peter Domone and John Illson, 507–26. London and New York: Spon Press, 2010.

Domone, Peter. 'Part 2 Metals and Alloys' (revision and update of chapter by previous authors: Bill Biggs, Ian McColl and Bob Moon). In *Construction Materials: Their Nature and Behaviour*, Fourth Edition, edited by Peter Domone and John Illston, 53–81. London and New York: Spon, 2010.

Domone, Peter. 'Part 3 Concrete'. In *Construction Materials: Their Nature and Behaviour*, Fourth Edition, edited by Peter Domone and John Illston, 83–208 (83). London and New York: Spon Press, 2010.

Dostoevsky, Fyodor. *Notes from the Underground* (1864), translated by Constance Garnett. In *The Norton Anthology of World Masterpieces*, edited by Maynard Mack, 1852–939. New York: W. W. Norton & Co., 1987.

Eatwell, Roger. *Fascism: A History*. London: Penguin Books, 1995.

Eco, Umberto. 'Function and Sign: The Semiotics of Architecture' (1973). In *Rethinking Architecture: A Reader in Cultural Theory*, edited by Neil Leach, 182–202. London and New York: Routledge, 1997.

Eco, Umberto. *The Open Work*, translated by Anna Cancogni. Cambridge: Harvard University Press, 1989.

Elliott, Cecil D. *Technics and Architecture: The Developments of Materials and Systems for Buildings*. Cambridge: MIT Press, 1992.

Ersoy, Ufuk. 'The Fictive Quality of Glass'. *Architectural Research Quarterly*, vol. 11, no. 3/4 (2007): 237–43.

Ersoy, Ufuk. 'Glass as Light as Air, As Deep as Water'. In *The Material Imagination: Reveries on Architecture and Matter*, edited by Matthew Mindrup, 155–67. Surrey: Ashgate, 2015.

Ersoy, Ufuk. 'To See Daydreams: The Glass Utopia of Paul Scheerbart and Bruno Taut'. In *Imagining and Making the World: Reconsidering Architecture and Utopia*, edited by Nathaniel Coleman, 107–37. Oxford and Bern: Peter Lang, 2011.

Etlin, Richard A. *Modernism in Italian Architecture, 1890–1940*. Cambridge: MIT Press, 1991.

Evans, Robin. 'Translations from Drawing to Building' (1986). In *Translations from Drawing to Building and Other Essays*, 152–93. London: Architectural Association, 1997.

Filarete, Antonio Averlino. *Treatise on Architecture*, translated by John R. Spencer. New Haven: Yale University Press, 1965.

Ford, Edward R. *The Architectural Detail*. New York: Princeton Architectural Press, 2011.

Forty, Adrian. *Concrete and Culture: A Material History*. London: Reaction Books, 2012.

Foster, Norman. *Rebuilding the Reichstag*. Woodstock: Overlook Press, 2000.

Frampton, Kenneth. 'Carlo Scarpa and the Adoration of the Joint'. In *Studies in Tectonic Culture: The Poetics of Construction in Nineteenth and Twentieth Century Architecture*, edited by John Cava, 299–332. Cambridge: MIT Press, 1995.

Frampton, Kenneth. 'Louis Kahn and the French Connection'. *Oppositions*, no. 22 (1980): 20–53. Reprinted in *Labor, Work and Architecture: Collected Essays on Architecture and Design*, 169–185. London and New York: Phaidon, 2002.

Frampton, Kenneth. *Modern Architecture: A Critical History*, Third Edition, New York: Thames and Hudson, 1992.

Frampton, Kenneth. *Modern Architecture, 1851–1945*. New York: Rizzoli, 1981.

Frampton, Kenneth. 'Six Points for an Architecture of Resistance'. In *The Anti-Aesthetic: Essays on Postmodern Culture* (1983), edited by Hal Foster, 17–34. New York: The New Press, 1998.

Frampton, Kenneth. *Studies in Tectonic Culture: The Poetics of Construction in Nineteenth and Twentieth Century Architecture*, edited by John Cava. Cambridge: MIT Press, 1995.

Francesco, di Giorgio Martini. *Trattati Di Architettura Ingegneria E Arte Militare*, a cura di Corrado Maltese, transcritzione di Livia Maltese Degrassi. Milano: Edizione Il Polifilo, 1967.

Frascari, Marco. *Eleven Exercises in the Art of Architectural Drawing: Slow Food for the Architect's Imagination*. London and New York: Routledge, 2011.

Frascari, Marco. 'A Heroic and Admirable Machine: The Theater of the Architecture of Carlo Scarpa, *Architetto Veneto*'. *Poetics Today*, vol. 10, no. 1 (Spring 1989): 103–26.

Frascari, Marco. 'The Lume Materiale in the Architecture of Venice'. *Perspecta*, vol. 24 (1988): 136–45.

Frascari, Marco. 'Review: *Carlo Scarpa the Complete Works*'. *Journal of Architectural Education*, vol. 41, no. 1 (Fall 1987): 54–6.

Frascari, Marco. 'The Tell-Tale Detail', *VIA*, vol. 7 (1984): 22–37.

Fraser, Peter Lovat. (The Rt Hon Lord Fraser of Carmyllie QC). *Spitting Tacks: Lord Fraser's Report into the Building of the Scottish Parliament*. London and New York: Tim Coates Books, 2004. Available online at: http://www.parliament.scot/SPICeResources/HolyroodInquiry.pdf (Accessed 26 April 2019).

Freud, Sigmund. *Civilization and its Discontents* (1929), edited and translated by James Strachey. New York: W.W. Norton, 1961.

Gay, Peter. *The Enlightenment: The Rise of Modern Paganism*. New York: W. W. Norton, 1966.

Gay, Peter. *The Enlightenment: The Science of Freedom*. New York: W. W. Norton, 1969.

Gentile, Emilio. 'Fascism, Totalitarianism and Political Religion: Definitions and Critical Reflections on Criticism of an Interpretation', translated by Natalia Belozentseva. *Totalitarian Movements and Political Religions*, vol. 5, no. 3 (2004): 326–75.

Gentile, Emelio. *The Sacralization of Politics in Fascist Italy*, translated by Keith Botsford. Cambridge: Harvard University Press, 1996.

Ghirardo, Diane. 'Italian Architects and Fascist Politics: An Evaluation of the Rationalist's Role in Regime Building'. *Journal of the Society of Architectural Historians*, vol. 39, no. 2 (May 1980): 109–27.

Ghirardo, Diane. 'Terragni, Conventions, and the Critics'. In *Critical Architecture and Contemporary Culture*, edited by William J. Lillyman, Marilyn F. Moriarty and David J. Neuman, 99–103. New York and Oxford: Oxford University Press, 1994.

Giedion, Sigfried. *Building in France, Building in Iron, Building in Ferro-Concrete* (1928), translated by J. Duncan Berry. Santa Monica: The Getty Center, 1995.

Giedion, Sigfried. *Space, Time and Architecture: The Growth of A New Tradition* (1941), Fifth Edition, Revised and Enlarged. Cambridge: Harvard University Press, 1982.

Glendinning, Miles. 'Towards a New Parliament'. In *The Architecture of Scottish Government: From Kingship to Parliamentary Democracy*, 316–64. Dundee: Dundee University Press, 2004.

Gray, Alasdair. *Independence: Why Scots Should Rule Scotland*. Edinburgh: Canongate Press, 1992.

Greig, Stuart. (Producer/Director). *The Holyrood Files*, (Documentary film). Scotland; Scottish Screen: IWC; BBC, 2005. Available online at: https://vimeo.com/185674169 (Accessed 26 April 2019).

Grigor, Murray. *Holyrood A New Parliament for Scotland – Informational Video on Miralles' Parliament Project*. Scotland: Scottish Parliament, 2001. Available online at: https://vimeo.com/38038463 (Accessed 26 April 2019).

Guedes, Pedro (Editor). *Encyclopedia of building Technology*. New York: McGraw-Hill, 1979.

Select Bibliography

Guillén, Mauro F. *The Taylorized Beauty of the Mechanical: Scientific Management and the Rise of Modernist Architecture*. Princeton: Princeton University Press, 2006.

Hall, Christopher. *Materials: A Very Short Introduction*. Oxford: Oxford University Press, 2014.

Hauser, Arnold. *Naturalism, Impressionism, The Film Age: The Social History of Art , Volume 4* (1958), translated by Stanley Goodman. London and New York: Routledge, 1999.

Hays, K. Michael. *Architecture's Desire: Reading the Late Avant-Garde*. Cambridge: MIT Press, 2009.

Hegger, Manfred, Hans Drexeler and Martin Zeumer. *Materials*. Basel: Birkhäuser, 2007.

Herdeg, Klaus. *The Decorated Diagram: Harvard Architecture and the Failure of the Bauhaus Legacy*. Cambridge: MIT Press, 1983.

Hitchcock, Henry-Russell, Jr and Philip Johnson. *The International Style* (1932). New York: W. W. Norton, 1995.

James-Chakraborty, Kathleen. *German Architecture for a Mass Audience*. London and New York: Routledge, 2000.

Jameson, Fredric. 'Architecture and the Critique of Ideology' (1982). In *Architecture, Criticism, Ideology*, edited by Joan Ockman, Deborah Berke, and Mary McLeod, 442–61. Princeton: Princeton Architectural Press, 1985.

Jameson, Fredric. 'The Constraints of Postmodernism', In *The Seeds of Time*, 129–205. New York: Columbia University Press, 1994.

Jameson, Fredric. 'Is Space Political?' In *Anyplace*, edited by Cynthia Davidson, 192–205. Cambridge: Anyone Corp/MIT Press, 1995.

Kahn, Louis I. '1973: Brooklyn, New York – Lecture at Pratt Institute'. *Perspecta* 19 (1982): 89–100. Reprinted in *Louis I. Kahn, Lectures, Writings, Interviews*, edited by Alessandra Latour, 320–30. New York: Rizzoli, 1991.

Kahn, Louis I. 'Lecture to Towne School of Civil and Mechanical Engineering, University of Pennsylvania, Philadelphia, Pennsylvania. 19 November 1968'. In *What Will Be Has Always Been, The Words of Louis I Kahn*, edited by Richard Saul Wurman, 33. New York: Access and Rizzoli, 1986.

Kahn, Louis I. *Light is the Theme* (1975). Comments on Architecture Compiled by Neil E. Johnson. Fort Worth: Kimbell Art Foundation, 2002.

Kahn, Louis I. *Writings, Lectures, Interviews*, edited by Alessandra Latour. New York: Rizzoli, 1991.

Klein, Florence. *Guide Mwakaa: The Pathways of Kanak Tradition*, translated by Stéphane Goiran. Nouméa, Nouvelle-Calédonie: Agence de Développementde la Culture Kanak, 2000.

Koolhaas, Rem. *Delirious New York: A Retroactive Manifesto for Manhattan* (1978). New York: Monacelli Press, 1994.

Koren, Leonard. *Undesigning the Bath*. Berkeley: Stone Bridge Press, 1996.

Kostof, Spiro. 'The Practice of Architecture in the Ancient World: Egypt and Greece'. In *The Architect: Chapters in the History of the Profession*, edited by Spiro Kostof, 3–27. New York and Oxford: Oxford University Press, 1977.

Laugier, Marc-Antoine. *An Essay on Architecture* (1753), translated by Wolfgang and Anni Hermann. Los Angeles: Hennessey & Ingalls, 1977.

Lawrence, A. W. *Greek Architecture*. Revised with additions by R. A. Tomlinson, Middlesex: Penguin, 1983.

Leatherbarrow, David. 'Architecture Its Own Discipline'. In *The Discipline of Architecture*, edited by Andrzej Piotrowski and Julia Williams Robinson, 83–102. Minneapolis: University of Minnesota Press, 2001.

Leatherbarrow, David. 'Material Matters'. In *Architecture Oriented Otherwise*, 69–94. New York: Princeton Architectural Press, 2009.

Leatherbarrow, W. J. 'Introduction: Dostoevskii and Britain'. In *Dostoevskii and Britain*, edited by W. J. Leatherbarrow, 1–38. Oxford and Providence: Berg, 1995.

Lefebvre, Henri. *Critique of Everyday Life Volume II, Foundations for a Sociology of the Everyday* (1961), translated by John Moore. London: Verso, 2008.

Lefebvre, Henri. *Introduction to Modernity* (1962), translated by John Moore. London: Verso, 1995.

Lefebvre, Henri. *Key Writings*, edited by Stuart Elden, Lebas and Kofman. New York: Continuum, 2003.

Lefebvre, Henri. *The Production of Space* (1974), translated by Donald Nicholson-Smith. Oxford: Blackwell, 1991.

Lefebvre, Henri. *Rhythmanalysis: Space, Time and Everyday Life* (1992), translated by Stuart Elden and Gerald Moore. London and New York: Continuum, 2004.

Lefebvre, Henri. 'Time and History' (1970), from *La Fin de l'histoire*. Paris: Éditions de Minuit, and Second Edition (2001), Paris: Anthropos. Reprinted in Henri Lefebvre, *Key Writings*, edited by S. Elden, E. Lebas and E. Kofman (unspecified translator), 177–87. New York: Continuum, 2003.

Lefebvre, Henri. *Writings on Cities*, translated by Kofman and Lebas. Oxford: Wiley-Blackwell, 1996.

Lingren, Hugo. 'ARCHITECTURE: A Little Fascist Architecture Goes a Long Way'. *The New York Times*, 12 October 2003.

Loos, Adolf. 'Architecture' (1910). In *On Architecture*, selected by Adolf and Daniel Opel, translated by Michael Michell, 73–85. Riverside: Ariadne Press, 2002.

Loos, Adolf. 'Building Materials' (1898). In *On Architecture*, selected by Adolf and Daniel Opel, translated by Michael Michell, 37–41. Riverside: Ariadne Press, 2002.

Loos, Adolf. 'Chairs' (1898). In *Ornament and Crime: Selected Essays*, selected by Adolf Opel, translated by Michael Michell, 63–7. Riverside: Ariadne Press, 1998.

Loos, Adolf. 'The Chicago Tribune Column' (1923). In *On Architecture*, selected by Adolf and Daniel Opel, translated by Michael Michell, 168–71. Riverside: Ariadne Press, 2002.

Loos, Adolf. 'Gentlemen's Hats' (1898). In *Ornament and Crime: Selected Essays*, selected by Adolf Opel, translated by Michael Michell, 89–93. Riverside: Ariadne Press, 1998.

Loos, Adolf. '*Heimatkunst*' (1912). In *On Architecture*, selected by Adolf and Daniel Opel, translated by Michael Michell, 110–18. Riverside: Ariadne Press, 2002.

Loos, Adolf. 'My First Building' (1910). In *On Architecture*, selected by Adolf and Daniel Opel, translated by Michael Michell, 70–2. Riverside: Ariadne Press, 2002.

Loos, Adolf. 'The New Style and the Bronze Industry' (1898). In *Ornament and Crime: Selected Essays*, selected by Adolf Opel, translated by Michael Michell, 457–60. Riverside: Ariadne Press, 1998.

Loos, Adolf. 'The Old and the New Style in Architecture' (1898). In *On Architecture*, selected by Adolf and Daniel Opel, translated by Michael Michell, 31–6. Riverside: Ariadne Press, 2002.

Loos, Adolf. 'Ornament and Crime' (1929 [1908]). In *Ornament and Crime: Selected Essays*, selected by Adolf Opel, translated by Michael Michell, 167–76. Riverside: Ariadne Press, 1998.

Loos, Adolf. 'Ornament and Education' (1924). In *Ornament and Crime: Selected Essays*, selected by Adolf Opel, translated by Michael Michell, 184–9. Riverside: Ariadne Press, 1998.

Loos, Adolf. 'The Potemkin City' (1898). In *On Architecture*, selected by Adolf and Daniel Opel, translated by Michael Michell, 26–8. Riverside: Ariadne Press, 2002.

Loos, Adolf. 'The Principle of Cladding' (1898). In *On Architecture*, selected by Adolf and Daniel Opel, Adolf. translated by Michael Michell, 42–7. Riverside: Ariadne Press, 2002.

Loos, Adolf. 'A Review of Applied Arts I' (1898). In *Ornament and Crime: Selected Essays*, selected by Adolf Opel, translated by Michael Michell, 134–39. Riverside: Ariadne Press, 1998.

Loos, Adolf. 'Rules for Social Housing Development' (1920). In *On Architecture*, selected by Adolf and Daniel Opel, translated by Michael Michell, 142–3. Riverside: Ariadne Press, 2002.

Loos, Adolf. 'Social Housing Development Day' (1921). In *On Architecture*, selected by Adolf and Daniel Opel, translated by Michael Michell, 159–63. Riverside: Ariadne Press, 2002.

Loos, Adolf. 'On Thrift' (1924). In *On Architecture*, selected by Adolf and Daniel Opel, translated by Michael Michell, 178–83. Riverside: Ariadne Press, 2002.

Loos, Adolf. 'Tours of the Austrian Museum' (1898), translated by Jane O. Newman and John H. Smith. In *Spoken Into the Void: Collected Essays 1897–1900*, 111–13. Cambridge: Oppositions Books/MIT Press, 1982.

Los, Sergio. *Carlo Scarpa: An Architectural Guide*, translated by Antony Shugaar. Venice: Arsenale Editrice, 1995.

Löwy, Michael and Robert Sayre. *Romanticism against the Tide of Modernity*, translated by Catherine Porter. Durham: Duke University Press, 2001.

MacDonald, William L. *The Architecture of the Roman Empire, Volume I: An Introductory Study*, Revised Edition. New Haven and London: Yale University Press, 1985.

MacDonald, William L. *The Pantheon*. Cambridge: Harvard University Press, 1976.

Marin, Louis. 'Utopic Degeneration: Disneyland'. In *Utopics: The Sociological Play of Textual Spaces*, translated by R. A. Vollrath, 239–59. Amherst and New York: Humanity Books, 1984.

Marinetti, Filippo Tommaso. 'The Futurist Speech to the English' ('*Un Discours Futuriste aux Anglais*'), Lyceum Club, London (December 1910). In *Futurism: An Anthology*, edited by L. Rainey, C. Poggi and L. Wittman, 70–4. New Haven and London: Yale University Press, 2009.

Masheck, Joseph. *Adolf Loos: The Art of* Architecture. London: I.B. Taurus, 2013.

Mazzariol, Giuseppe and Giuseppe Barbieri. 'The Life of Carlo Scarpa'. In *Carlo Scarpa: The Complete Works*, edited by Francesco Dal Co and Giuseppe Mazzariol, 9–23. Milano and New York: Electa/Rizzoli, 1985.

Mertins, Detlef. 'The Enticing and Threatening Face of Prehistory: Walter Benjamin and the Utopia of Glass'. *Assemblage*, no. 29 (1996): 6–23.

Middleton, Robin and David Watkin. *Neoclassical and 19th Century Architecture: The Enlightenment in France and in England* (1980). New York: Electa/Rizzoli, 1987.

Middleton, Robin and David Watkin. *Neoclassical and 19th Century Architecture/2*. New York: Electa/Rizzoli, 1980.

Miotto, Luciana. *Carlo Scarpa: I Musei*. Venezia: Marsilio, 2006.

Missac, Pierre. 'Glass Architecture'. In *Walter Benjamin's Passages*, translated by Shierry Weber Nicholsen, 147–72. Cambridge: MIT Press.

More, Thomas. *Utopia* (1516). Norton Critical Edition, Second Edition, translated and edited by Robert M. Adams. New York: W. W. Norton, 1992.

More, Thomas. *Utopia* (1516). *Cambridge Texts in the History of Political Thought, Third Edition*, edited by George M. Logan, translated by Robert M. Adams. Cambridge: Cambridge University Press, 2016.

Mostafavi, Moshen and David Leatherbarrow. *On Weathering: The Life of Buildings Through Time*. Cambridge: MIT Press, 1993.

Moya, Enric Miralles. Concept Design, Scottish Parliament Building. Proposed Team: EMBT Architects Associates; RMJM; Ove Arup & Partners Scotland. The Scottish Parliament, 1998. Available online at: https://www.parliament.scot/VisitorInformation/4.Enric_Miralles_Moya. pdf (Accessed 26 April 2019).

Ockman, Joan and Edward Eigen (Editors). *Architecture Culture 1943–1968, A Documentary Anthology*. New York: Columbia/Rizzoli, 1993.

Palladio, Andrea. *The Four Books on Architecture* (1738), translated by Issac Ware. New York: Dover Publications, 1965.

Pallasmaa, Juhani. *The Eyes of the Skin: Architecture and the Senses*. Chichester: Wiley & Sons, 2005.

Pallasmaa, Juhani. *The Thinking Hand: Existential and Embodied Wisdom in Architecture.* Chichester: Wiley & Sons, 2009.

Panofsky, Erwin. *Gothic Architecture and Scholasticism* (1957). New York: Meridian, 1985.

Pérez-Gómez, Alberto. *Architecture and the Crisis of Modern Science.* Cambridge: MIT Press, 1984.

Pérez-Goméz, Alberto and Louise Pelletier. *Architectural Representation and the Perspective Hinge.* Cambridge: MIT Press, 1997.

Perrault, Claude. *Ordonnance For the Five Kinds of Columns After the Methods of The Ancients* (1683), translated by Indra Kagis McEwen. Santa Monica: Getty Center, 1993.

Pevsner, Nikolaus. *An Outline of European Architecture* (1943). London: Penguin Books, 1990.

Pevsner, Nikolaus. *Pioneers of Modern Design: From William Morris to Walter Gropius* (1936). London: Penguin, 1991.

Pevsner, Nikolaus. *The Sources of Modern Architecture and Design.* London: Penguin Books, 1968.

Powrie, Phil. 'The Surrealist *Poème-Objet*'. In *Surrealism: Surrealist Visuality*, edited by Silvano Levy, 57–77. Great Britain: Keele University Press, 1996.

Prina, Francesca. *Architecture: Elements, Materials, Form* (unnamed translator). Princeton and Oxford: Princeton University Press, 2008.

Rasmussen, Steen Eiler. Experiencing Architecture, Second Edition. Cambridge: MIT Press, 1964.

Ricoeur, Paul. 'Architecture of Narrativity' (1996). *Études Ricoeuriennes/Ricoeur Studies*, vol. 7, no. 2 (2016): 31–42. Available online at: http://ricoeur.pitt.edu/ojs/index.php/ricoeur/article/view/378/196 (Accessed 16 April 2018).

Ricoeur, Paul. *From Text to Action: Essays in Hermeneutics II*, translated by Kathleen Blamey and John B. Thompson, 25–52. Evanston: Northwestern University Press, 1991.

Ricoeur, Paul. 'Universal Civilization and National Cultures'. In *History and Truth*, translated by Charles A. Kelbley, 271–84. Evanston: Northwestern University Press, 1965.

Rowe, Colin and Fred Koetter. *Collage City.* Cambridge: MIT Press, 1978.

Ruskin, John. 'The Nature of Gothic' (1853). In *Unto this Last and Other Writings*, edited by Clive Wilmer, 77–109. London: Penguin, 1985.

Ruskin, John. *The Seven Lamps of Architecture* (1849), Second Edition (1880). New York: Dover, 1989.

Ruskin, John. *The Stones of Venice* (1851–53), edited by J. G. Links. New York: Da Capo Press, 2003 (1960).

Rycroft, Charles. *A Critical Dictionary of Psychoanalysis.* London: Penguin, 1995.

Rykwert, Joseph. *On Adam's House in Paradise: The Idea of the Primitive Hut in Architectural History* (1972). Cambridge: MIT Press, 1981.

Rykwert, Joseph. *The Dancing Column: On Order in Architecture.* Cambridge: MIT Press, 1996.

Rykwert, Joseph. 'The Dark Side of the Bauhaus' (1968); and 'The Nefarious Influence on Modern Architecture of the Neo-Classical Architects Boullée and Durand' (1972). In *The Necessity of Artifice*, 44–9; 60–5. New York: Rizzoli, 1982.

Rykwert, Joseph. *The First Moderns: The Architects of the Eighteenth Century*, Cambridge: MIT Press, 1980.

Rykwert, Joseph. 'Meaning and Building'. *Zodiac* 6 (1957). Reprinted in *The Necessity of Artifice*, 9–16. New York: Rizzoli, 1982.

Rykwert, Joseph. 'The Modern Movement in Italian Architecture' (1956). In *The Necessity of Artifice*, 19–22. New York: Rizzoli, 1982.

Rykwert, Joseph. *The Seduction of Place: History and Future of the City.* New York: Vintage Books, 2002.

Saarinen, Eero. *Eero Saarinen on His Work*, Revised Edition, edited by Aline B. Saarinen. New Haven: Yale University Press, 1968.

Sahin, Esra. 'Exchange of forces: Environmental definition of materials in the works of Vitruvius, Alberti, Le Corbusier, and Peter Zumthor' (PhD diss., University of Pennsylvania, Philadelphia, 2009).

Sargent, Lyman Tower. 'Review: Is there only one utopian tradition', *Journal of the History of Ideas*, vol. 43, no. 4. (October–December 1982): 681–9.

Scarpa, Carlo. 'Transcripts', including: 'Letter of the Venetian Rationalists' (1931), 'Can Architecture Be Poetry?' (1976), 'A Thousand Cypresses' (1978), 'Interview with Carlo Scarpa' (1978). In *Carlo Scarpa: The Complete Works*, edited by Francesco Dal Co and Giuseppe Mazzariol, 279–303. Milano and New York: Electa/Rizzoli, 1985.

Scheer, David Ross. *The Death of Drawing: Architecture in the Age of Simulation*. London and New York: Routledge, 2014.

Scheerbart, Paul. *Glass Architecture* (1914), translated by James Palmes. In *Glass Architecture* by Paul Scheerbart and *Alpine Architecture* by Bruno Taut, edited by Dennis Sharp, 41–74. New York: Praeger Publishers, 1972.

Schnapp, Jeffrey T. 'The People's Glass House'. *South Central Review*, vol. 25, no. 3 (2008): 45–56.

Schroyer, Trent. 'Foreword'. In *Adorno, Jargon of Authenticity*, vii–xvi. Evanston: University of Chicago Press, 1973.

Schumacher, Thomas L. *Surface and Symbol: Giuseppe Terragni and the Architecture of Italian Rationalism*. New York: Princeton Architectural Press, 1991.

Scott, Donald. *The Psychology of Fire*. New York: Charles Scribner's Sons, 1974.

Scott, Geoffrey. *The Architecture of Humanism: A Study in the History of Taste* (1924). New York: Norton Library, 1974.

Semper, Gottfried. 'The Four Elements of Architecture': A Contribution to the Comparative Study of Architecture' (1851). In *The Four Elements of Architecture and Other Writings*, translated by Harry Francis Mallgrave and Wolfgang Herrmann, 74–129. Cambridge: Cambridge University Press, 1989.

Sennett, Richard. *The Craftsman*. London: Allen Lane, 2008.

Sloterdijk, Peter. *In the World Interior of Capital* (2005), translated by Wieland Hoban. Cambridge: Polity, 2013.

Smith, Roch C. *Gaston Bachelard: Philosopher of Science and Imagination*, Revised and Updated. Albany: SUNY, 2016.

Smithson, Alison (Editor). *Team 10 Primer*. Cambridge: MIT Press, 1968.

Stewart, Janet. *Fashioning Vienna: Adolf Loos's Cultural Criticism*. London and New York: Routledge, 2000.

Stile, Alexander. *Benevolence to Betrayal*, New York: Summit Books, 1991.

Storchi, Imona. "'Il Fascismo É Una Casa di Vetro'": Giuseppe Terragni and the Politics of Space in Fascist Italy'. *Italian Studies*, vol. 62, no. 2 (2007): 231–45.

Suger (Abbot Suger). *On the Abbey Church of St.-Denis and its Art Treasures*, edited and translated by Erwin Panofsky, Second Edition by Gerda Panofsky-Soergel. New Jersey: Princeton University Press, 1979.

Sullivan, Louis H. *Kindergarten Chats and Other Writings* (1918). New York: Dover, 1979.

Summerson, Sir John. 'Foreword'. In *The Architecture of Adolf Loos*, edited by Safran, Yehuda and Wilfried Wang, 6–7. London: Arts Council of Great Britain, 1985.

Summerson, Sir John. 'The Mischievous Analogy' (1941). In *Heavenly Mansions and Other Essays on Architecture*, 195–218. New York and London: W. W. Norton, 1963.

Summerson, Sir John. 'Neo-Classicism: Britons Abroad'. In *Architecture in Britain: 1530–1830*, 377–437. London and New York: Pelican History of Art, 1983.

Tafuri, Manfredo. *Architecture and Utopia: Design and Capitalist Production* (1973), translated by Barabara Luigia La Penta. Cambridge: MIT Press, 1975.

Tafuri, Manfredo. 'Carlo Scarpa and Italian Architecture'. In *Carlo Scarpa: The Complete Works*, edited by Francesco Dal Co and Giuseppe Mazzariol, 79–95. Milano and New York: Electa/ Rizzoli, 1985.

Tafuri, Manfredo. 'Giuseppe Terragni: Subject and "Mask"', translated by Diane Ghirardo. *Oppositions*, vol. 11 (1977): 1–25.

Tafuri, Manfredo. *History of Italian Architecture, 1944–1985* (1982), translated by Jessica Levine. Cambridge: MIT Press, 1989.

Tafuri, Manfredo. *The Sphere and the Labyrinth: Avant-Gardes and Architecture from Piranesi to the 1970s* (1980), translated by Pellegrino d' Acierno and Robert Connolly. Cambridge: MIT Press, 1987.

Tanizaki, Jun'ichirō. *In Praise of Shadows* (1933), translated by Thomas Harper and Edward Seidensticker. London: Vintage Books, 2001.

Taut, Bruno. *Alpine Architecture* (1917), translated by Shirley Palmer. In *Glass Architecture* by Paul Scheerbart and *Alpine Architecture* by Bruno Taut, edited by Dennis Sharp, 74–127. New York: Praeger Publishers, 1972.

Taut, Bruno. *The City Crown* (1919). In *The City Crown by Bruno Taut*, edited and translated by Matthew Mindrup and Ulrike Altenmüller-Lewis, 73–114. Surrey: Ashgate, 2015.

Taut, Bruno. 'A Programme for Architecture' (1918), translated by Michael Bullock. In *Programs and Manifestoes on 20th-Century Architecture*, edited by Ulrich Conrads, 41–3. Cambridge: MIT Press, 1970.

Taylor, G. D. *Materials in Construction: An Introduction*. Harlow: Longman, 2000.

Terragni, Giuseppe. 'L Contruzione della Casa del Fascio di Como'. *Quadrante*, 35/36, no. 8 (October 1936): 5–27.

Terragni, Giuseppe. 'The Construction of the Casa del Fascio in Como', translated by Debra Dolinski. In Thomas L. Schumacher, *Surface and Symbol: Giuseppe Terragni and the Architecture of Italian Rationalism*, 142–70. New York: Princeton Architectural Press, 1991.

Thomas, Katie Lloyd. 'Introduction: Architecture and Material Practice'. In *Material Matters: Architecture and Material Practice*, edited by Katie Lloyd Thomas, 2–12. New York and London: Routledge, 2007.

Trilling, Lionel. *Sincerity and Authenticity*. Cambridge: Harvard University Press, 1973.

Unrau, John. *Looking at Architecture With John Ruskin*. London: Thames and Hudson, 1978.

Valéry, Paul. 'The Problem of Museums' (1923). In *The Collected Works of Paul Valéry Volume 12*: *Degas, Manet, Morisot*, edited by Jackson Mathews, translated by David Paul, 202–6. London: Routledge & Keegan Paul: 1960.

van Eyck, Aldo. 'Steps Toward A Configurative Discipline', *Forum* (August 1962). Reprinted in Aldo van Eyck, *Collected Articles and Other Writings: 1947–1998*, edited by Vincent Ligtelijn and Francis Struaven, 327–43. Amsterdam: Sun, 2008.

Vattimo, Gianni. 'Utopia Dispersed', translated by Colin Anderson. *Diogenes*, vol. 53, no. 18 (2006): 18–23.

Vitruvius Pollio, Marcus. *The Ten Books on Architecture*, translated by Morris Hicky Morgan (1914). New York: Dover, 1960.

von Simpson, Otto. *The Gothic Cathedral: Origins of the Gothic Cathedral and the Medieval Concept of Order* (1956). Princeton: Bolligen/Princeton University Press, 1962.

Welter, Volker M. *Ernst L. Freud, Architect: The Case of the Modern Bourgeois Home*. New York and Oxford: Berghahn, 2011.

Whorf, Benjamin Lee. *Language Thought & Reality, Selected Writings*, edited by John B. Carroll. Cambridge: MIT Press, 1956.

White, R. B. *Prefabrication: A History of Its Development in Great Britain*. National Building Studies, Special Report 36. London: Her Majesty's Printing Office, 1965.

Select Bibliography

Williams, Tod and Billie Tsien. *The Architecture of the Barnes Foundation*, edited by Octavia Giovannini-Torelli. New York: Skira/Rizzoli, 2012.

Williams, Tod and Billie Tsien. 'Quiet Light' (1995 project description). *TOD WILLIAMS BILLIE TSIEN Architects | Partners* website. Available online at: http://twbta.com/work/quiet-light (Accessed 02 April 2018).

Williams, Tod and Billie Tsien. 'Slowly (improving) Vision'. In *Williams and Tsien Works: 2G International Architectural Review*, vol. 1, no. 9 (1999): 138–43.

Williams, Tod and Billie Tsien. Unpublished author interview with Tod Williams and Billie Tsien conducted by Nathaniel Coleman, TWBTA Studio, New York City, March 2008 (Digital voice recording).

Williams, Tod and Billie Tsien. *Work Life*, edited by Hadley Arnold. New York: The Monacelli Press, 2000.

Wise, Michael J. *Capital Dilemma: Germany's Search for a New Architecture of Democracy*, New York: Princeton Architectural Press, 1998.

Wittkower, Rudolf. 'Le Corbusier's Modulor' (1961). In *In the Footsteps of Le Corbusier*, edited by Carlo Palazzola and Ricardo Vio, 11–19. New York: Rizzoli, 1991.

Wright, Frank Lloyd. 'The Architect and the Machine' (1894 speech). In *Frank Lloyd Wright Collected Writings: Volume 1, 1894–1930*, edited by Bruce Brooks Pfeiffer, 20–6. New York: Rizzoli, 1992.

Wright, Frank Lloyd. 'Architect, Architecture, and the Client' (1896). In *Frank Lloyd Wright: Collected Writings, Volume 1: 1894–1930*, edited by Bruce Brooks Pfeiffer, 27–38. New York: Rizzoli, 1992.

Wright, Frank Lloyd. 'The Art and Craft of the Machine' (1901). In Catalogue, *14th Annual Exhibition Chicago Architectural Club*, March 1901. Reprinted in *Frank Lloyd Wright Collected Writings: Volume 1*, 1894–1930, edited by Bruce Brooks Pfeiffer, 58–69. New York: Rizzoli, 1992

Wright, Frank Lloyd. 'In the Cause of Architecture I: The Architect and the Machine'. In *The Architectural Record*, vol. 61, no. 5 (May 1927): 394–6. Reprinted in *Frank Lloyd Wright Collected Writings: Volume 1, 1894–1930*, edited by Bruce Brooks Pfeiffer, 225–9. New York: Rizzoli, 1992.

Wright, Frank Lloyd. 'In The Cause of Architecture III – The Meaning of Materials: Steel'. *Architectural Record*, vol. 62, no. 2 (August 1927): 163–66. Available online at: https://www.arc hitecturalrecord.com/articles/11513-in-the-cause-of-architecture-iii-steel (Accessed 18 July 2018).

Wright, Frank Lloyd. 'In the Cause of Architecture IV: The Meaning of Materials – Wood'. *The Architectural Record*, vol. 63, no. 5 (May 1928): 481–8.

Wright, Frank Lloyd. 'In the Cause of Architecture V: The Meaning of Materials – The Kiln', *The Architectural Record*, vol. 63, no. 6 (June 1928). Reprinted in *Frank Lloyd Wright: Collected Writings, Volume 1: 1894–1930*, edited by Bruce Brooks Pfeiffer, 284–9. New York: Rizzoli, 1992.

Wright, Frank Lloyd. 'In the Cause of Architecture: VI. The Meaning of Materials – Glass'. *The Architectural Record*, vol. 64, no. 1 (July 1928): 11–16. Available online at: https://www.arc hitecturalrecord.com/ext/resources/news/2016/01-Jan/InTheCause/Cause-PDFs/In-the-Caus e-of-Architecture-1928-07.pdf (Accessed 28 June 2018).

Wright, Frank Lloyd. 'In the Cause of Architecture VII: The Meaning of Materials – Concrete'. *Architectural Record*, vol. 64, no. 2 (August 1928): 98–104. Available online at: https://www.arc hitecturalrecord.com/articles/11507-in-the-cause-of-architecture-vii-the-meaning-of-materi alsconcrete (Accessed 16 July 2018).

Zambonini, Giuseppe. 'Notes for a Theory of Making in a Time of Necessity'. *Perspecta*, vol. 24 (1988): 13–23.

Zambonini, Giuseppe. 'Process and Theme in the Work of Carlo Scarpa'. *Perspecta*, vol. 20 (1983): 21–42.

Zamyatin, Yevgeny. *We* (1924), translated by Mirra Ginsburg. New York: Avon Books, 1972.

Zevi, Bruno. *Giuseppe Terragni*. Bologna: Zanchelli, 1980.

Zipes, Jack. 'Toward a Realization of Anticipatory Illumination'. In *Ernst Bloch, The Utopian Function of Art and Literature: Collected Essay*s, translated by Jack Zipes and Frank Mecklenburg, 11–43. Cambridge: MIT Press, 1988.

Zumthor, Peter. *Atmospheres: Architectural Environments – Surrounding Objects*. Basel: Birkhäuser, 2006.

Zumthor, Peter. *Peter Zumthor Therme Vals*. Zurich: Scheidegger & Spiess, 2007.

Zumthor, Peter. *Peter Zumthor Works: Buildings and Projects, 1979–1997*. Basel: Birkhäuser, 1998.

Zumthor, Peter. 'The Tension of Not Being Specific: Tod Williams and Billie Tsien in Conversation with Peter Zumthor'. *2G International Architecture Review*, no. 9 (1999): 8–23.

Zumthor, Peter. *Thinking Architecture*, Second Expanded Edition, translated by Maureen Oberon-Turner and Catherine Schoenberg. Basel: Birkhäuser, 2006.

INDEX

Index

brick   8, 177, 189, 191–2, 196, 197–9, 201–5, 192
  Fig. 9.2, 203 Fig. 9.6
  as artificial stone   198, 202–3
  baking, bread-making, brickmaking   7, 189,
    191, 194, 199, 201–2, 204–5
  as captured fire, heat, light, warmth   189,
    191–2, 194, 197, 199, 201
  earthy origins (clay)   189, 191, 194
  encompasses ancient four elements   191,
    201, 203
  fireplace, hearth   191–2, 199, 201, 205
  handmade (formed by hand)   8, 204
  hand-scaled, human-scaled, scale   7, 189, 196,
    199, 203
  Imperial Roman brick   190 Fig. 9.1, 216–18
  machine-made (mass-produced, mechanized
    production of)   8, 189, 203–4
  manufacture of   190, 194, 198–9, 201, 203
  reminders of warmth and origins   190, 196, 199
  significance (associations, material imaginaries,
    material meaning)   7–8, 191–2, 196–7,
    199, 201
building(s)   15–16, 31, 281
  as art object   7, 55
  as city brand (icon)   7, 143
  construction (practices)   72, 190, 227, 270
  construction separate from drawing   281, 285
  as distinct from architecture   281, 285
  industrialized production of   21, 27, 38, 104,
    207, 284
  industry   9, 15, 20, 28, 32, 55, 68, 71, 88, 106,
    116, 128, 144, 152, 155, 158, 189, 256,
    279, 285
  machine production of, machine-made   20,
    22, 27, 32, 55, 136, 161, 189, 215,
    228, 249
  machine-work   21–2
  mass produced elements, mass production,
    of   18–20, 27, 33, 38, 66, 177, 204, 211,
    221, 227, 233
  material reality of   281, 283, 287 (see
    also architecture)
  mechanized production of   9, 26, 182, 203
  as products (objects) of exchange   7, 74, 97
  standardization of   9, 285
built environment   5–7, 11, 15, 18, 20, 22, 26–9,
    155, 189–90, 199, 212
bureaucratic rationality   56, 73, 130, 147, 157, 161,
    172, 209, 216, 232, 251, 269

capitalism, capitalist   6–7, 30, 33, 68, 109, 129,
    145, 161, 209, 218, 232, 238, 257–9, 261,
    263, 267–9
Casa del Fascio   250, 263–4, 264 Fig 12.8, 265 Fig.
    12.9, 266–8, see also glass; Terragni

catastrophe, the   29, 52, 87, 105, 205, see also
    Holocaust, the
Chernyshevsky, Nikolai   257–9, 261
  and Crystal Palace   257–8
  What is to be Done?   257
Chicago   43, 191, 192 Fig 9.2, 230, 236, 242
Christo and Jean Claude   267–8
Chrysler Building (William Van Alen)   230, 232
  (Fig. 11.3)   246
CIAM (Congrès internationaux d'architecture
    moderne)   52
cladding   18, 21, 45–6, 53, 99–101, 105, 118–19,
    125, 169, 174, 183–4, 204, 223, 227, 236,
    241, 271, 286
Collage City (Colin Rowe and Fred Koetter)   154
column(s)   4, 24, 43, 50, 69, 79, 150, 169, 173,
    180, 199, 209, 222, 228–9, 255, 278,
    284, 286
community   7, 9, 29, 40, 93, 162, 173–4, 183, 195,
    196, 199, 217, 266, 278, 285
concept of centre   27, 57, 133, 135, 139, 145, 154,
    156, 160, 174, 192, 197–9, 209, 215
concrete
  aggregate   122, 207, 214 Fig. 10.4, 216, 223
  amalgam (gloopy)   214, 223
  arches   214, 220
  domes   217, 220 Fig. 10.5
  exposed   208 Fig. 10.1, 216, 233
  expressionist   221–2
  formwork, shuttering   101, 172, 212, 216,
    221, 242
  Imperial Roman architecture   215–17
  and infrastructure   208–9, 211
  Le Corbusier's use of   23, 26–7, 208 Fig 10.1
  as liquid stone (recollection of traditional
    masonry)   101, 214 Fig. 10.4, 215, 223
  material qualities and associations of   177,
    179, 207–8, 211–13, 215–17, 221–3,
    234, 241–2
  monotonous   135, 221
  as pervasive   177, 207, 215
  plasticity   208, 213, 216, 223–4
  reinforced   69, 213, 230, 233 Fig. 11.4, 241,
    245, 249, 255
  solidity   208, 211
  vaulted architecture, vaults   148, 151, 207,
    210–11, 213, 215–21, 234
construction
  architectural significance in relation to   16, 19
  architecture as   283
  as assembly of prefabricated parts   19, 228
  compromises of   129, 279
  conditions of (real world of)   99, 219, 282
  contemporary   30, 122, 143
  drawing (anticipates) guides   74, 86

306

Index

Index

Index

Index

Index

Index